DEVICE

RECONSTRUCTED

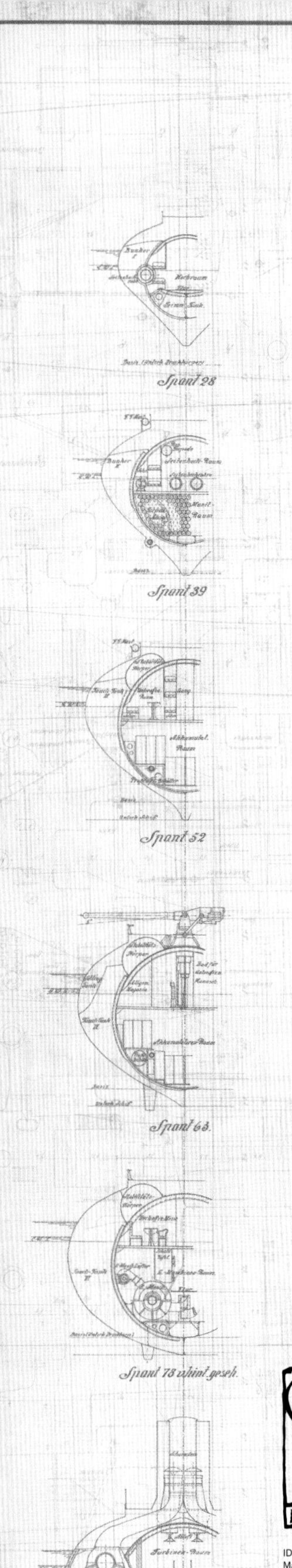

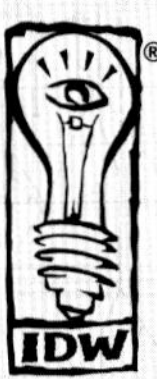

ISBN: 978-1-60010-559-3

12 11 10 09 01 02 03 04 05

www.idwpublishing.com

IDW Publishing: Operations: Ted Adams, Chief Executive Officer • Greg Goldstein, Chief Operating Officer • Matthew Ruzicka, CPA, Chief Financial Officer • Alan Payne, VP of Sales • Lorelei Bunjes, Dir. of Digital Services • AnnaMaria White, Marketing & PR Manager • Marci Hubbard, Executive Assistant • Alonzo Simon, Shipping Manager • Angela Loggins, Staff Accountant • Editorial: Chris Ryall, Publisher/Editor-in-Chief • Scott Dunbier, Editor, Special Projects • Andy Schmidt, Senior Editor • Justin Eisinger, Editor • Kris Oprisko, Editor/Foreign Lic. • Denton J. Tipton, Editor • Tom Waltz, Editor • Mariah Huehner, Associate Editor • Carlos Guzman, Editorial Assistant • Design: Robbie Robbins, EVP/Sr. Graphic Artist • Neil Uyetake, Art Director • Chris Mowry, Graphic Artist • Amauri Osorio, Graphic Artist • Gilberto Lazcano, Production Assistant

DEVICE VOLUME 2: RECONSTRUCTED. JULY 2009. FIRST PRINTING. Device Volume 2: Reconstructed © 2009 Device Gallery. All Rights Reserved. © 2009 Idea and Design Works, LLC. All artwork © 2009 their respective artist. IDW Publishing, a division of Idea and Design Works, LLC. Editorial offices: 5080 Santa Fe St., San Diego, CA 92109. The IDW logo is registered in the U.S. Patent and Trademark Office. All Rights Reserved. Any similarities to persons living or dead are purely coincidental. With the exception of artwork used for review purposes, none of the contents of this publication may be reprinted without the permission of Idea and Design Works, LLC. Printed in Korea.
IDW Publishing does not read or accept unsolicited submissions of ideas, stories, or artwork.

Material Condition°	Cutting Speed, fpm	
	HSS	Carbide
HR, A	150	600
CD	160	625
HR, A	130	500
CD	120	545
HR, A, N, CD	120	400
Q and T	75	300
Q and T	50	225
Q and T	40	200
HR, A, N, CD	140	550
HR, A, N, CD	145	560
N, CD	110	400
HR, A, N, CD	120	450
HR, A, N, CD	110	400
HR, N, CD	90	350
CD	70	300
HR, A, N, CD	100	375
HR, A, N, CD	85	325
N, CD, Q and T	70	275
Q and T	60	200
Q and T	40	160
Q and T	30	140
HR, A, N, CD	100	370
HR, A, N, CD	80	320
N, CD, Q and T	65	220
Q and T	50	180
Q and T	35	150
Q and T	30	130
HR, A, N, CD	110	400
HR, N, CD	90	350
Q and T	65	300
Q and T	50	225
Q and T	40	165
HR, A, N, CD	120	430
HR, N, CD	100	380
Q and T	75	275
Q and T	55	230
Q and T	50	200
HR, A, N, CD	100	400
HR, N, CD	90	350
CD, N, Q and T	70	300
Q and T	60	250
Q and T	50	200
Q and T	35	175

Drill Diameter Factors: F_T for Thrust; F_M for Torque

Inch Units

Drill Diam., in.	F_T	F_M	Drill Diam., in.	F_T	F_M
.063	.110	.007	.875	.899	.786
.094	.151	.014	.938	.950	.891
.125	.189	.024	1.000	1.000	1.000
.156	.226	.035	1.063	1.050	1.116
.188	.263	.049	1.125	1.099	1.236
.219	.297	.065	1.250	1.195	1.494
.250	.330	.082	1.375	1.290	1.774
.281	.362	.102	1.500	1.383	2.075
.313	.395	.124	1.625	1.475	2.396
.344	.426	.146	1.750	1.565	2.738
.375	.456	.171	1.875	1.653	3.100
.438	.517	.226	2.000	1.741	3.482
.500	.574	.287	2.250	1.913	4.305
.563	.632	.355	2.500	2.081	5.203
.625	.687	.429	2.750	2.246	6.177
.688	.741	.510	3.000	2.408	7.225

SI Metric Units

Drill Diam., mm	F_T	F_M	Drill Diam., mm	F_T	F_M
1.60	1.46	2.33	22.00	11.86	260.8
2.40	2.02	4.84	24.00	12.71	305.1
3.20	2.54	8.12	25.50	13.34	340.2
4.00	3.03	12.12	27.00	13.97	377.1
4.80	3.51	16.84	28.50	14.58	415.6
5.60	3.97	22.22	32.00	16.00	512.0
6.40	4.42	28.26	35.00	17.19	601.6
7.20	4.85	34.93	38.00	18.36	697.6
8.00	5.28	42.22	42.00	19.89	835.3
8.80	5.96	50.13	45.00	21.02	945.8
9.50	6.06	57.53	48.00	22.13	1062
11.00	6.81	74.90	50.00	22.86	1143
12.50	7.54	94.28	58.00	25.75	1493
14.50	8.49	123.1	64.00	27.86	1783
16.00	9.19	147.0	70.00	29.93	2095
17.50	9.87	172.8	76.00	31.96	2429

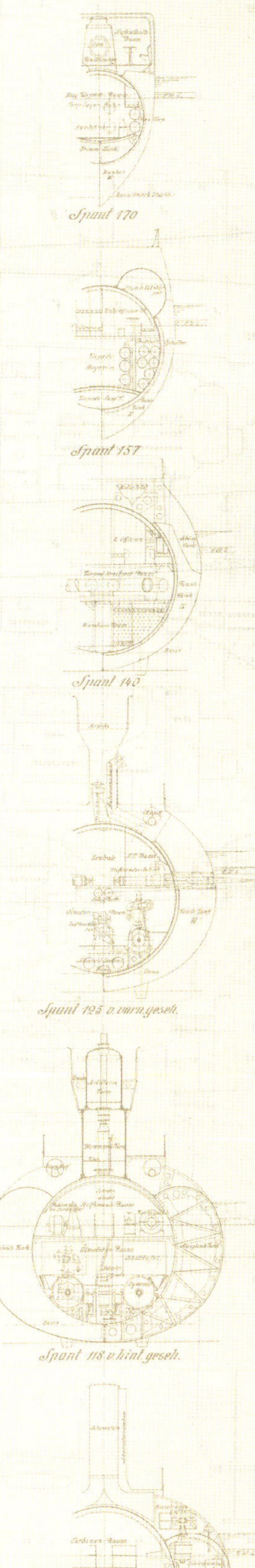

Techno-Temporal Mash-Ups and Bringing the Tinfoil
by Gareth Branwyn

"When I think about the future, all I wanna know is: when do we get to wear the tinfoil?"

That statement was uttered by a friend of mine, a New York artist and fashion designer, during a conversation in the early 1990s. It floored me because it was so simultaneously funny, quaint, quirky, honest, and cynical about projections of the future. It called to mind so many Ed Wood-worthy '50s and '60s films about the future where everybody ran around in silver lamé flight suits with fishbowls on their heads.

I was so inspired by the statement that I created a page for my art zine, *Going Gaga: art/information/noise*, made out of aluminum foil, with this question printed on clear sticker paper and stuck to the foil page. I brought the tinfoil, so the future could be delivered without further delay.

I thought of this anecdote, looking at the amazing collection of "mechanical animism," assembled here for *Device Volume 2: Reconstructed*. The artists represented seem similarly intent on delivering the tinfoil now, or at least delivering a heady dose of all of the projections, expectations, disappointments, fears, fetishistic obsessions, utopian hopes, and all the other associative baggage we have about the future we dream of (or lose sleep over).

Like the collection found in *Device Volume 1: Fantastic Contraption*, the work here comes from no apparent school, no labeled movement. It has issued no manifestoes. It has no house organ. The closest we get to anything tying it all together into a discernible mélange of work is the impressive curatorial eye of the Brothertons, their Device Gallery, and this dazzling series of books. Each volume explores a pattern recognition, and is a meditation on some aspect(s) of the collected work. The koan for that meditation is encoded in the name of each volume. *Fantastic Contraption* was just that, a beautiful piece of artistic machinery made of sub-assemblies from sixteen artists' sculptures, paintings, and digital work. Each piece was a human/animal cum machine, or a machine becoming something alive or mystical. Otherworldly. It was about biology and machinery changing state. It was about the oscillations from the mundane to the fantastic. Although a number of the artists here are back from Volume I, and the work mines many similar veins, *Reconstructed* offers up a different koan.

Living in the Matrix

While we were busy waiting to wear the tinfoil, looking up at the skies for the future to arrive via a pie plate held on a string by a grip, the future arrived through a most unlikely place. It came over the phone lines. The Internet and the digital revolution changed everything. There is probably no area of human endeavor that hasn't been significantly changed by computers, instantaneous global communications, and personal multimedia publishing. The reverb on all this is endless, but one thing especially concerns us here while considering our koan of *Reconstucted*: the notion of cut and paste. It didn't take netizens too long to figure out that cutting and pasting didn't just apply to email and word processing. In a digital universe, where a copy can clone as perfectly as the original, any medium can be cut, copied, pasted, edited, recompiled, and reissued. The digital world is suddenly one big mash-up, a dynamic act of reconstruction.

But this is nothing new for nature. Creation has always been an act of recombinism. One of the most mind-blowing, life-changing thoughts I've ever been gifted came from a cyberneticist I met once (who was also something of a stoner). He told me to try looking at the living world as a "conversation between elements and processes, a nexus, a matrix in which these elements are held and find expression." It sure sounded good, as did the apparent quality of whatever it was he was smoking. But one night, with my nose buried deep in a riotous bunch of spring flowers my wife had arranged on our dinning room table, I had an epiphany. I understood—I actually felt—exactly what he was talking about. I understood that the flowers I was looking at were the overlapping point at which all of these feedback loops of "elements and processes" (water, sunlight, soil, photosynthesis, the information being meted out by the seeds defining the protocols by which these elements interacted) came together and "had a conversation." The result of that conversation was the deliriously beautiful and fragrant nature-art in which I enthusiastically had my head buried. I had a visceral sense of these elements recombining, constantly, dynamically, in some cosmic lambada by which nature is constructed.

While "meditating" on the collection assembled in these pages, I had a similar sense of almost being able to see the active entrainment of elements as they came together to create the sculptural objects assembled here.

Look at the dense, wiry constructions of Andrew Smith and tell me you don't almost feel the electromagnetic force by which they have seemingly assembled themselves out of the cast off materials they managed to draw to them. As if to drive home the temporal nature of these pieces, some of them, such as *High Rise Billiards* and *Nine to Five*, are kinetic; they are always reconstructing themselves.

Looking at a piece of Greg Brotherton's work is like simultaneously peering into a 3D piece of fine art, an absurdly expensive hand-built luxury car from some retro golden age that hasn't happened yet, and into the fever-dreams of a '40s industrial designer. And that's just the first wave of impressions. The thing you can't get over is the technical virtuosity in evidence. In pieces like the Sisyphian *Pushed Around*, with its sense of movement aggressively offered, yet denied (the piece does not move), and the vertigo-inducing *Migraine Machine II*, which you'd rather didn't move (at least its subject would rather it didn't), but it does, we experience clever tweaks to our expectations while the craftmanship wows our aesthetic senses and feeds our appreciation of impressive engineering.

Christopher Conte's work is almost geniunely scary, with such beautifully rendered, precisely engineered techno-sculptures calling to mind some cyborged, componentized future. Then you learn of Christopher Conte's experience in engineering prosthetic devices, building artificial limbs for amputees. The horrible beauty of it all kicks into overdrive, like some stim injection from a cyberpunk novel.

Rich Muller, Jeremy Mayer, Lewis Tardy, Nemo Gould, Olivier Pauwels, Paul Loughridge, and Stéphane Halleux all aesthetically mine a similar vein of rich techno-temporal mythology: over five decades of the robot. In speaking about the rights of digital artists to mash-up existing work to create new work—reconstruction, in other words—Mark Hosler of the audio-collage band Negativland once talked about the legitimate emergence of folk art whenever physical objects, codes, and signs reach such a level of saturation that they become the available raw material through which a culture expresses itself. So, in a third-world country, aluminum from Pespsi and Coke cans and rubber from imported tires are just as likely to show up in the artwork as indigenous materials—it's what's at hand. While robot components have barely reached the outskirts of modern, first-world culture, so saturation is minimal, robot codes and signs have been thoroughly penetrating our consciousness for decades. These Device artists have decided to use all of their creative powers to bring the robot tinfoil, to recombine the found objects, the future forward household appliances, electronic components, and other everyday elements cast from our lives to create the robots we always wanted. They all do it in very unique and inspired ways, from the '50s-looking constructions of Rich Muller's sweet and personable knuckle-draggers and Paul Loughridge's sparky little bots, to Jeremy Mayer's incredibly-detailed typewriter recombinism, to Lewis Tardy's quicksilvery, Art Decoesque robotic humans and animals. Nemo Gould's work is packed with whimsy and deals in defiance of initial impressions. His art (and a lot of the work here) is usually an act of promising one thing and delivering something different, like a joke that's funny because the set-up creates an expectation and the payoff comes from a completely different direction. A comedian once told me that the distance between the expectation and payoff dictated the size of the laugh. In kinetic pieces like *The Performer #2* and *Re:animated*, the distance traveled is satisfyingly great.

Olivier Pauwels and Stéphane Halleux draw from a similar box of objects, but recombine them to a very different effect. Olivier's work is much darker, more innervating. Although the subject matter of Stéphane's work is no less potentially sinister, there's a sense of wonder and charm about it that adds a note of sweetness. He's probably heard it too many times before, but there's something extremely Burton-esque about the world Stéphane Halleux creates.

If much of the work in this collection trades on the reconstruction of components found in the adult world, Kris Kuksi's constructions recombine the content of a child's. Army men, vehicles, dolls, plastic models, and other similar components coalesce into unimaginably dense Bosch-worthy sculptures that speak to decidedly adult themes. Not surprisingly, given these raw materials, war, death, and the depths of human suffering infuse these pieces. If the Devil had had an adolescence, this would have been his playset.

Rounding out the collection is Mike Libby's increasingly well-known, and deservedly so, cyborged, watchwork bugs, along with some new constructions heading in a very different direction. This is represented here by *Recycled Ruins*, constructed of little paper boxes, and *Stegosaurus*, a dinosaur model built from Bible pages.

Crossing Jules Verne's rivets and brass Nautilus with Italian surrealist Luigi Serafini's visions (with a little Yellow Submarine thrown in for good measure) might approximate the flavor of Michihiro Matsuoka's work. As with all of the artists in this collection, the quality of the construction, the obsessive attention to detail, is as impressive as the ideas being expressed.

There is something Lovecraftian about Steve Brudniak's pieces, an old (Old) world menace, a discernible chill that creeps along the walls upon which much of the work hangs. These are devices that give you the impression that, as you're looking at them, they might be looking back. Closer examination, peering into the worlds on the other side of their windows, offer payoffs not anticipated—again, a twist of rusty wire that threads itself through this entire collection.

Jud Turner weaves together contradictions as deftly as he weaves the welding rod used in many of his figurative pieces. His flip-sided, wall-mounted assemblages reveal the opposites his work embraces.

Tom Haney's handcarved automata dutifully bring up the rear, with antique-style robotic wood and metal servants going about their robotic business, from behind antique glass. Watching these automata in action offers up a strange feeling of both sadness at the rote drudgery of the tasks these mechanical humans are perpetually performing, but also a sliver of hope for the nobility found ever-present in the human spirit.

In the end, looking at Haney's automata, some of the other kinetic works in this collection, and the robot and cyborg sculptures, we're reminded of one of the things that attracts us so strongly to robots and personified machinery in the first place—the extent to which we identify with them. And in a world that's becoming increasingly cut and paste, reconstructed, to the point that the cutting and pasting has come to include us, it's only fitting that the Device artists are bringing the tinfoil—if for no other reason than for us to decide if we really want to wear it.

Gareth Branwyn writes on the intersection of art, technology, and culture. He wrote for Wired *for 12 years and has written or edited more than 10 books on technology, media, culture, and humor. He is currently a Senior Editor at MAKE magazine.*

GREGORY **BROTHERTON**

Migraine Machine II — 11" x 15" (2009)

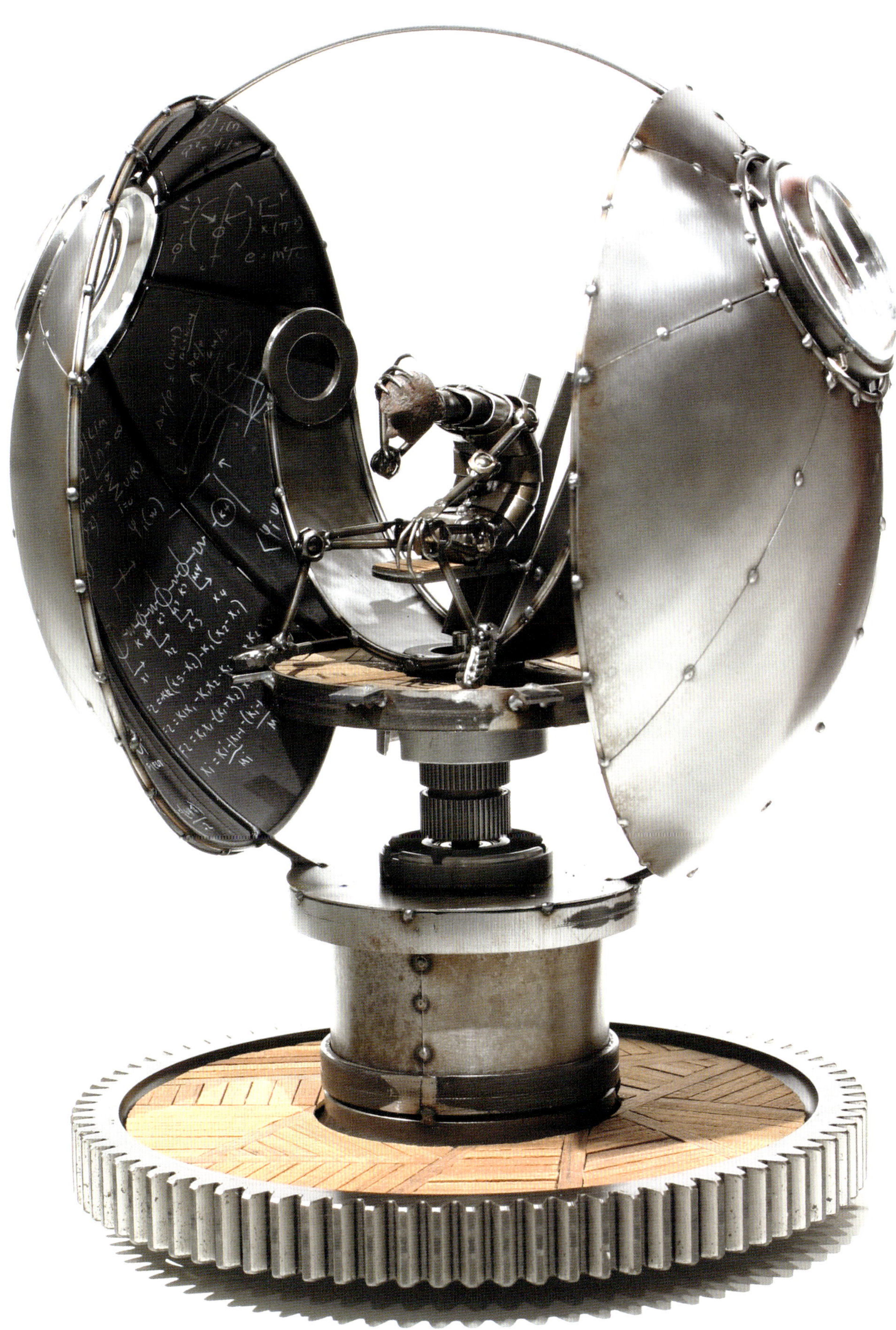

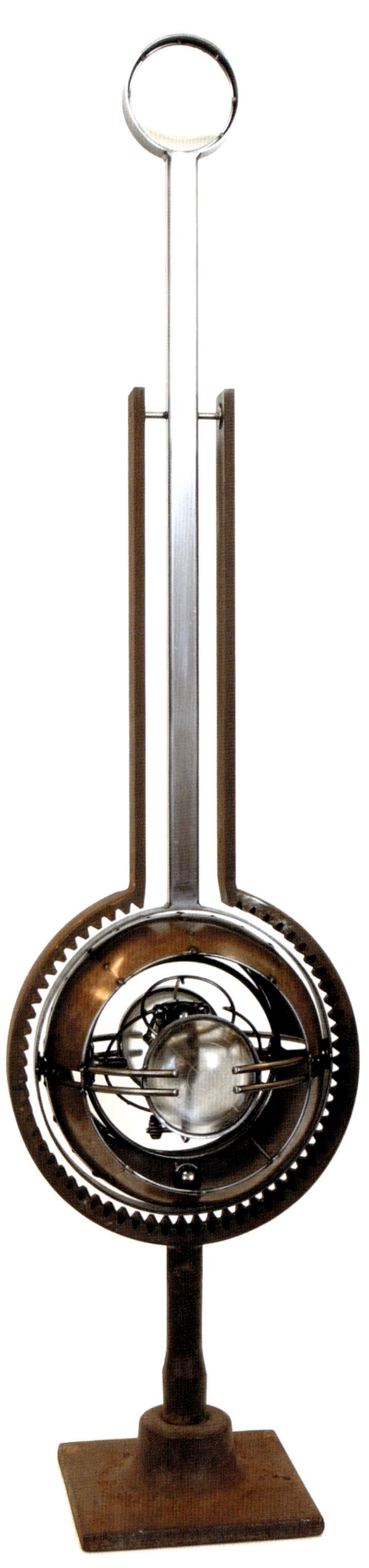

Pendulum – 47" x 13" x 9" welded steel, found object, surplus lenses (2008)

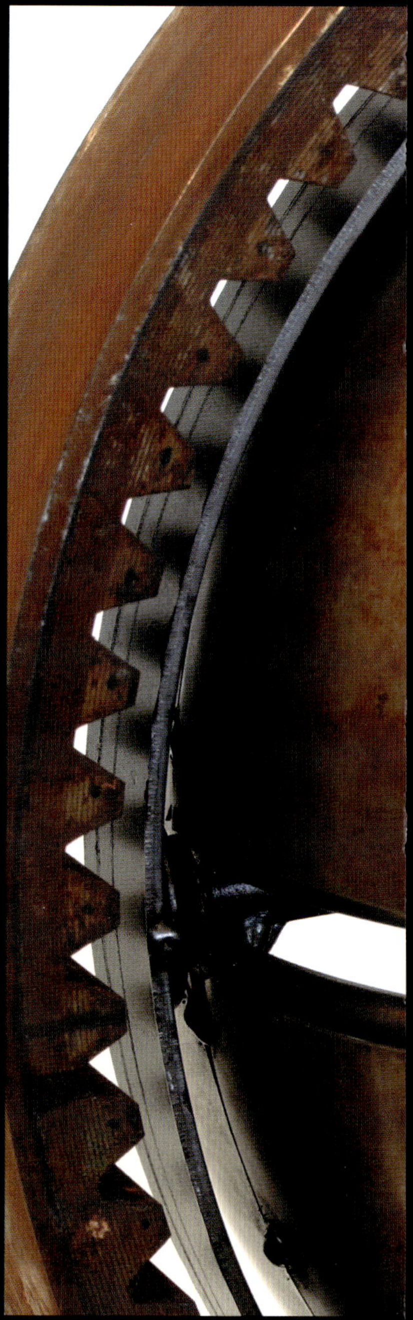

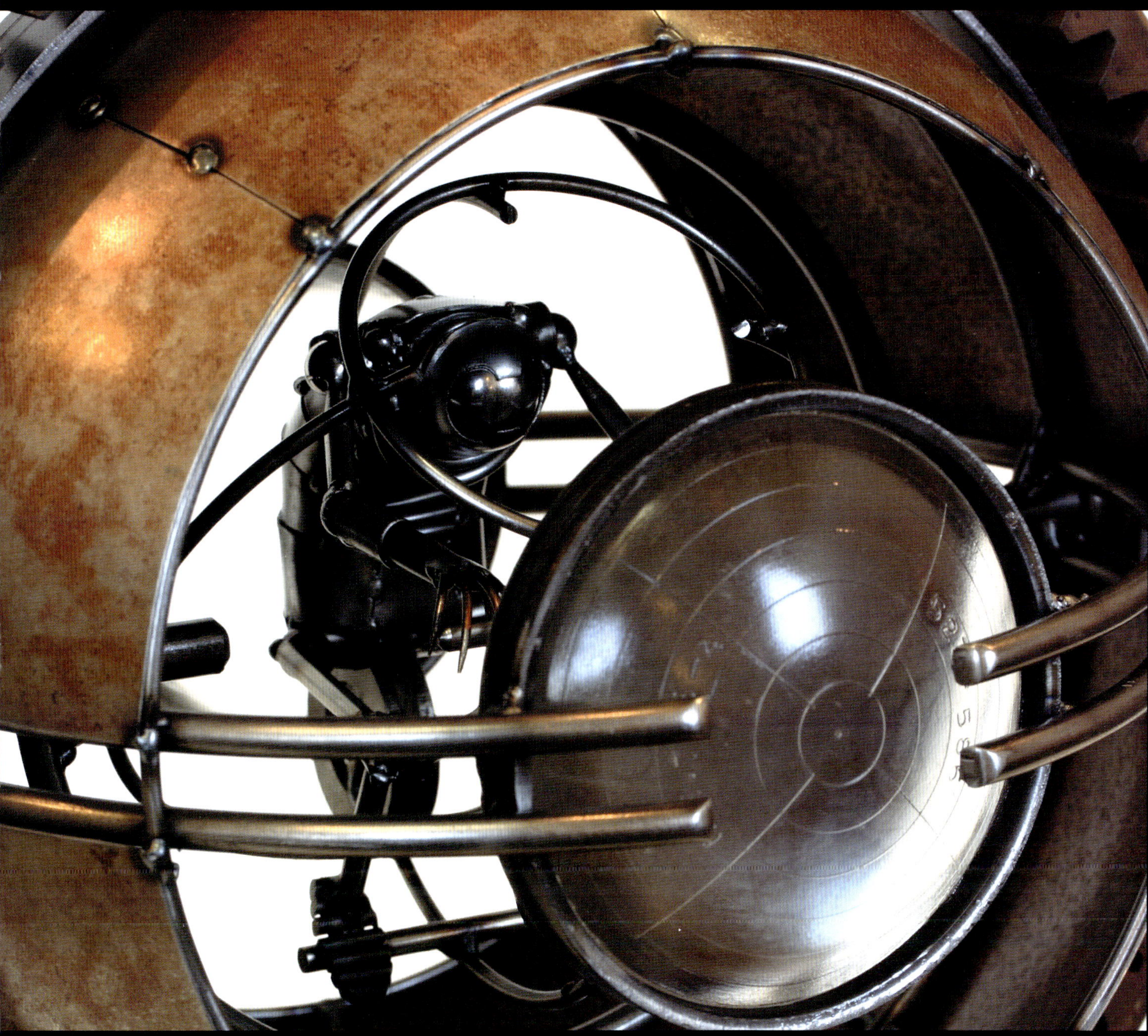

Gregory **Brotherton**

"Inspired by human curiosity and the wonderful mechanisms that curiosity brings about, my work explores relationships of emotion and technology. The forms I present emerge from a disordered mechanical history, often revealed through a dystopian lens."

Born in Aims, Iowa, in 1968, Greg experienced a somewhat nomadic childhood, spending the majority of his youth in Utah and Colorado. His interest in the mechanical surfaced at age five, when he began disassembling anything with screws in it. By twelve he had taught himself to mine his backyard with homemade explosives (no injuries!). Then, after being successfully ejected from a series of public and private learning institutions, Greg, with equivalency test in hand, entered the Colorado Academy of Art, beginning his undergraduate studies at sixteen.

In 1987, after receiving a degree in graphic design, Greg set off for California. Over the next two decades, he forged a successful career as an award-winning commercial artist, while honing his skills as a sculptor.

With a consuming drive to build things, which often escalate in complexity as they take shape, Greg's work is compulsive. Working with hammer-formed steel and repurposed objects, his themes tend to be mythological in nature, revealed through a Dystopian view of pop culture.

Greg's work has received international recognition and has been exhibited throughout the United States. In 2007, he was invited to serve as the featured artist at the Technology, Entertainment, Design (TED) Conference in Monterey, California, joining the ranks of some of the most prestigious artists, luminaries, and scientists of our time.

He currently resides in San Diego, California, where he continues to sculpt and experiment and is owner of the Device Gallery.

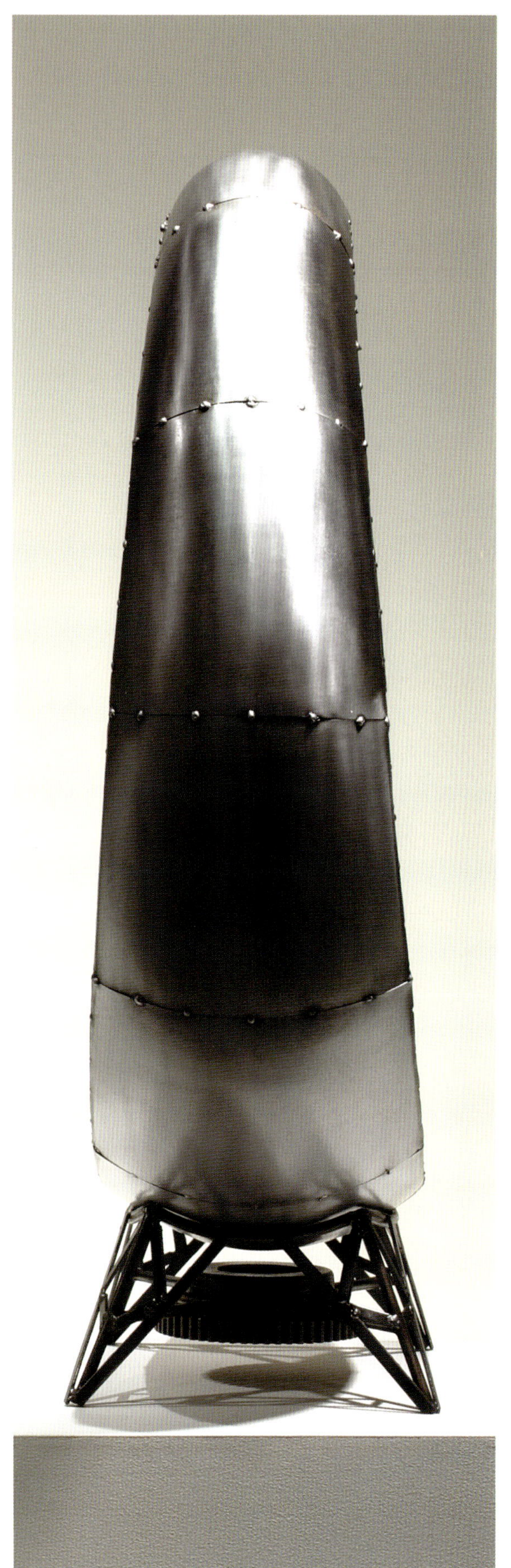

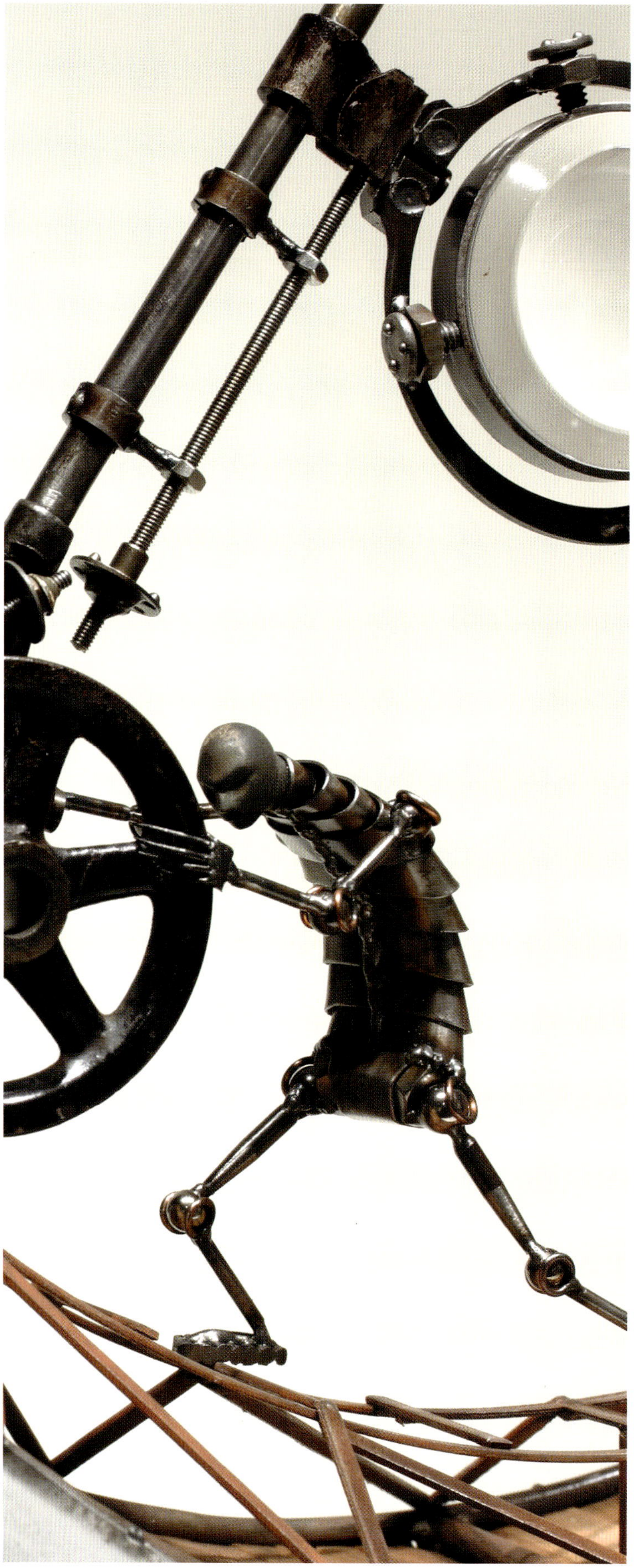

Pushed Around – welded steel, teak, surplus lens, iron (2009)

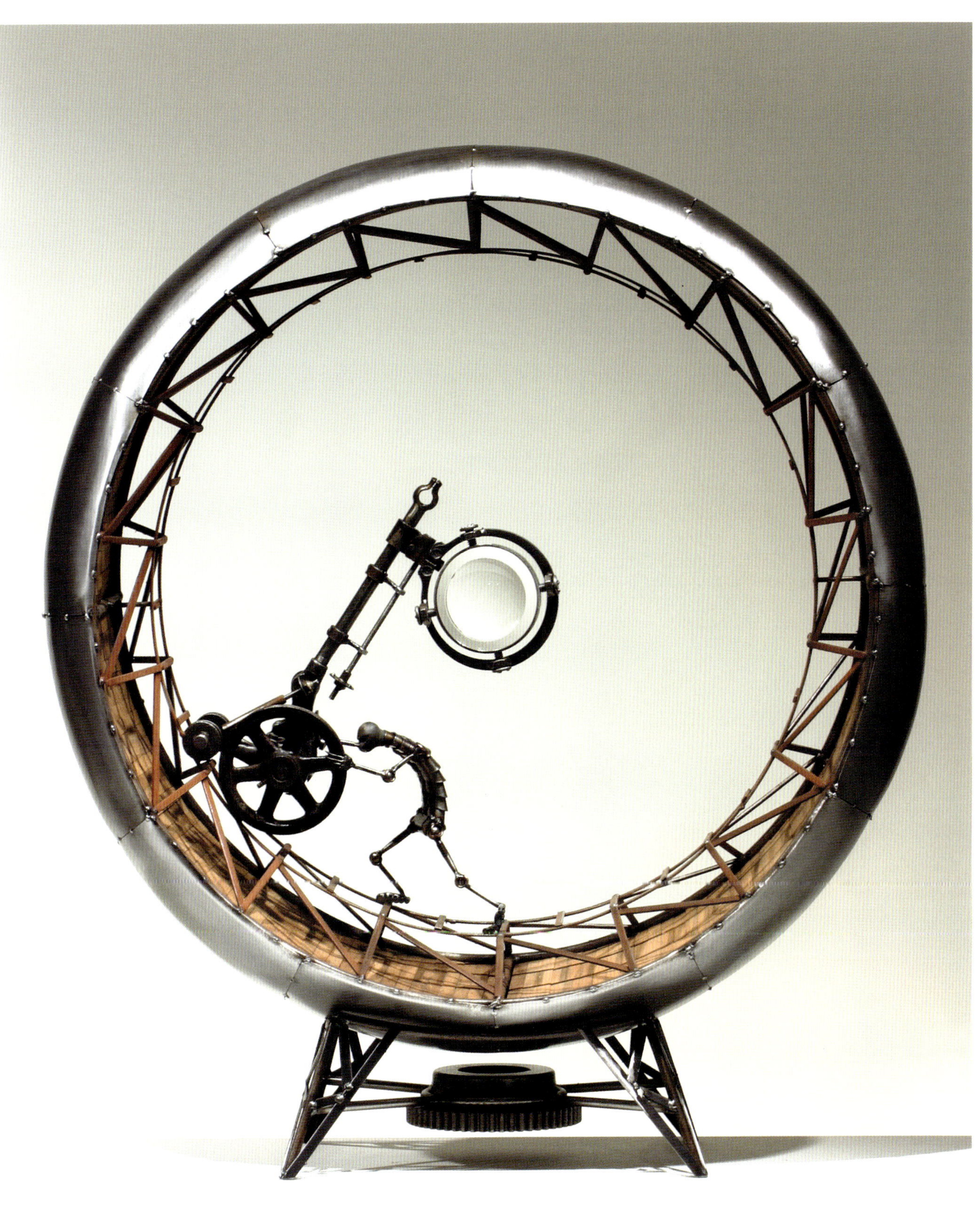

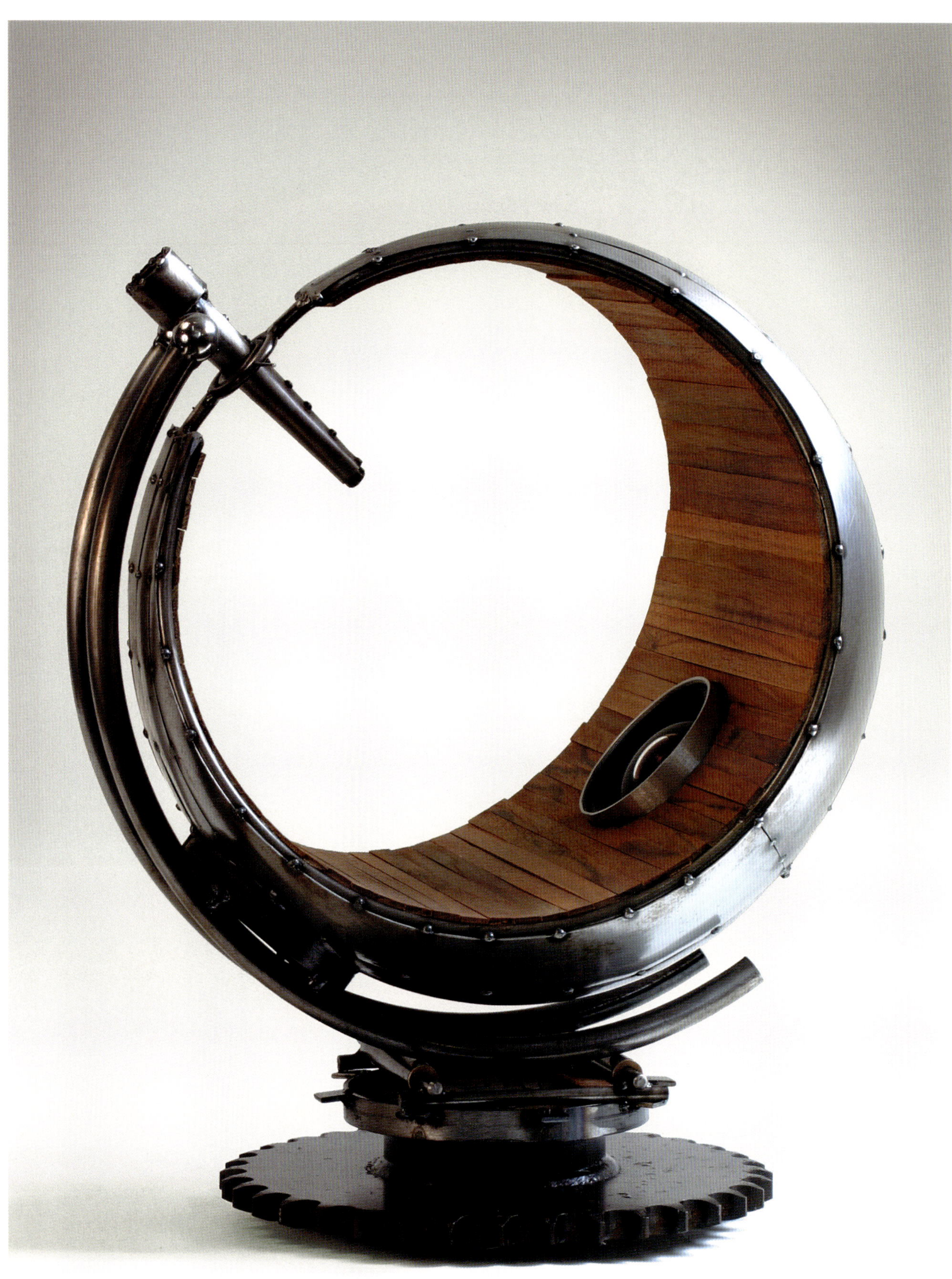

Observatory I – 16" x 15" x 9" welded steel, teak, surplus lens (2008)

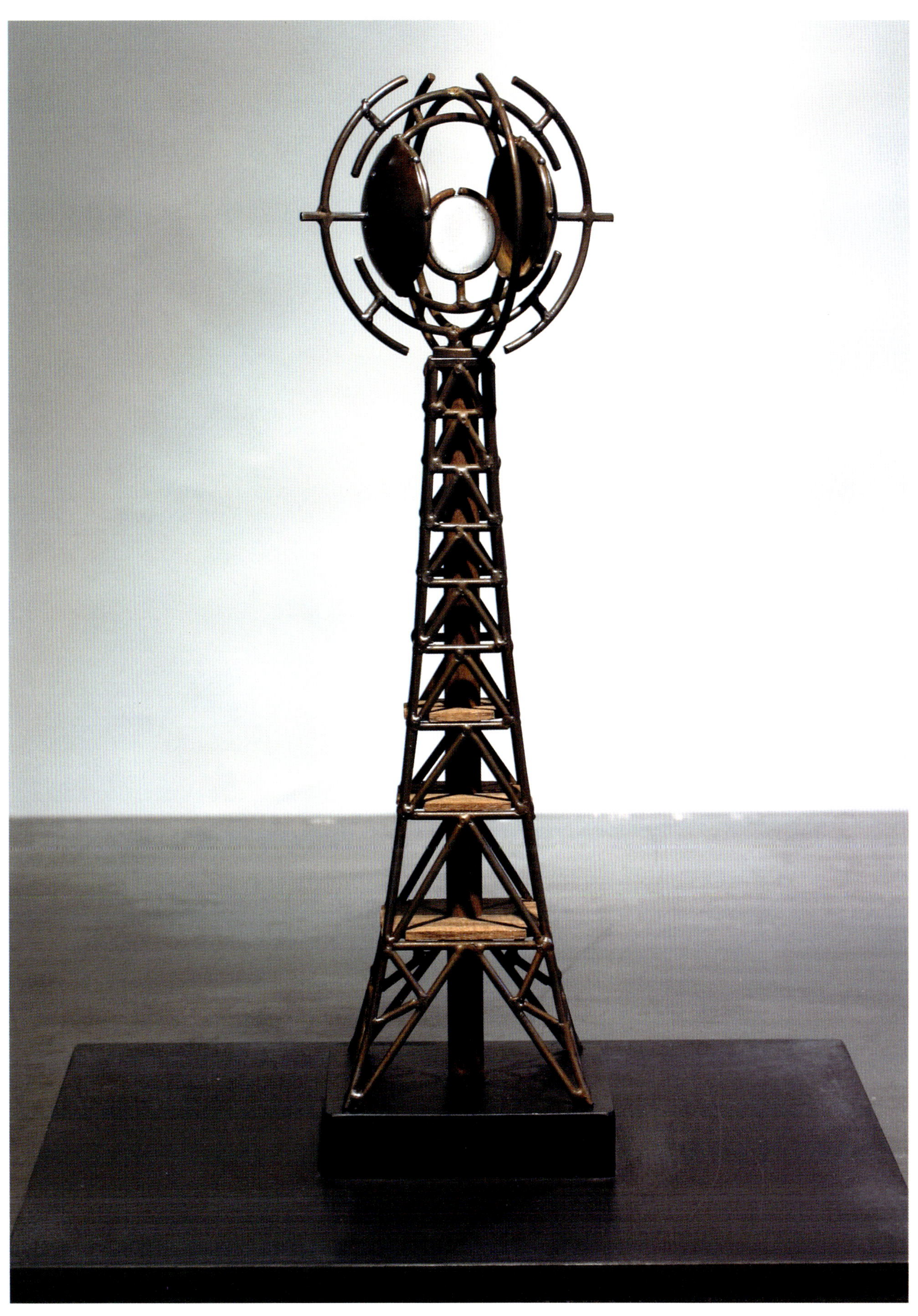

Lost Signal – welded steel, teak, surplus lens (2009)

STEVE**BRUDNIAK**

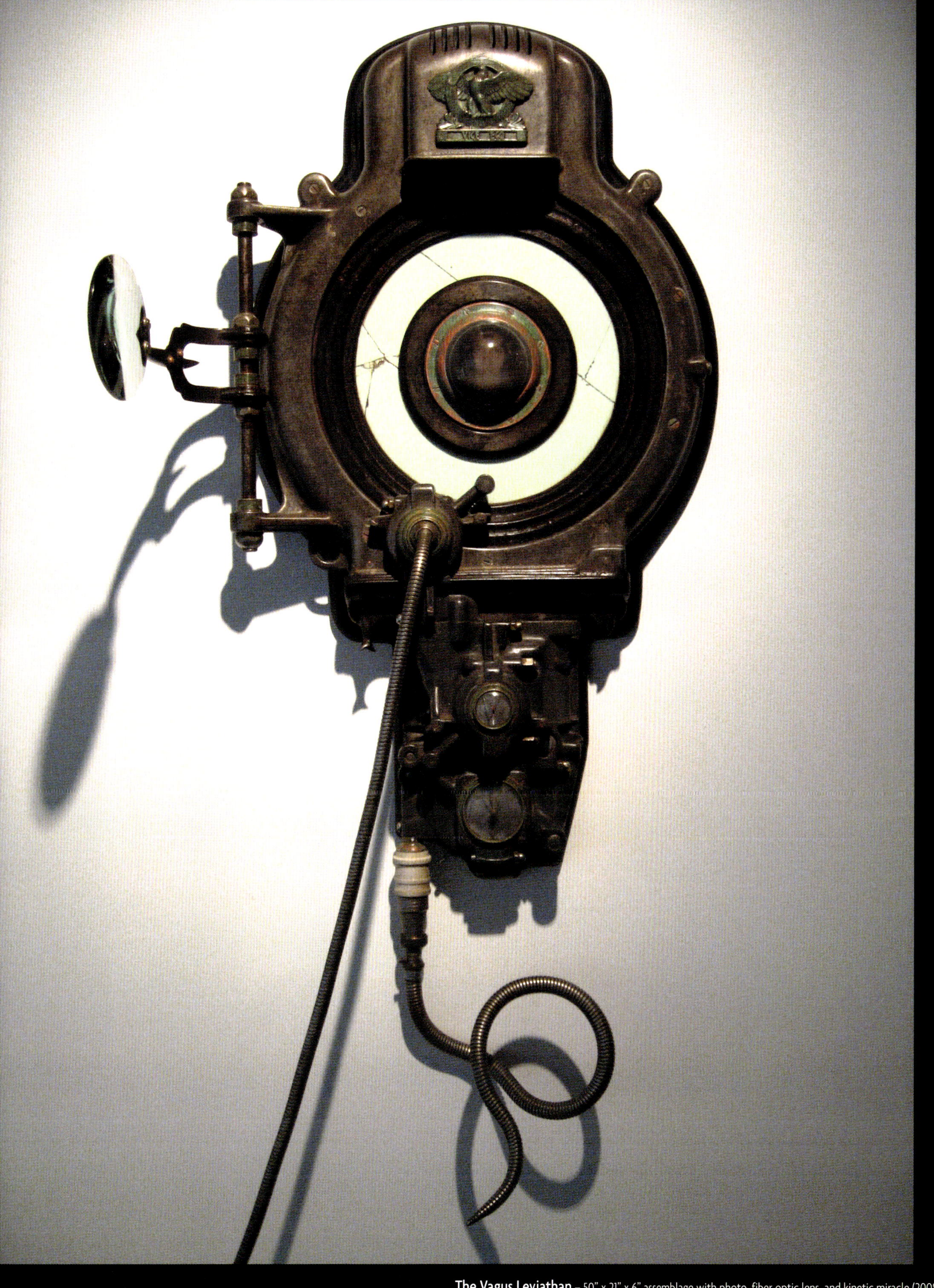

The Vagus Leviathan – 50" x 21" x 6" assemblage with photo, fiber optic lens, and kinetic miracle (2008)
Collections of Richard Garriott, Richard Linklater, and Wiley Wiggins

Steve **Brudniak**

Steve Brudniak (born April 9 1961, Topeka, Kansas) is an American contemporary artist and filmmaker known mostly for highly crafted assemblage sculpture invested with active science elements and other unusual characteristics. His work is distinguished by the use of found objects and that the finished pieces do not resemble collage but rather machines, devices, or ritual objects of some fictional surreal origin. Brudniak pioneered the use of many unconventional mediums in art including Tesla coil lightning, magnetic ferro fluid, gyro mechanics, ancient and modern biological preservations, fiber optic materials and high voltage and laser applications. Pieces often generate ideas and themes of spirituality and psychological function and dysfunction and borrow elements from the surrealist and industrialist movements.

His early years were spent in Houston, Texas, where he cultivated an interest in film, writing, acting, and music. In 1981, after a short stint in the graphic arts industry, he opened a recording studio and also began making his first assemblages. By the mid '80s his work was gaining exposure and making its way into important collections including the Houston Museum of Fine Arts and local and international art publications such as Art in America.

In 1988, Brudniak moved to Austin, Texas, to begin full-time production on his sculpture. He remains involved in performance, music, filmmaking and acting and can be seen in many film and documentary productions—notably, in Rick Linklater's *Waking Life* and in Eric Frodsham's *More Moments the Go*, which he co-directed and produced, as well.

Today, books, calendars, documentaries, films, and hundreds of publications and websites feature his assemblages which can be found in the collections of the San Antonio Museum of Art, The El Paso Museum of Art and The Art Museum of South Texas at Corpus Christi, as well as in the Houston Museum and many private and corporate collections worldwide. In 2008, his *Astrogeneris Mementos* became the first assemblage sculpture in outer space when it was taken on board the International Space Station by entrepreneur and space tourist Richard Garriott.

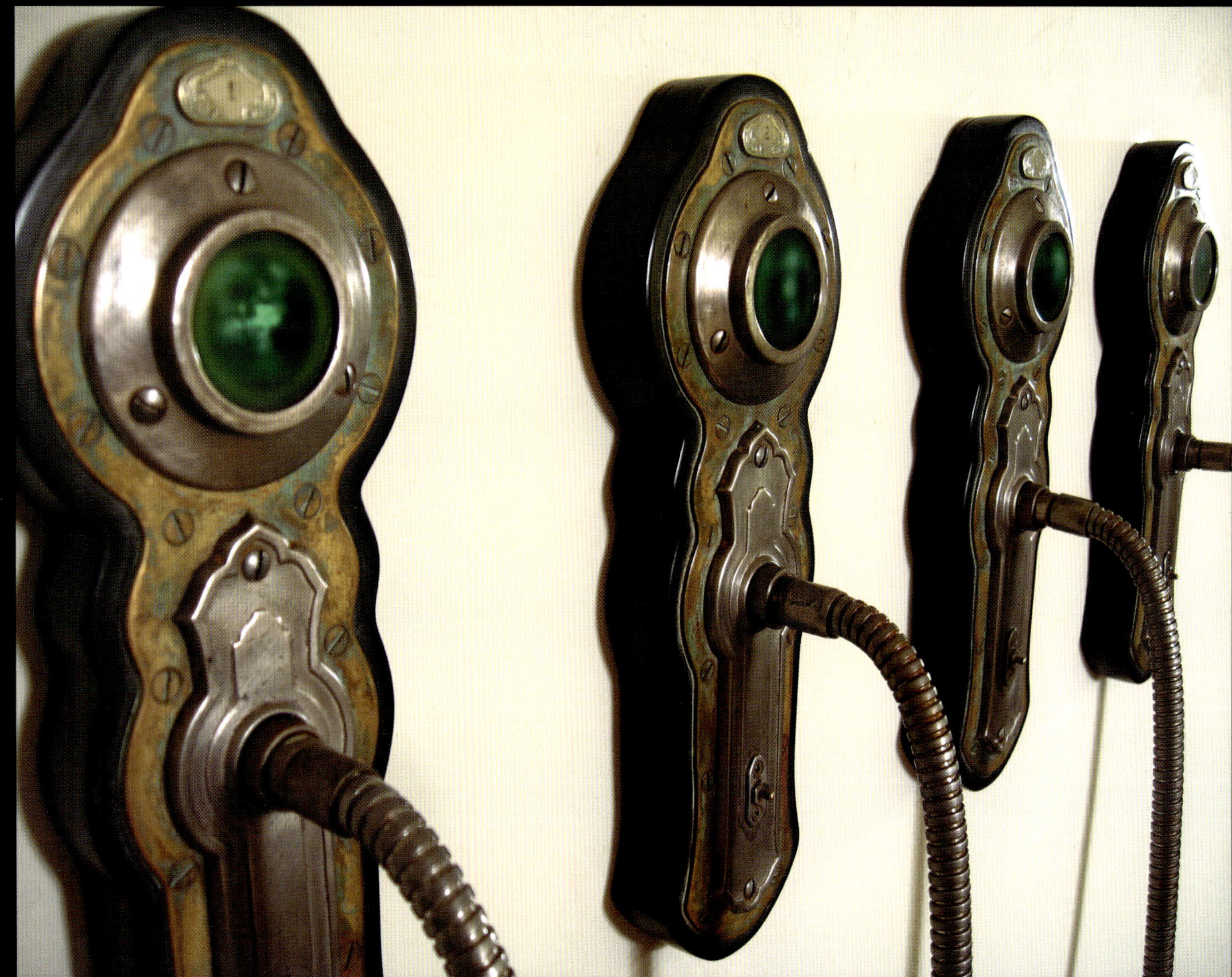

Canal Dreams (Edition of Four) – Each 12" x 4" x 4" + electrical cord. Assemblage with slide photo, fiber optic lens, and electroluminescent light (2006)
Collections of Richard Garriott, Richard Linklater, and Wiley Wiggins

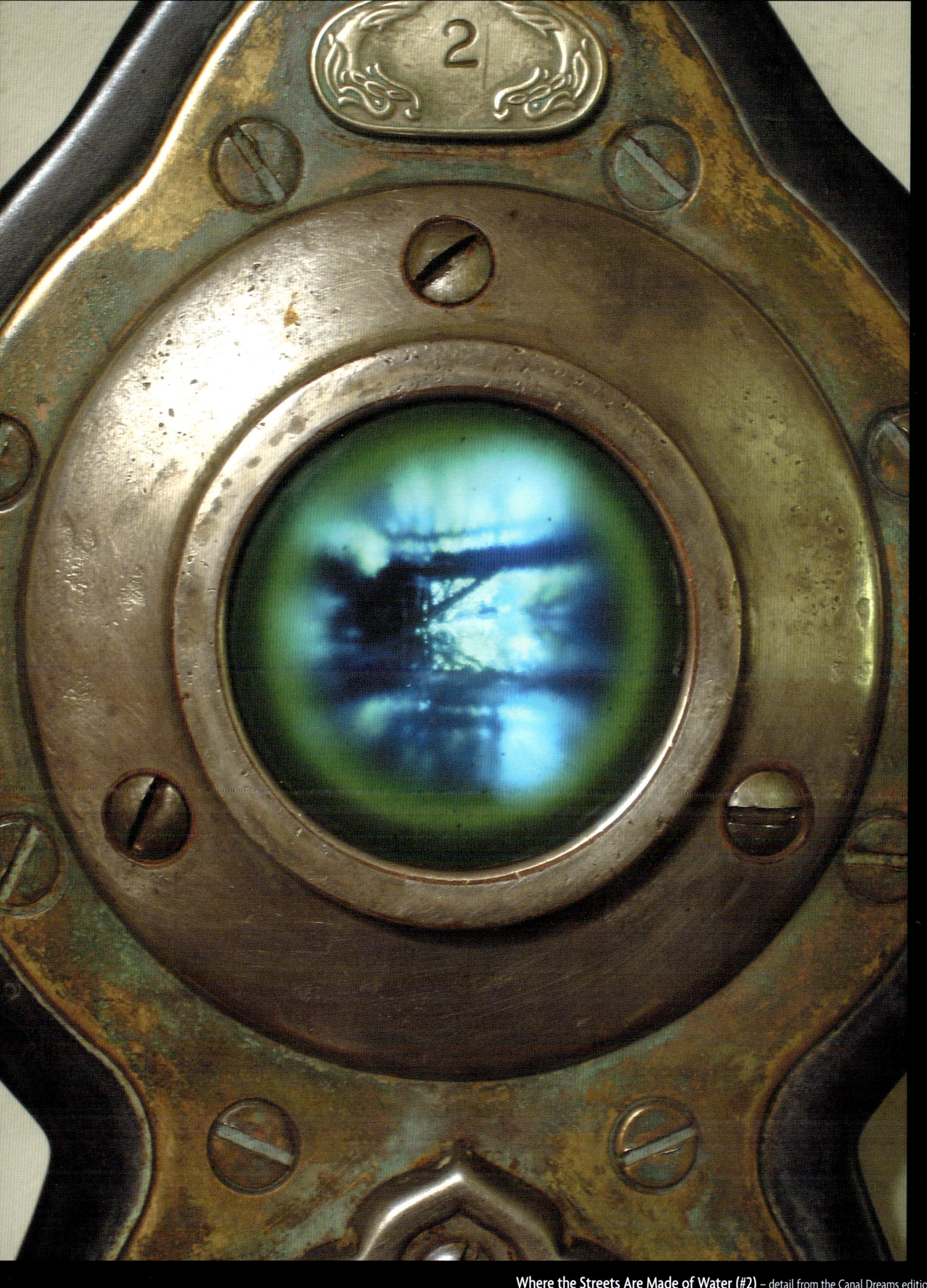

Where the Streets Are Made of Water (#2) – detail from the Canal Dreams edition
Collection of Richard Linklater

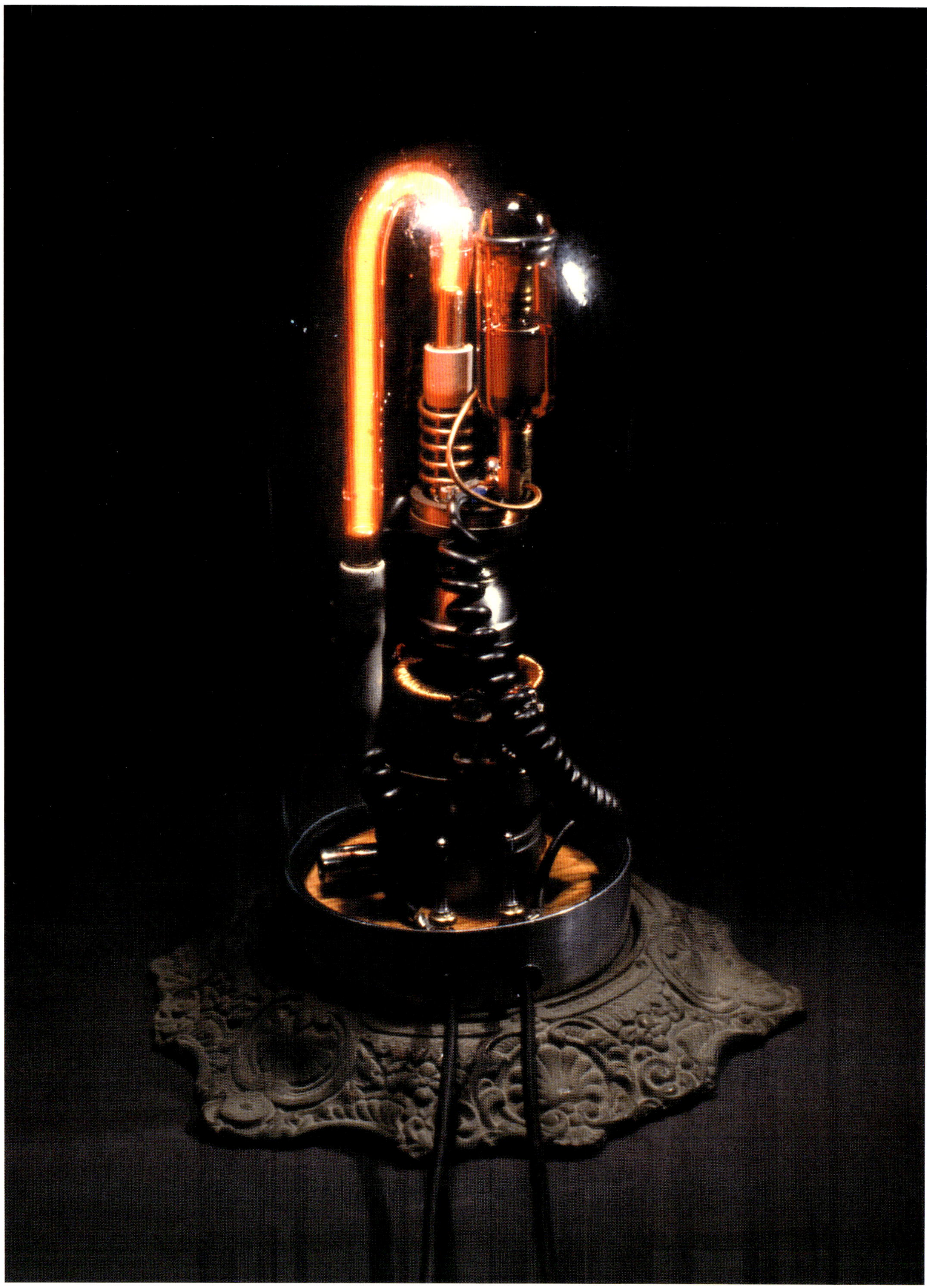

1936 Science Fiction Device – 13" x 10" x 10" assemblage with neon (1984)

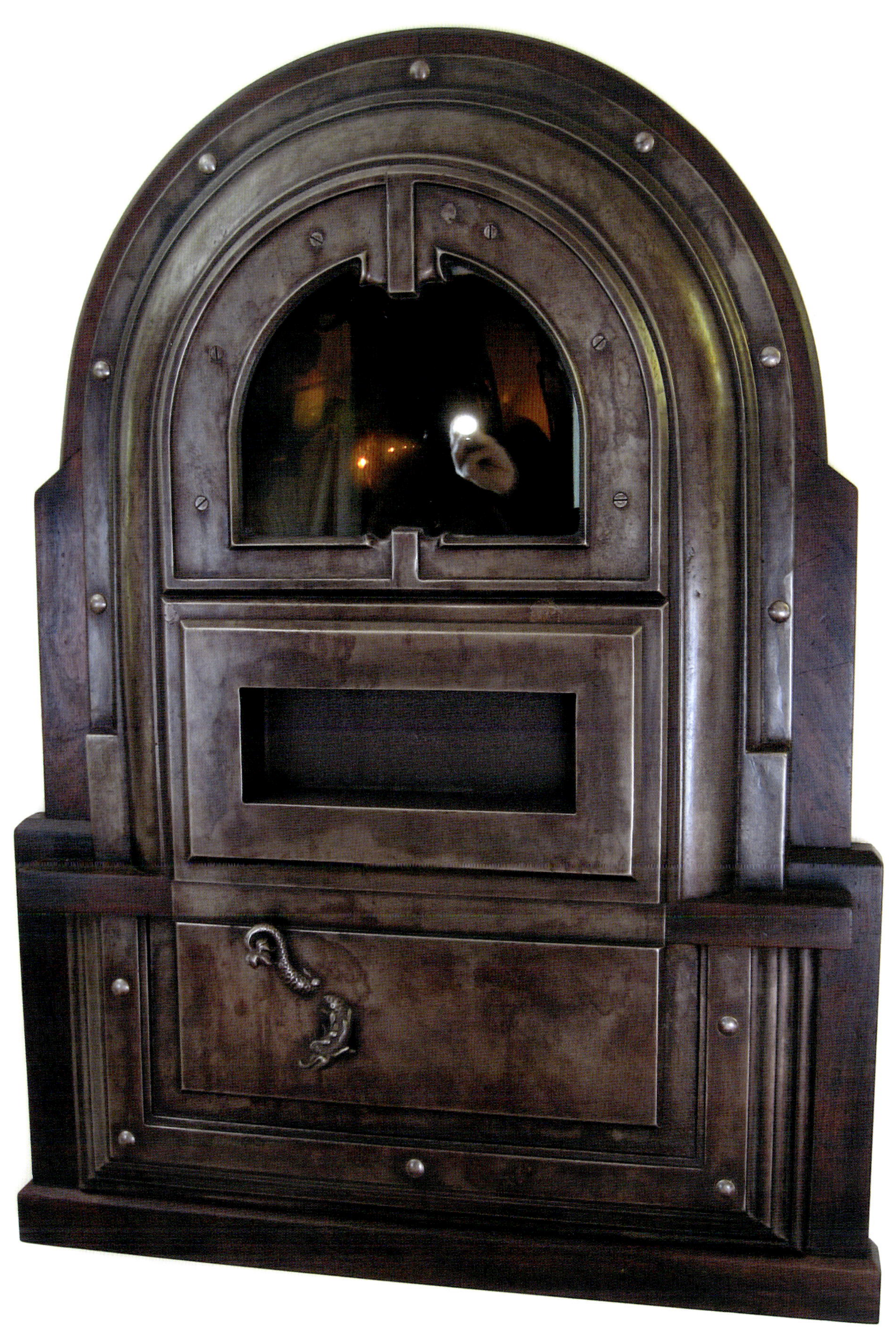

Noumenon – 45" x 34" x 36" iron and ipe wood assemblage with emanating reflection optical lens (2006)
Collection of Everett and Karen Anschutz

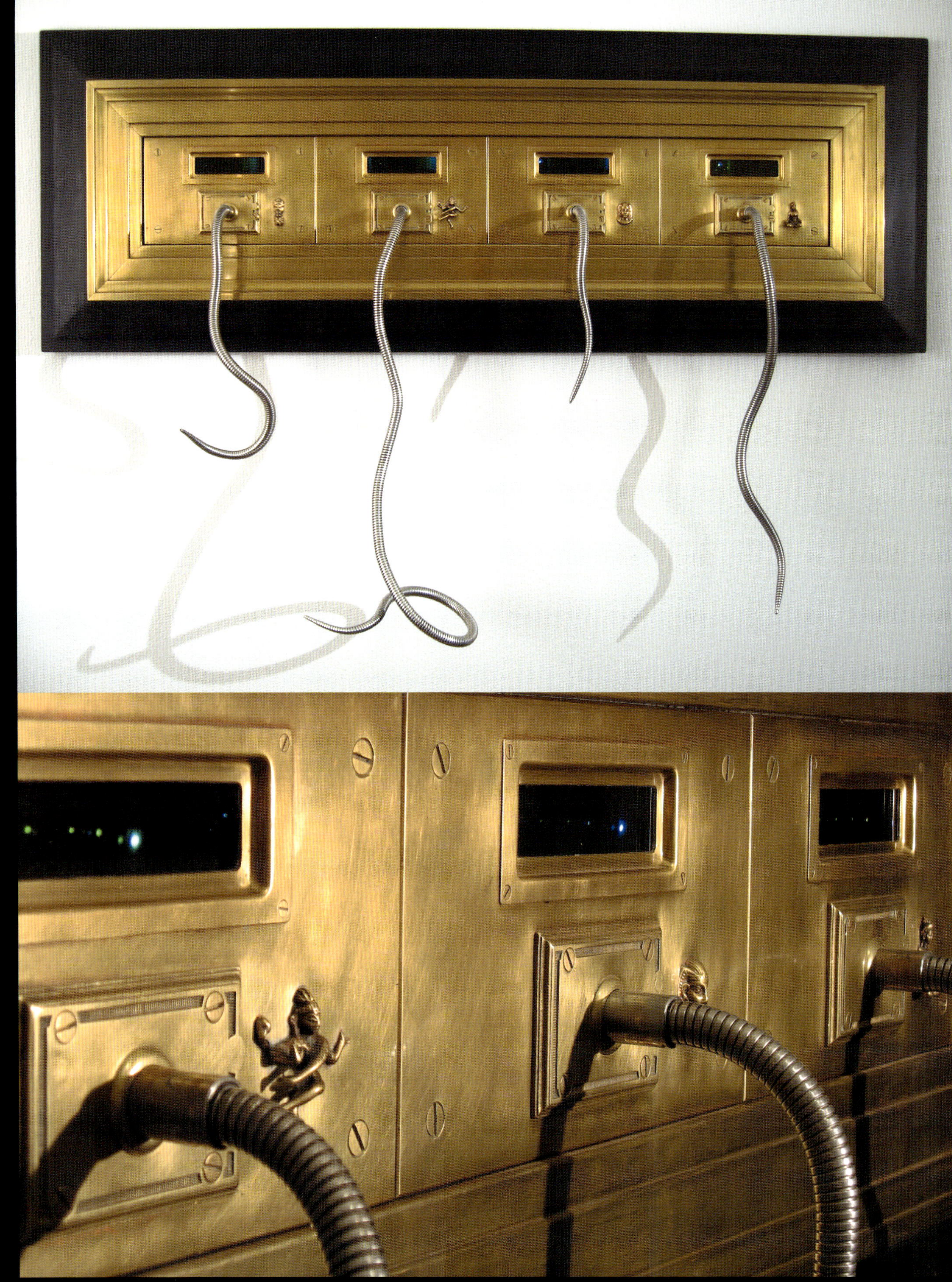

Noumenon Objectifying in Four Parts – 48" x 19" x 6" assemblage with emanating reflection optical lenses (2005)
Collection of Dr. Donovan and Catarina Sigerfoos

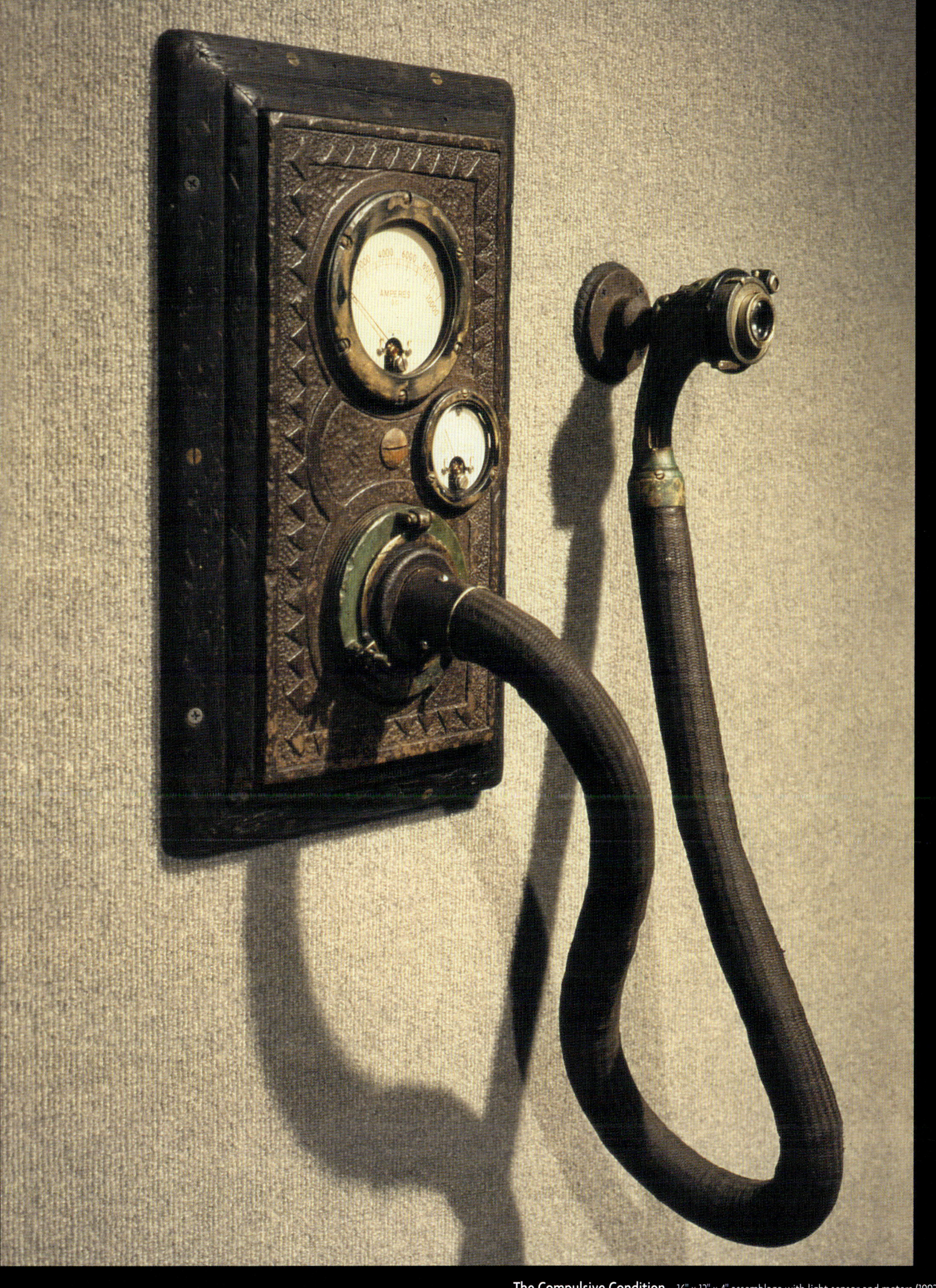

The Compulsive Condition – 16" x 12" x 4" assemblage with light sensor and meters (1992)
Collection of William Farr

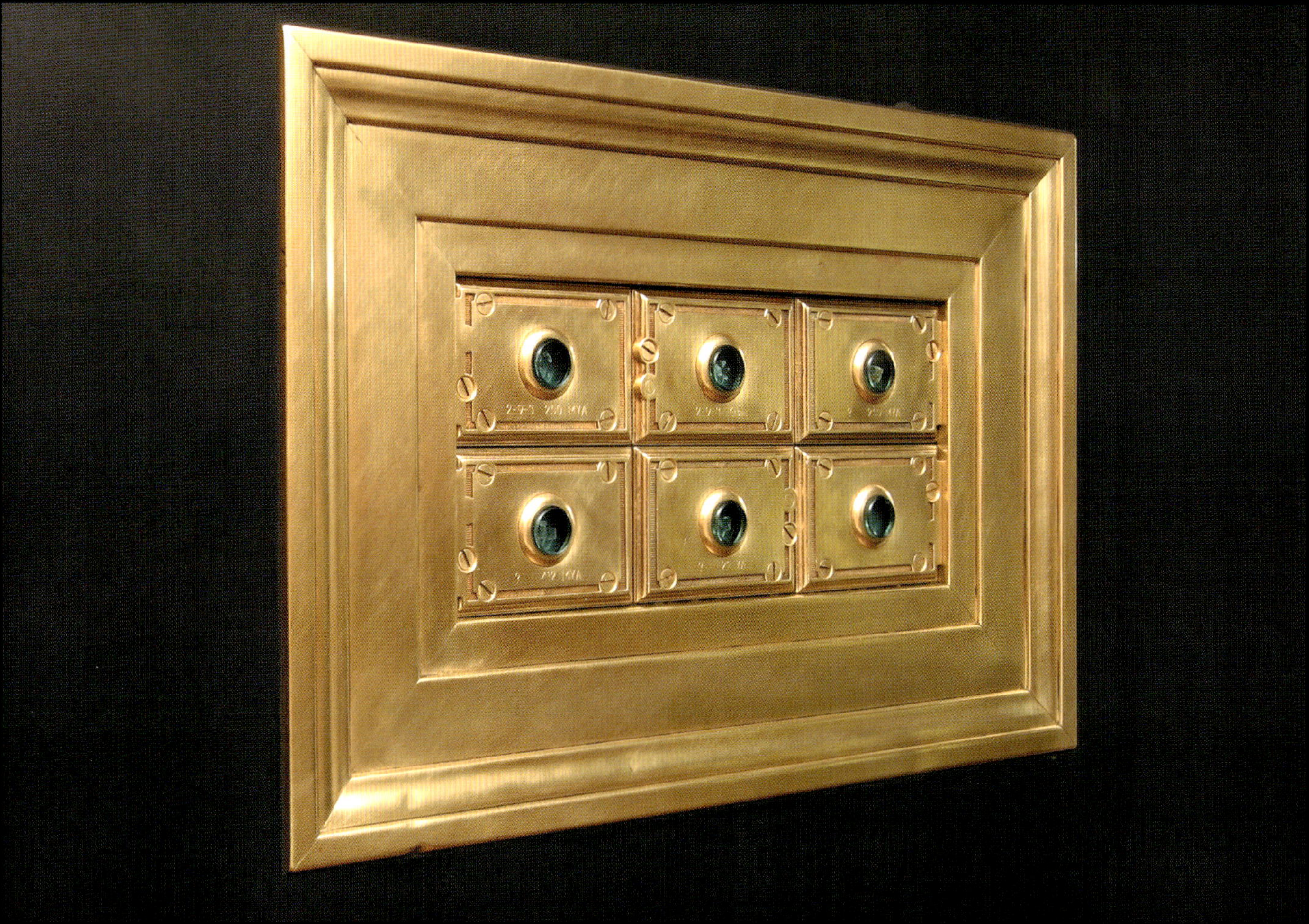

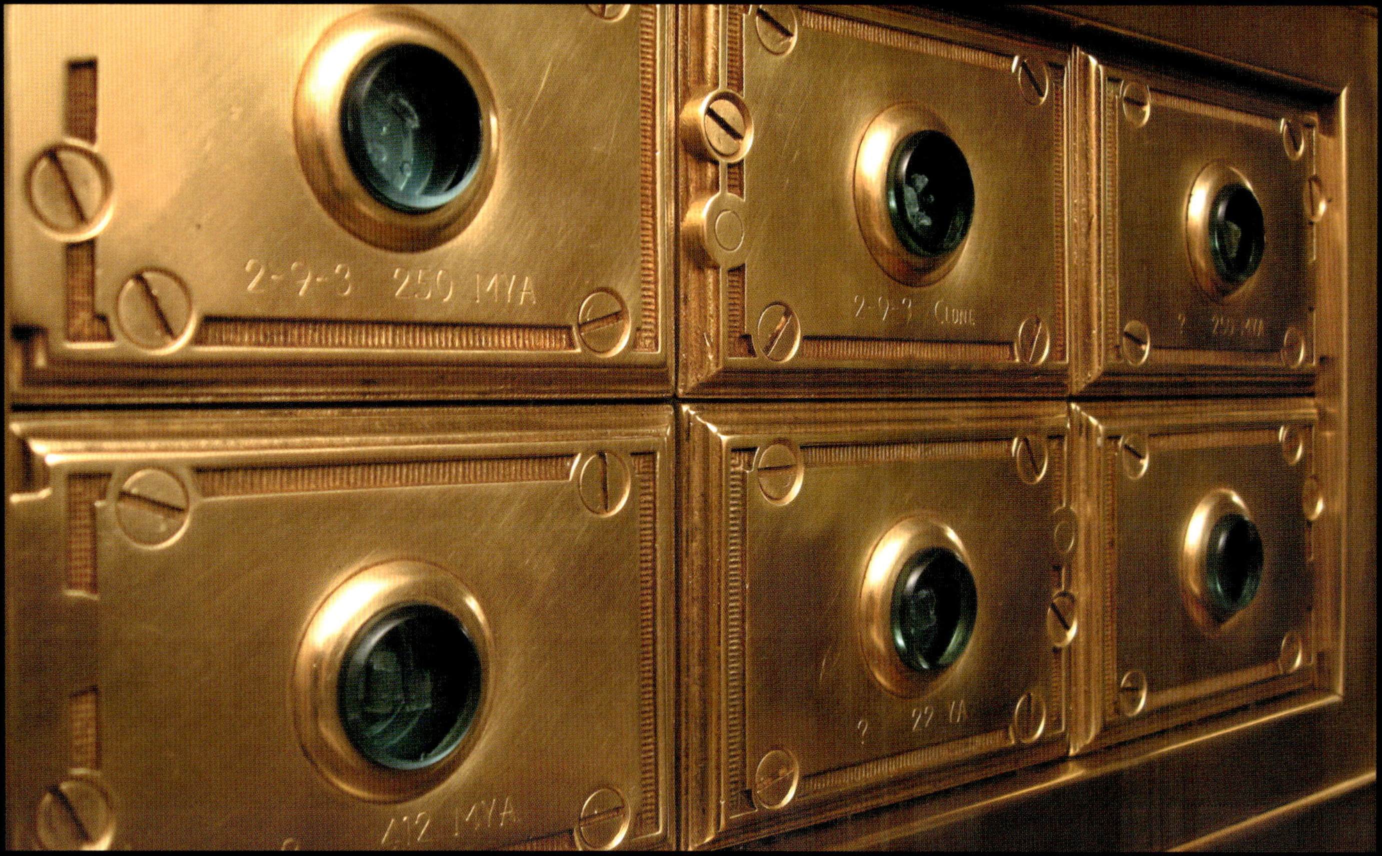

The Menagerie of Eternal Life – 25" x 32" x 3" assemblage with salt crystals containing dormant living bacteria,
including the 250 million year old 2-9-3 strain discovered in 2000, which is the oldest living thing known (2006)

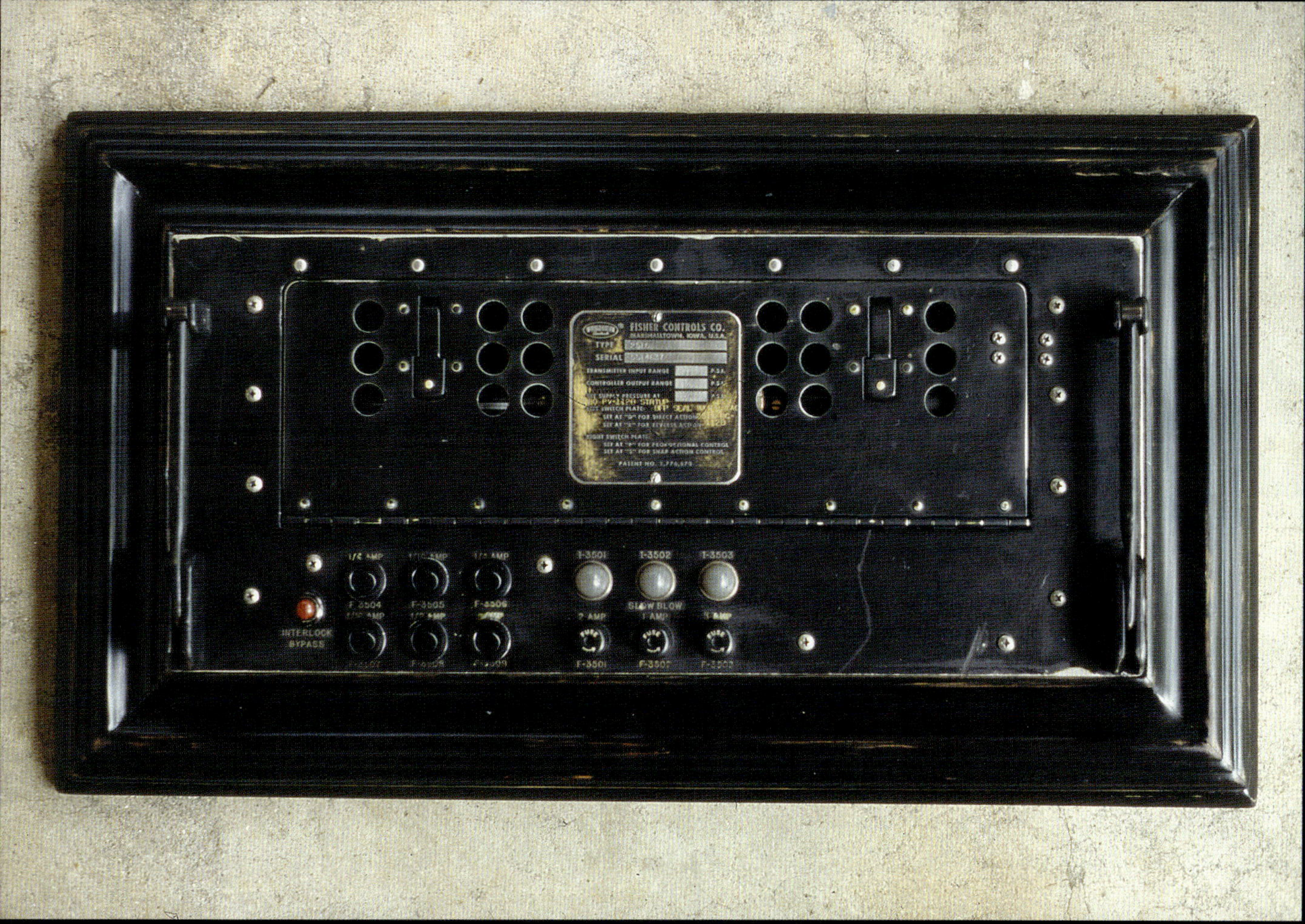

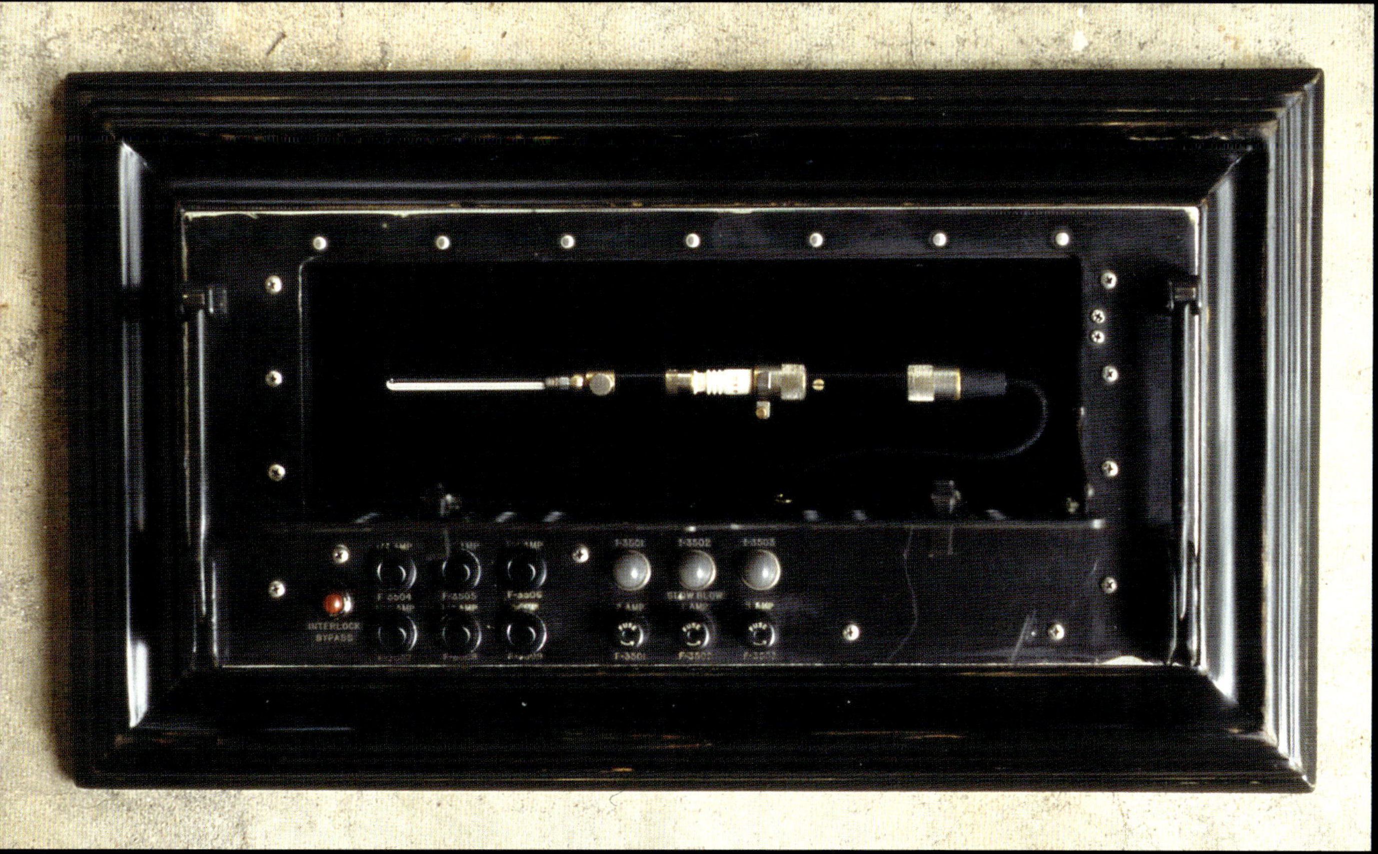

Probe with Apparatus – 14" x 24" x 6" assemblage (1994)
Collection of Peter and Bunny Van Bavel

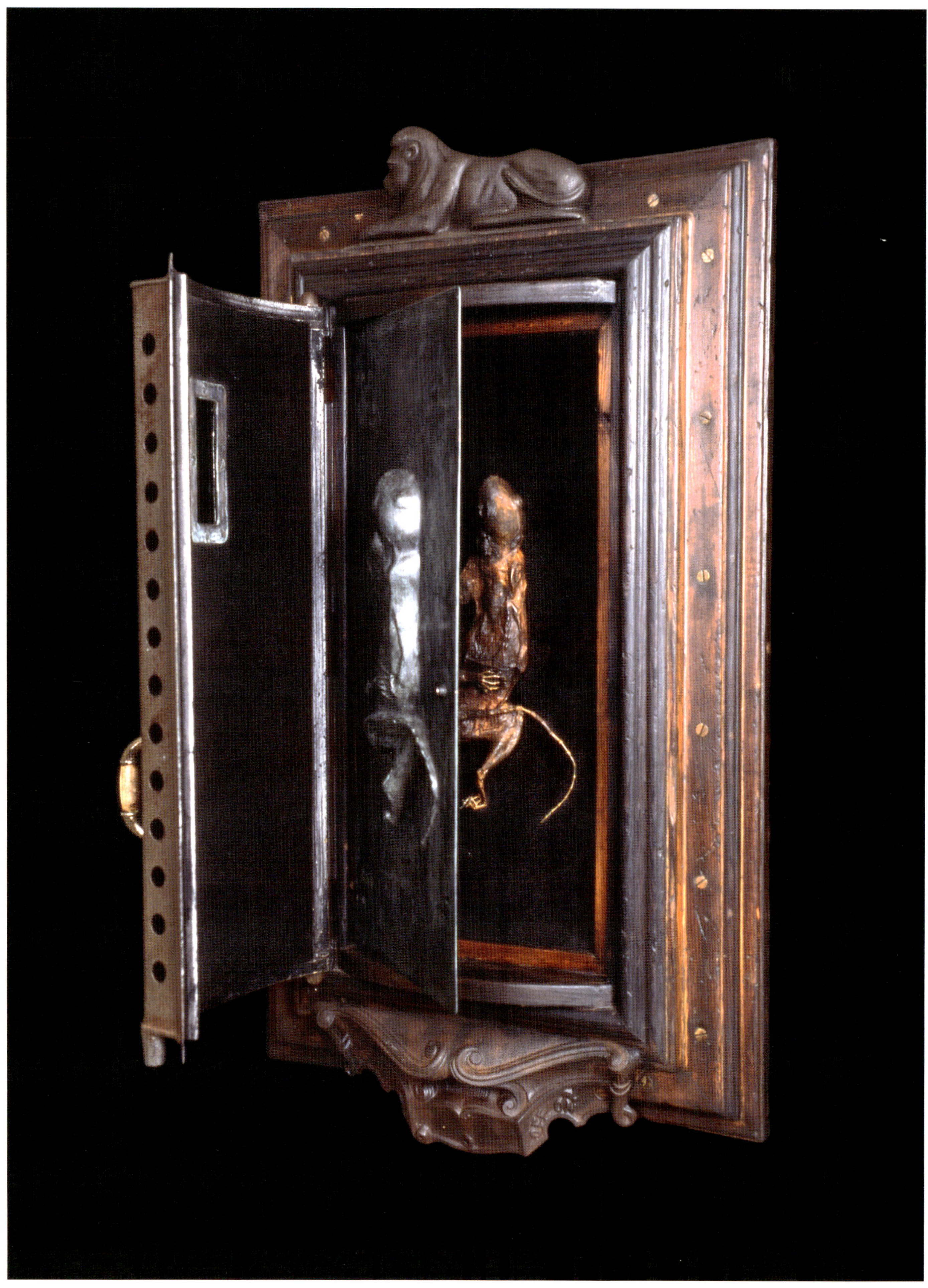

Zeitgeist – 34" x 24" x 36" assemblage with mummified squirrel and bronze squirrel cast (1996)
Collection of Edward Gage

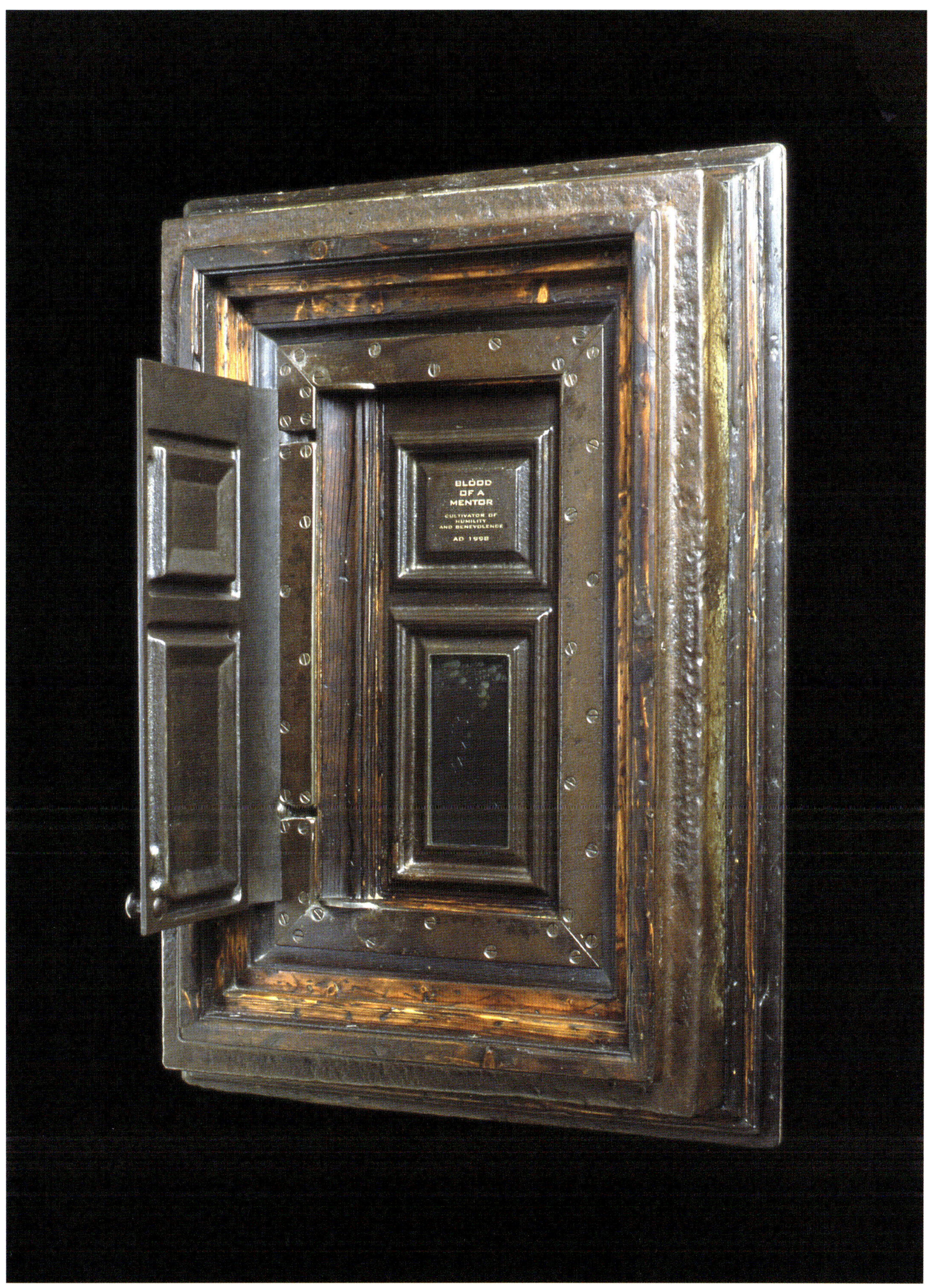

Blood of a Mentor: Cultivator of Humility and Benevolence (From the Blood of Reliquary series) – 23" x 32" x 5" assemblage with human blood (1999)

Collection of Richard Linklater

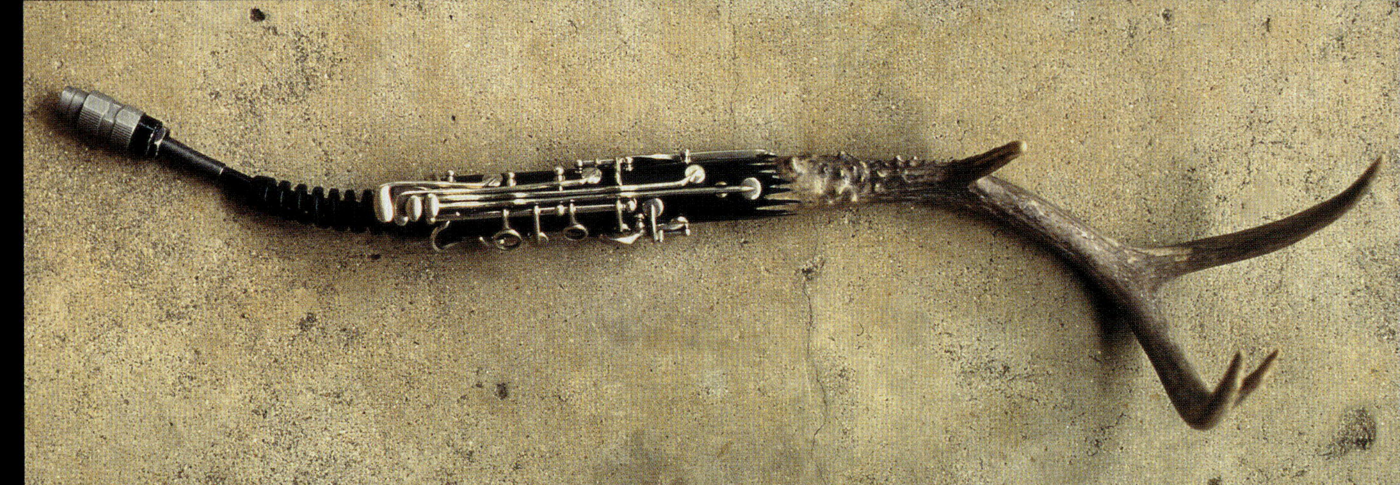

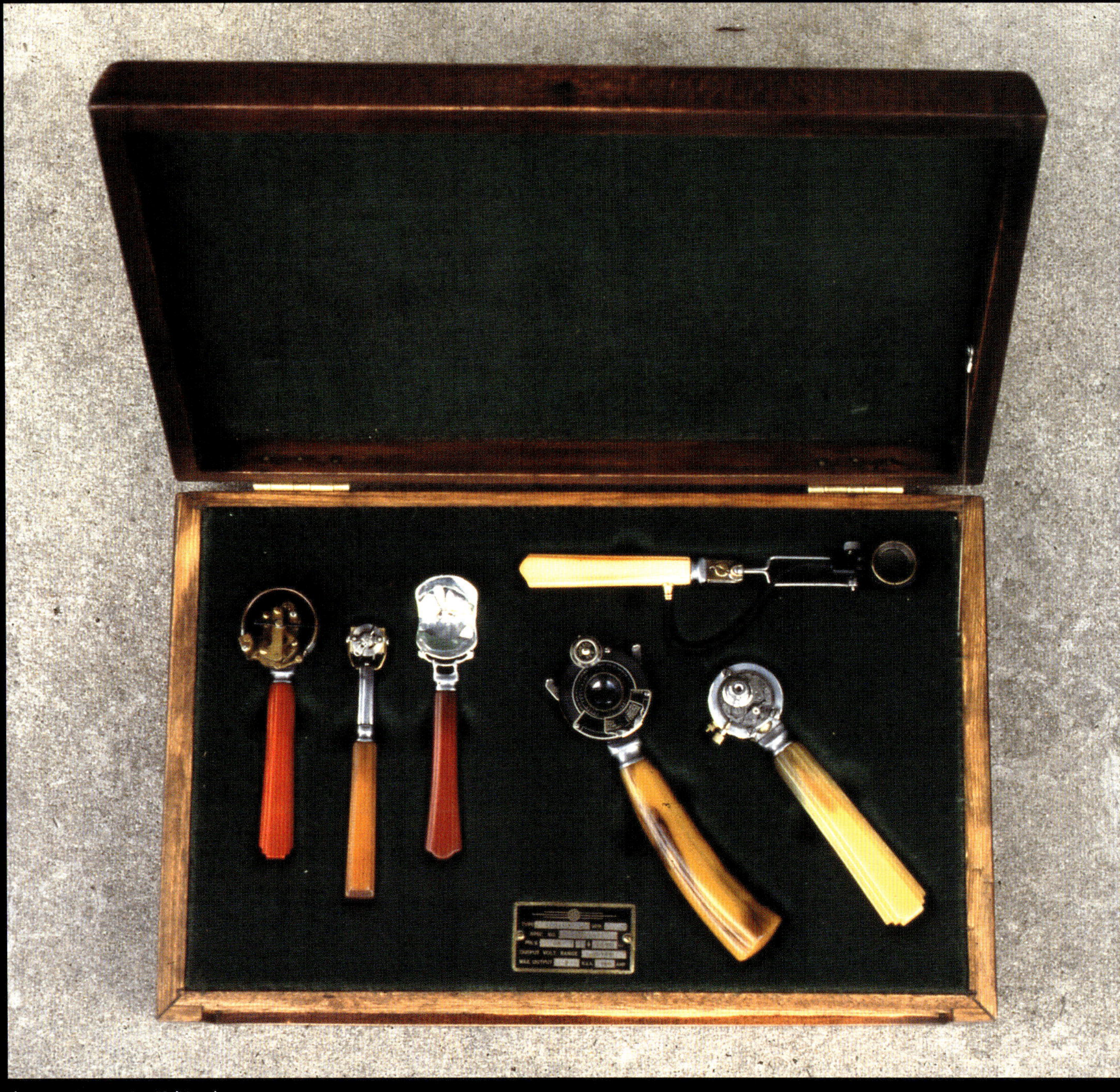

Homologous Monstrosity #2 (Horn) – 3" x 3" x 20" assemblage with antler and clarinet (1995) (top) Collection of Julie Speed
Divining Implements for Prophets, Messiahs and Physicians – 14" x 10" x 3" assemblage (1989) (bottom) Collection of The Museum of Fine Arts, Houston

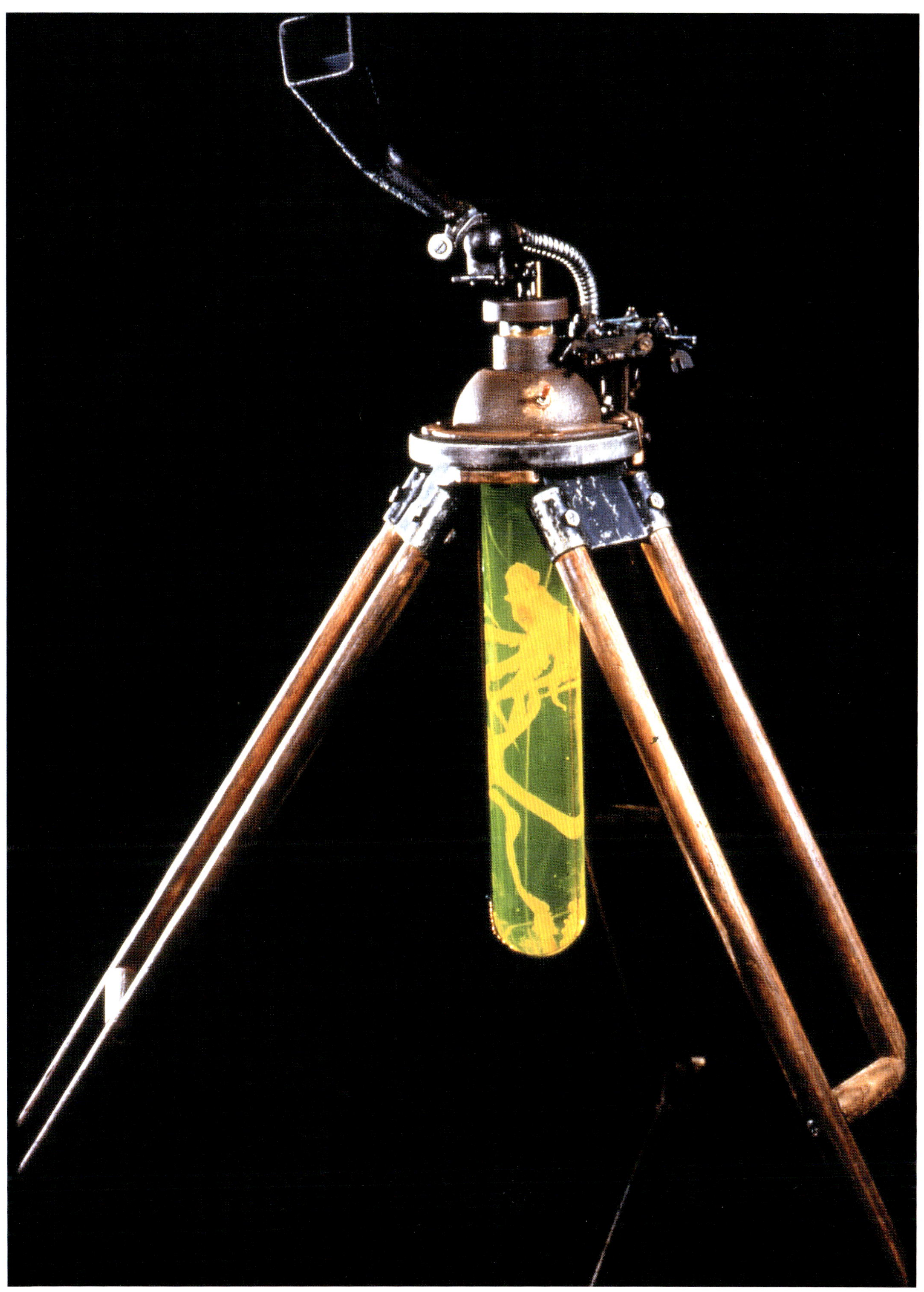

I think but What am I? – 58" x 64" x 64" assemblage with squid in propylene glycol and film projection (1990)

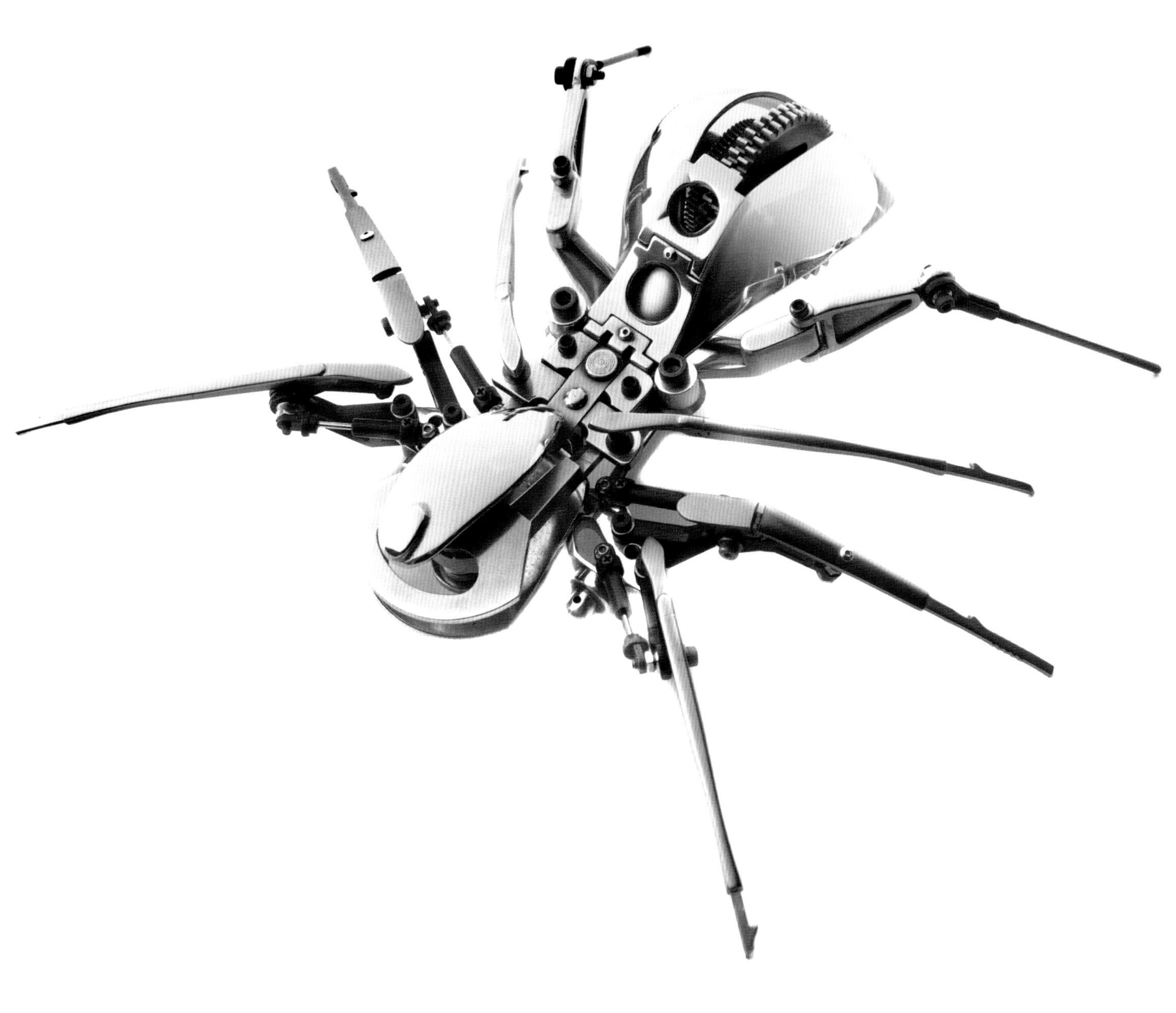

Steel Widow – 8″ x 8″ x 2″ stainless steel, carbon steel, glass-filled nylon, aluminum, and brass (2008)

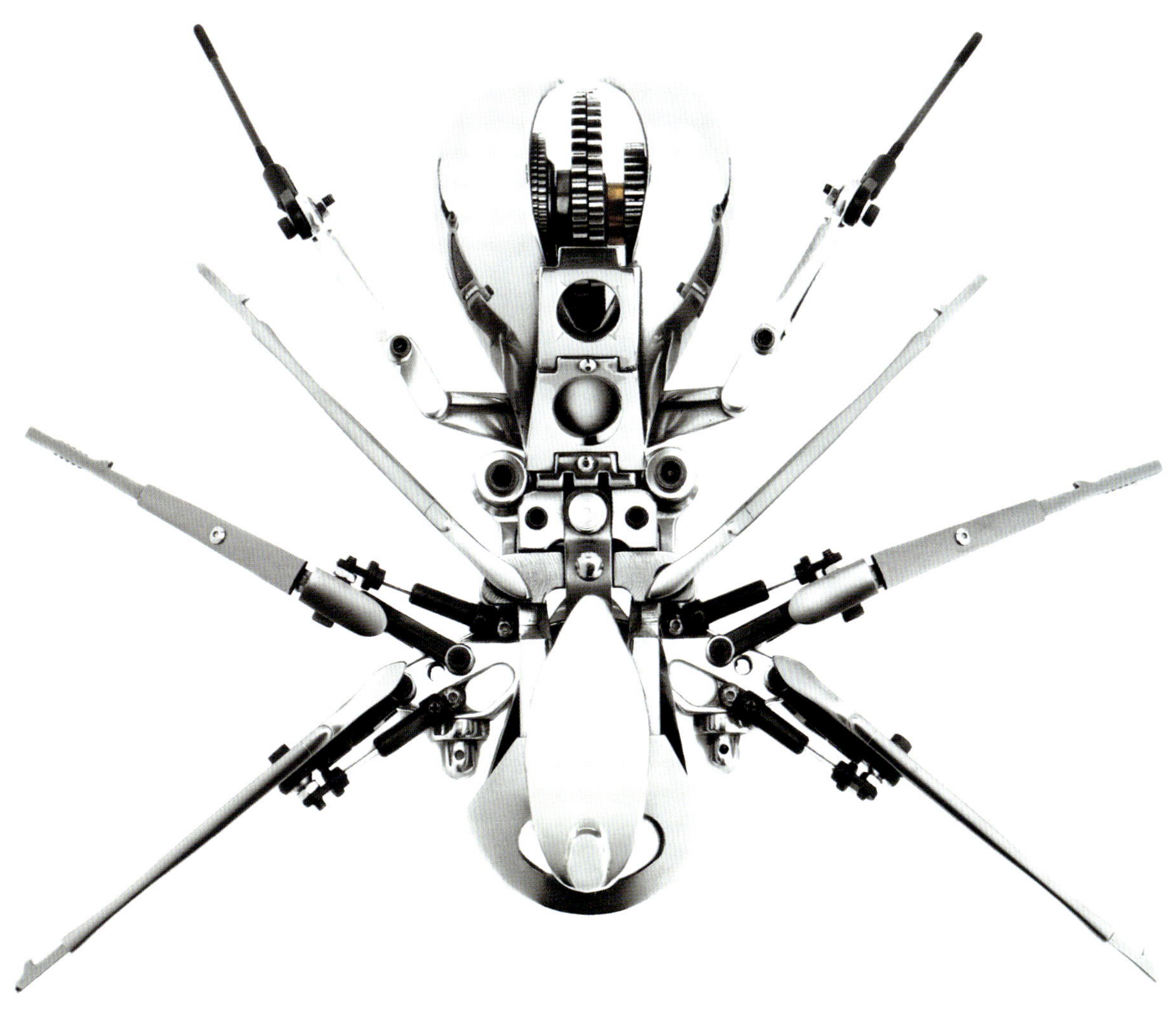

CHRISTOPHER**CONTE**

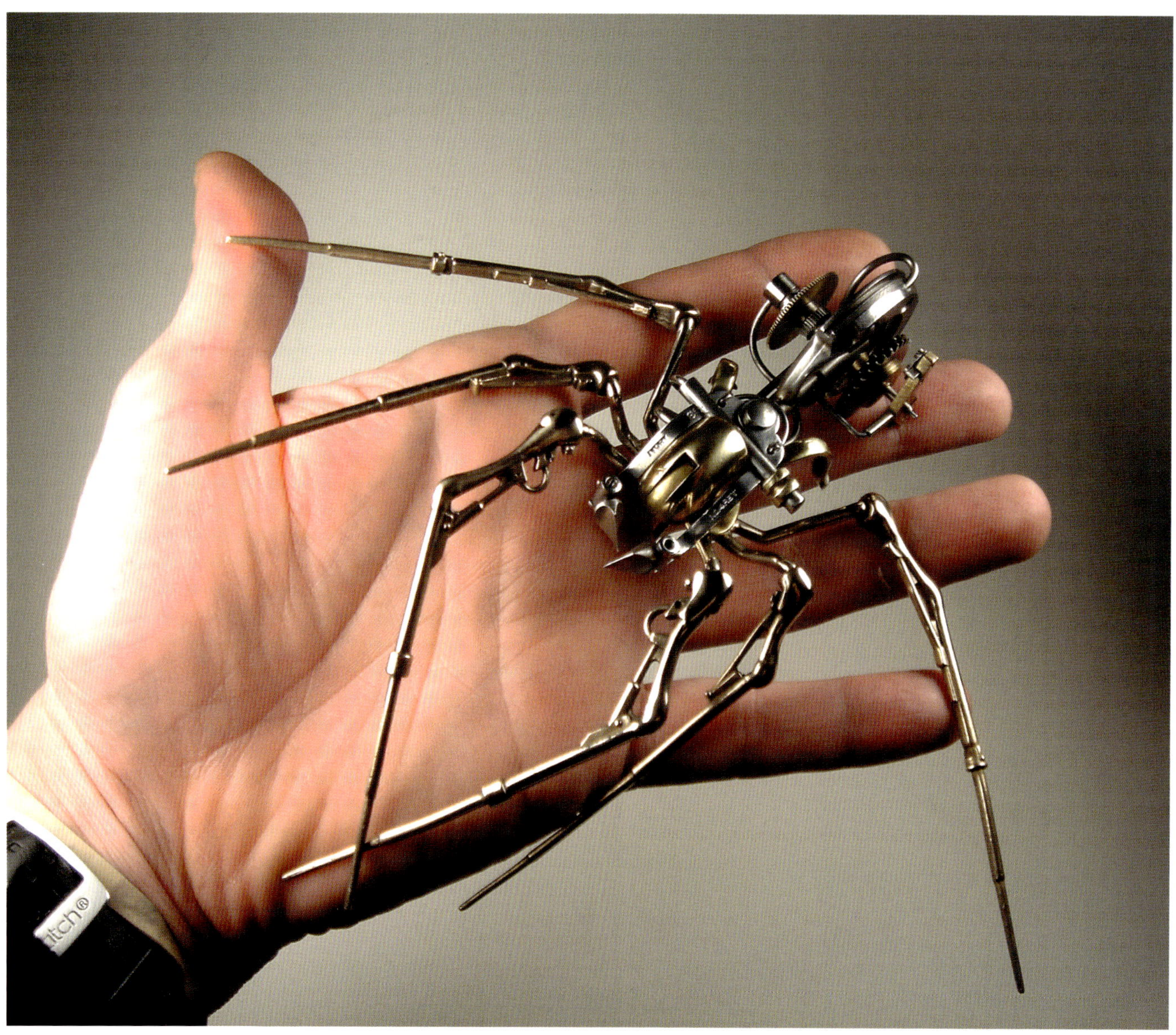

Christopher **Conte**

Christopher Conte was born in Bergen, Norway, where he began drawing at age 3. At age 6, shortly after moving to New York, he started taking college art classes at Hofstra University, following a recommendation from his first grade teacher.

While an illustration major at Pratt Institute, Christopher began creating his first mechanical sculptures as illustrations. His professors strongly encouraged this new direction and by his senior year, most of his work was three-dimensional.

After earning a Bachelors Degree in Fine Art (BFA) from Pratt Institute, he entered the prosthetics field and began making artificial limbs for amputees in New York. Along with a combined love for sculpture, medical science, and biomechanics, the field enabled Christopher to apply his natural talents to help amputees for 16 years as a certified prosthetist.

Christopher uses a wide range of experience along with diverse materials and construction techniques to create his one-of-a-kind pieces. The work is usually a combination of original cast components with found/recycled parts using materials ranging from bronze to carbon fiber. Many of the exotic materials used in both the aerospace industry and the prosthetics field have found their way into his work.

Decodroid – (Revised with articulated Legs) – 3" x 5" x 3.5" cast bronze with stainless steel and brass components (2008)

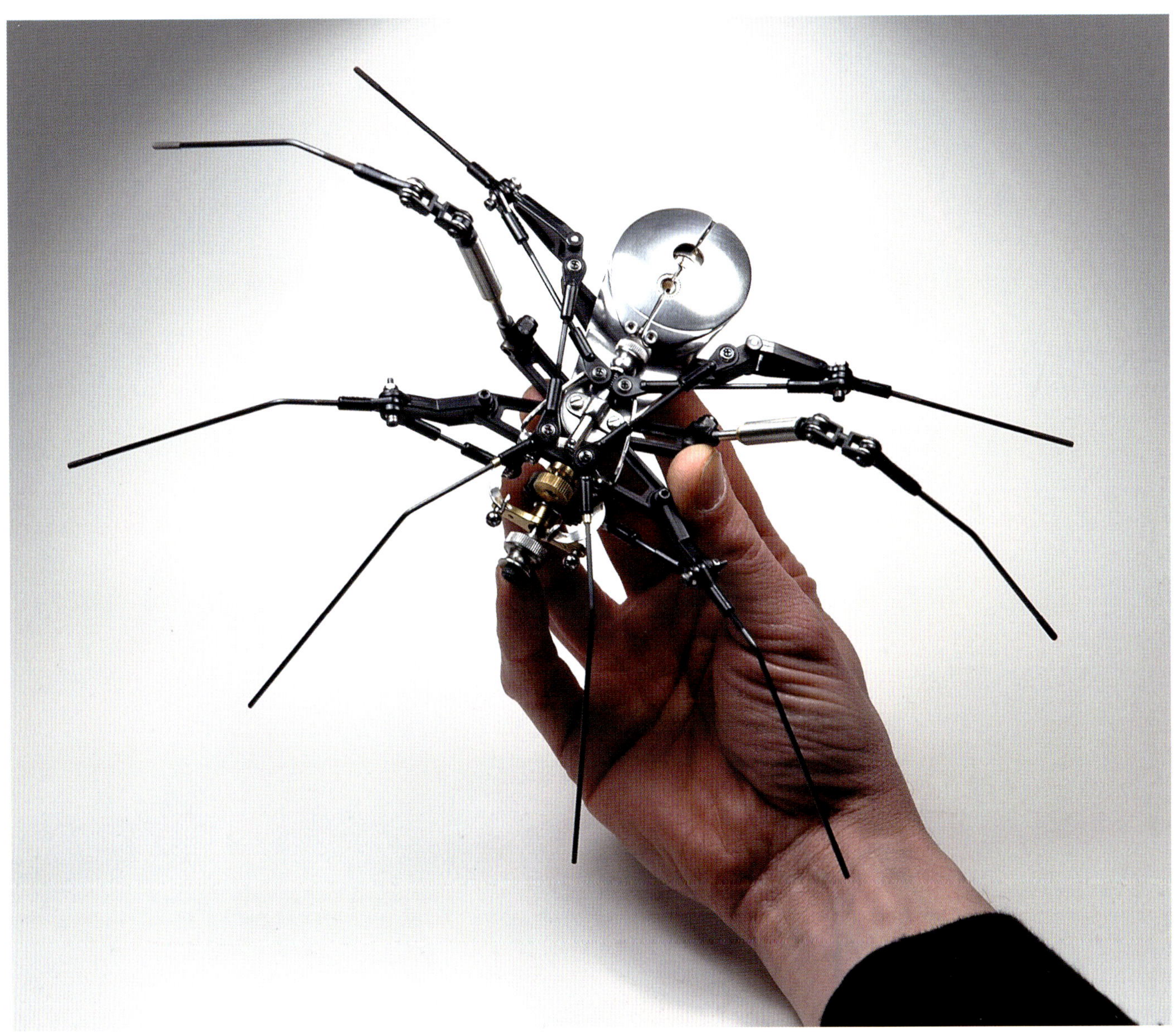

While a strong connection with robotics and technology is present in all of Christopher's work, ancient techniques such as lost-wax bronze casting have become an integral part of the process as well. The process involved in creating just one sculpture can often take months, sometimes, in the case of a series, several years to evolve.

In 2007, Christopher began offering these unique pieces for sale through galleries for the first time. Since then, his sculptures have been displayed at the National Museum in Washington, DC, and have appeared on The Discovery Channel, Discover Magazine, The Learning Channel, MTV Networks and in *Popular Science* and *Wired* magazines.

In March 2009, Christopher participated in an international technology and design conference in Sweden called Material Fusion. In June 2009, he will be loaning several of his sculptures to the oldest museum in the United States, the Peabody Essex Museum in Salem, Massachusetts, for a one-year exhibition.

Black Widow 1 – 10" x 8" x 4" stainless steel, glass-filled nylon, blackened steel, brass, and vintage parts (2008)

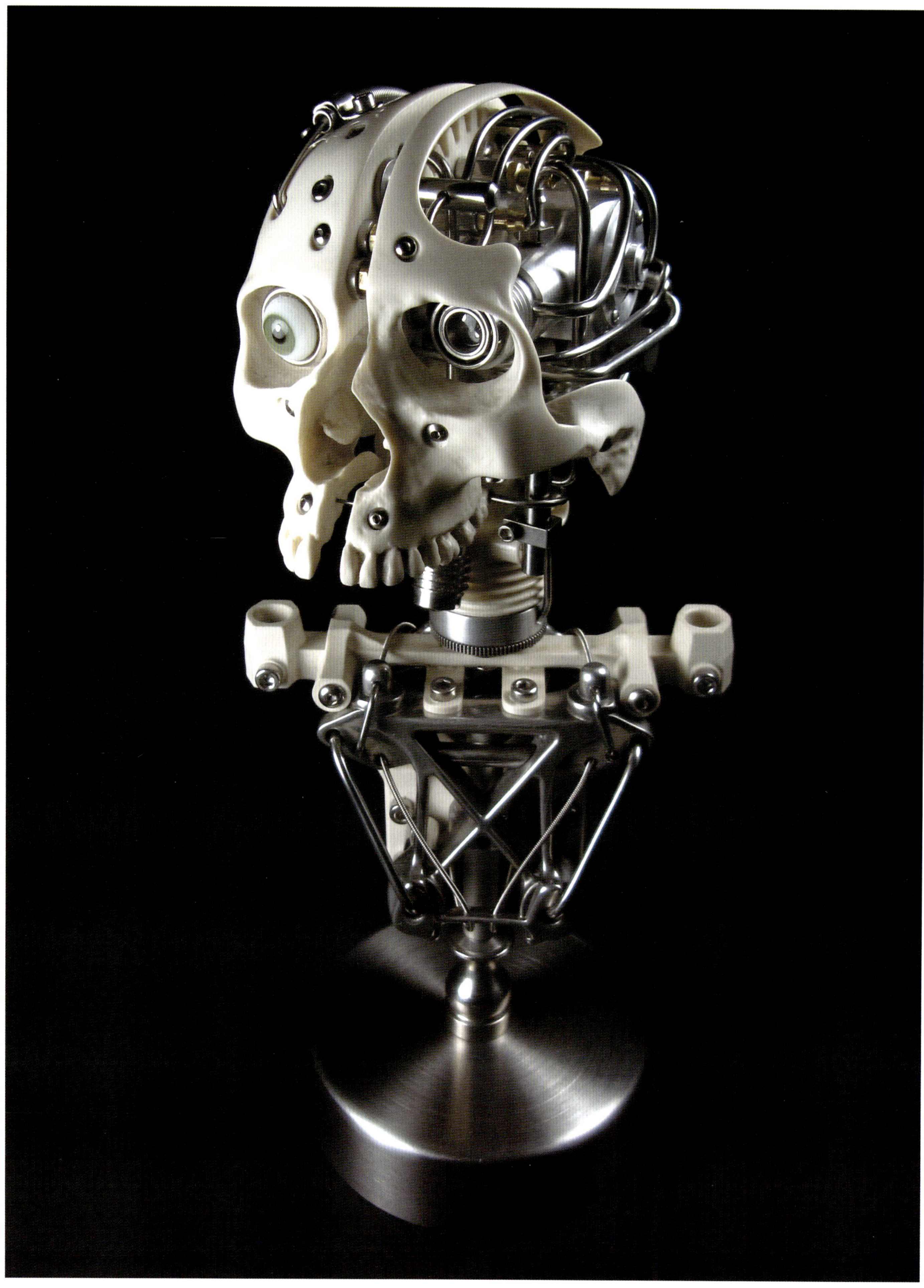

Cynthetic Cutaway – 4" x 7" x 3.5" aircraft-grade aluminum and titanium, medical grade stainless steel, and carbon-steel with cast polyurethane (2009)

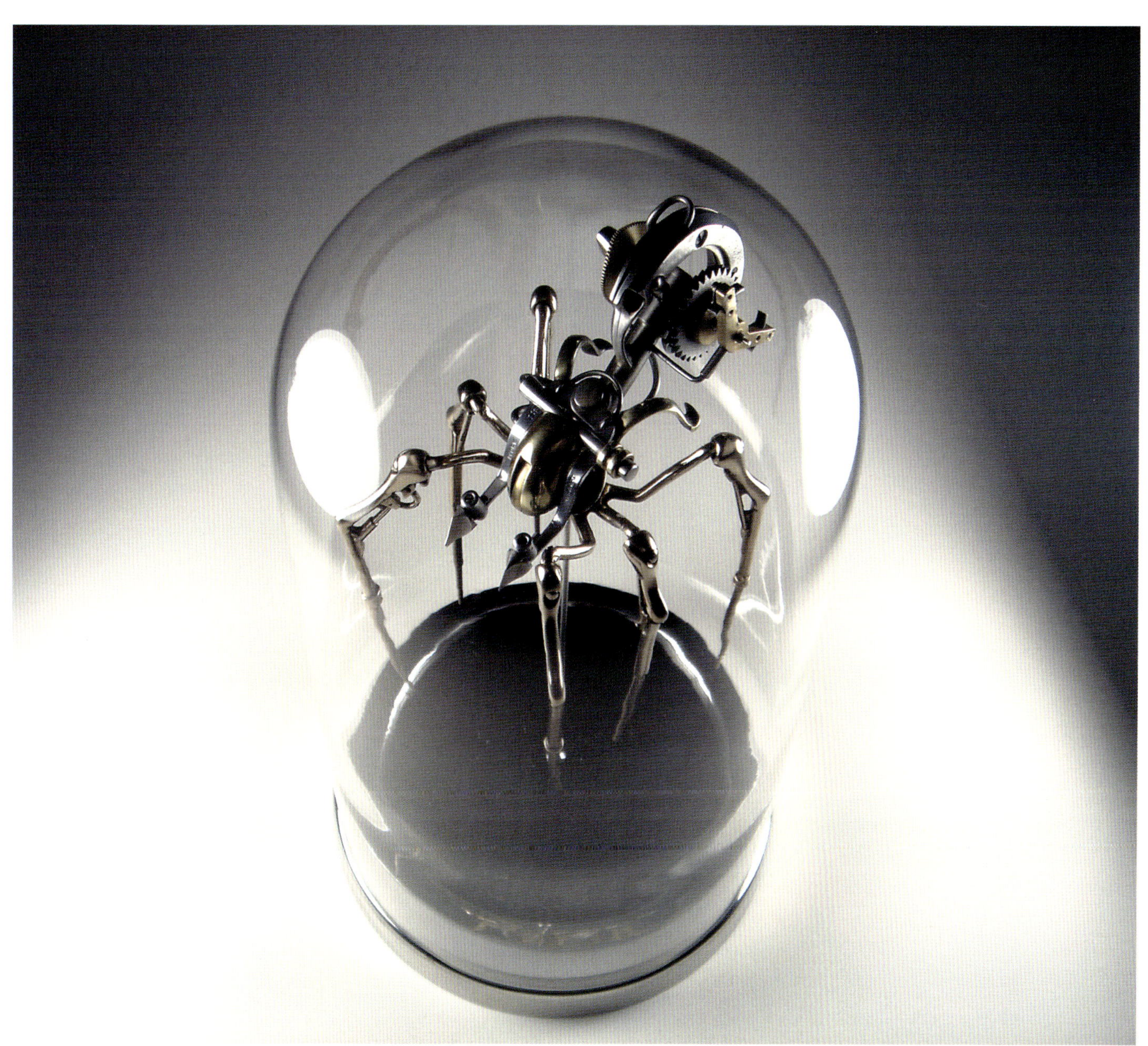

Decodroid (Revised with articulated Legs) – 3" x 5" x 3.5" cast bronze with stainless steel and brass components (2008)

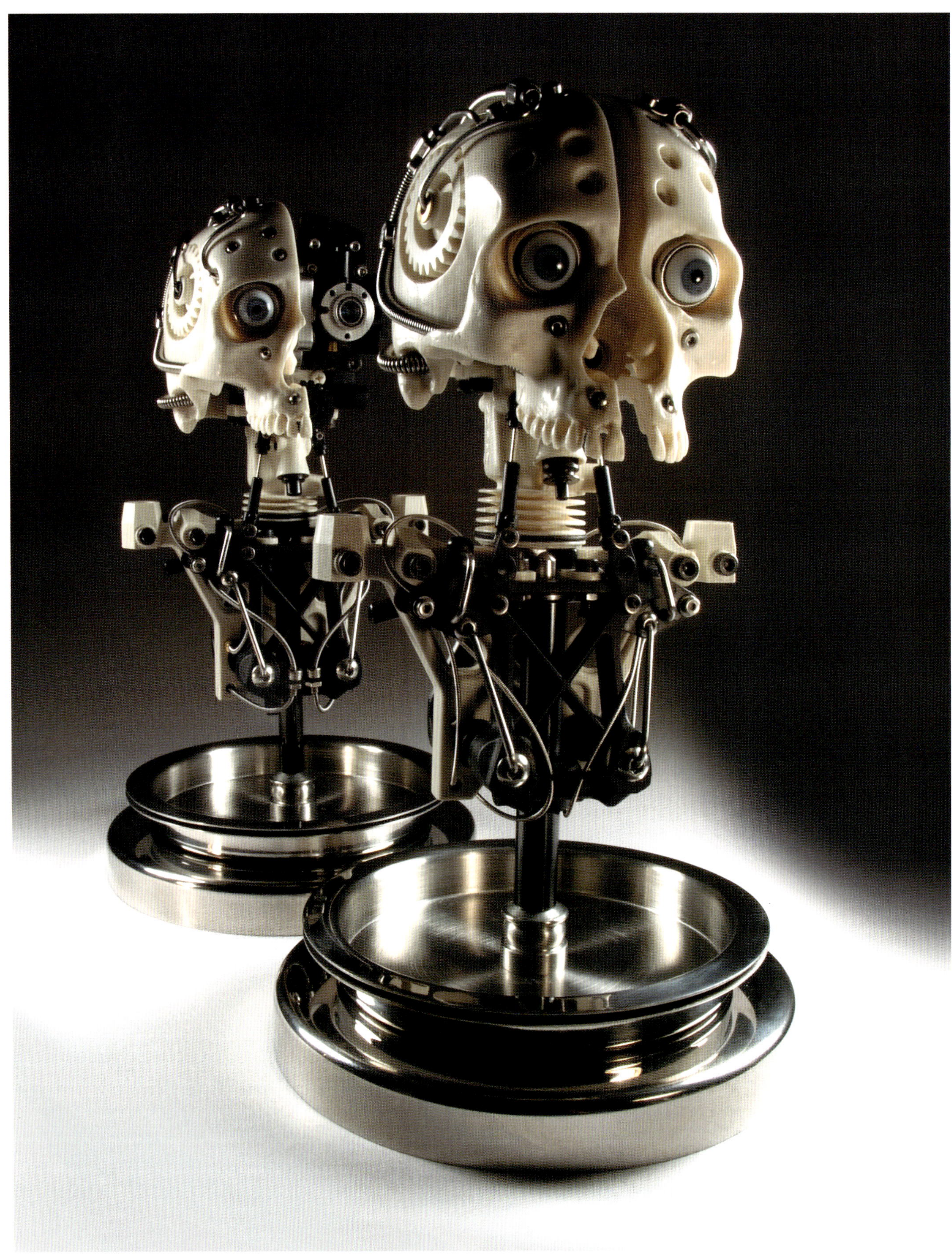

Cynthetic, Version 1, 2 – 4" x 7" x 3.5" cast polyurethane, glass-filled nylon, and stainless steel components

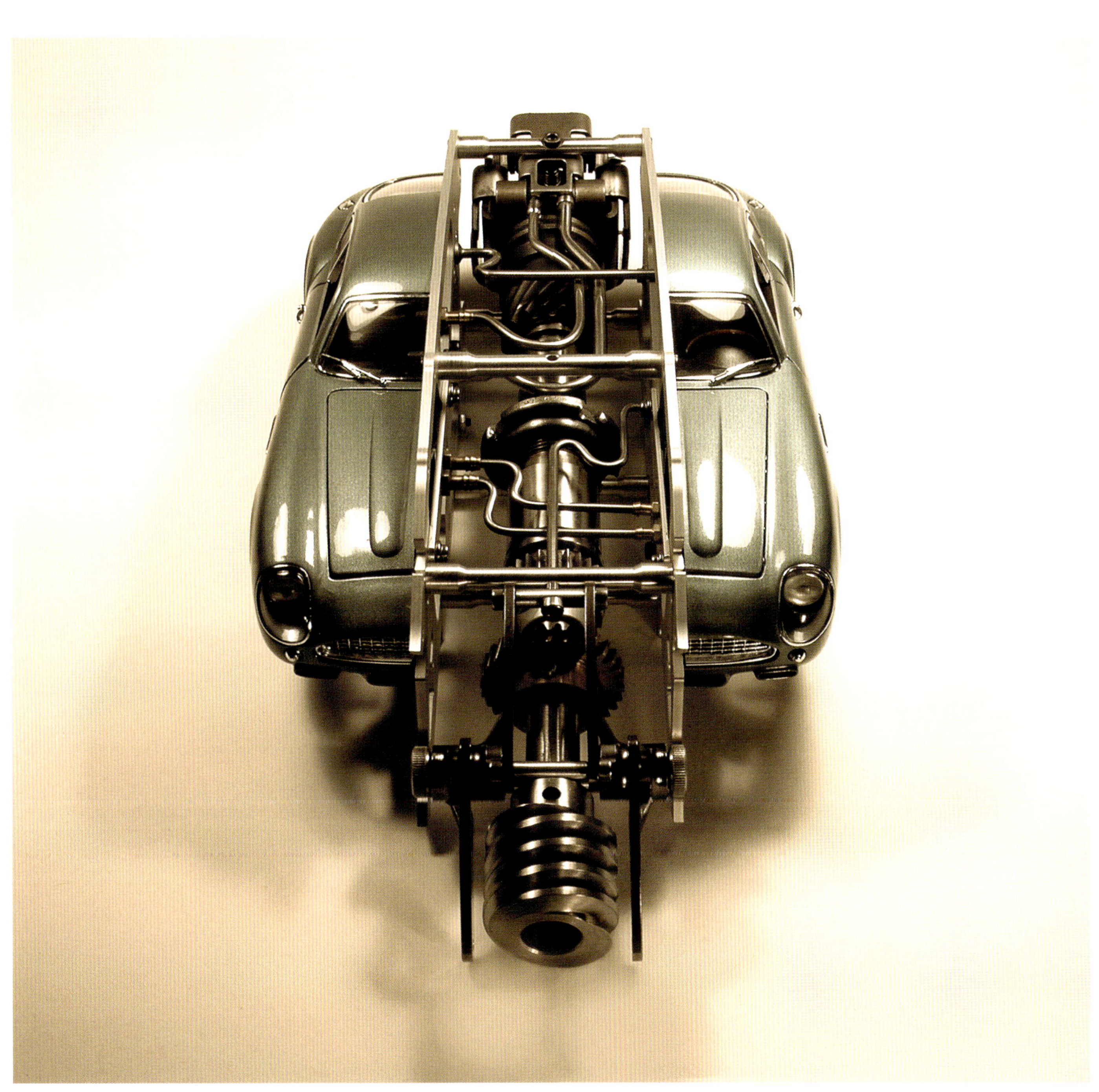

Aston Martin Turbine (created for the book, *Carnivora* by Leslie Barany) – 6" x 4" x 12" dissected 1:18 scale model car with stainless steel and aluminum components (2007)

NEMO**GOULD**

Psychos-O-Matic – 45" x 17" x 17" electric drill, glass planter, outdoor light fixture, cigar box, mechanical counter, record player lid, chair legs, auto parts, gear motor, neon sign transformer, ice cream scoops, salad tongs, phenolic, brass hardware, bicycle brake parts, LEDs, switches (2009)

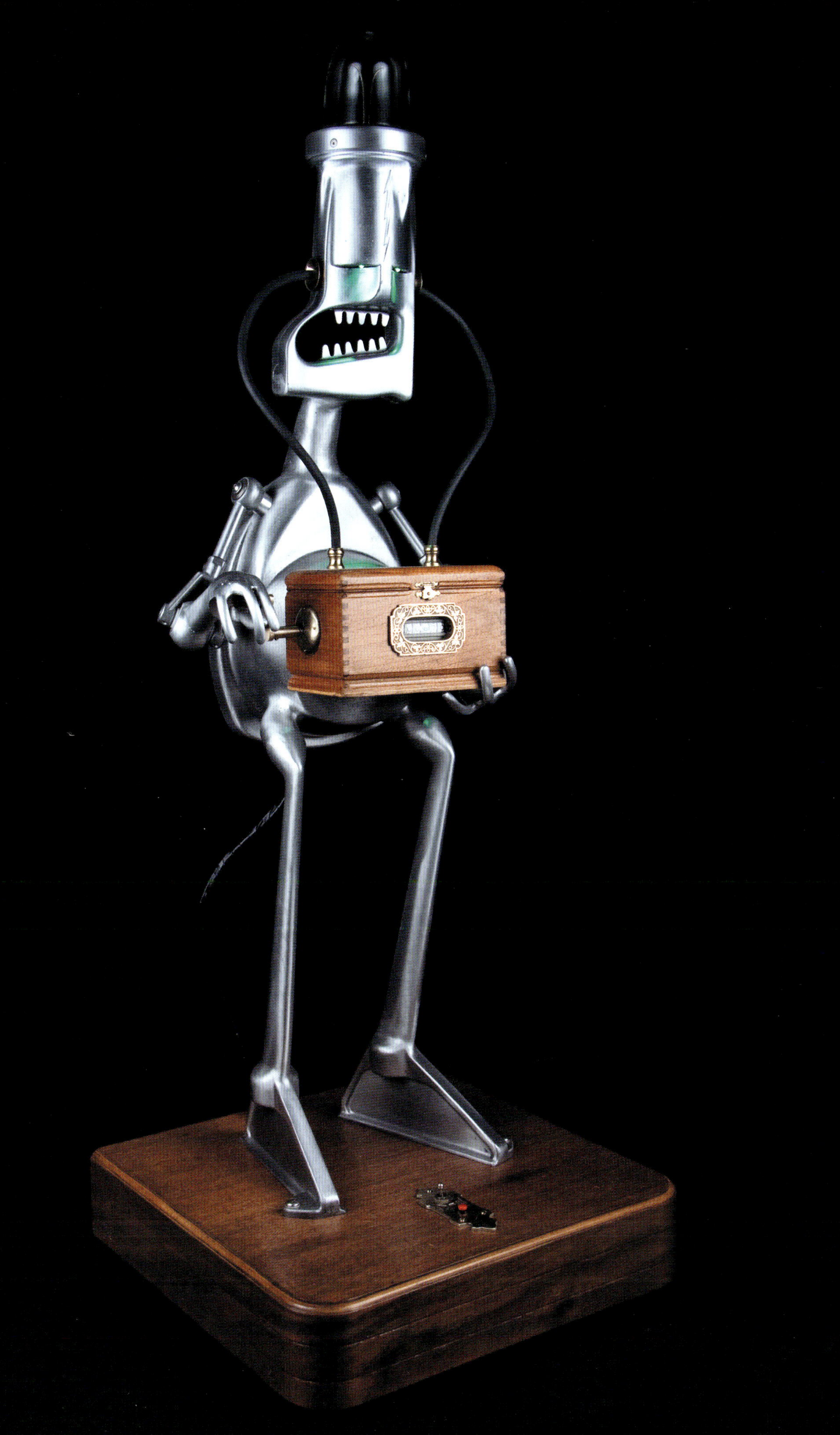

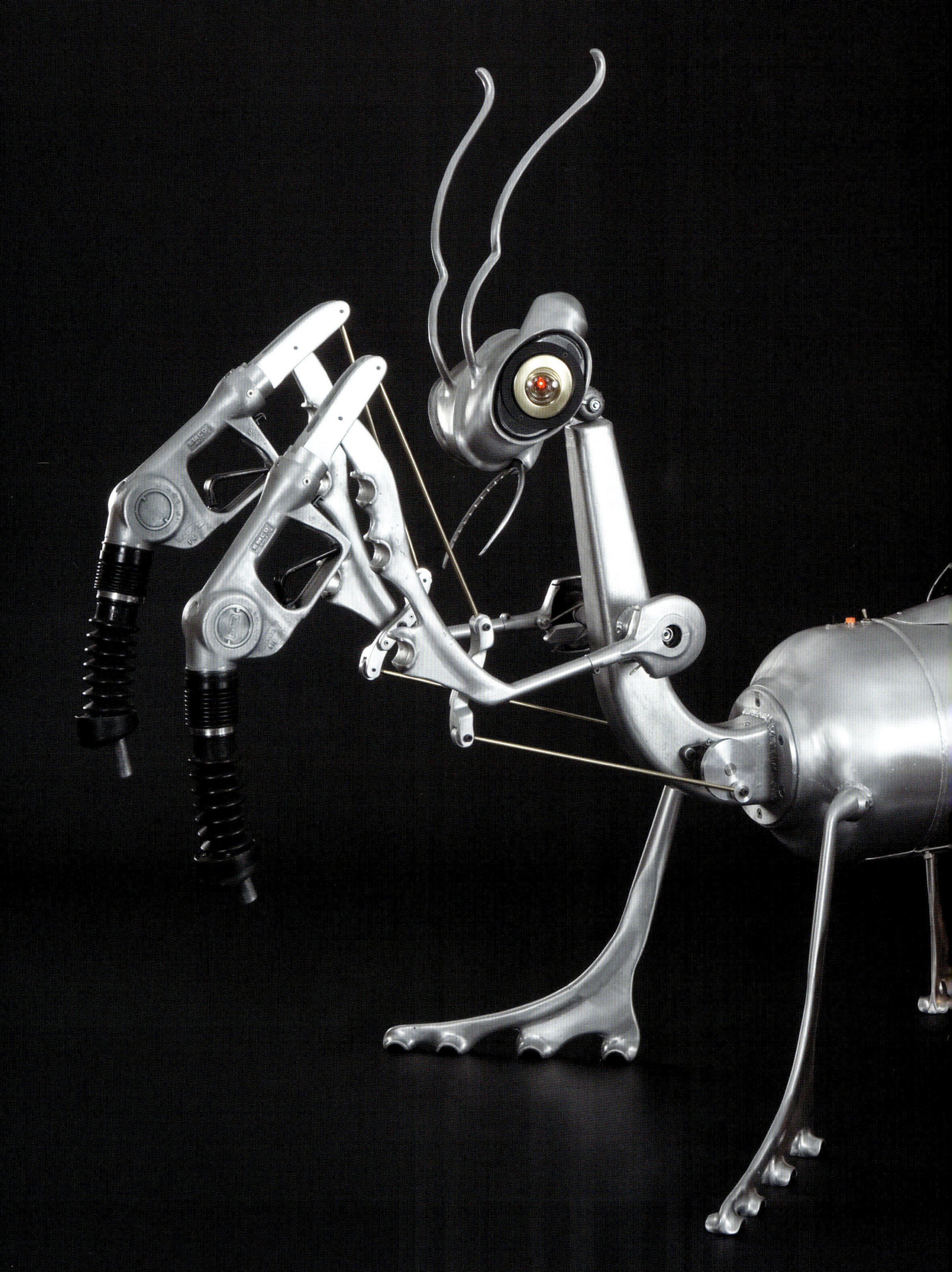

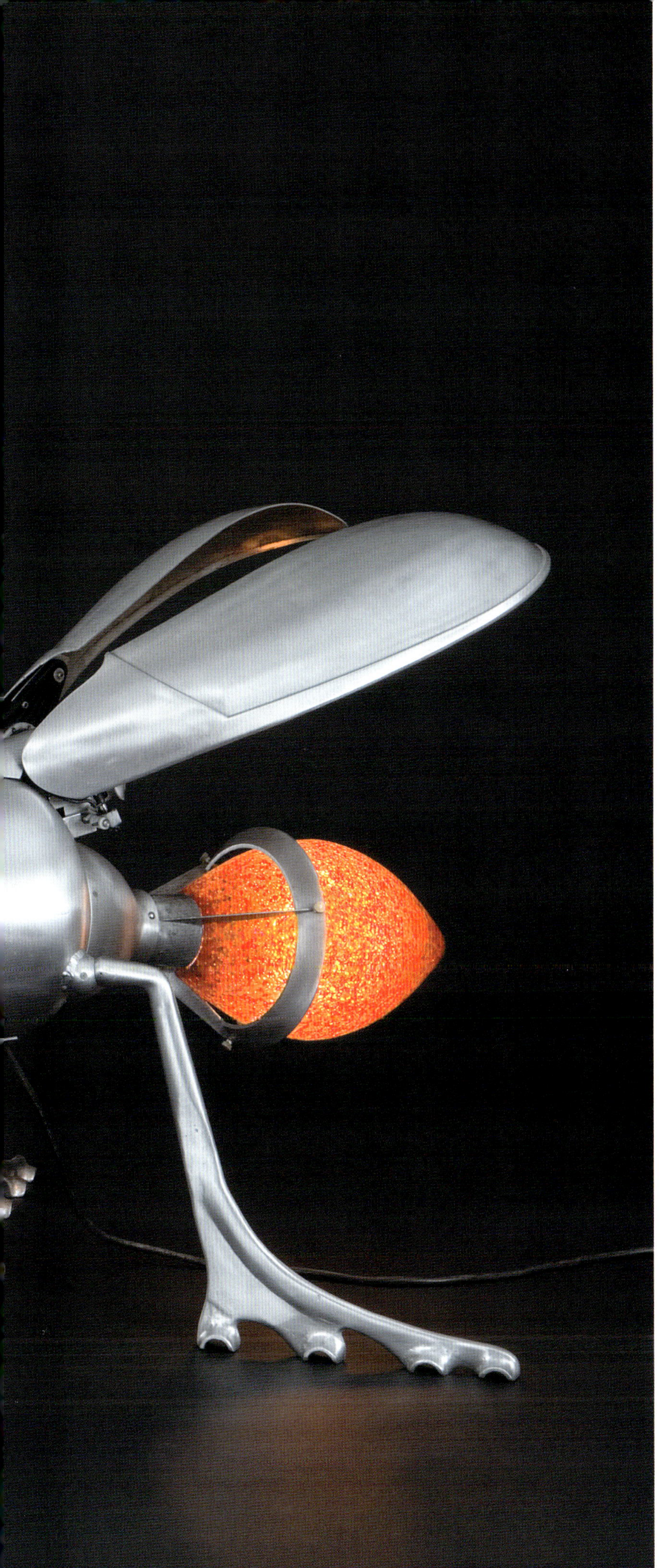

Nemo **Gould**

Nemo Gould was born to artist parents in 1975, in Minneapolis, Minnesota. Named after the protagonist in Windsor McKay's comic strip "Little Nemo in Slumberland," Gould's work has fittingly evolved to reflect the images and mythology of comic books and Science Fiction. Parallel to these influences was an irrepressible tendency towards collecting and dismantling anything with moving parts.

Gould earned his Bachelor of Fine Arts degree at the Kansas City Art Institute in 1998, and his Master of Fine Arts degree at U.C. Berkeley in 2000. Once he was free of the constraints of contemporary art education he quickly threw himself into the pursuit of his childhood dreams. "My work appeals to the 7-year-old boy mind, because I still have one... I take silly very seriously."

In the ensuing years he has produced a prolific body of work that attempts to reconcile the innocent wonder of youth with the dull complexity of the adult experience. "Most adults are dangerously lacking in wonder. As we age and learn more of the answers to life's mysteries, I think we lose part of what keeps us alive. When I am working, I am always trying to make things that can produce a child like response from a jaded adult—it's a matter of life and death!"

Gould's work has been featured frequently in national media and is shown in Galleries and Museums throughout the U.S. and abroad.

Praying Mantis – 72"x 42" x 3" gas pumps, drafting table hardware, door security peep holes, rod brackets, propane tank, vacuum cleaner bag attachments, lamp parts, street lamp housing, massage chair mechanism, cake stand, television parts, gear motor, LEDs, brass and aluminum stock switches (2009)

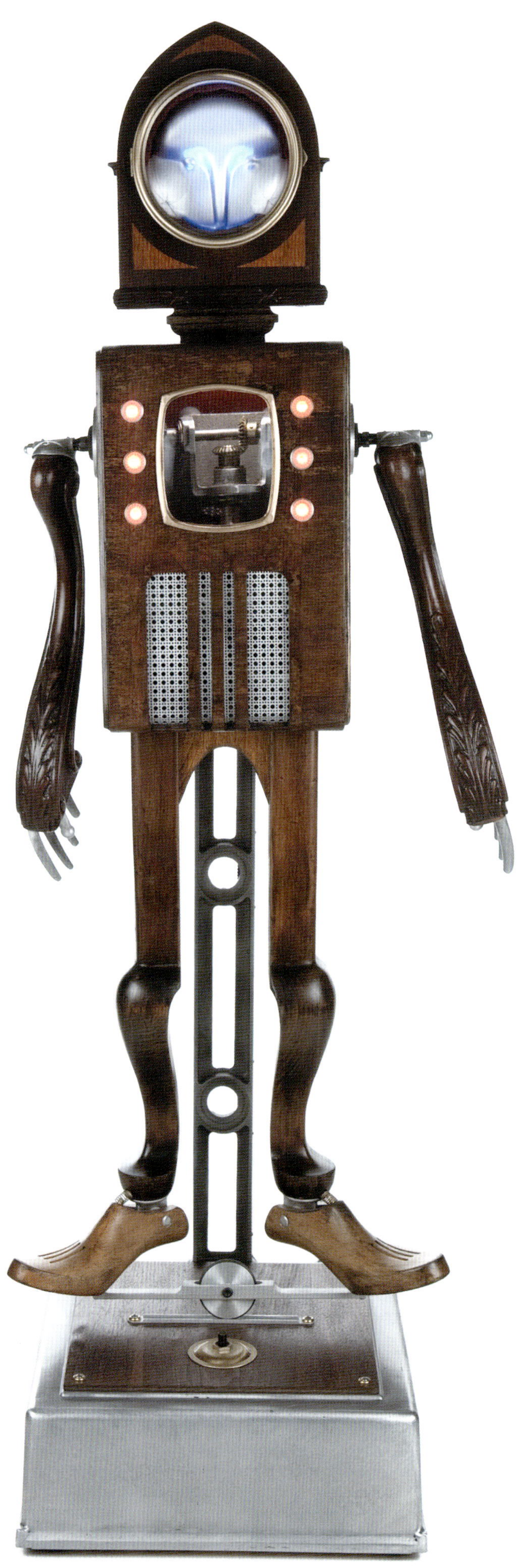

The Performer #2 – 49" x 18" x 14" radio cabinet, clock cabinet, bed legs, chair arms, garden tools, ice cream scoops, ash tray, bubble level, shoe forms, electrical box, gears, motors, velvet, LEDs (2008)

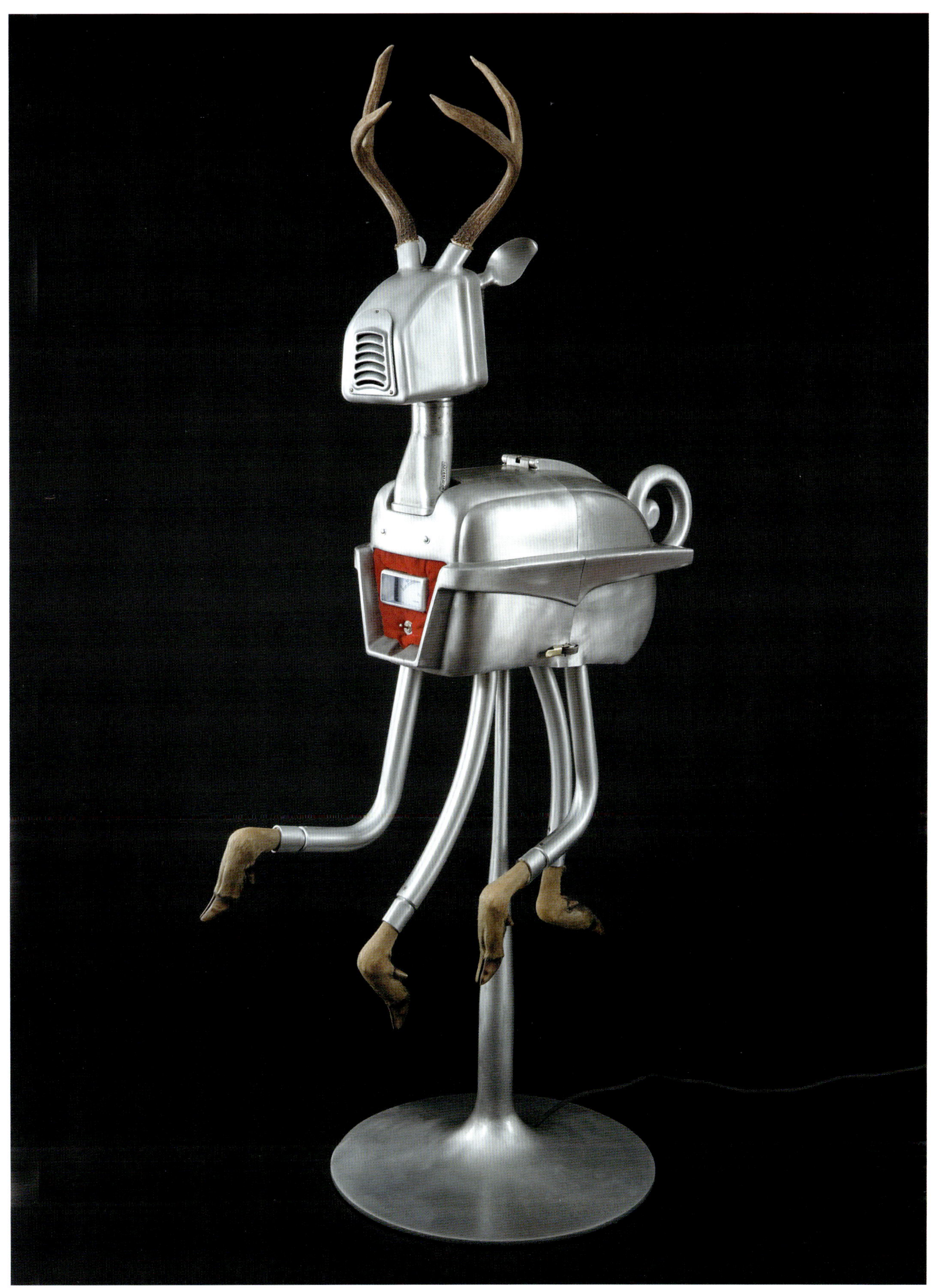

Re: Animated – 69" x 36" x 22" slide projector, antlers, ice cream scoops, motor boat motor housing, railing sections, deer hoofs, baseball bat, table stand, velvet, motor, motion sensor, amp meter, drive in movie speaker case, LEDs, switches, aluminum stock (2009)

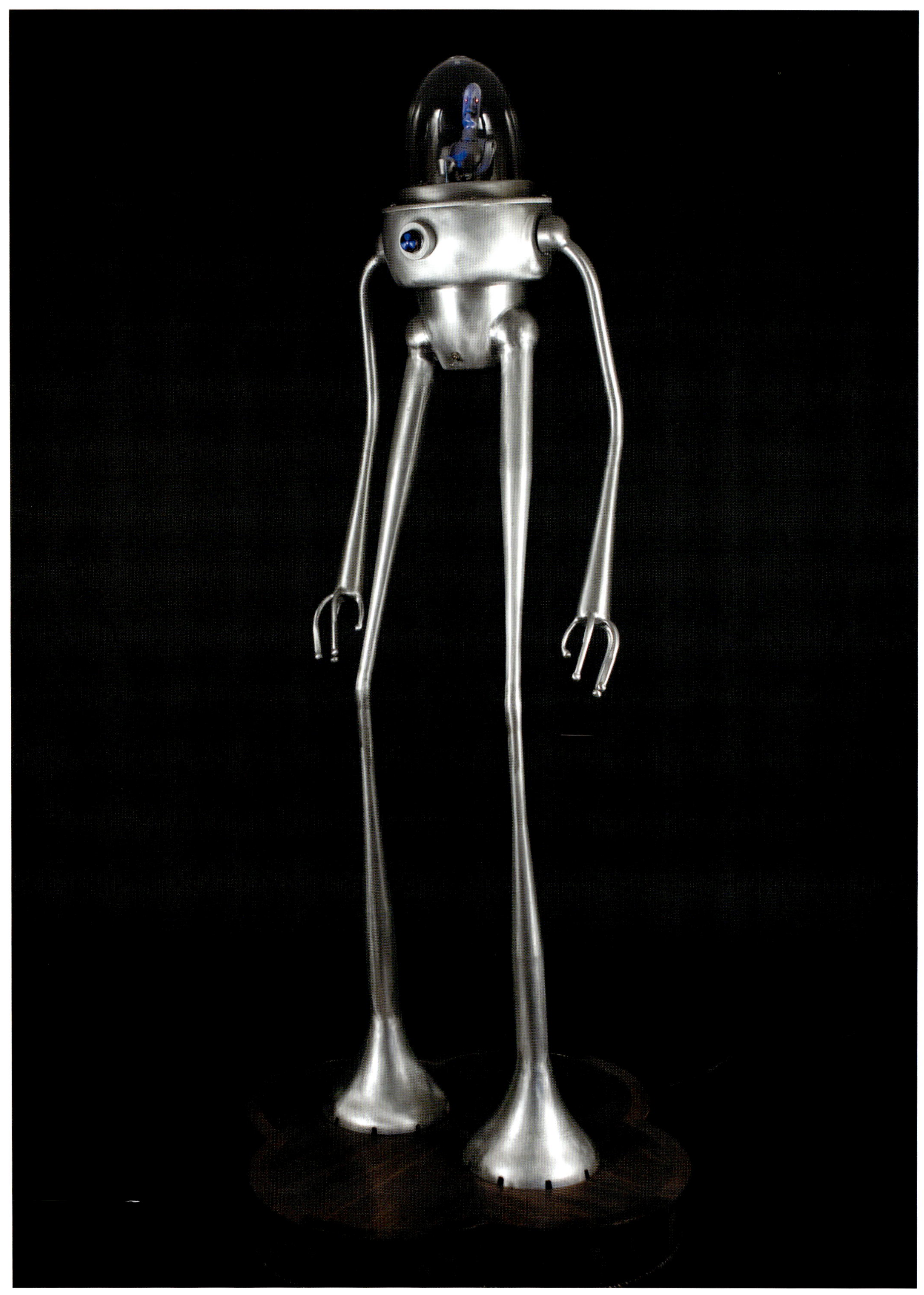

Above It All – 5'8" x 2'4" x 11" cooking pots, baseball bats, coffee table, lamp parts, bicycle brake parts, electric massager, screen door latch, motors, LEDs (2008)

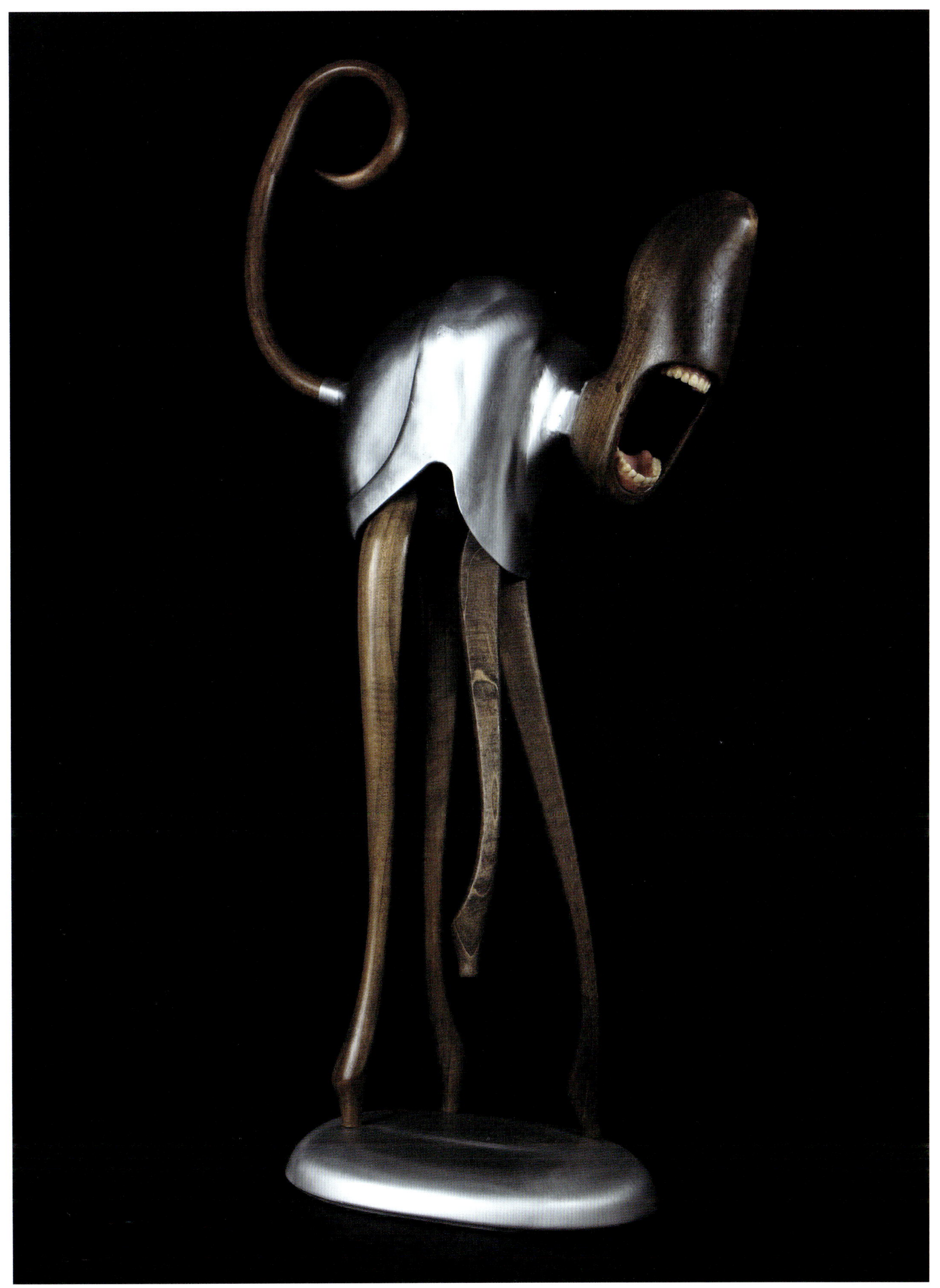

Skittish –39" x 21"x 10" clog, weather head, bean scoops, table legs, broiling pan lid, chair parts, dentures, velvet (2008)

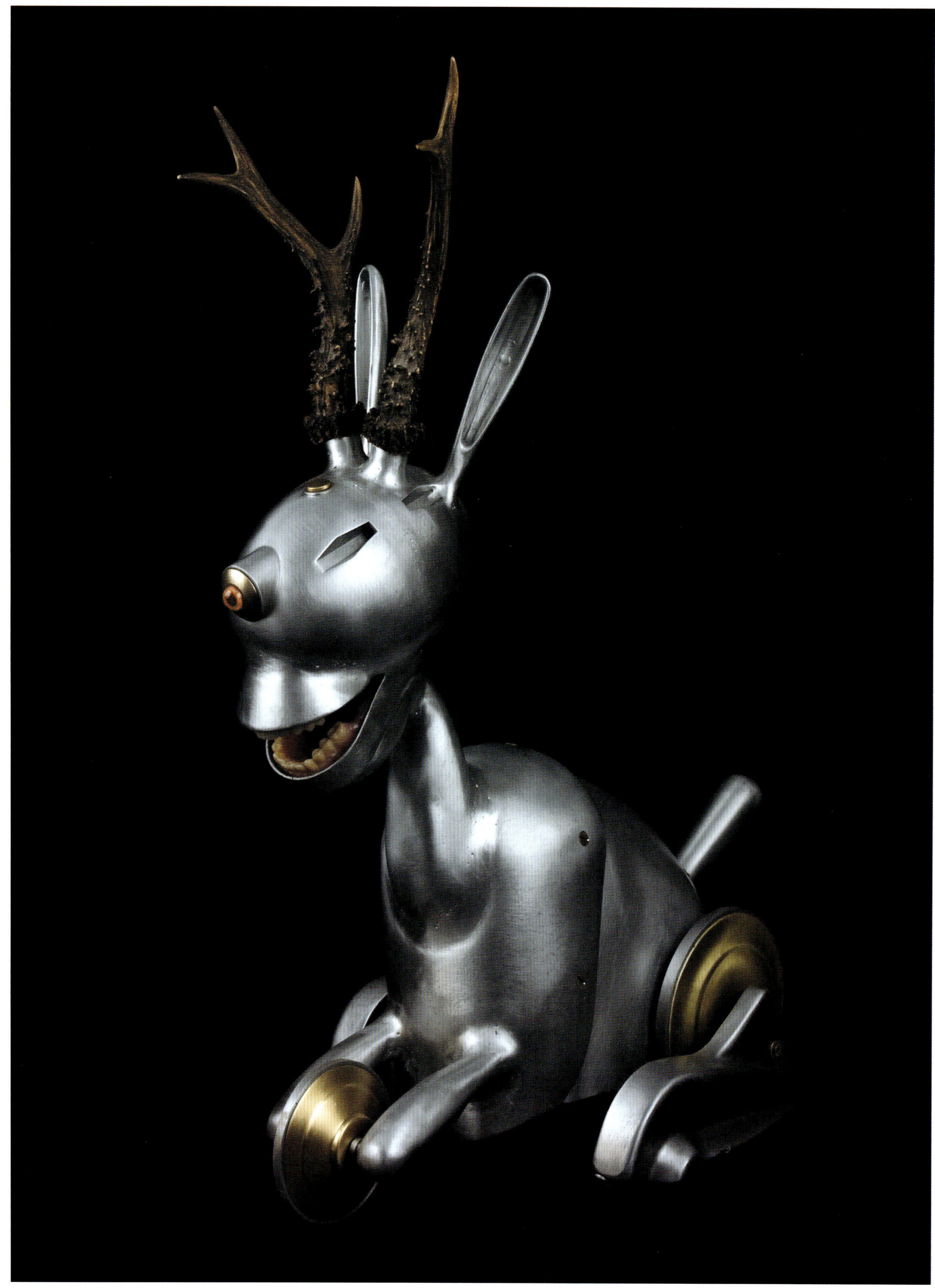

One Eyed Jack –28" x 18" x 11" food processor, bean scoop, float switch, weather head, teapot spout, brass lamp parts, antlers, cheese slicer handles, motor boat parts, glass eye (2008)

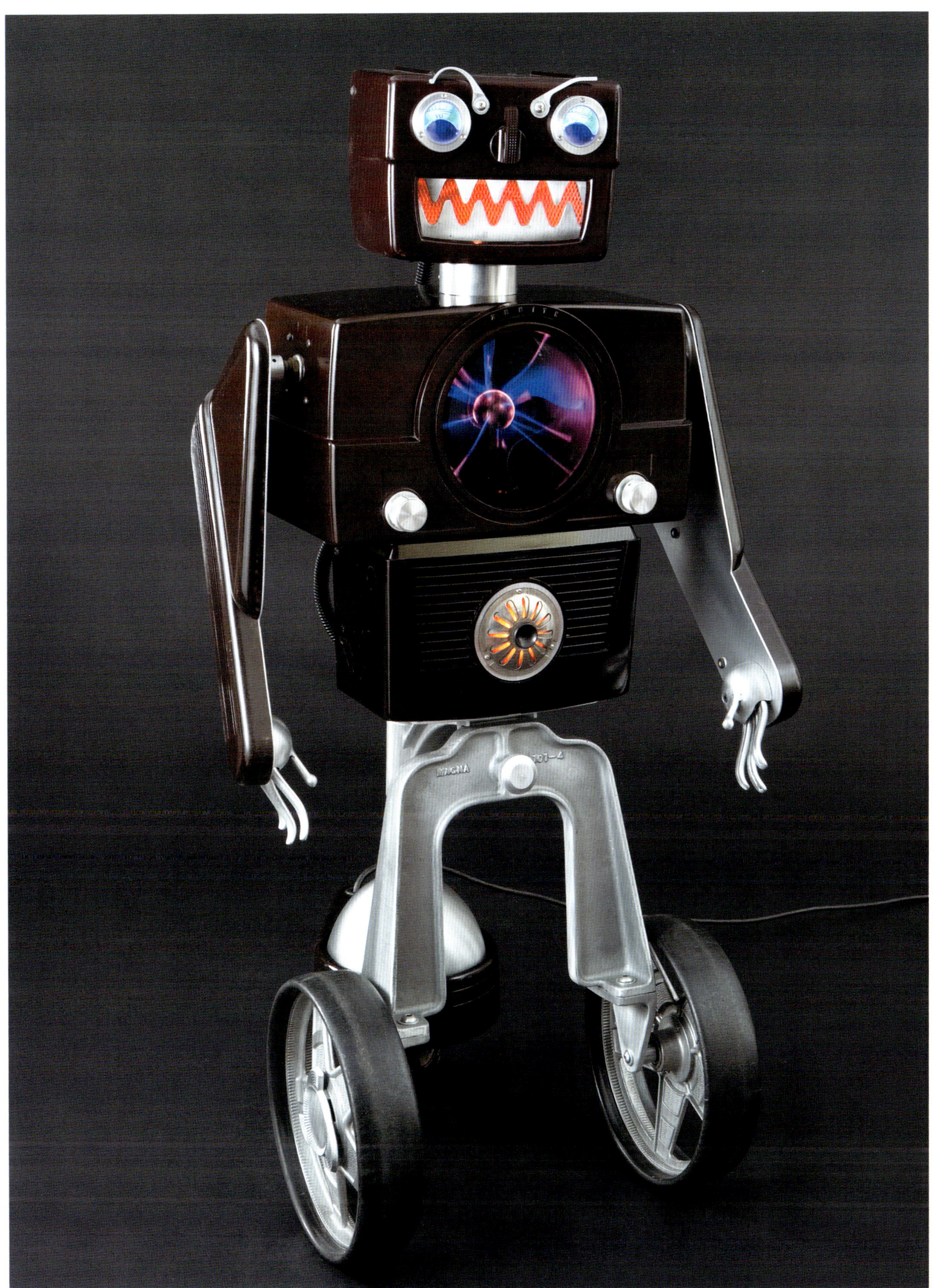

Bake-O-Lite – 43" x 21" x 30" bakelite radios, record player, golf caddy cart wheels, bicycle brake levers, VU meters, windshield wiper motors, plasma globe, tricycle part, bandsaw part, asphalt rake, ice cream scoops, cooking pan lids, stock aluminum, LEDs, switches, knobs (2009)

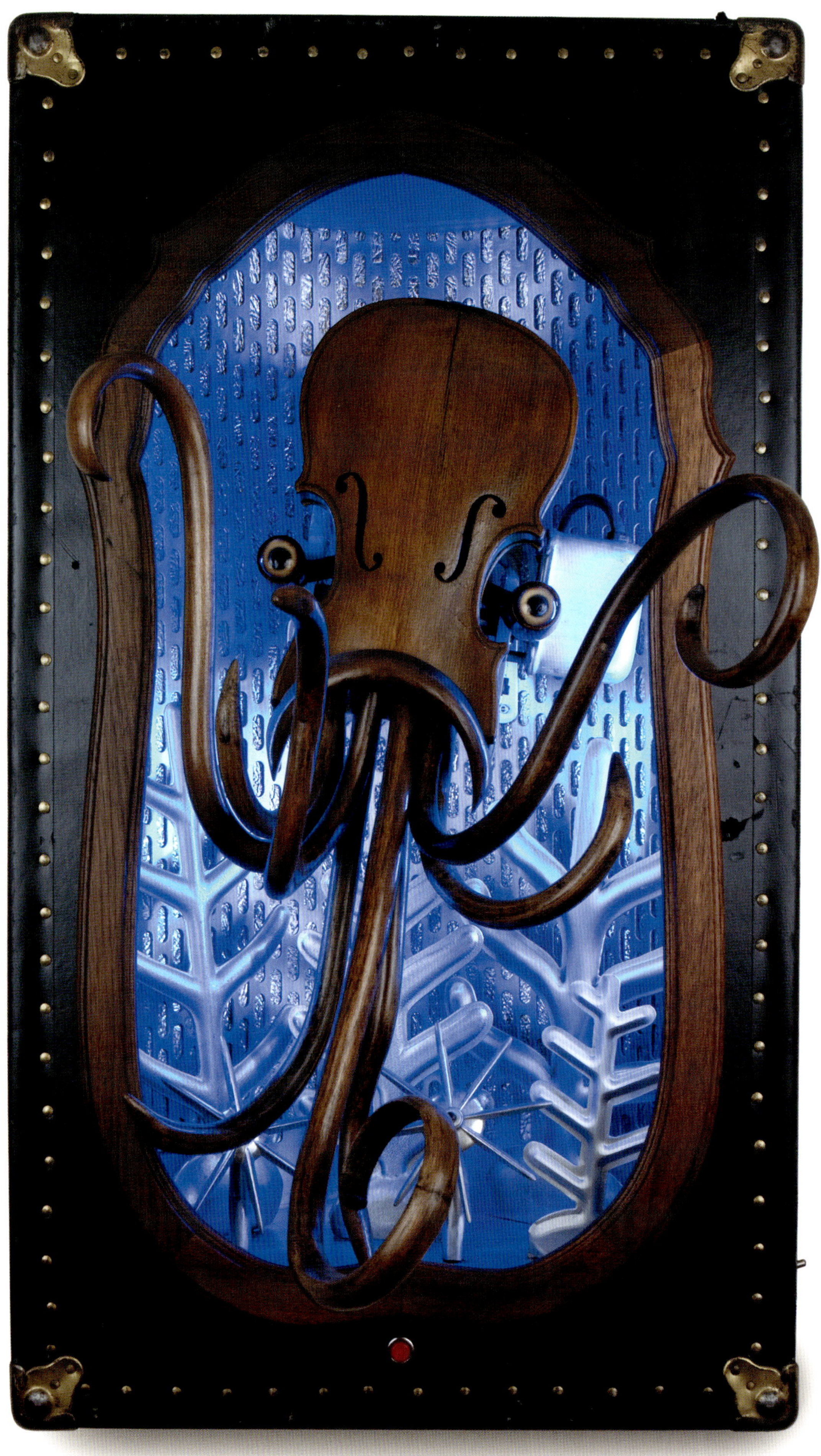

Octovarius – 36" x 21" x 21" steamer trunk, violin, chair parts, tobacco pipes, taxidermy eyes, steak serving platters, motor, semi truck exhaust guard, cold cathode light tubes (2008)

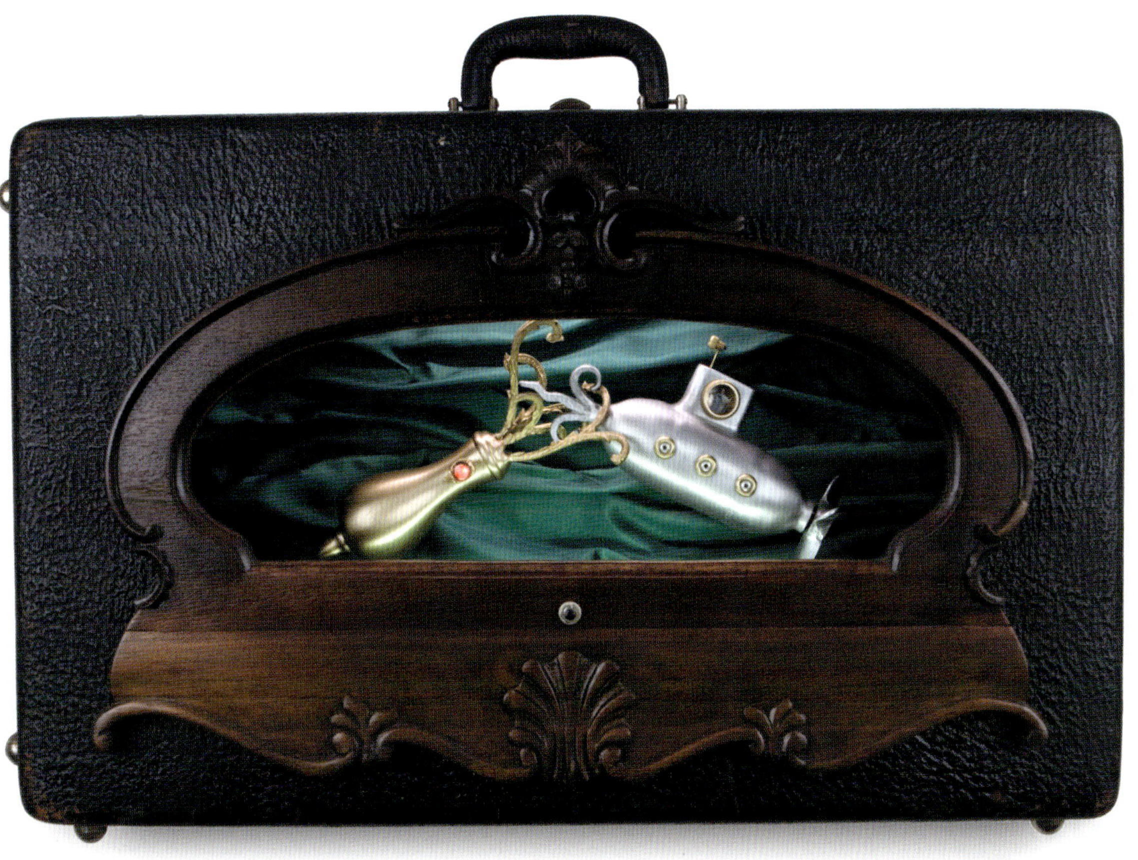

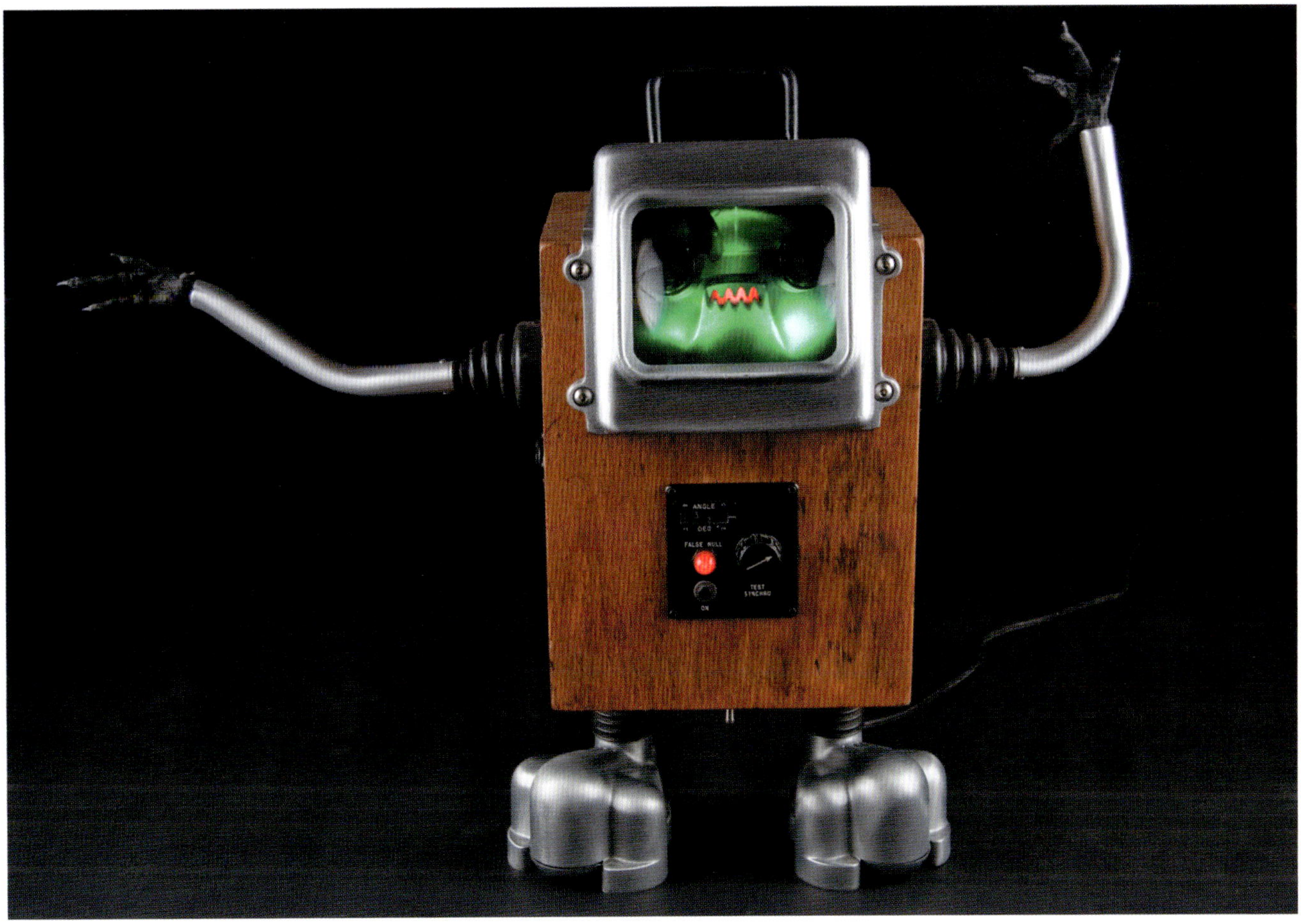

Captain Nemo #2 – suitcase, mirror frame, brass lamp parts, motors, aluminum condenser, rivets, magnifying lens, model railroad engineer, LEDs, computer scanner lights (2008) (top)

Boogeyman – 20" x 26" x 9" equipment case, juicer, navy throat mic, desk lamp clamps, rubber linkage boots, radio equipment salvage, massage tool motor, folding chair sections, dried chicken feet, LEDs, gear motor, switches, oscilloscope housing, overhead projector lens (2009) (bottom)

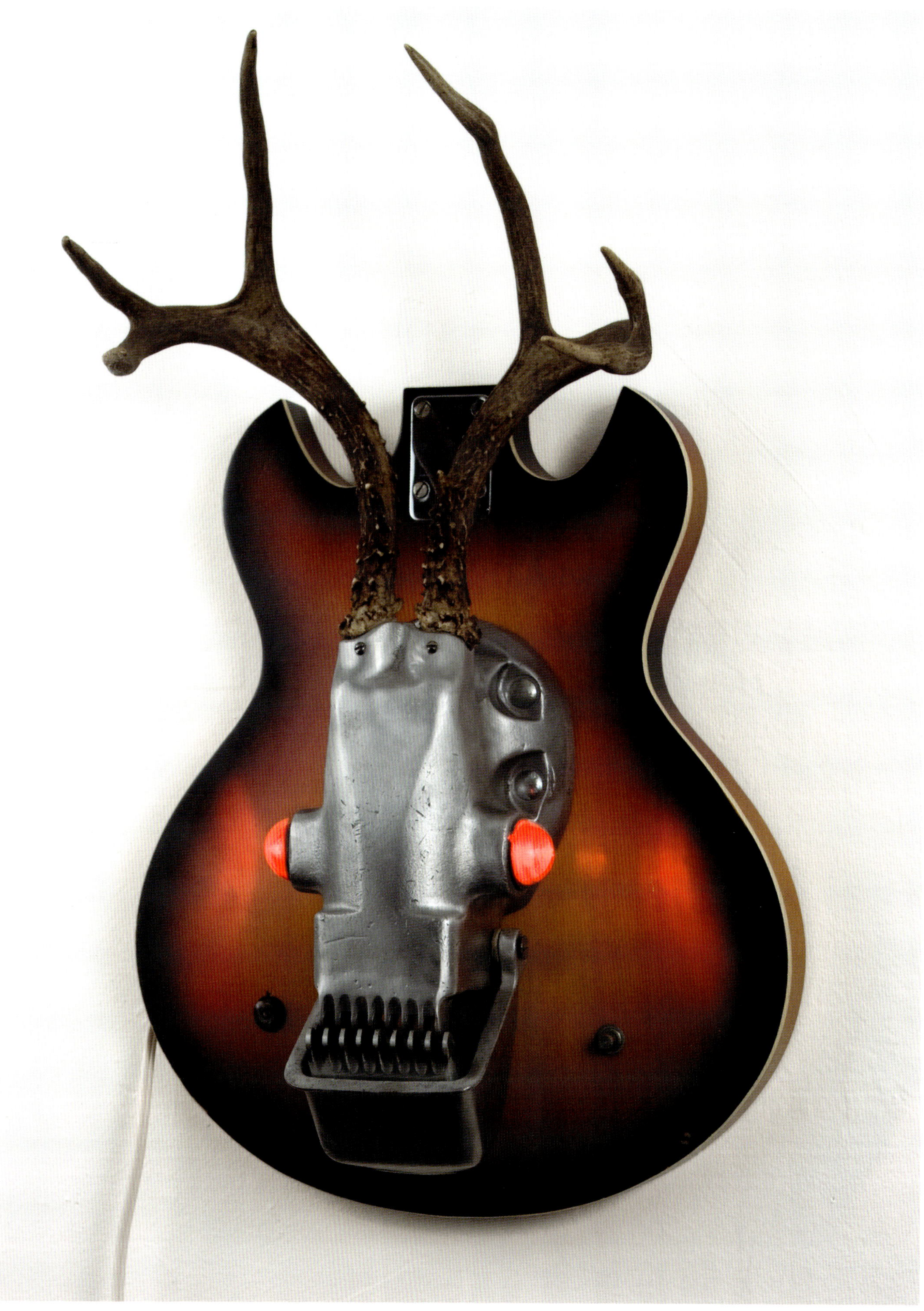

Heavy Metal – *22" x 15" x 11" electric guitar, electric jackhammer, vacuum cleaner parts, engine parts, antlers, toy motor, LED lights, antlers (2007)*

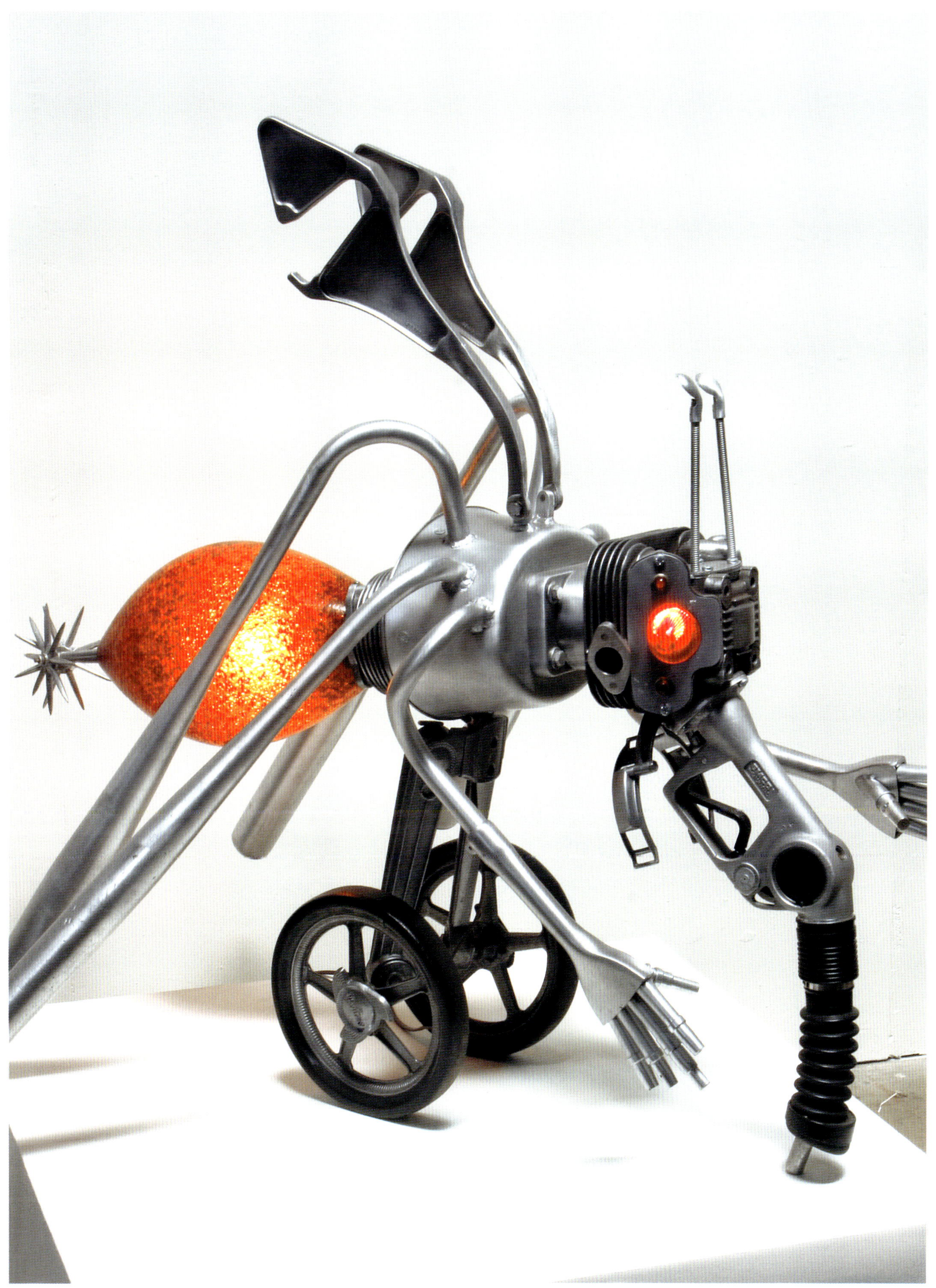

Guzzler – 41" x 48" x 38" floor lamp, golf caddy cart, baseball bats, bicycle handle bars, vacuum cleaner parts, gas pump, small engine parts, baking pan, soil aerator, extension ladder parts, brake light covers (2007)

TOM**HANEY**

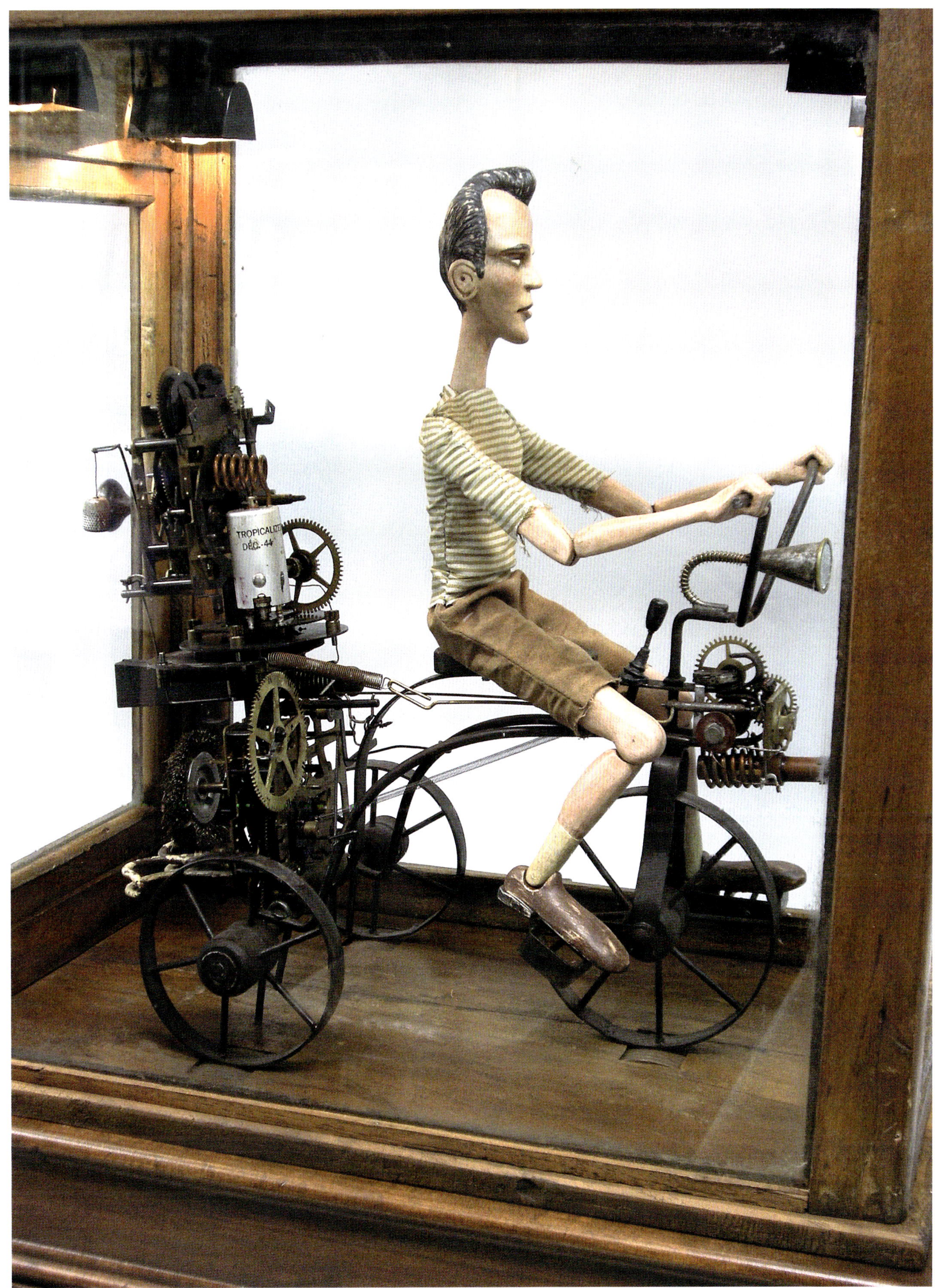

Tinguely's Dream – 18" x 21" x 13" (2008)

Tom **Haney**

"Much of my work is unseen. Whether it's an intricate part of a mechanism or the curve of a leg; so much of what I do is not instantly apparent. On a kinetic piece, 50%–60% of my time is spent on the mechanism hidden inside the work. I hand-carve the bodies of all my figures and sculpt each head one at a time, doing things the old-fashioned way. No corners are cut, no shortcuts taken. When making a piece that moves, I aspire to produce a piece that will operate for years to come. A great deal of time is spent perfecting the mechanisms to ensure I will never have to spend my time repairing them.

The special people who collect my art understand what goes into creating it. They appreciate the hours, days, weeks, and sometimes months of dedication it takes to create these unique pieces.

Woodcarving was my initial approach to creating the figures, but lately I've found myself using materials as diverse as fabric, polymer clay, and found objects. Electrical motors, miniature lights, and motion-detectors have been added to my mechanical repertoire.

For the most part, I approach my work searching for that characteristic of the human spirit that struggles to overcome anything fate can throw its way. I've always been on the side of the underdog, rooting for the little guy. Their lives and stories inspire me."

Some of Haney's earliest memories are of creating things (toys, games, etc.). He has always been fascinated with anything mechanical, often taking household items apart, much to his parents' disapproval. He took art classes in high school and received a BS in Industrial Design from the University of Cincinnati.

Prior to becoming a full-time artist in 2000, Haney's professional work consisted of making props and models for television commercials and still photography for advertising. He created things that couldn't be found anywhere else. This included a five-foot ping pong paddle for a Japanese television show, miniature laser printers for a magazine ad, and marionettes for TNT's "Rudy and Go-Go's World Famous Cartoon Show." He attributes his skill at aging partially to the experience he gained working on the John Sayles' movies, *Eight Men Out* and *City of Hope*.

Born in Cincinnati, Ohio, 1962. Tom Haney currently resides in Atlanta, Georgia.

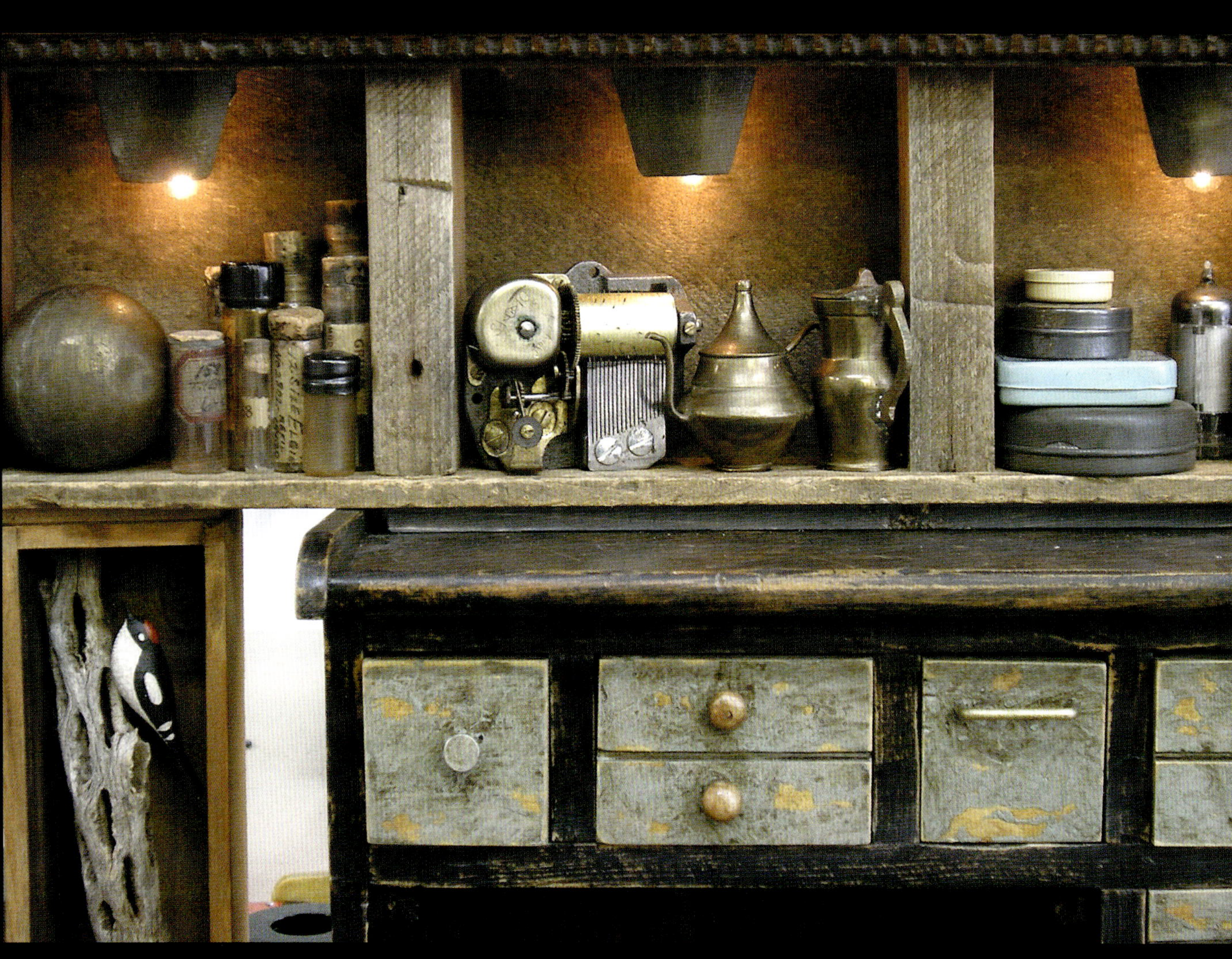

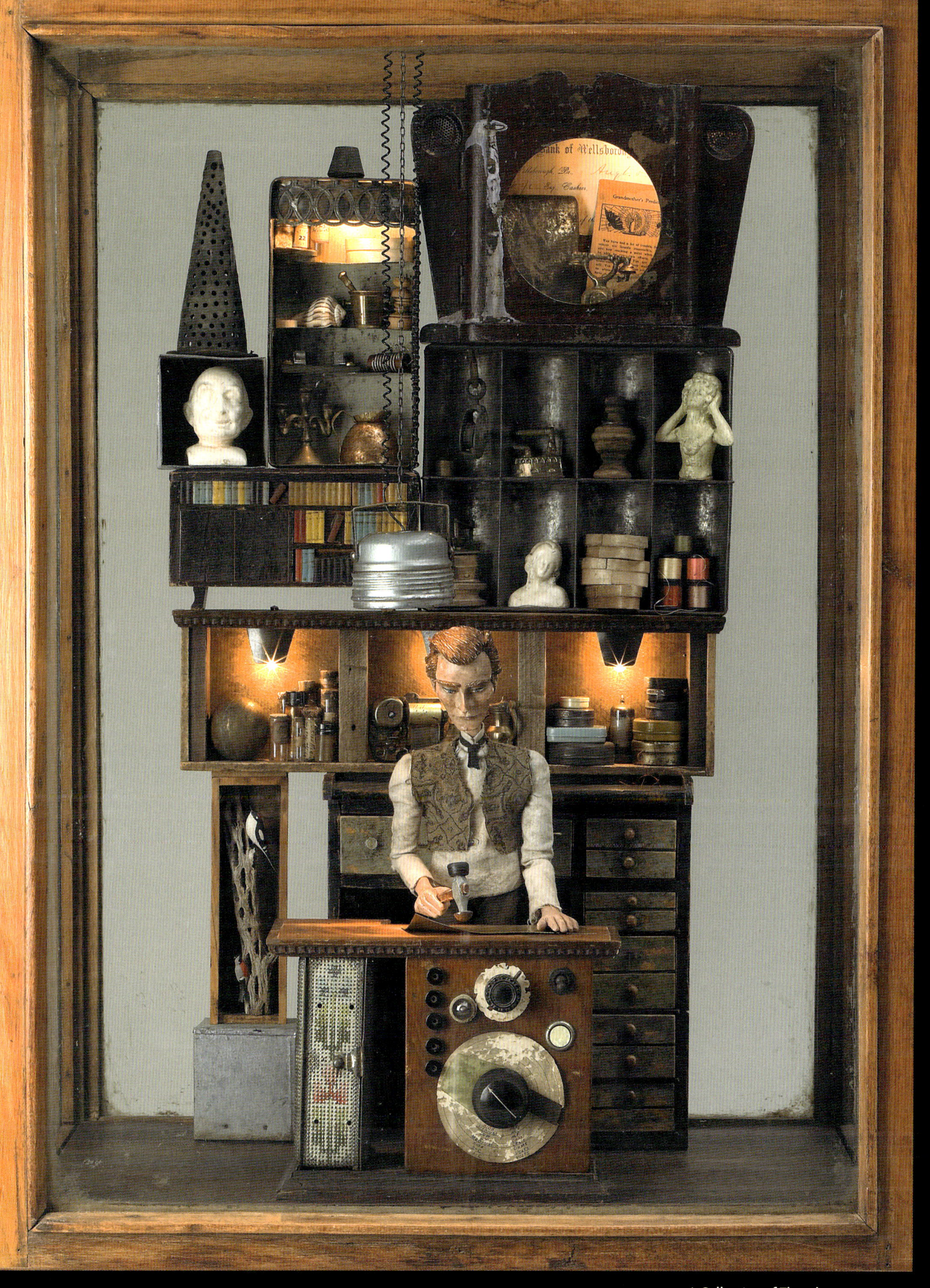

A Collection of Thoughts – 26" x 38" x 19" (2008)

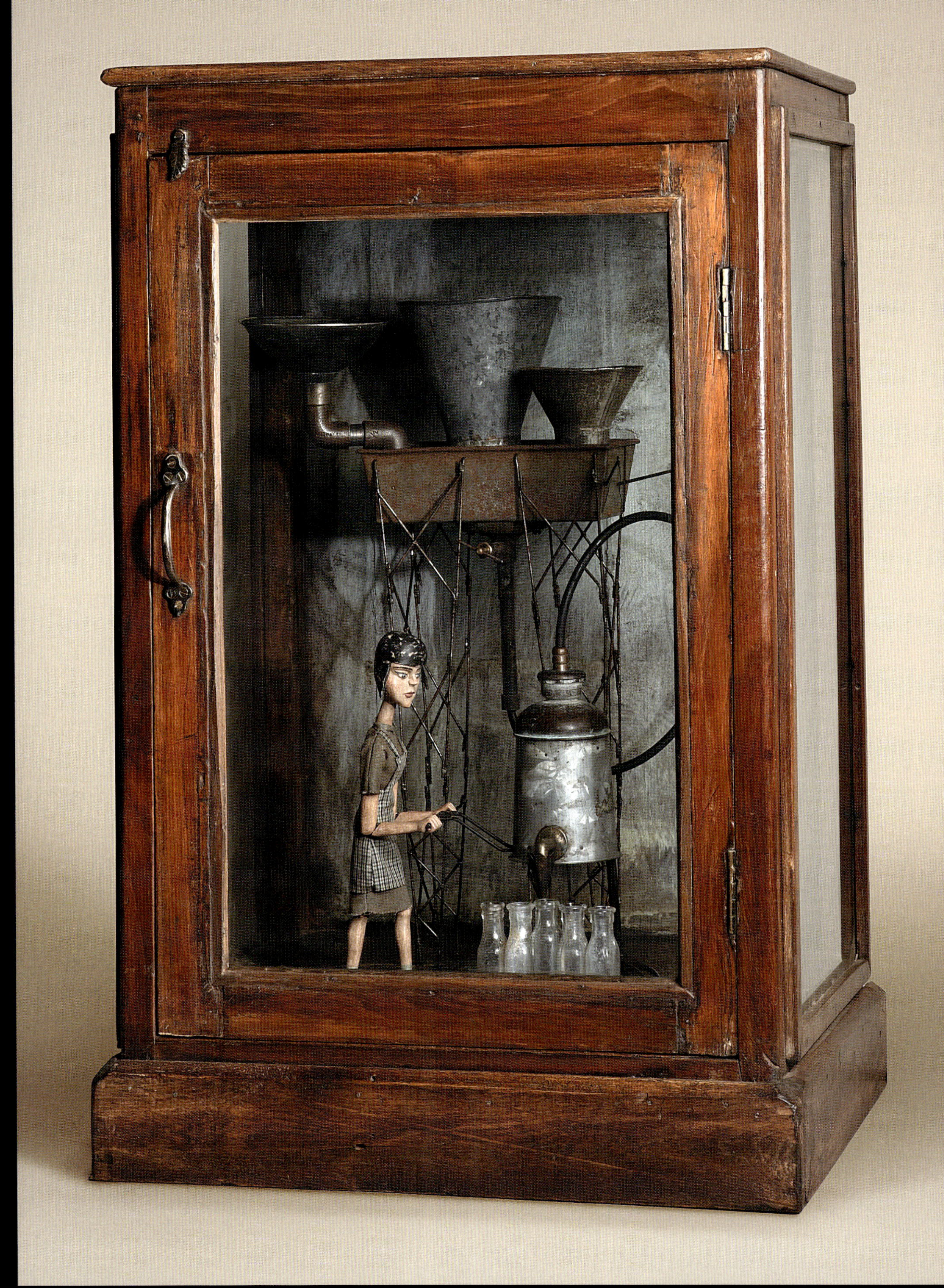

Accumulation – 19" x 29" x 15" (2008)

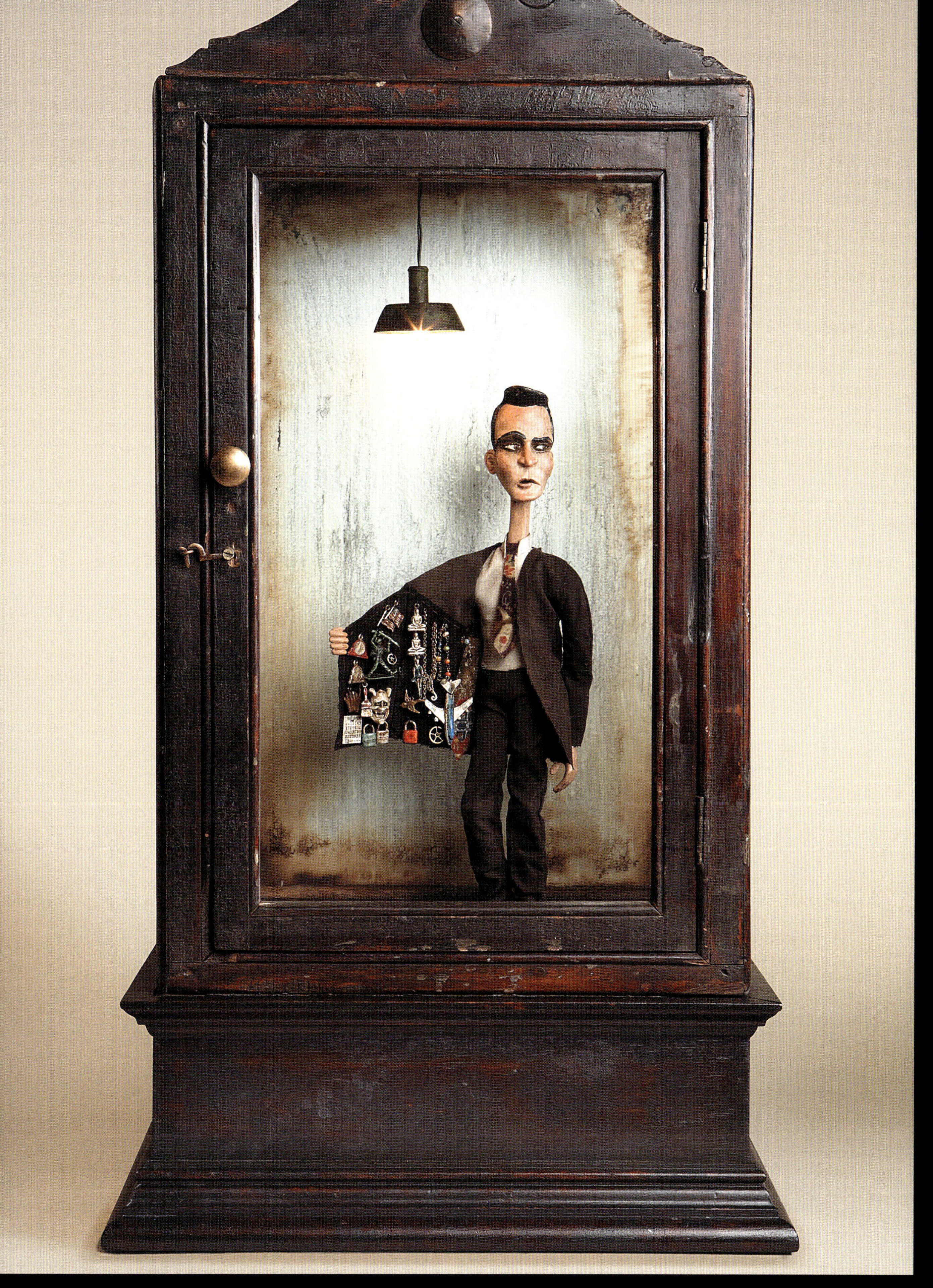

Dubious – 16" x 29" x 11" (2008)

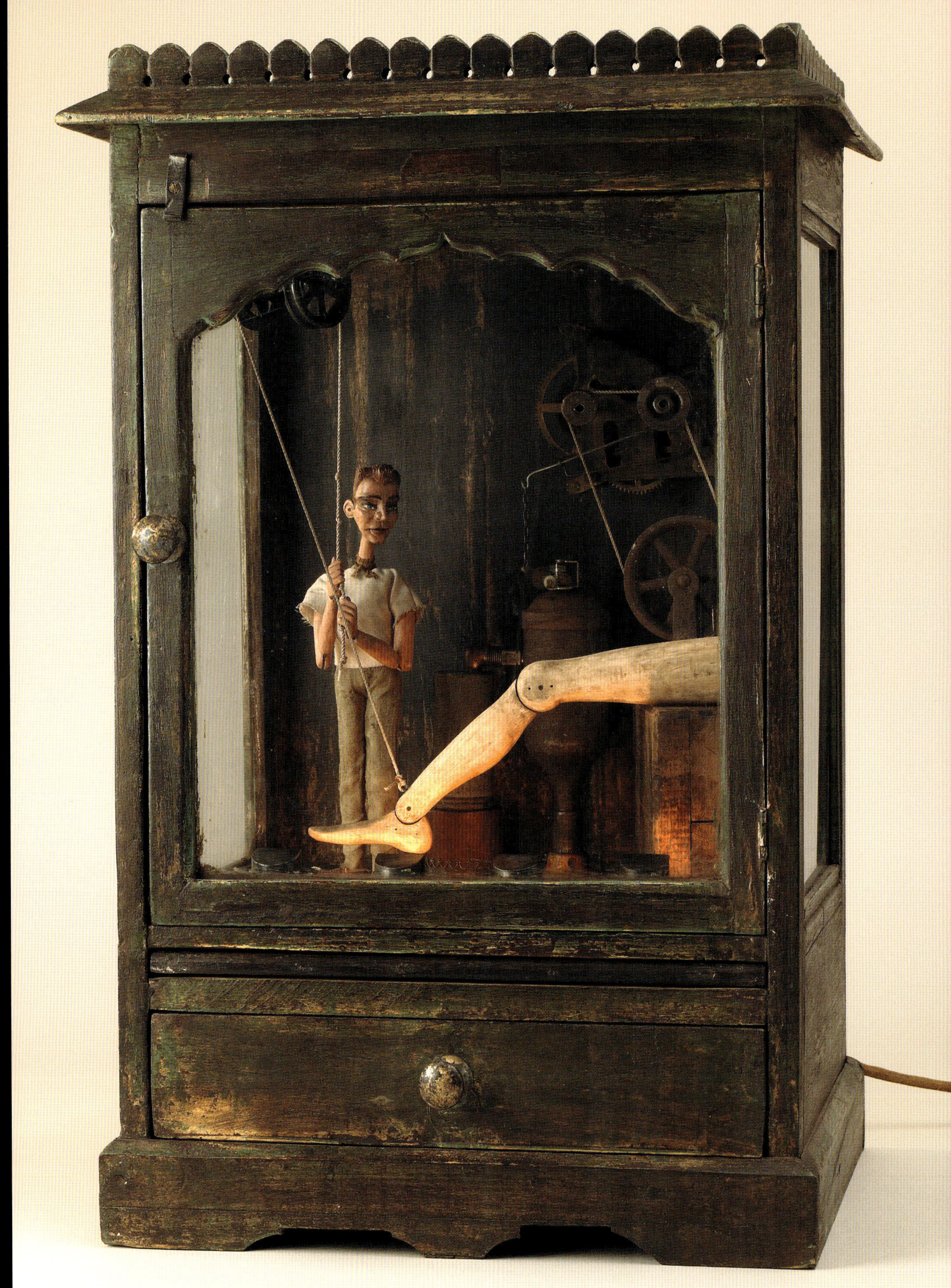

Introspection – 16" x 25" x 13" (2008)

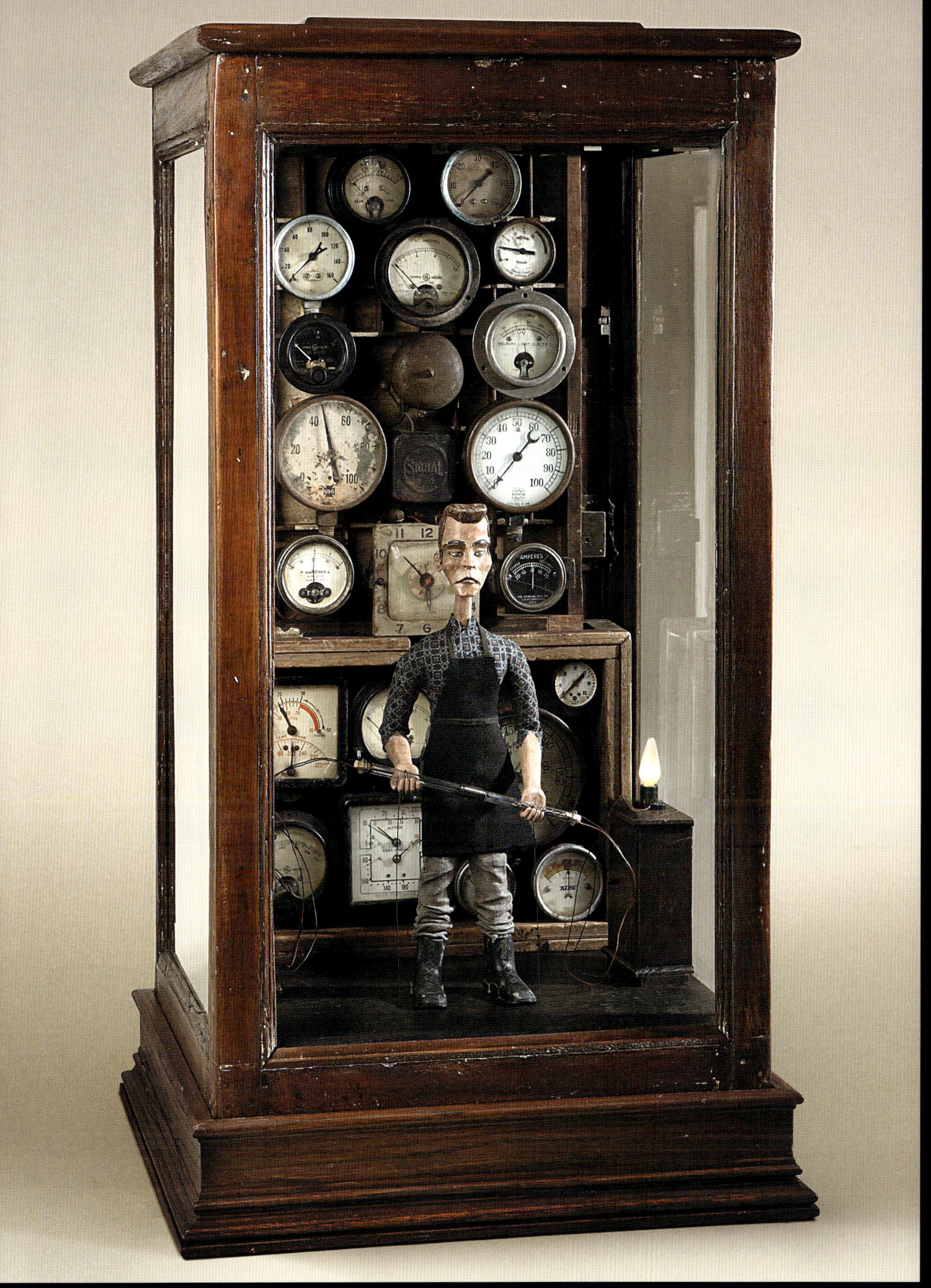

Contrivance – 19" x 34" x 19" (2008)

STÉPHANE**HALLEUX**

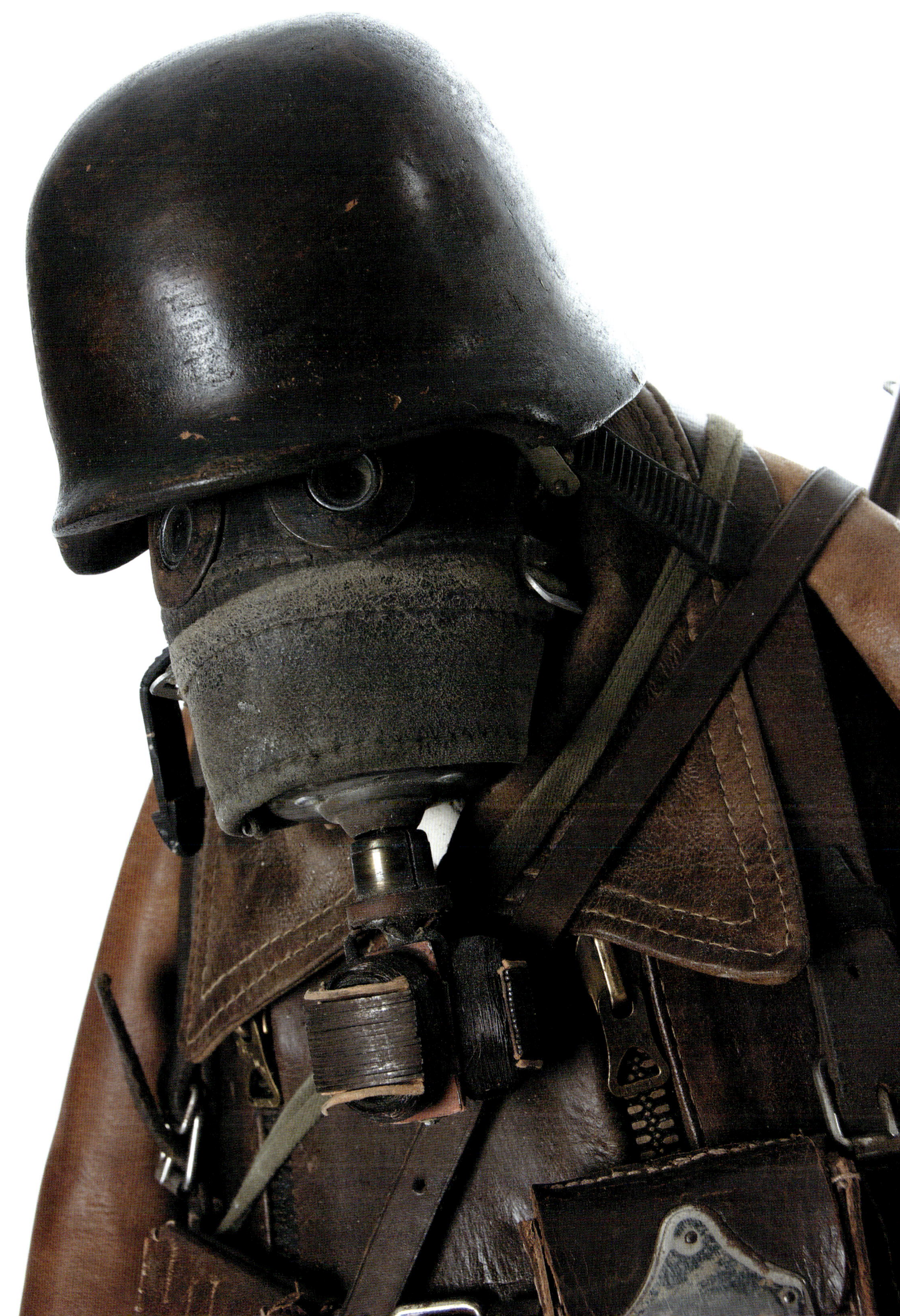

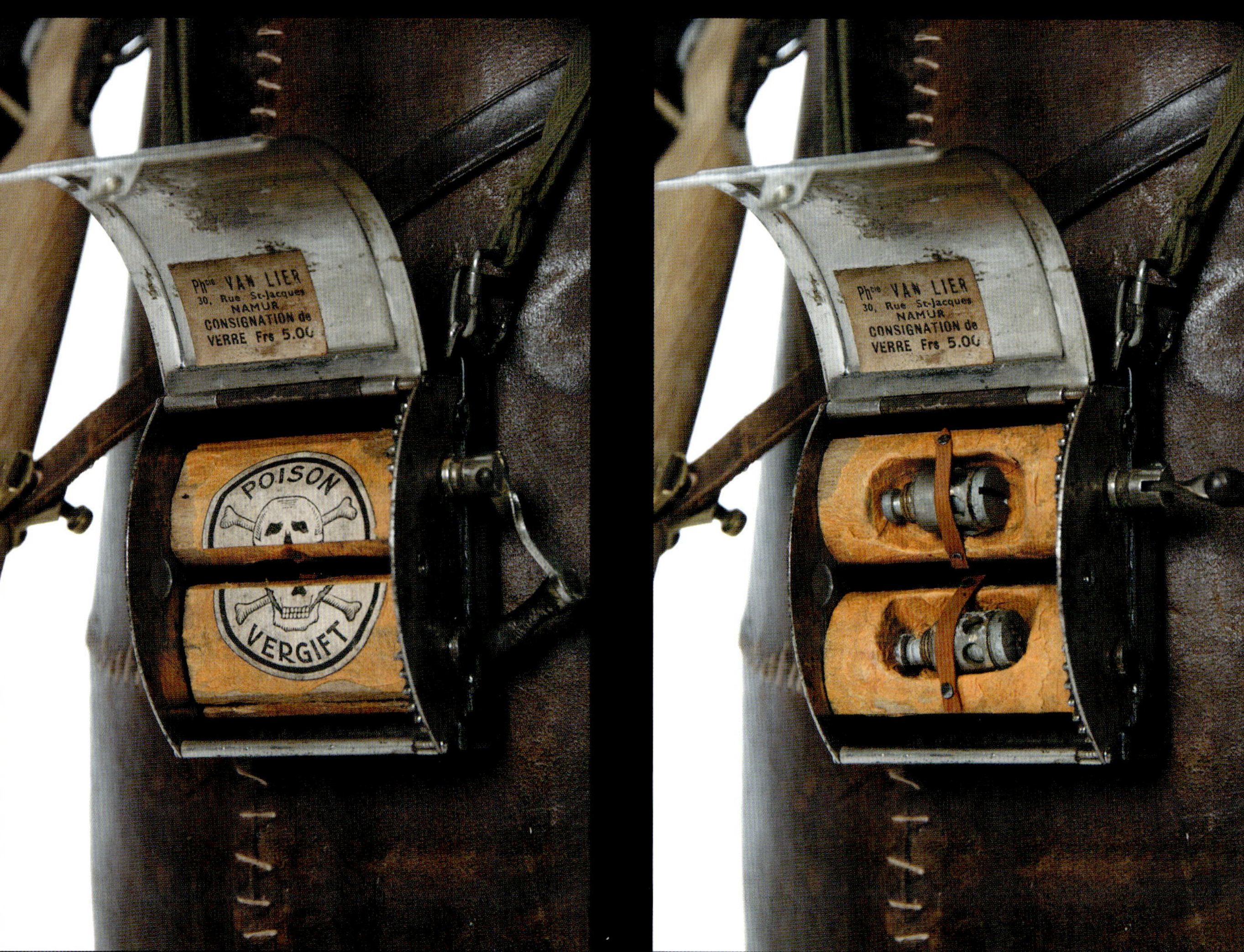

Phcie VAN LIER
30, Rue St-Jacques
NAMUR
CONSIGNATION de
VERRE Frs 5.00
POISON
VERGIFT

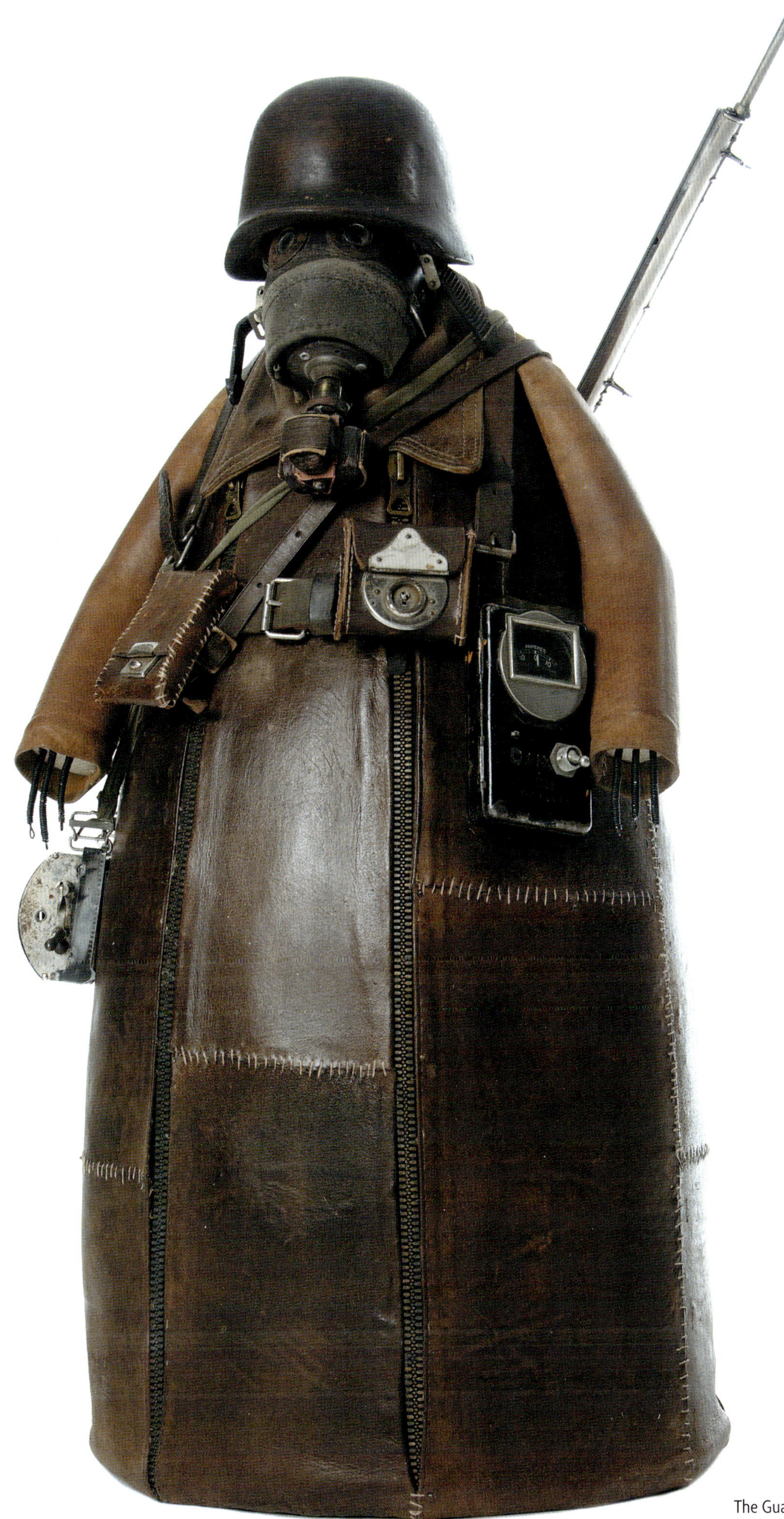

The Guard – 31.5” x 13.8” x 13.8” (2009)

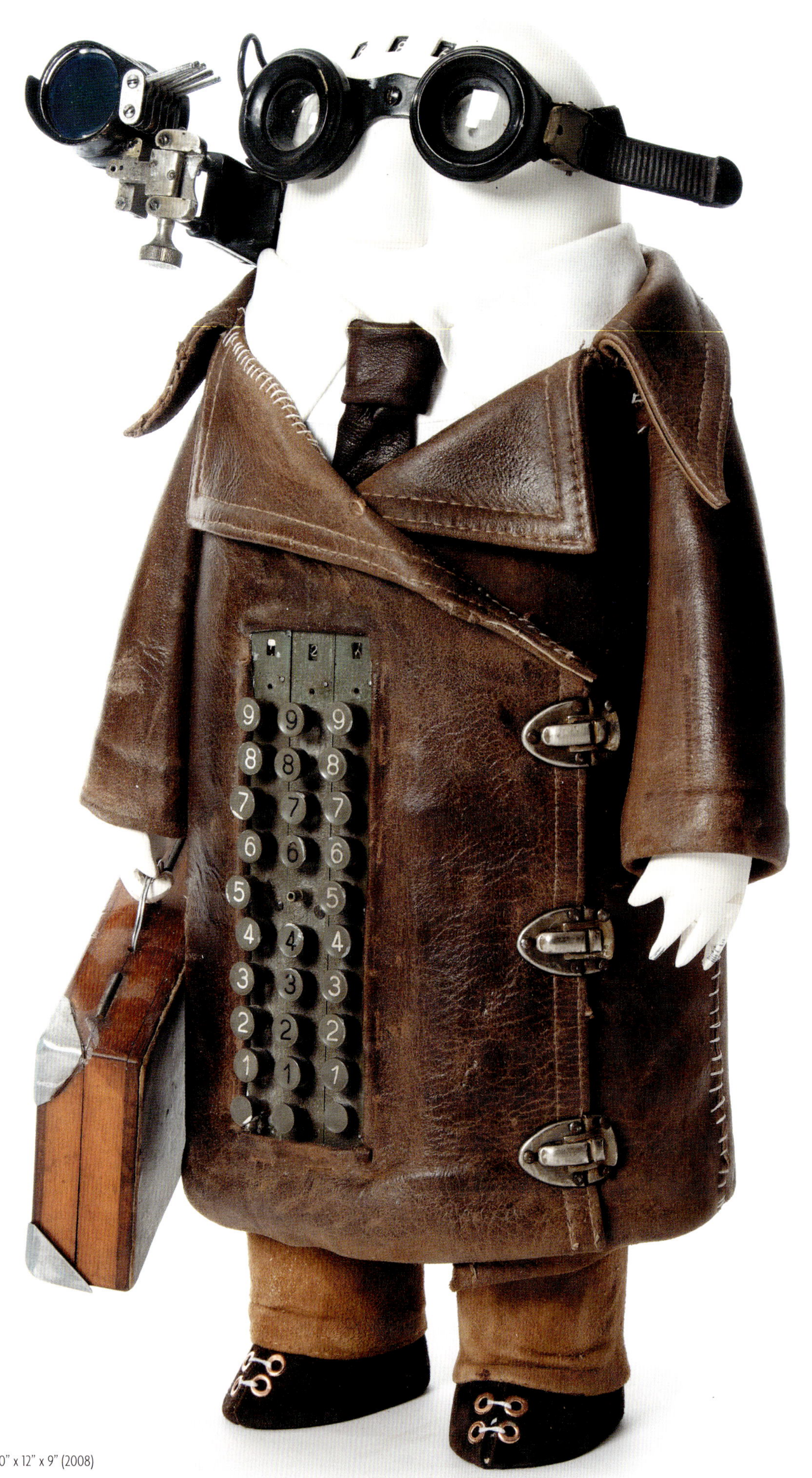

Monsieur Hublot – *20" x 12" x 9" (2008)*

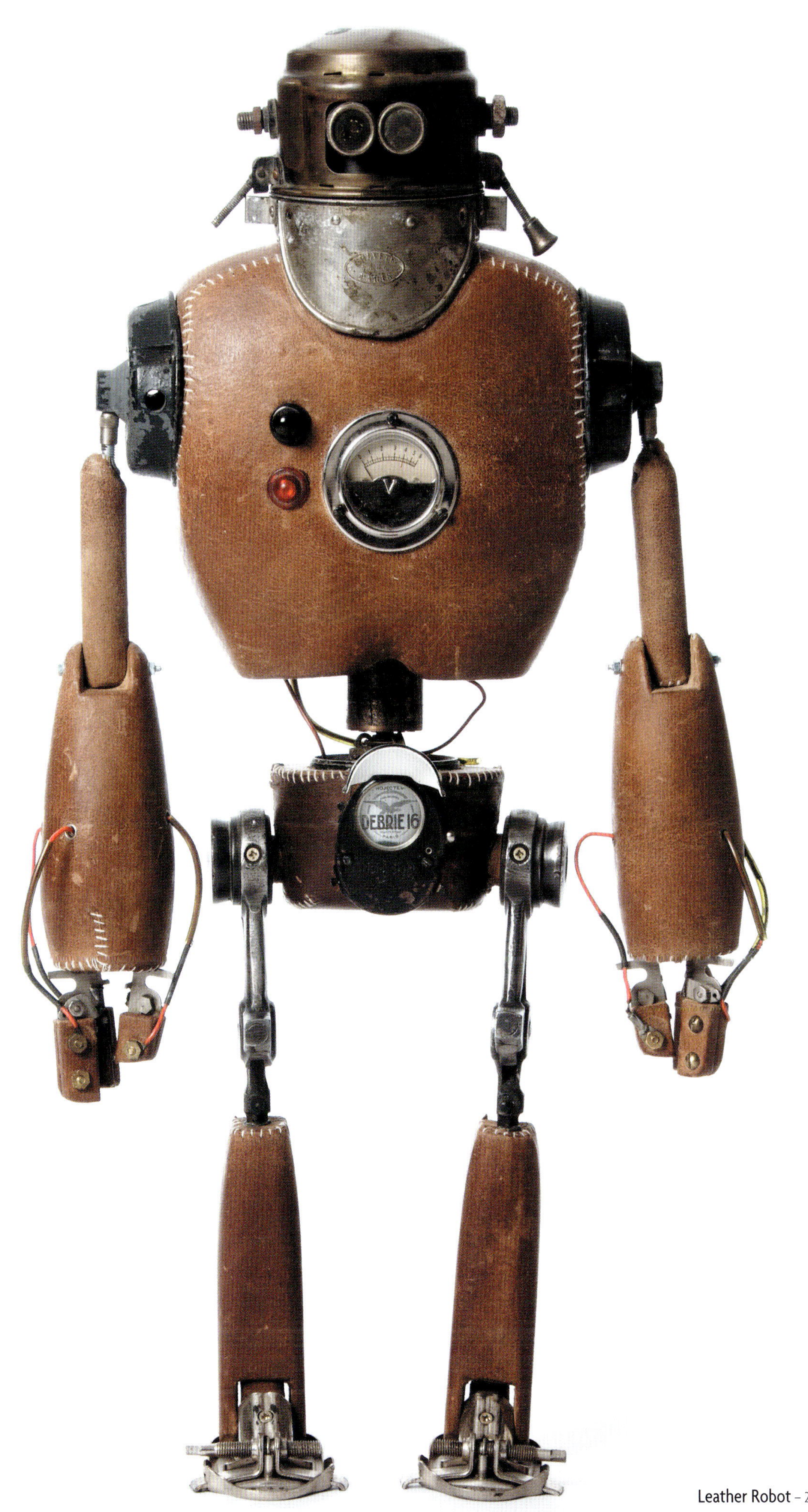

Leather Robot – 28" x 6.3" x 15.3" (2008)

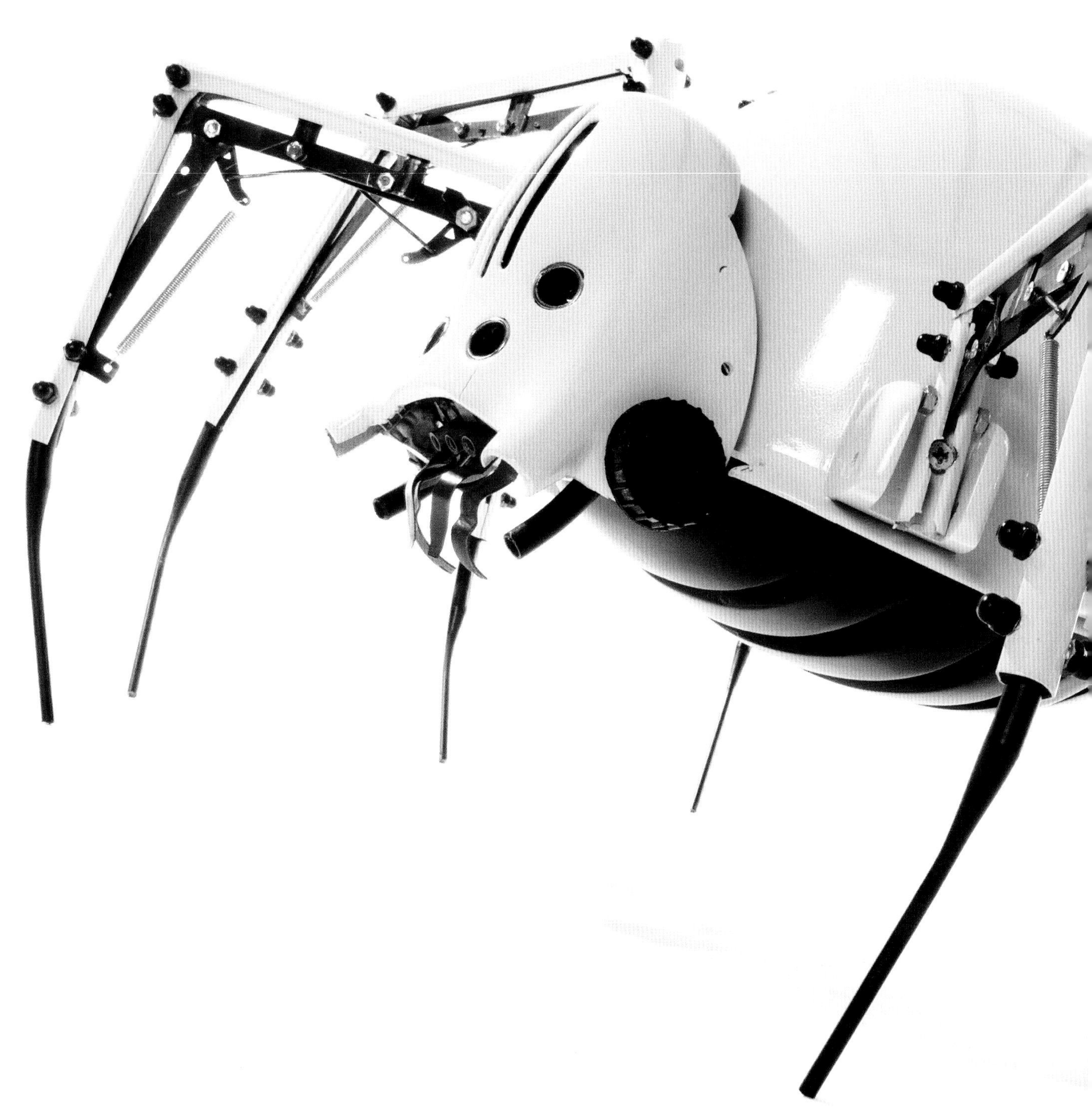

Araignée de l'empire (Spider Empire) – 13.4" x 27.5" x 17.7" (2008)

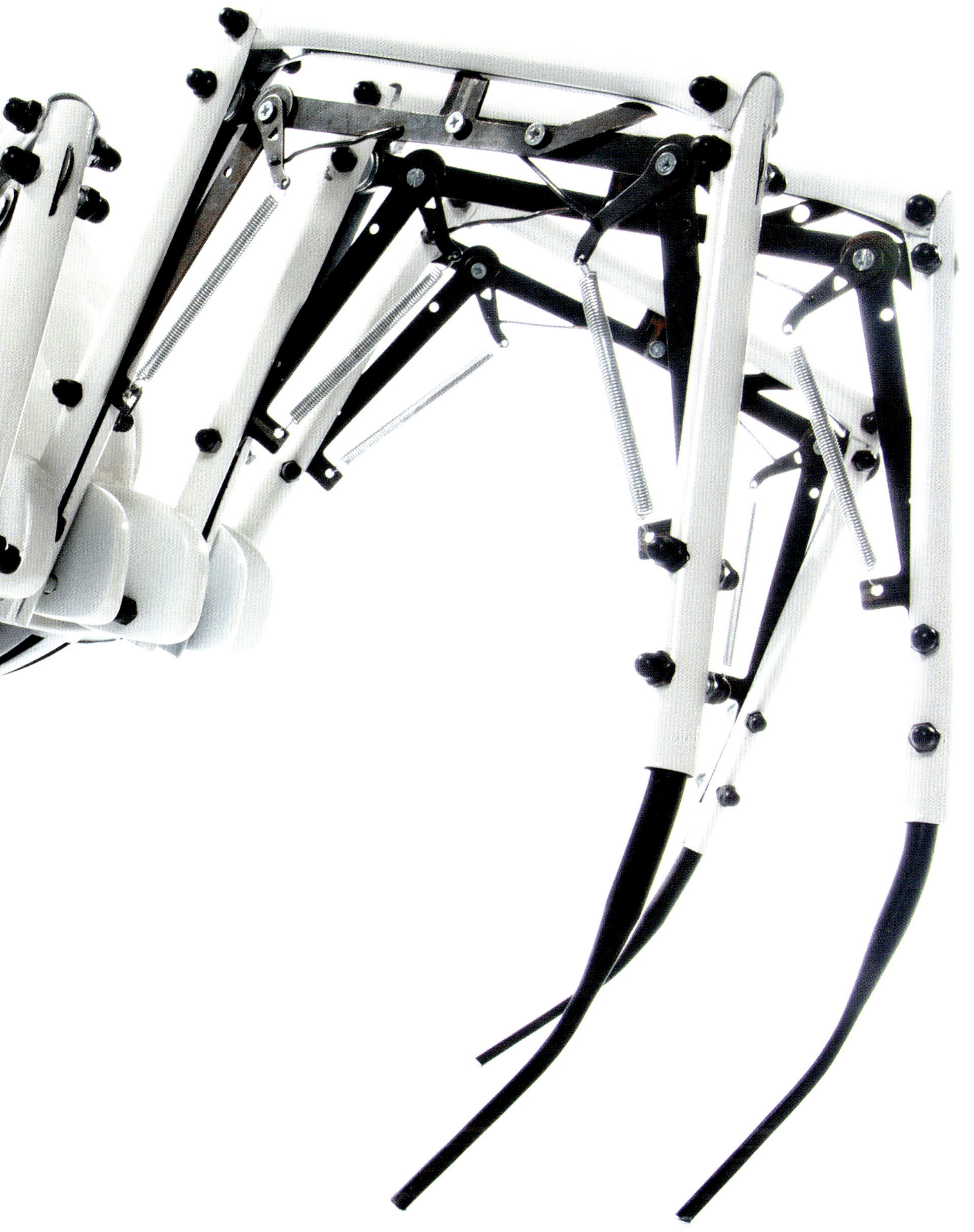

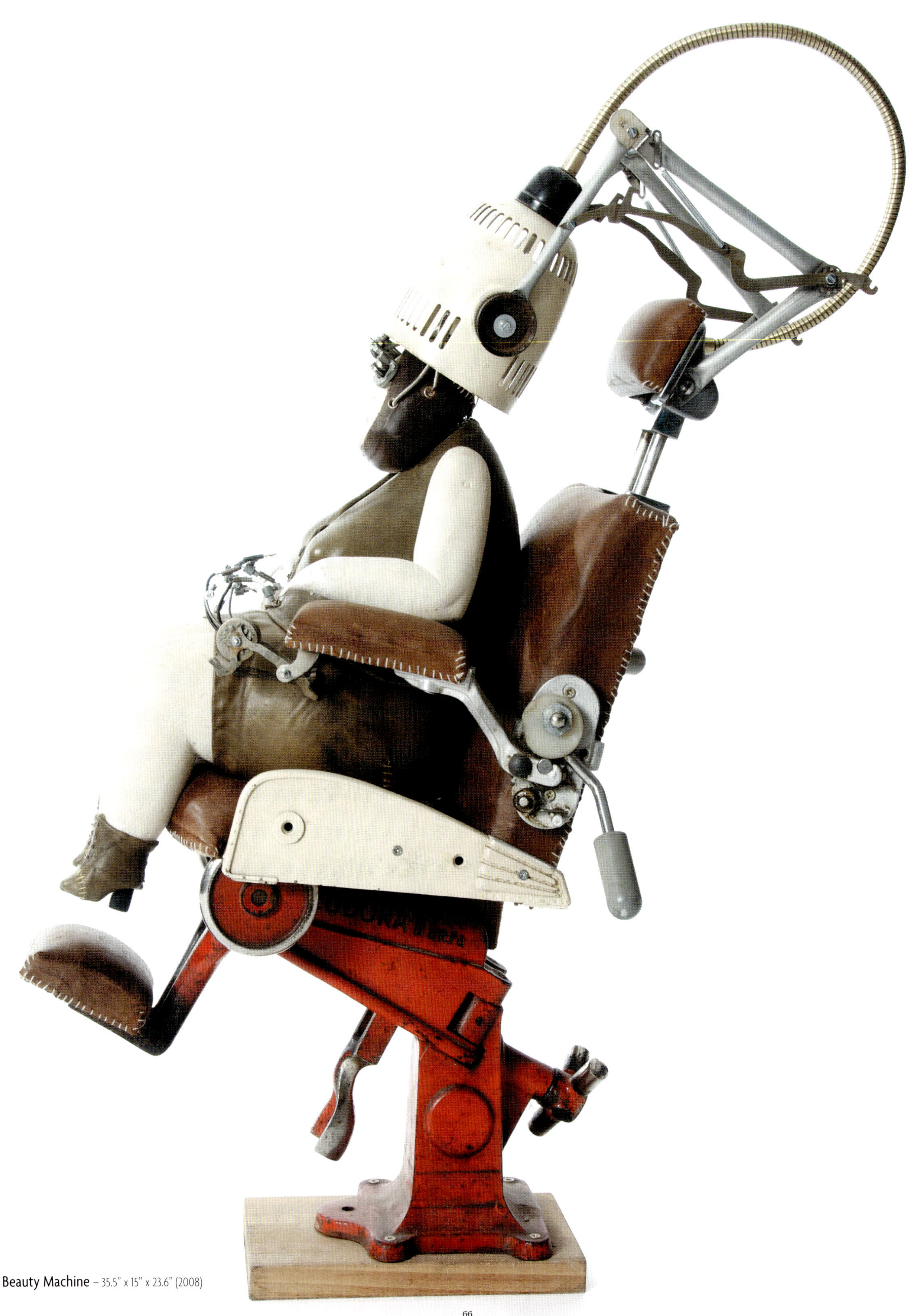

Beauty Machine – 35.5" x 15" x 23.6" (2008)

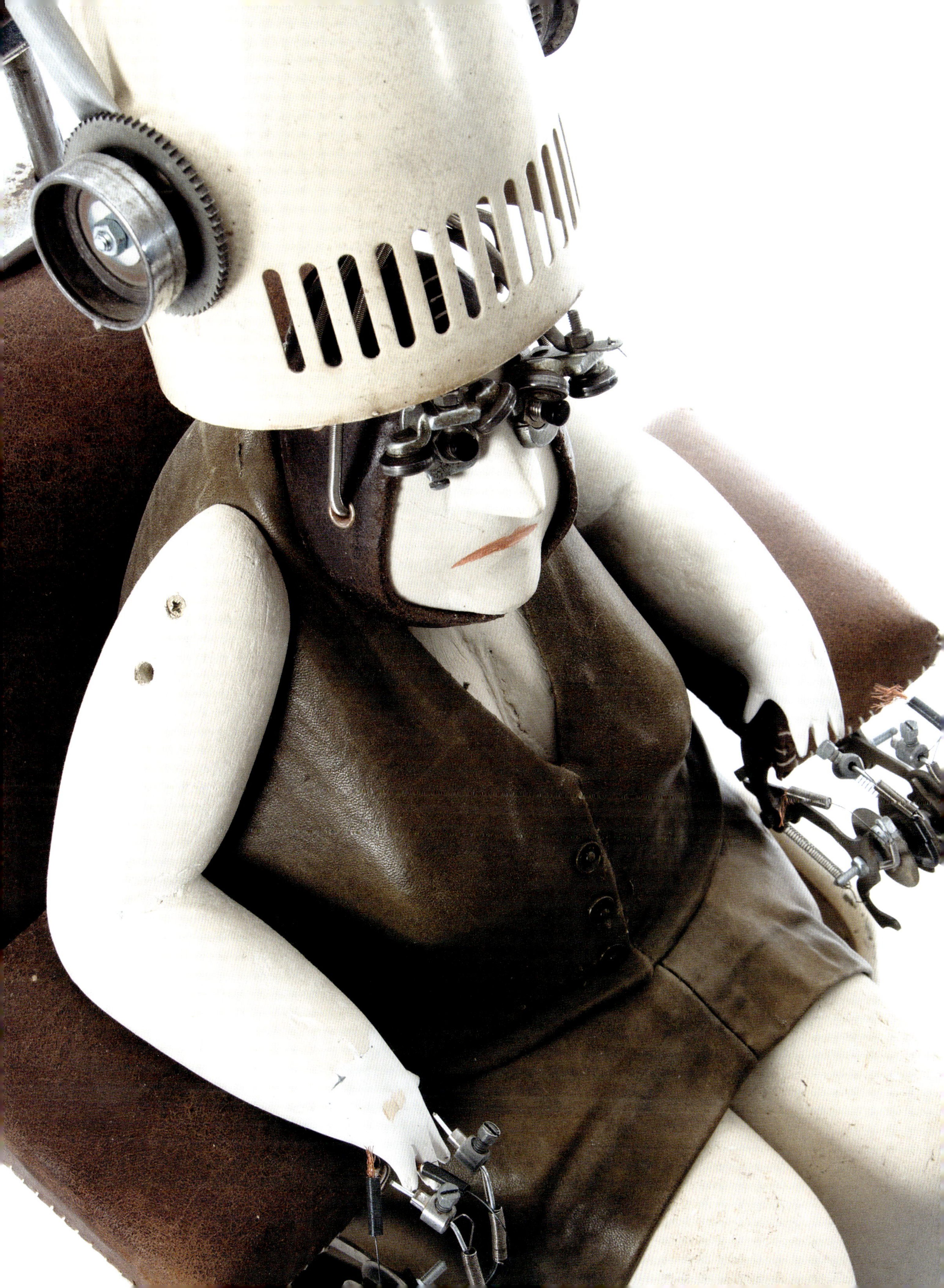

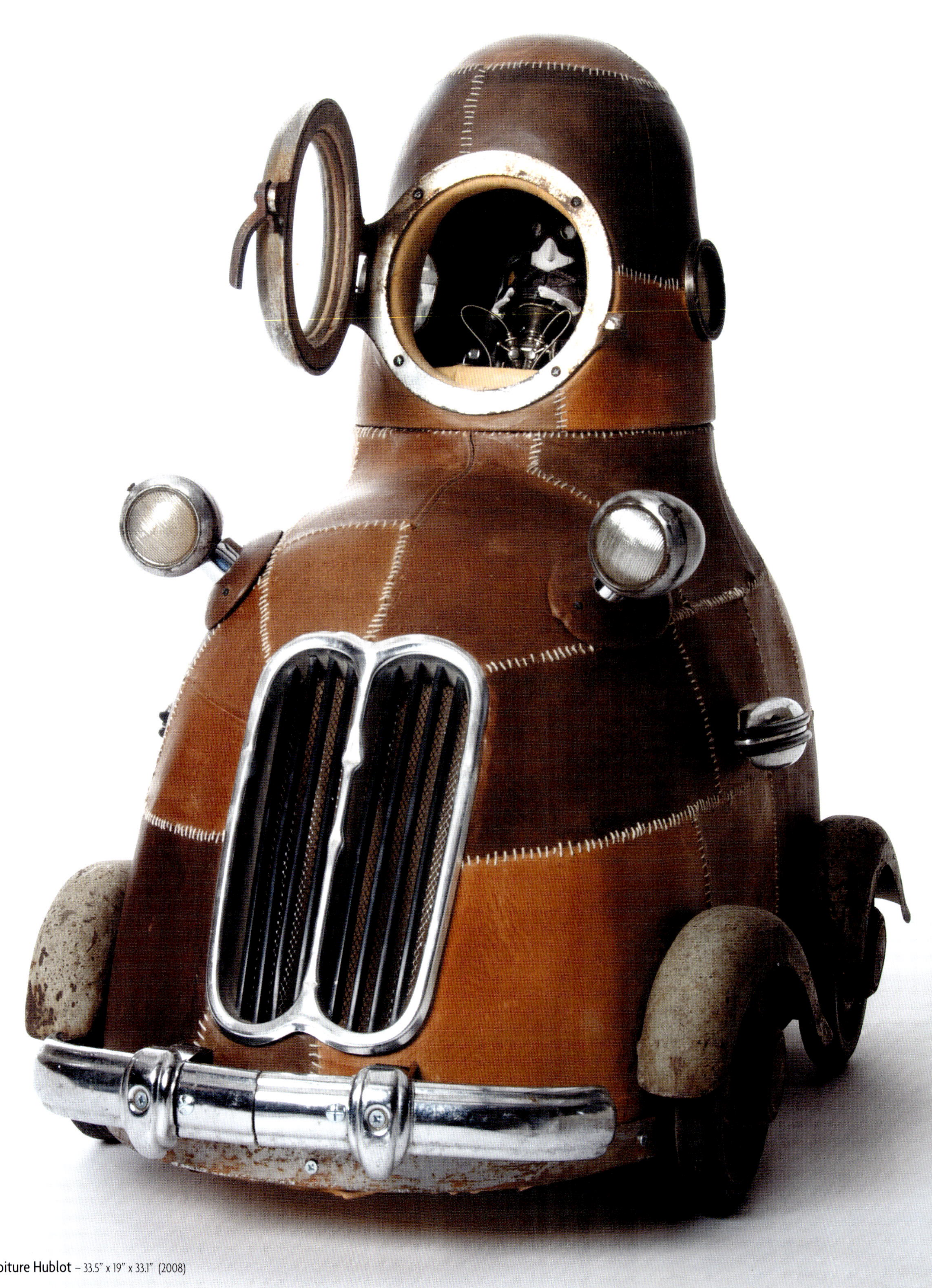

Voiture Hublot – 33.5" x 19" x 33.1" (2008)

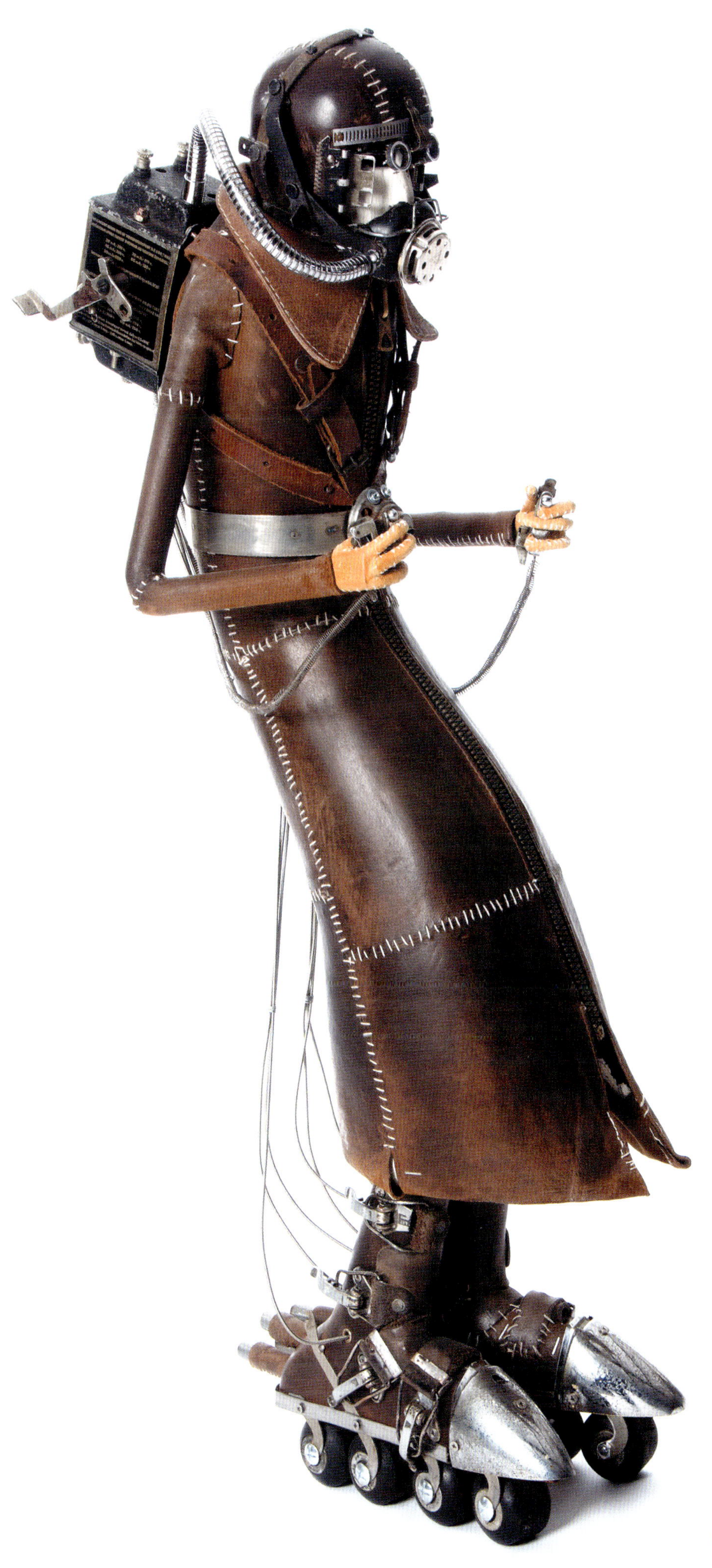

Rouleur de patins – 32″ x 12″ x 10″ (2008)

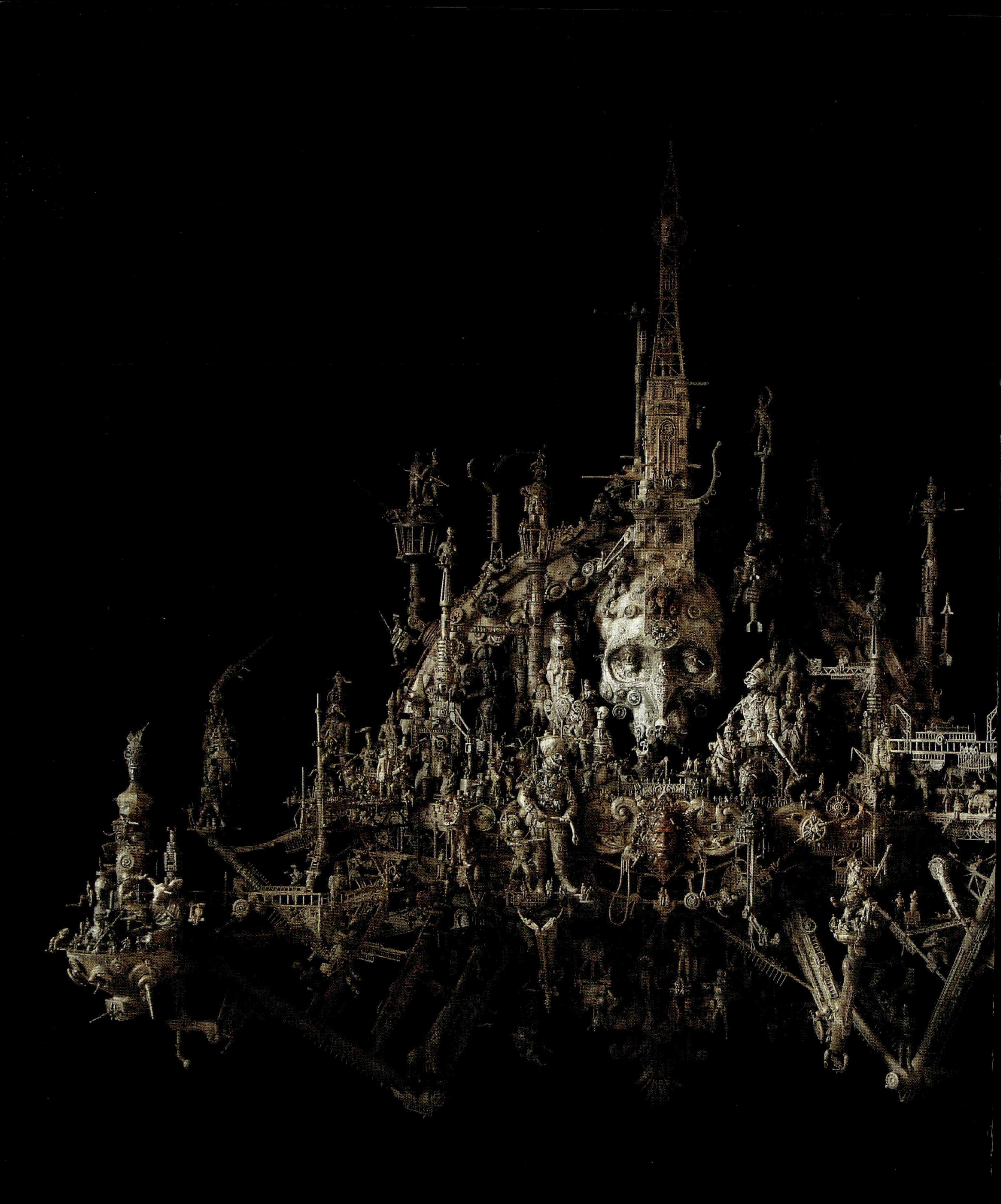

Sanctuary of the Bewildered – 38" x 36" x 16" (2009)

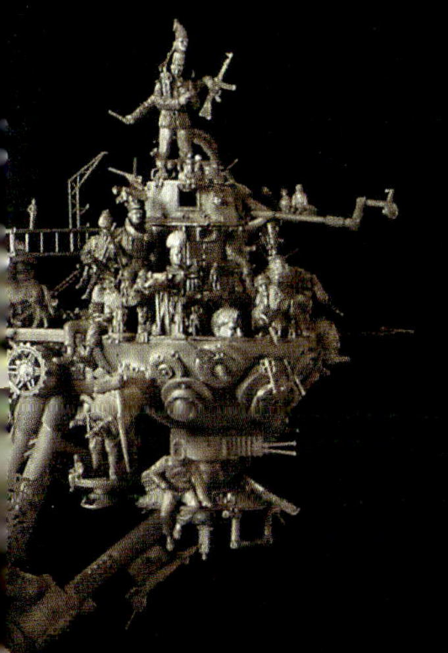

KRIS**KUKSI**

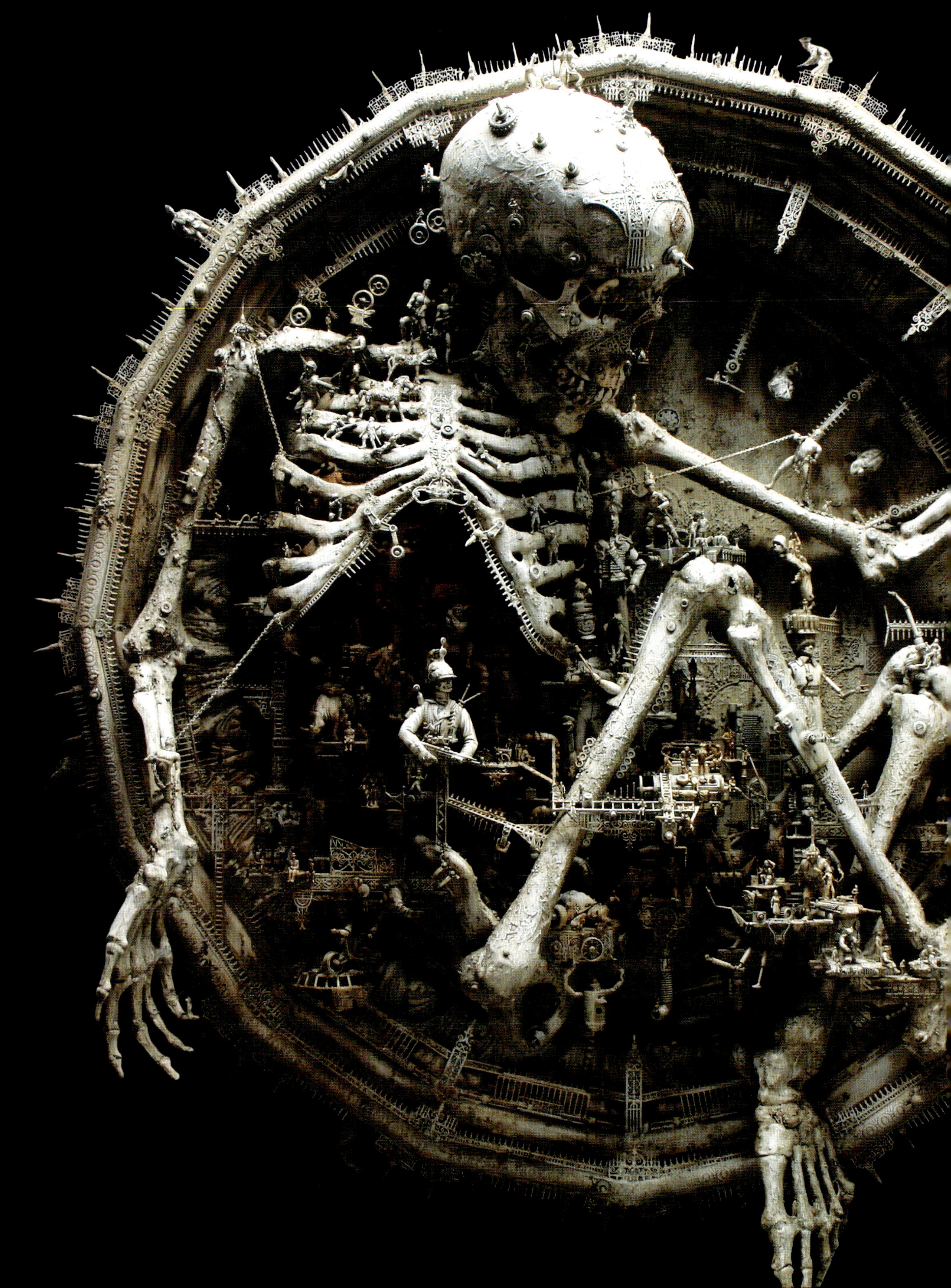

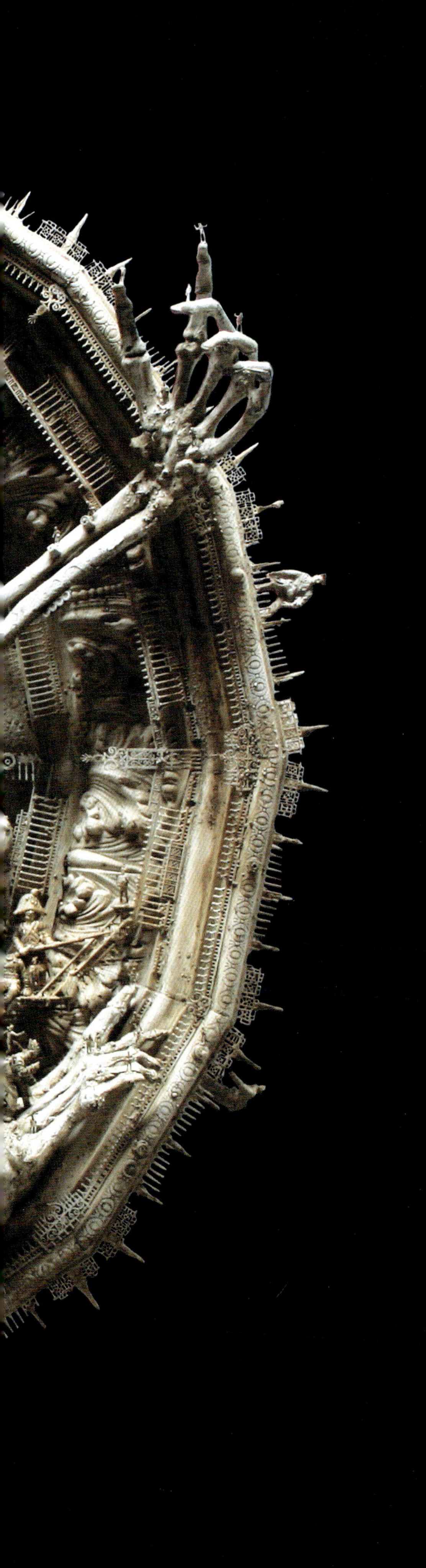

Kris **Kuksi**

"I get inspired by the industrial world, all the rigidity of machinery, the network of pipes, wires, refineries, etc. Then I join that with an opposite of flowing, graceful, harmonious, and pleasing design of the Baroque and Rococo. And, of course, I add a bit of weirdness and the macabre. It's all about how I see the evolution of what man makes his created environment look like. I had such a major emphasis in painting and drawing earlier in my career, and had a great time with it, but I always felt something was missing. I knew deep inside I was a builder, and so my 3D work is the expansion into that realm. I still enjoy painting and doing figurative work, but those moments are reserved for special times. Yet, sculptural works are wonderfully intricate constructions of pop culture effluvia like plastic model kits, injection molded toys, dolls, plastic skulls, knick-knack figurines, miniature fencing, toy animals, mechanical parts, and ornate frames or furniture parts, assembled into grotesque tableaux that look a bit like an explosion in Hieronymus Bosch's attic."

Kuksi's art speaks of a timelessness—potentiality and motion attempting to reach on forever, and yet pessimistically delayed—forced into the stillness of death and eternal sleep. He treats morbidity with a sympathetic touch and symbolizes the paradox of the death of the individual by objective personification of death. There is a fear of this consciousness because it drops in upon us without mercy, and yet there is a need to appeal to it in order to provide a sense of security, however deluded that sense may be. Kuksi's art warns us that this appeal is irrelevant, and that we should be slow to create a need for it. His themes also teach us that although death may pursue us arbitrarily, we should never neglect to mourn the tremendous loss of individual potential.

In personal reflection, Kuksi feels that in the world today much of mankind is oftentimes a frivolous and fragile being driven primarily by greed and materialism. He hopes that his art exposes the fallacies of Man, unveiling a new level of awareness to the viewer. His work has received several awards and prizes and has been featured in over 100 exhibitions in galleries and museums worldwide including the Smithsonian's National Portrait Gallery. Kris's art can also be seen in a number of international art magazines, book covers, and theatrical posters, and is featured in both public and private collections in the United States, Europe, and Australia that include such collectors as Mark Parker (Nike CEO), Kay Alden (three-time Emmy award winning writer for *The Young and The Restless* and *The Bold and the Beautiful*), Fred Durst (musician, and film director), and Chris Weitz (movie director *The Golden Compass* and *American Pie*).

Antics & Mechanical Frolic – 34" diameter (2008)

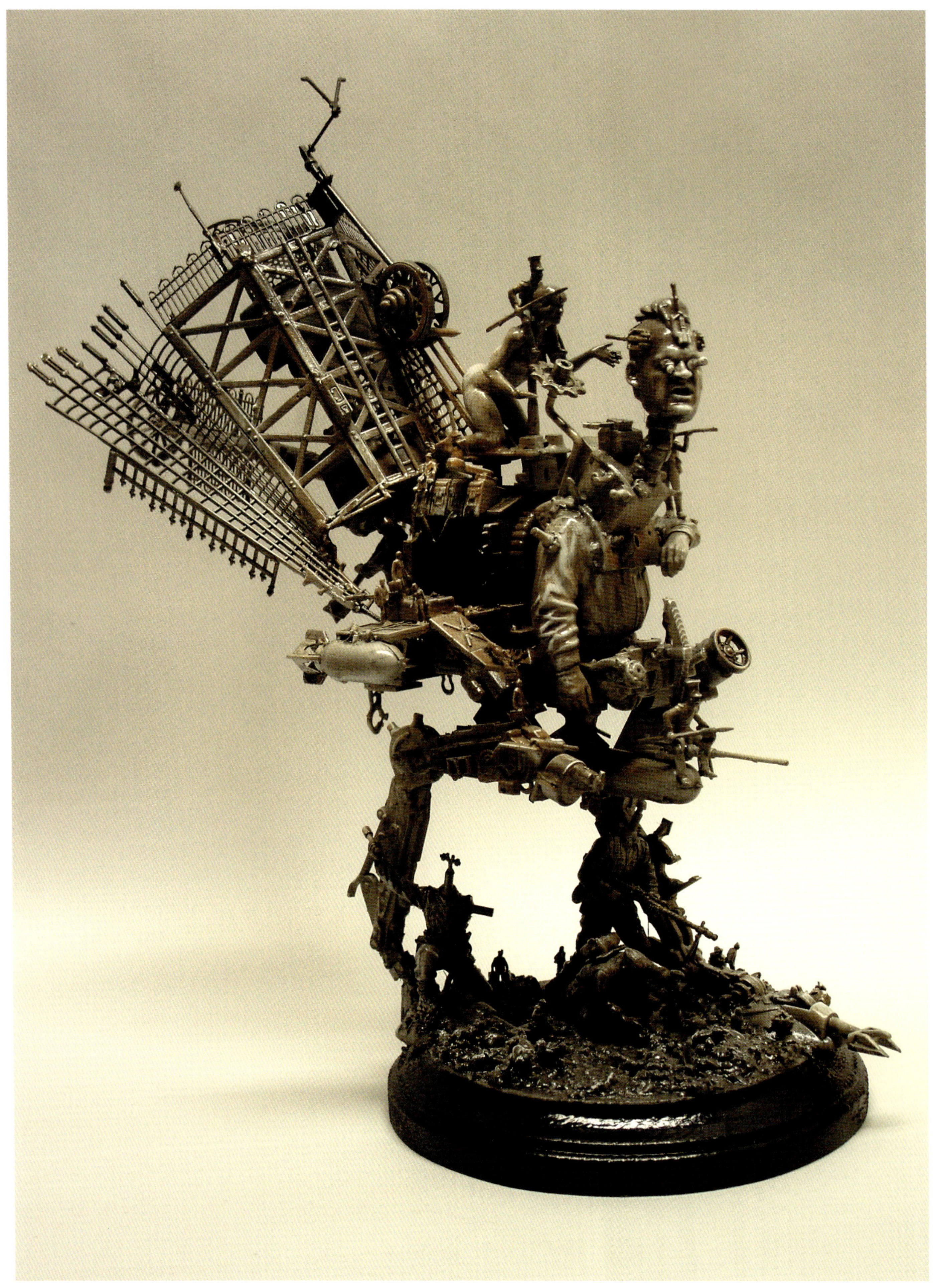

Oblivion Scout – 4" x 10" (2008)

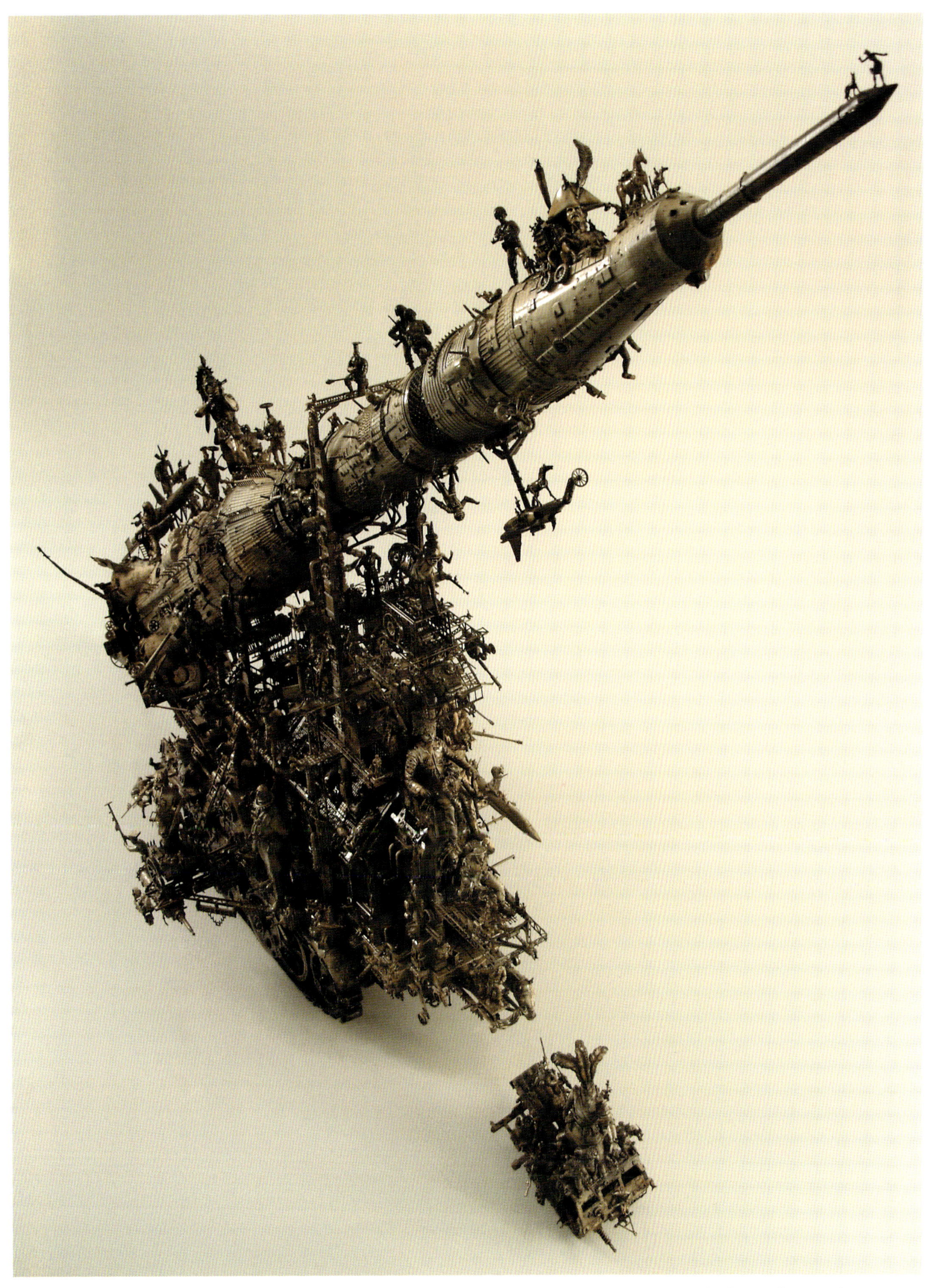

Intercontinental Ballistic Defiance Machine – 46" x 60" (2008)

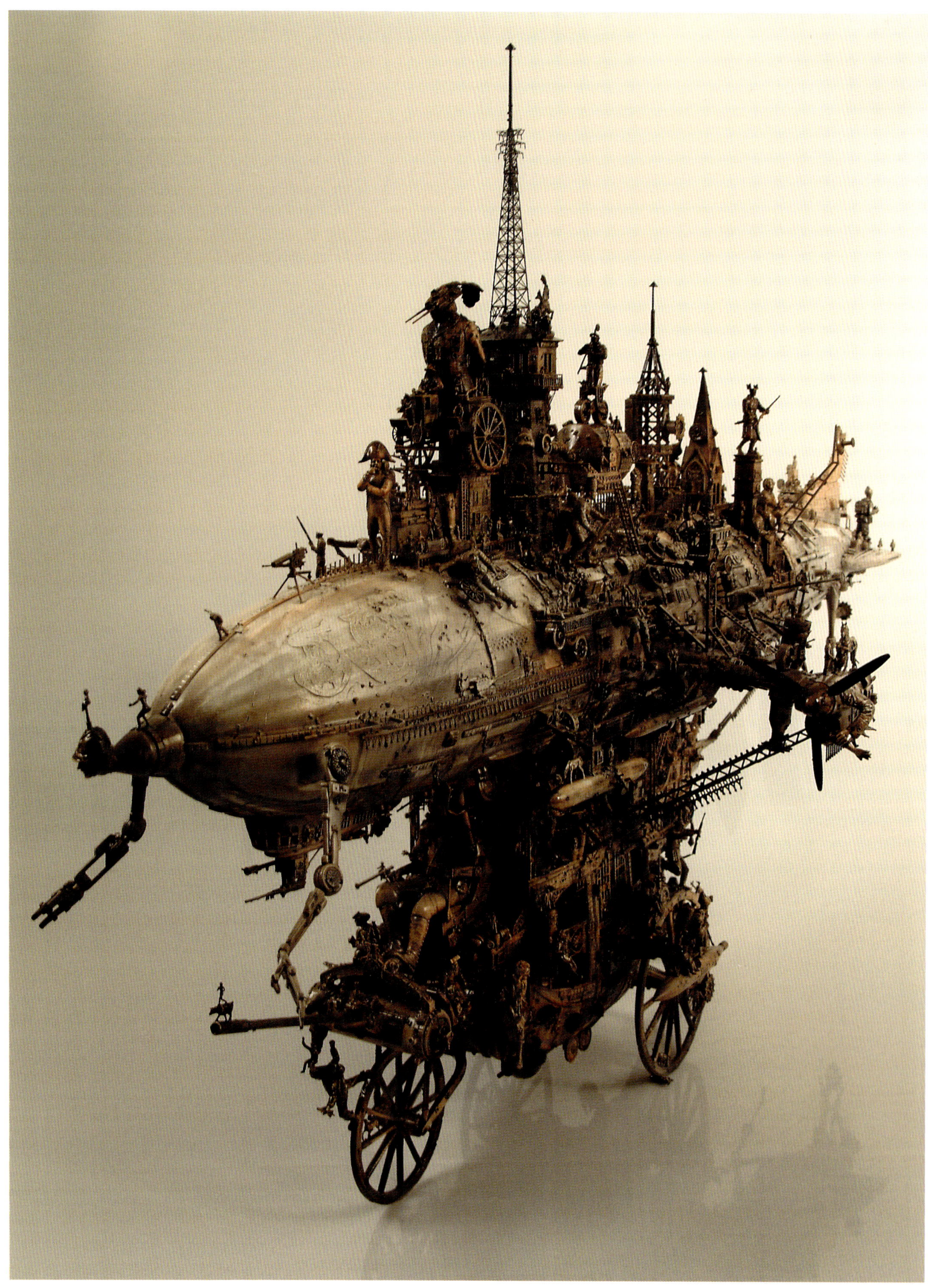

Caravan Assault Apparatus – 39" x 28" (2008)

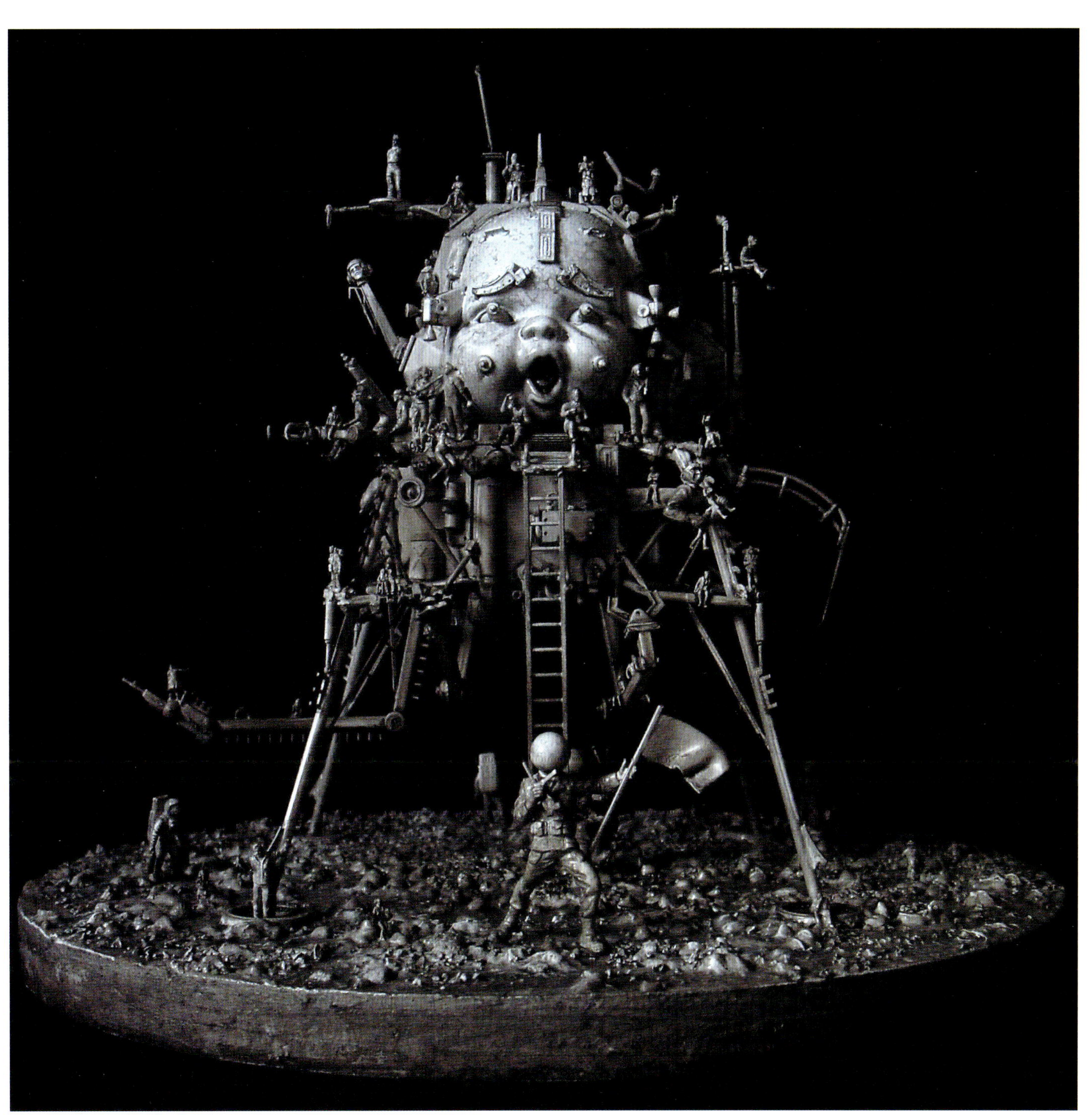

Lunatic Lander I – (2008)

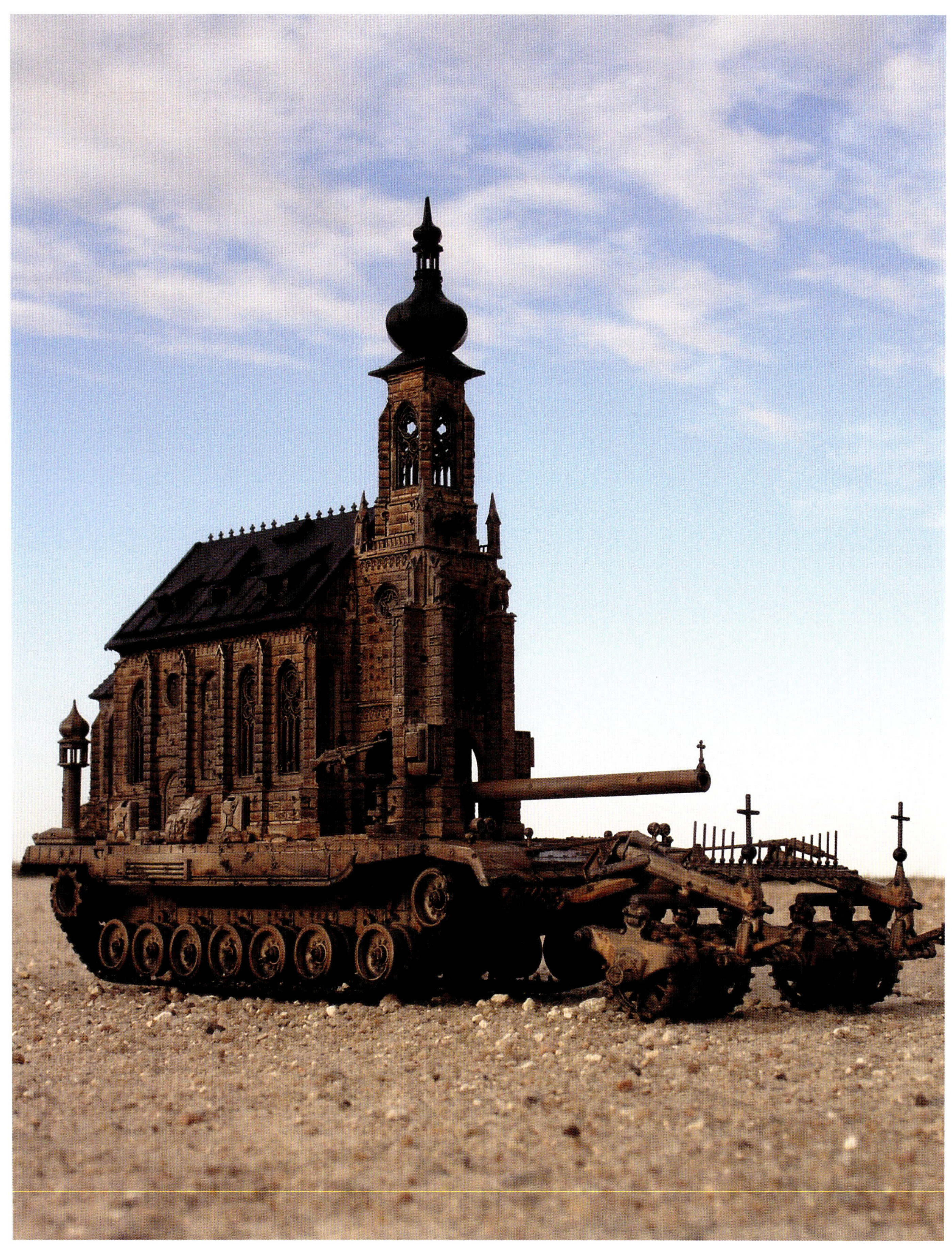

Church Tank 6.6F – 9.75" x 4.25" x 14" (2008)

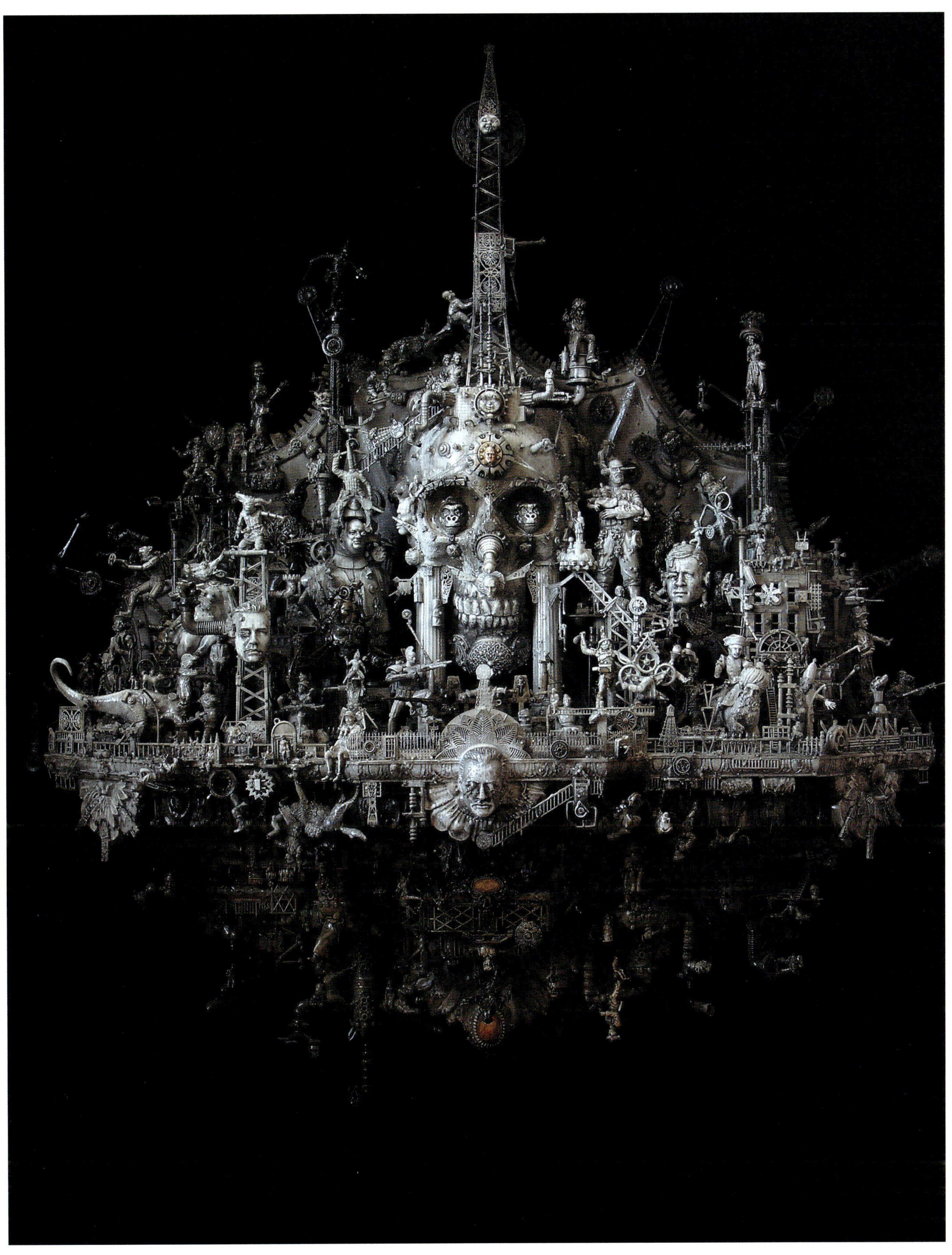

Phantasma – 27" x 32" x 9" (2008)

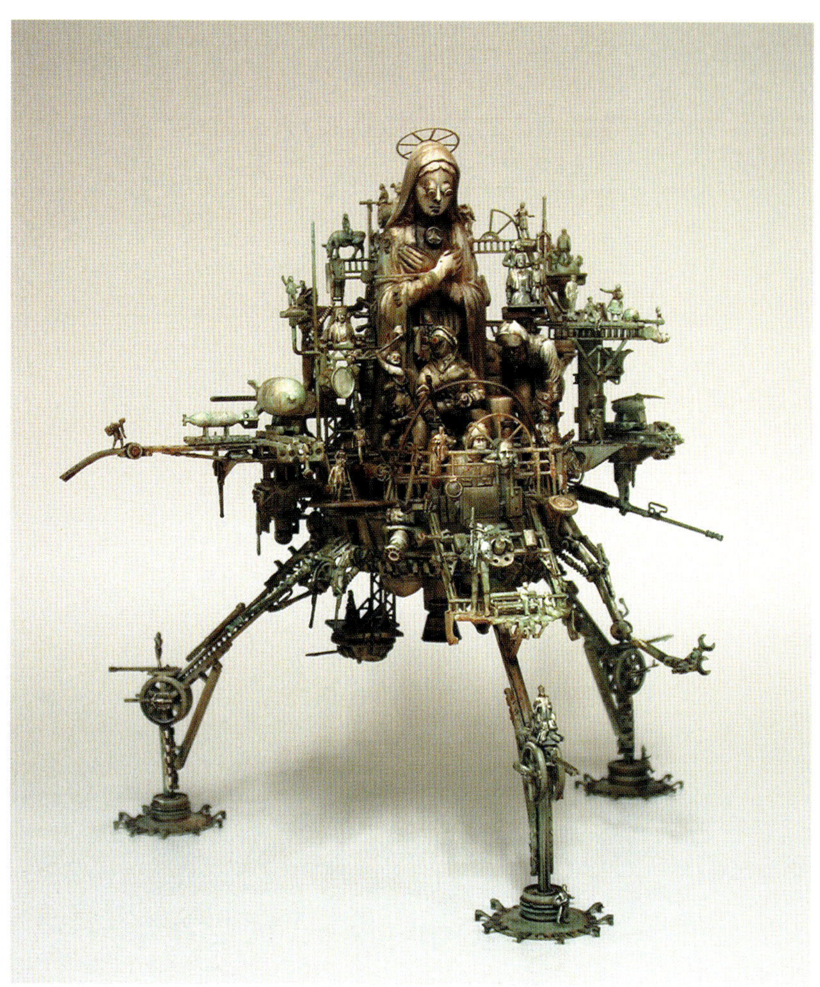

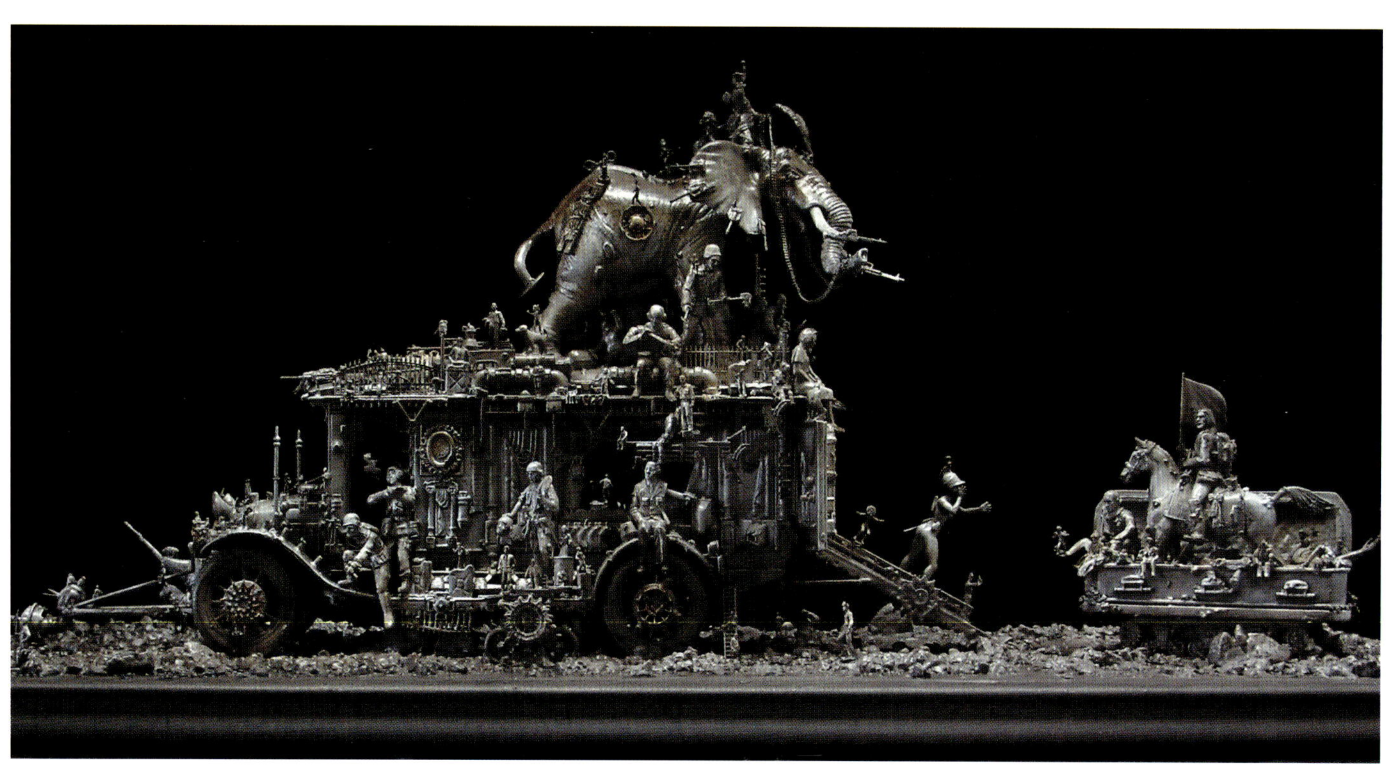

Mary Militia – 6" x 7" (2006) (top)
After World Transporter – 26" x 12" (2008) (bottom)

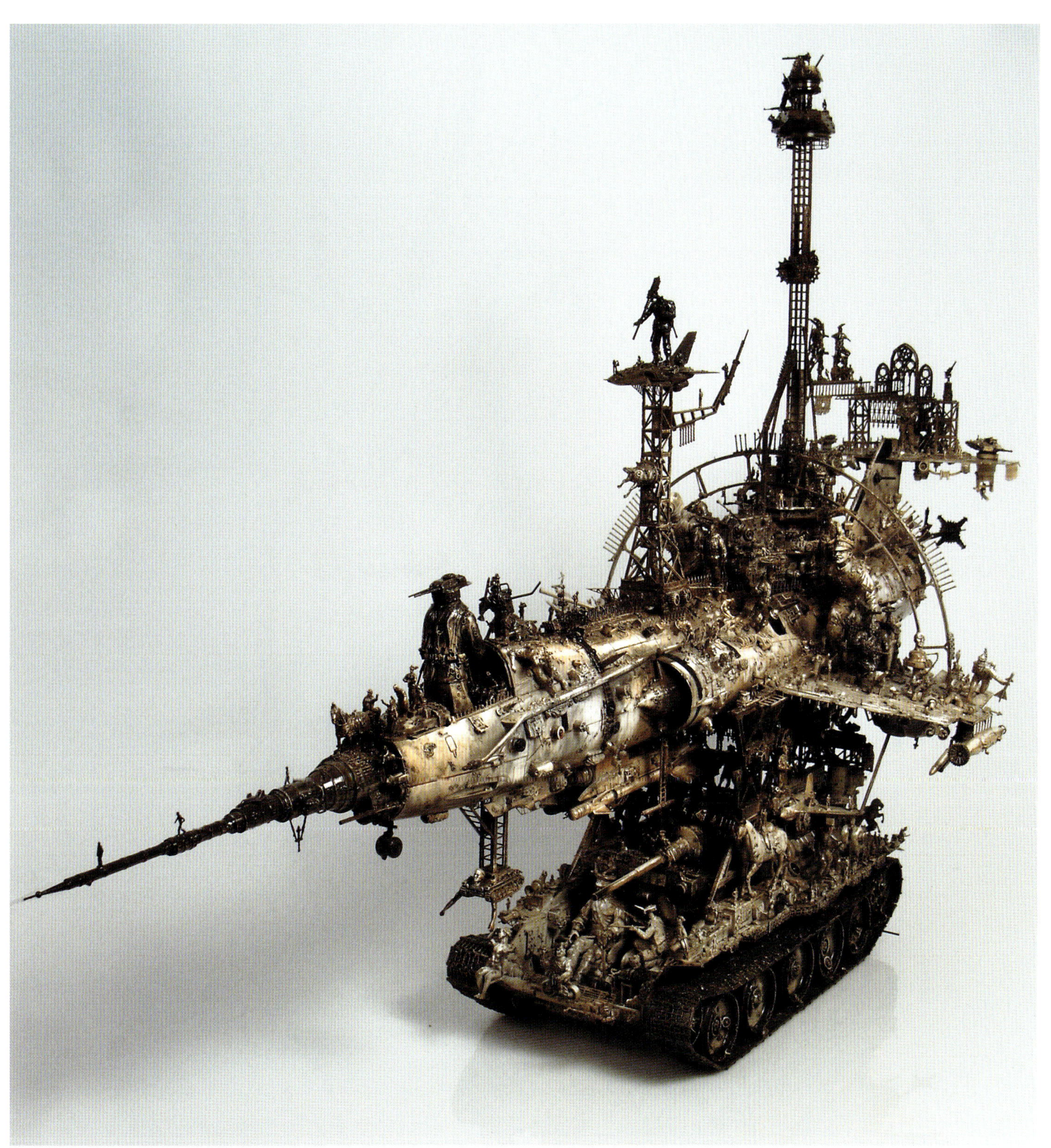

Sub-Sonic Dissidence Propulsion Device – 41" x 28" (2008)

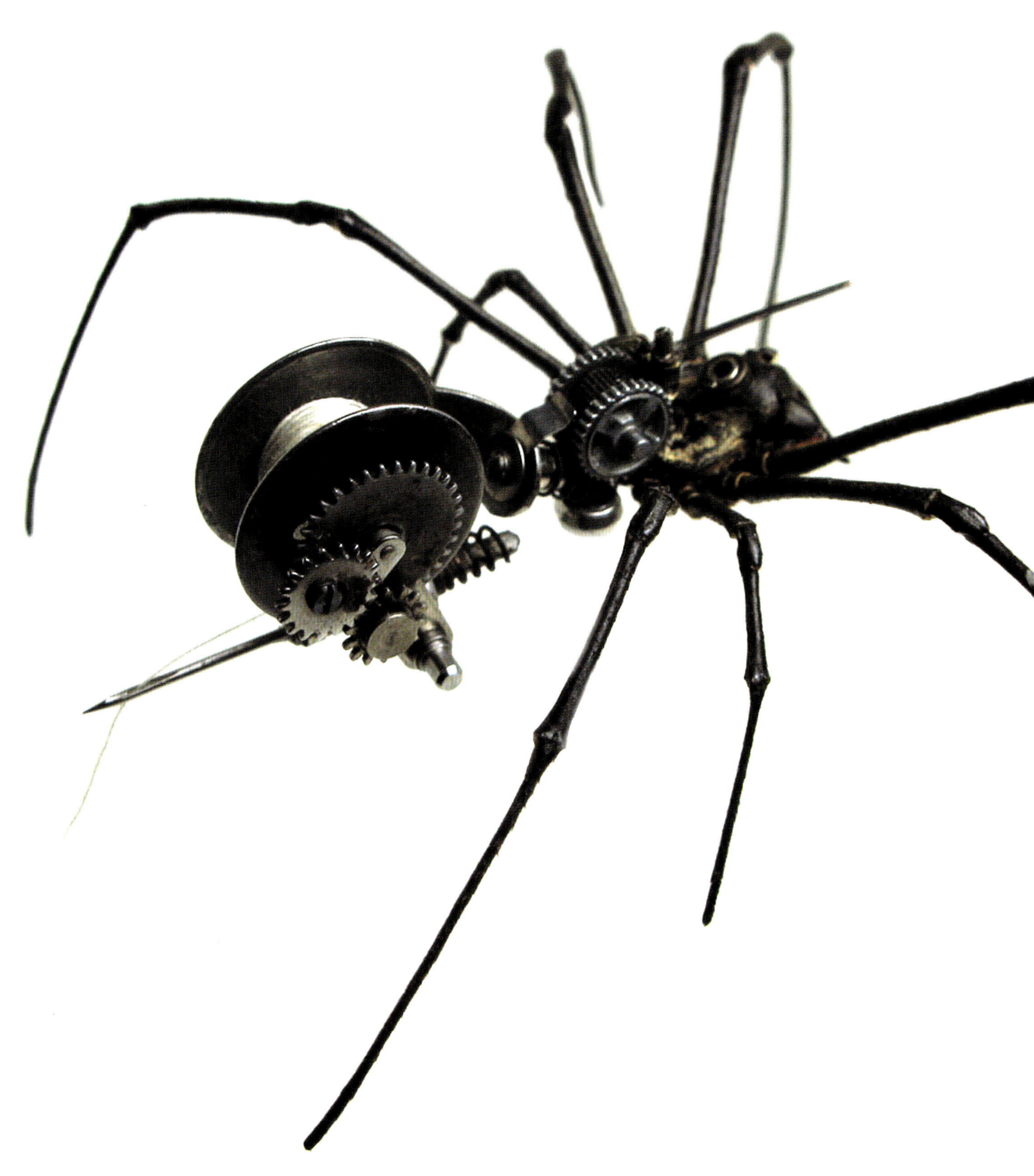

Arachnidae: Nephila Maculata – 5" x 5" x 3" spider, antique watch parts and gears, sewing machine parts, and thread (2008)

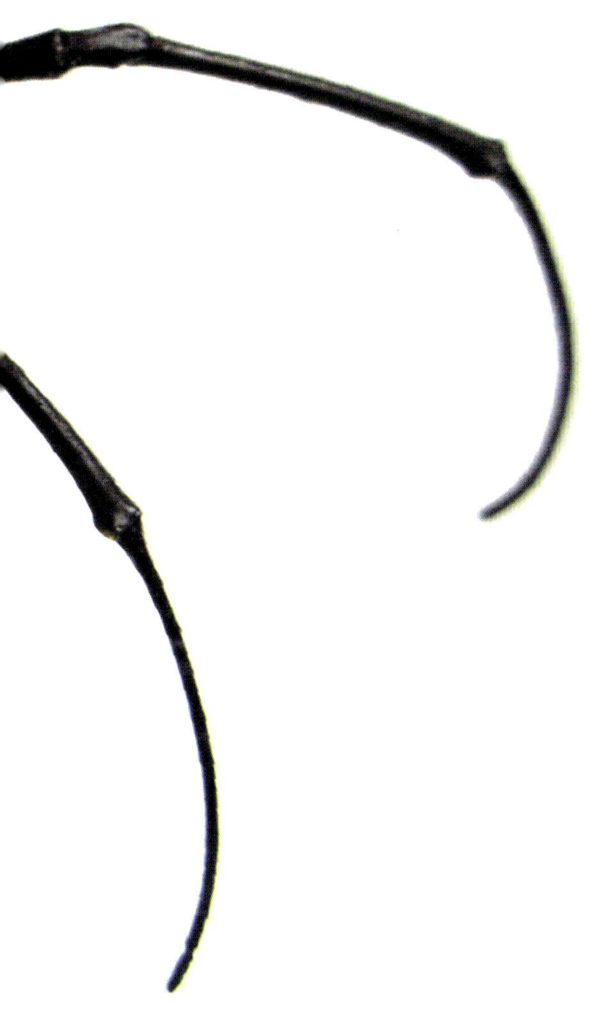

MIKE**LIBBY**

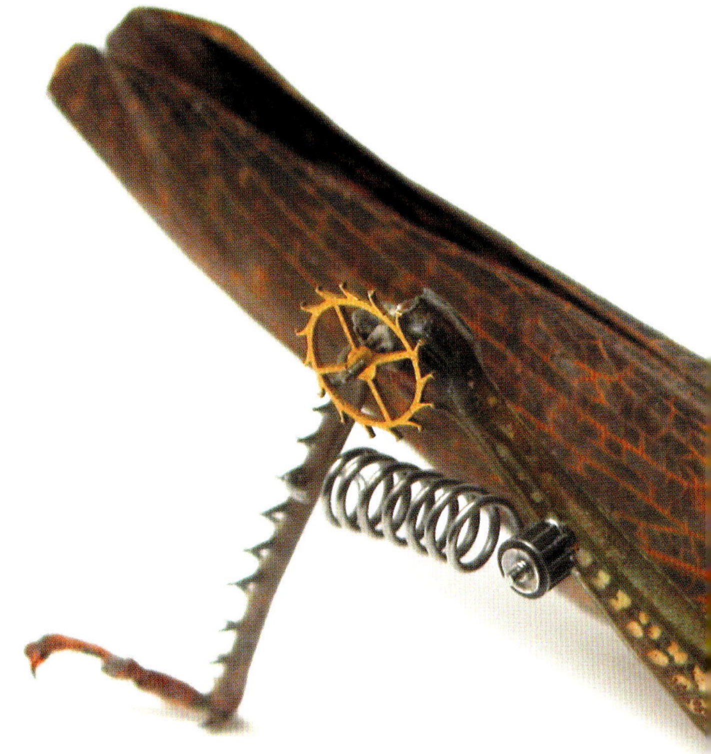

Mike **Libby**

Mike Libby makes sculptures, models, collages, and drawings. Using everyday materials and varied processes of fabrication, Libby explores cultural and personal themes of science, nature, fantasy, history, and autobiography, highlighting acute and awkward correspondences between them.

For the past five years, in addition to developing his main work, Libby has maintained the side project of Insect Lab. In this special series, antique watch parts and electronic components are customized onto preserved insect specimens. This series compliments Libby's ongoing investigation into how culture perceives (and thereby distorts) biology, natural resources and phenomena to various human ends.

Libby graduated with a degree in Sculpture from the Rhode Island School of Design (RISD) in 1999, has since attended the Vermont Studio Center, and was artist-in-residence at the University of Maine. He has been in many solo and group exhibits throughout the U.S. and Canada, and is in collections worldwide. His work was presented alongside Damien Hirst, Dorothy Cross, and Carolyn Chambers at Rutgers University's SPECIMEN exhibit in 2008, and in early 2009 he received the Exhibitor's Choice Award at the Smithsonian Craft Show. Born in 1976, he currently resides and works in Southern Maine.

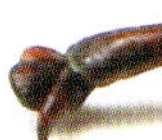

Orthoptera: Tropidacris Dux – 5" x 3" x 1" grasshopper, antique watch parts, gears, and springs (2008)

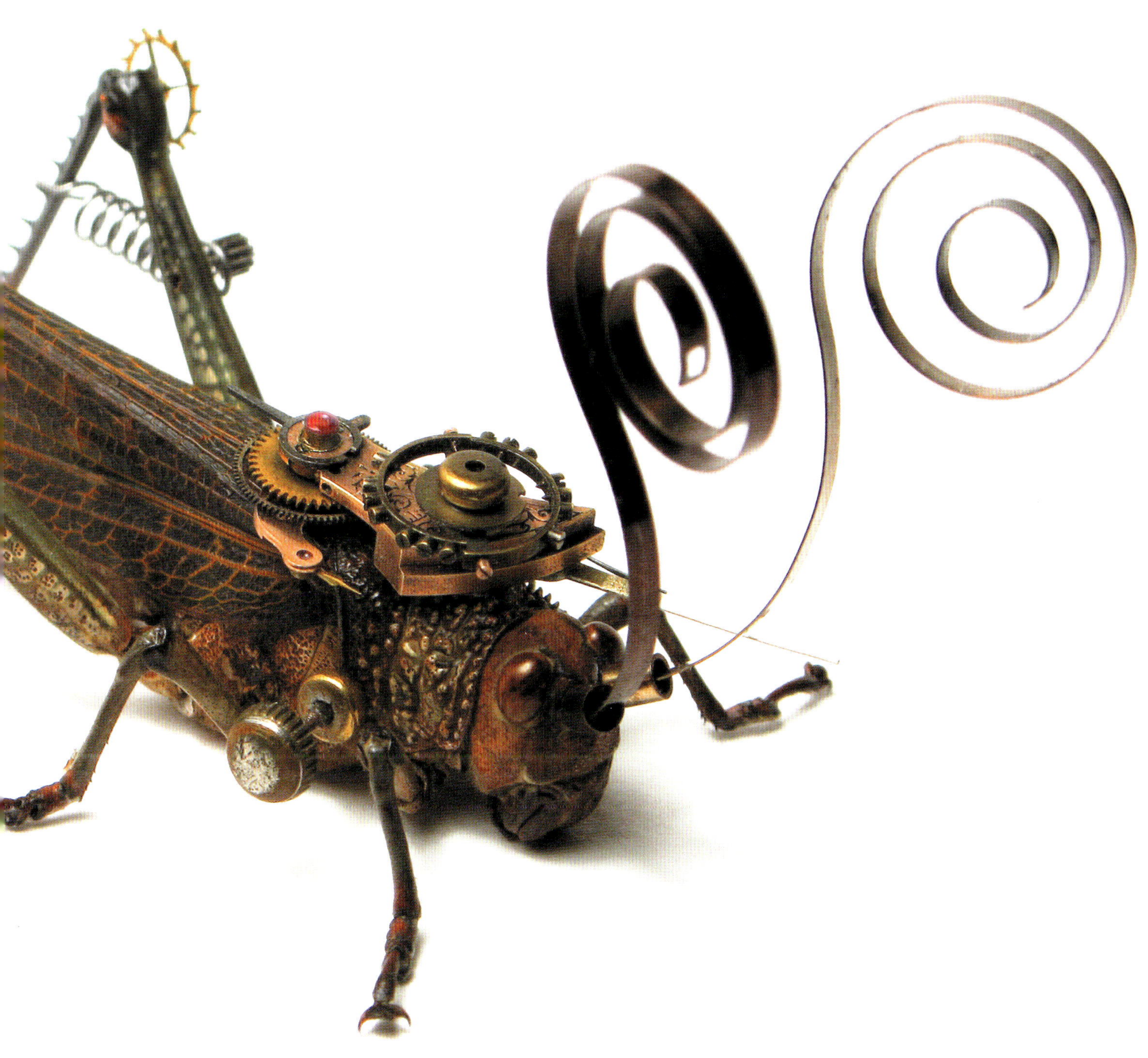

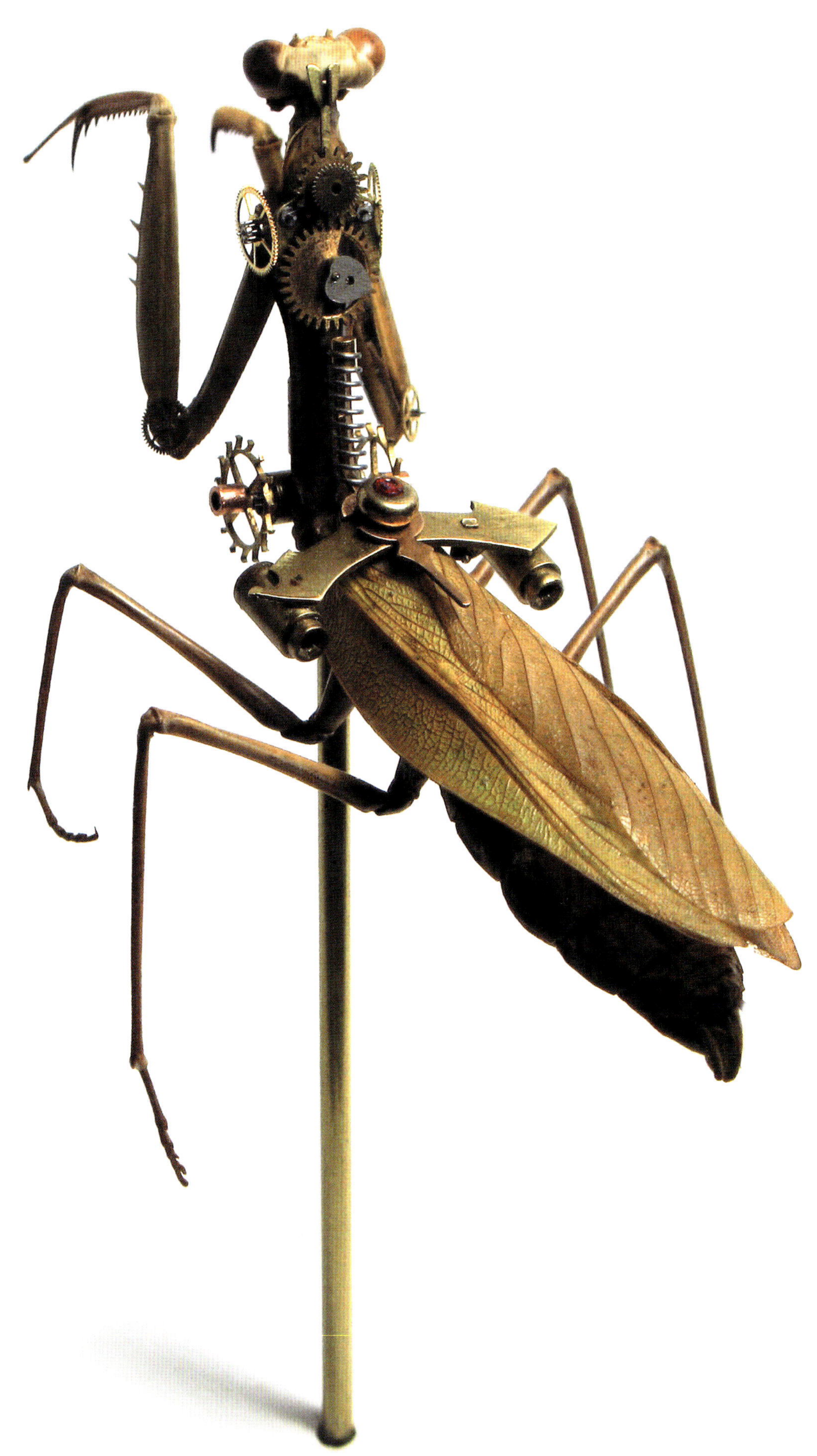

Mantidae: Tenodera Supertitiosa – 5.5" x 2" x 2.5" praying mantis, antique watch parts, gears, and jewel (2008)

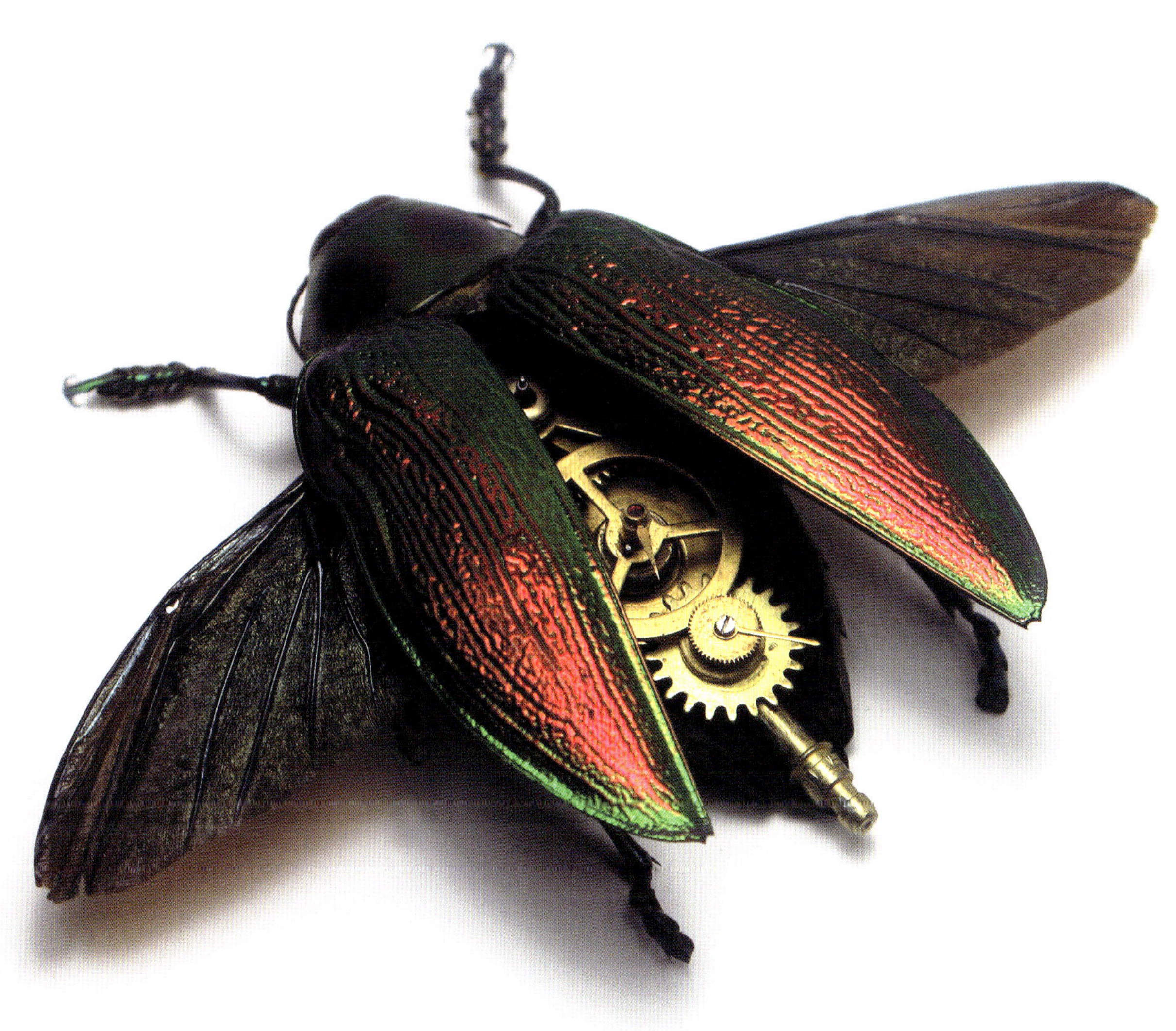

Buprestidae: Euchroma Gigantae – 4" x 3" x 1" jewel neetle, antique watch parts, and gears (2008)

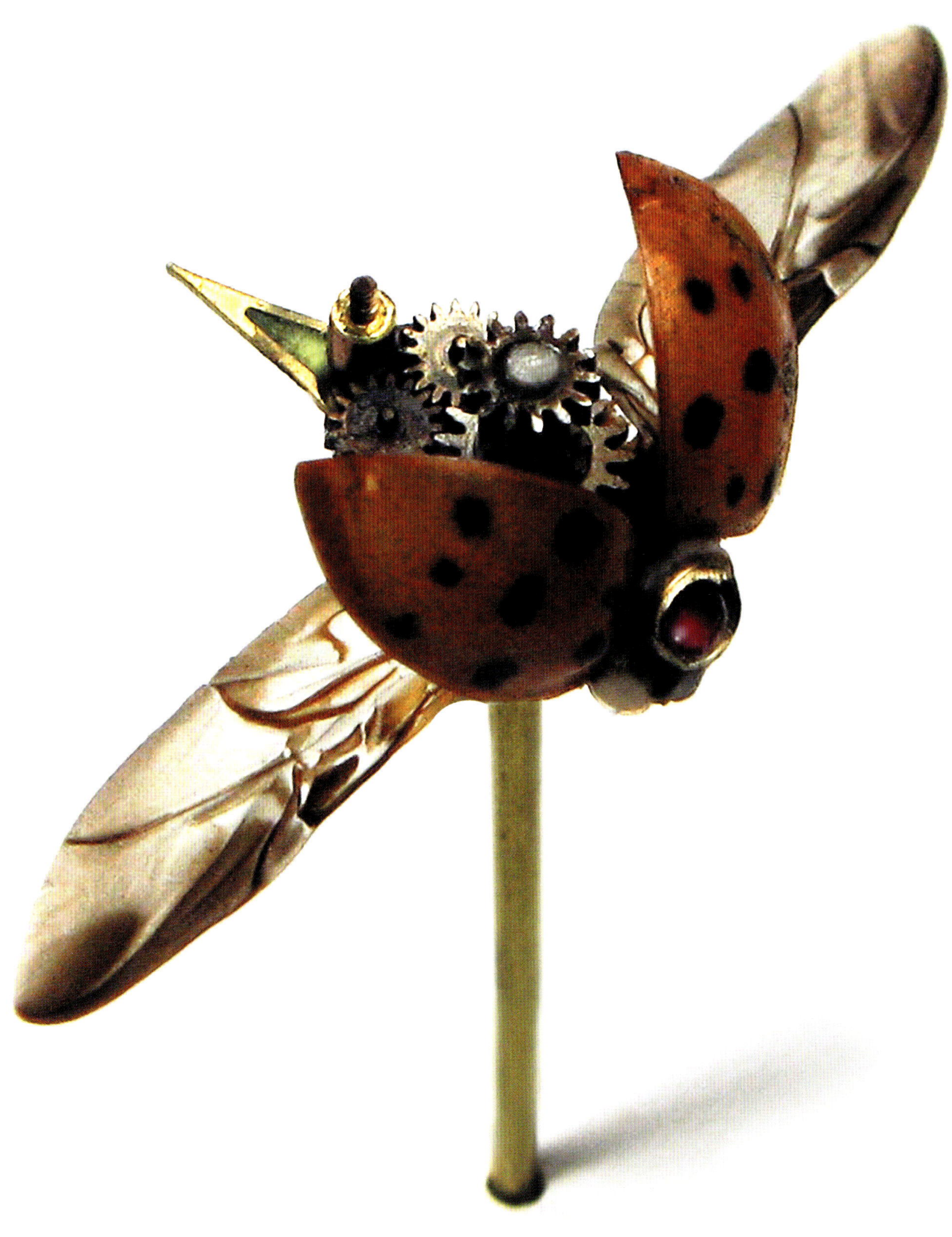

Ladybug – .5" x .25" x .25" flower beetle, antique watch parts, gears, and glow in the dark dial

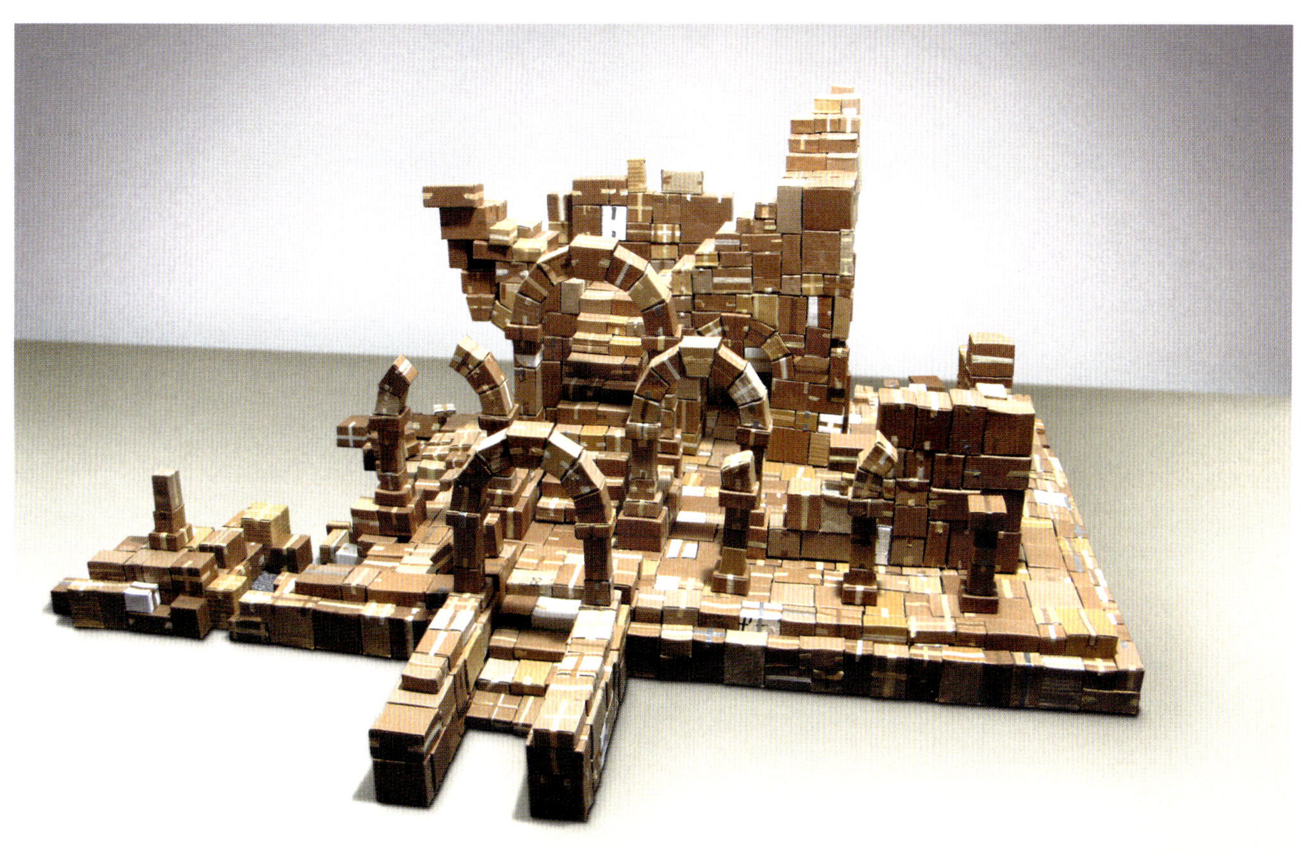

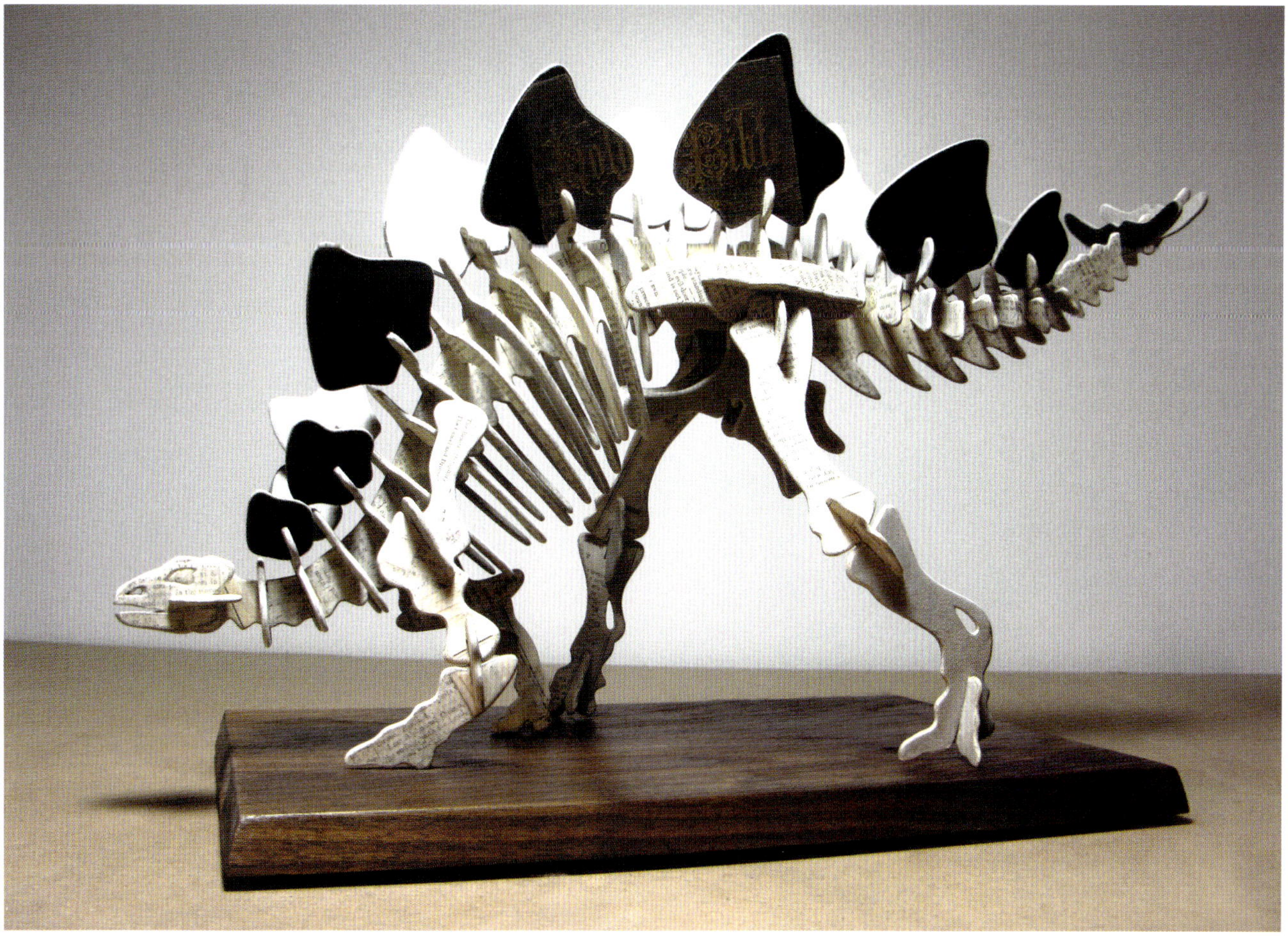

Recycled Ruins – 45" x 40" x 22" cardboard, glue, and tape (2008) (top)
Stegosaurus (Tanniyn Series) –24" x 12" x 10" laminated bible pages, and black walnut (2009) (bottom)

PAUL**LOUGHRIDGE**

Walter (aka The Lung) – antique opera glasses, aluminum bicycle brake housing, and a vintage photo enlarger light housing. His backpack: mini cake pan, a pair of galvanized flanges, brass compression fittings, "carbon-fiber-looking" coaxial cable, toggle switch, and rubber-coated cable guide. Ol' Walter is 19" tall. (2008)

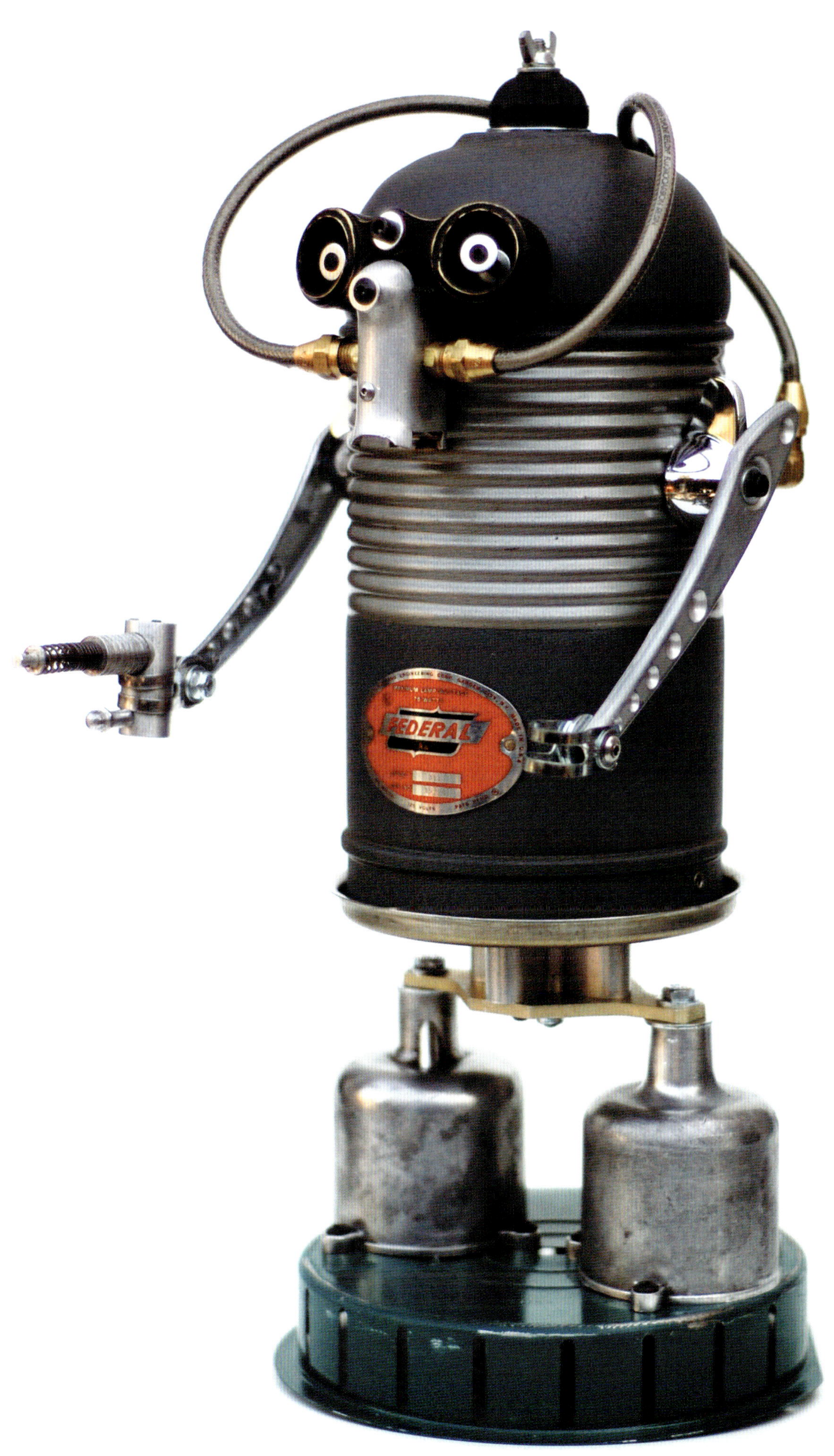

FEDERAL

Paul **Loughridge**

"Some of my fondest memories have me and my brothers tearing our toys and bikes apart just so we could figure out how things worked. Then armed with youthful confidence and my Dad's off-limits tools we set about recreating a "better product." This early industrial education while feeding my inquisitive nature also provided me with a strong sense of scale and balance. I still feel strongly about this concept and strive to inject that sense of proportion into all of my work. My creative process consists of dry-fitting objects from my extensive urban stash collection until I attain that natural looking fit. If executed properly I believe a distinct personality emerges from the sculpture. I find this creative process satisfying on many levels and since the raw materials which I seek out are in such abundance I don't see myself stopping anytime soon."

From his Northern California lab, Paul Loughridge (pronounced Lok-rij) transforms what most people would consider junk into one-of-a-kind, surreal, cyber/steam punk assemblage sculptures. During this creative journey, Paul develops a unique character and personality for each sculpture. Whether it's giving his found-object assemblage sculptures a silly smirk or a forceful stare, there is often a humorous element to much of his work. This ability to re-engineer cold, metal parts into playful art pieces is fueled by his childhood diet of sci-fi space movies and TV. Paul stocks his "laboratory" with elements of forgotten, retired, or otherwise discarded paraphernalia by frequenting flea markets, garage sales, and old warehouses. All of his pieces are carefully "cold" assembled, void of any soldering or welding.

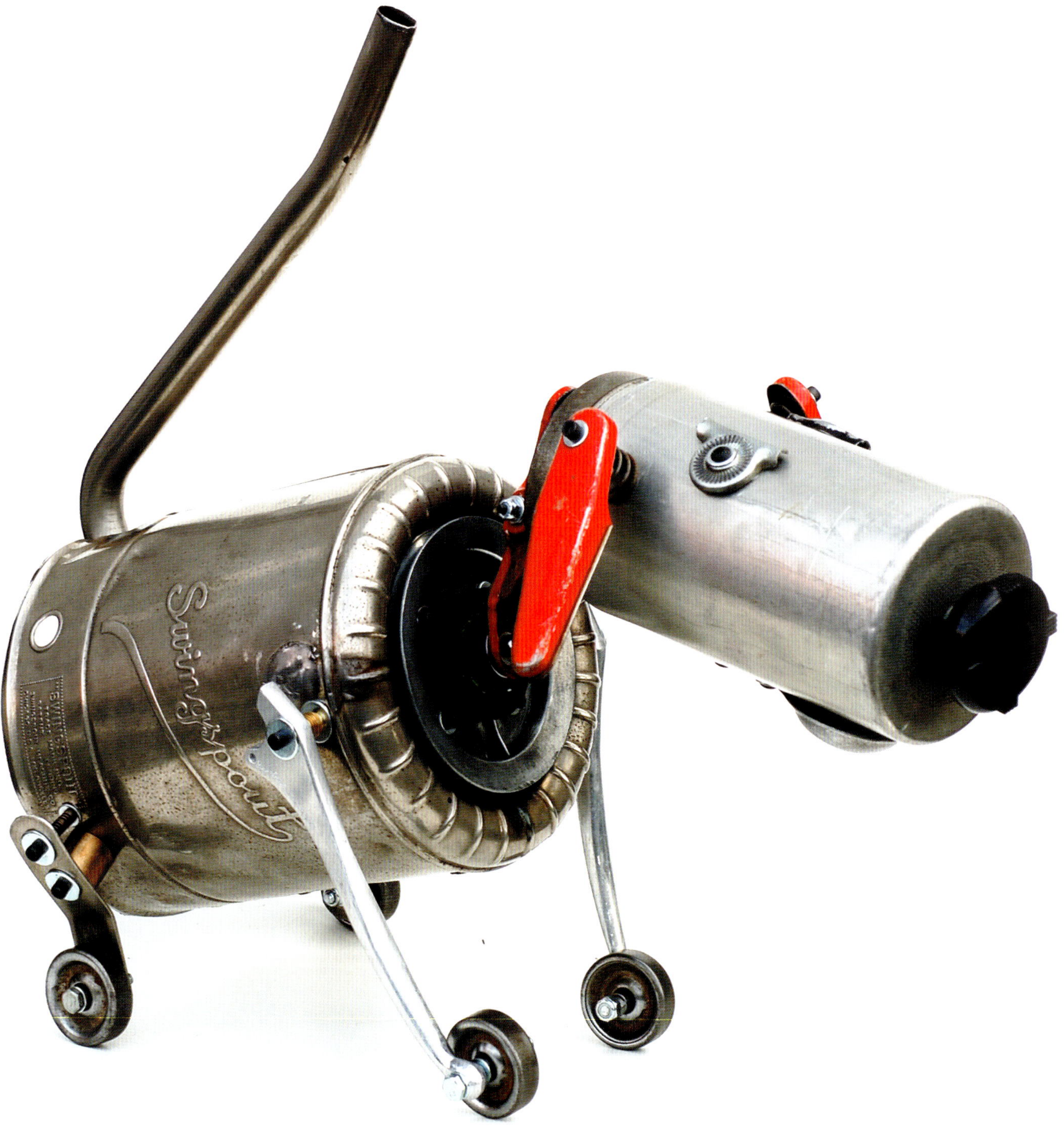

Springer… spaniel – 24" x 15" Here's a K9 fabricated from an old "Swingspout" oil can. Nose to tail: old TV knob, coffee urn basket, bicycle seat hardware, toy washing machine legs, vintage bike rack bracket, water valve handle, belt pulley, motorcycle brake levers and one roller skate worth of wheels, a bunch of nuts/bolts/washers and of course, Springs!… not counting the tail. (2008)

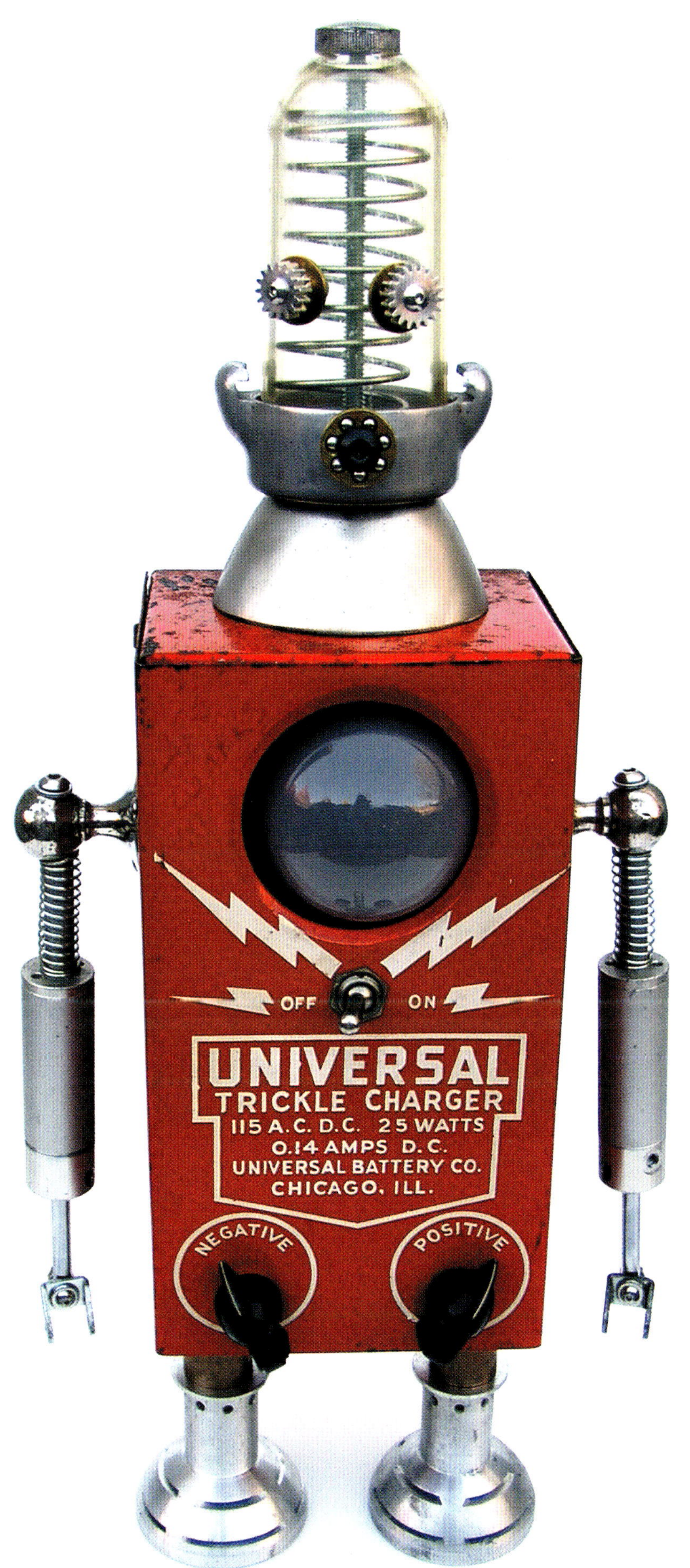

Trickle the Robot – 18" tall. I think the graphics on this old battery trickle charger look cool but I still had to go ahead and muck it up with a head, arms, and legs. Is nothing sacred? (2006)

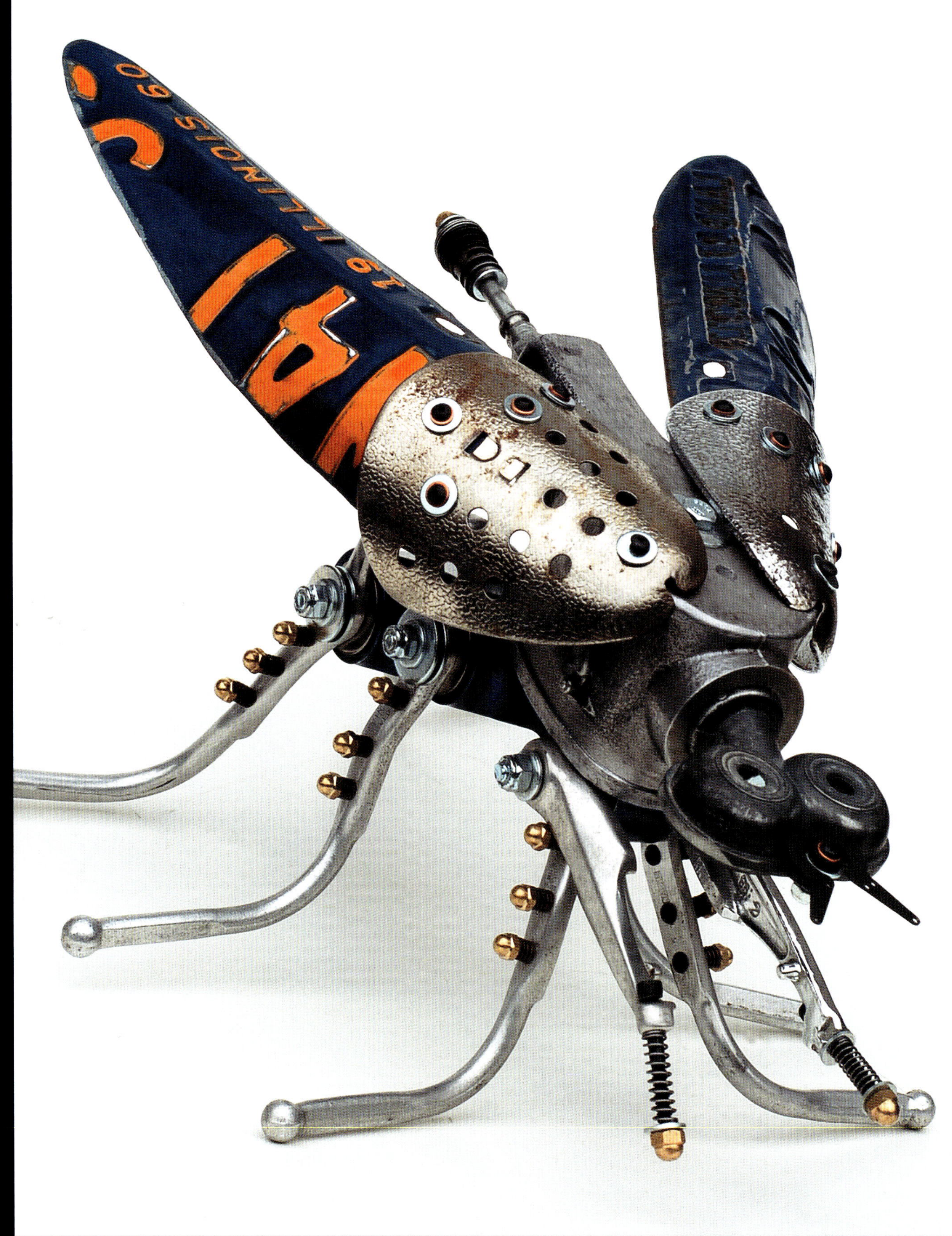

Spark Plug Bug – 10" x 12" x 16" Fashioned from pneumatic spark plug cleaner, Illinois license plate, shoe trees, lawn sprinkler, bicycle brake levers, model airplane engine cylinder, mt. bike suspension pivot, and old typewriter parts. (2009)

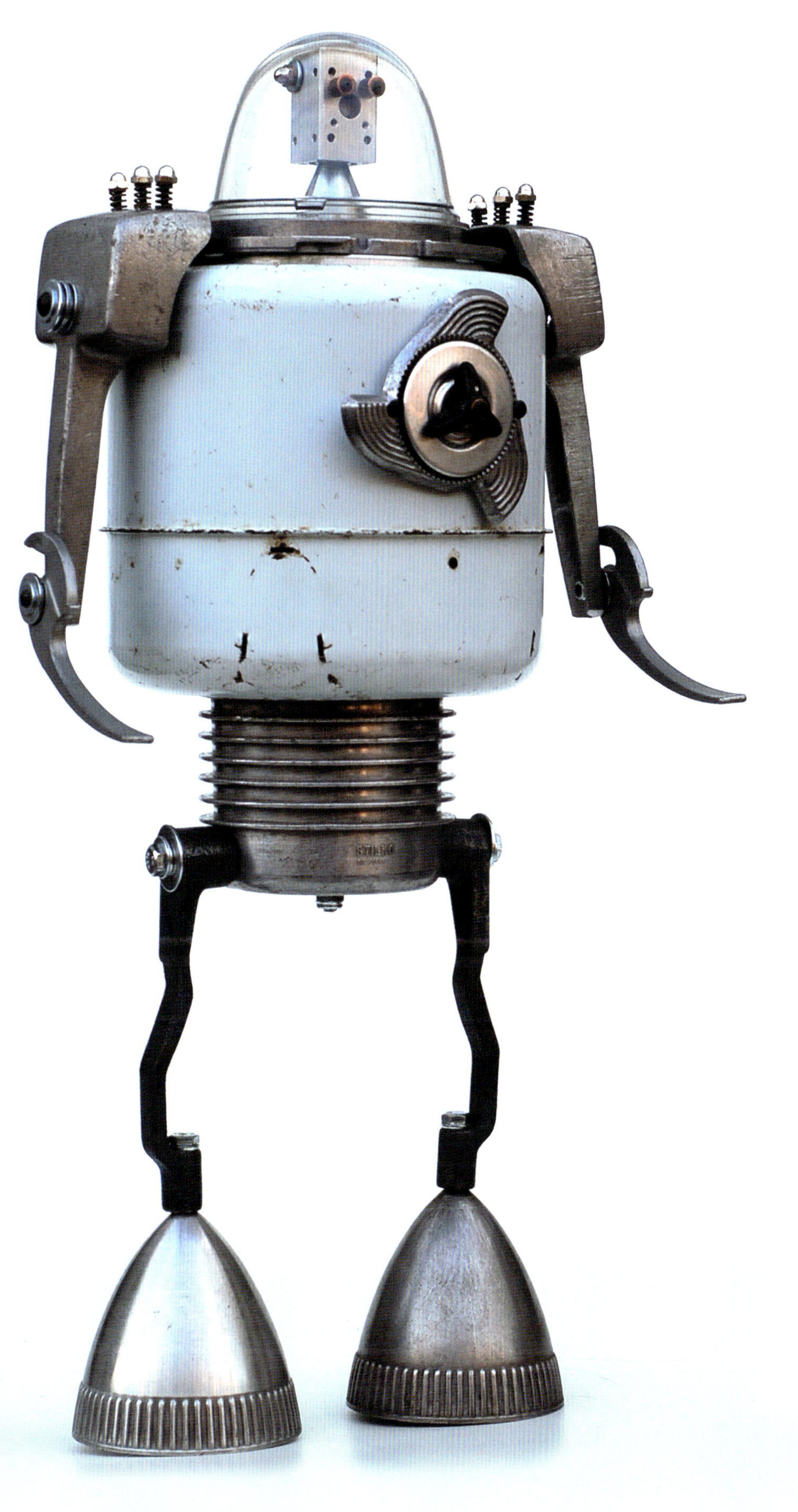

Stilko Robot – 21" tall. Stilko is named for his finned aluminum torso—an old add-on car filter which was designed to utilize a roll of bum paper as the disposable filter. The body is a vintage child's tin washing machine. (2009)

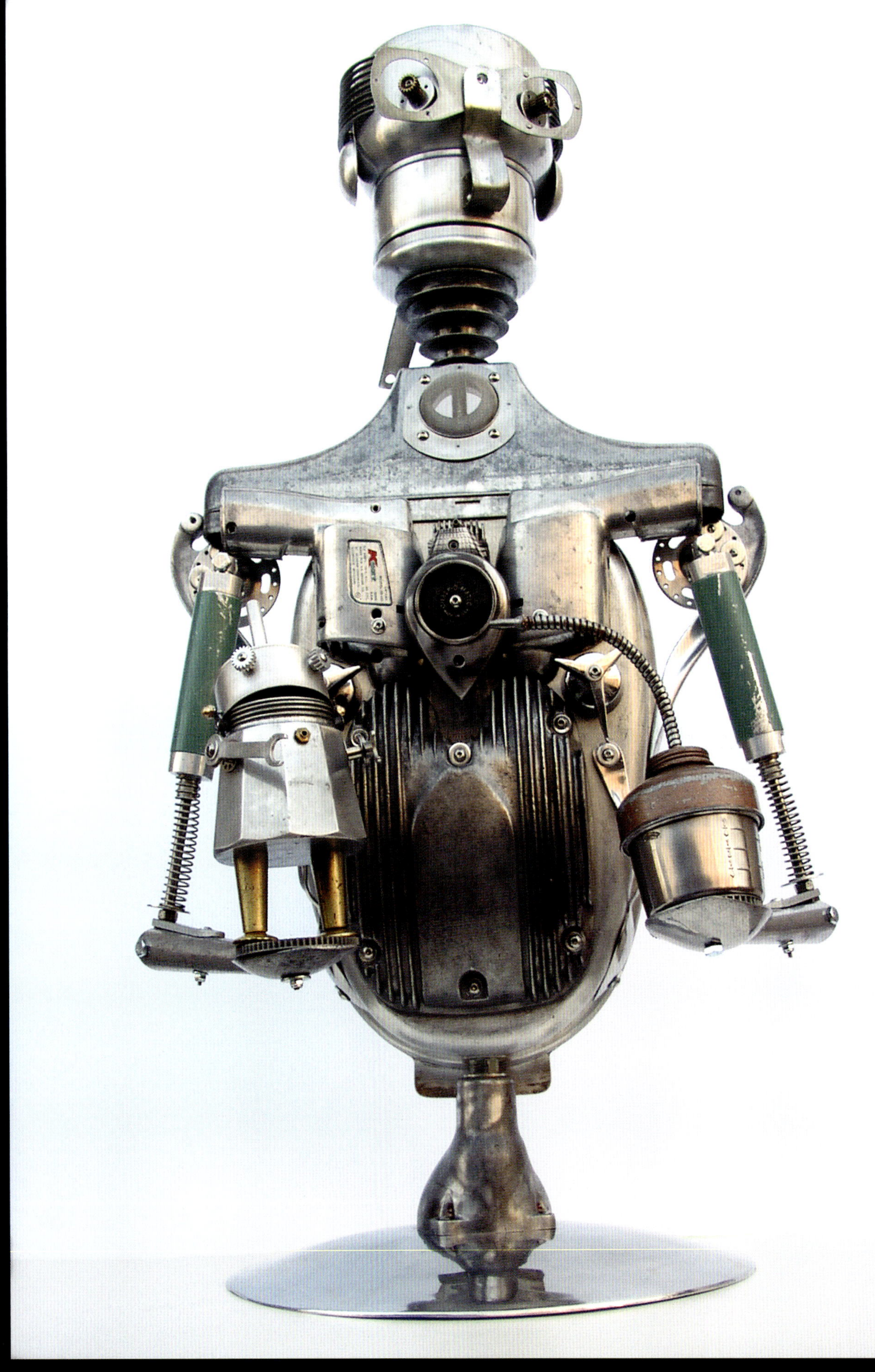

Recycle Man and Son Robot – 37" tall. My father/son tribute was fashioned from a double boiler pot, potato tongs, measuring spoons, pulley spindle, assorted gears, vintage vacuum cleaner, power drill housing, chalk line reel, BSA valve cover, roasting pan, ice cream scoops, espresso maker, retro furniture legs, and a couple of wrenches. (2007)

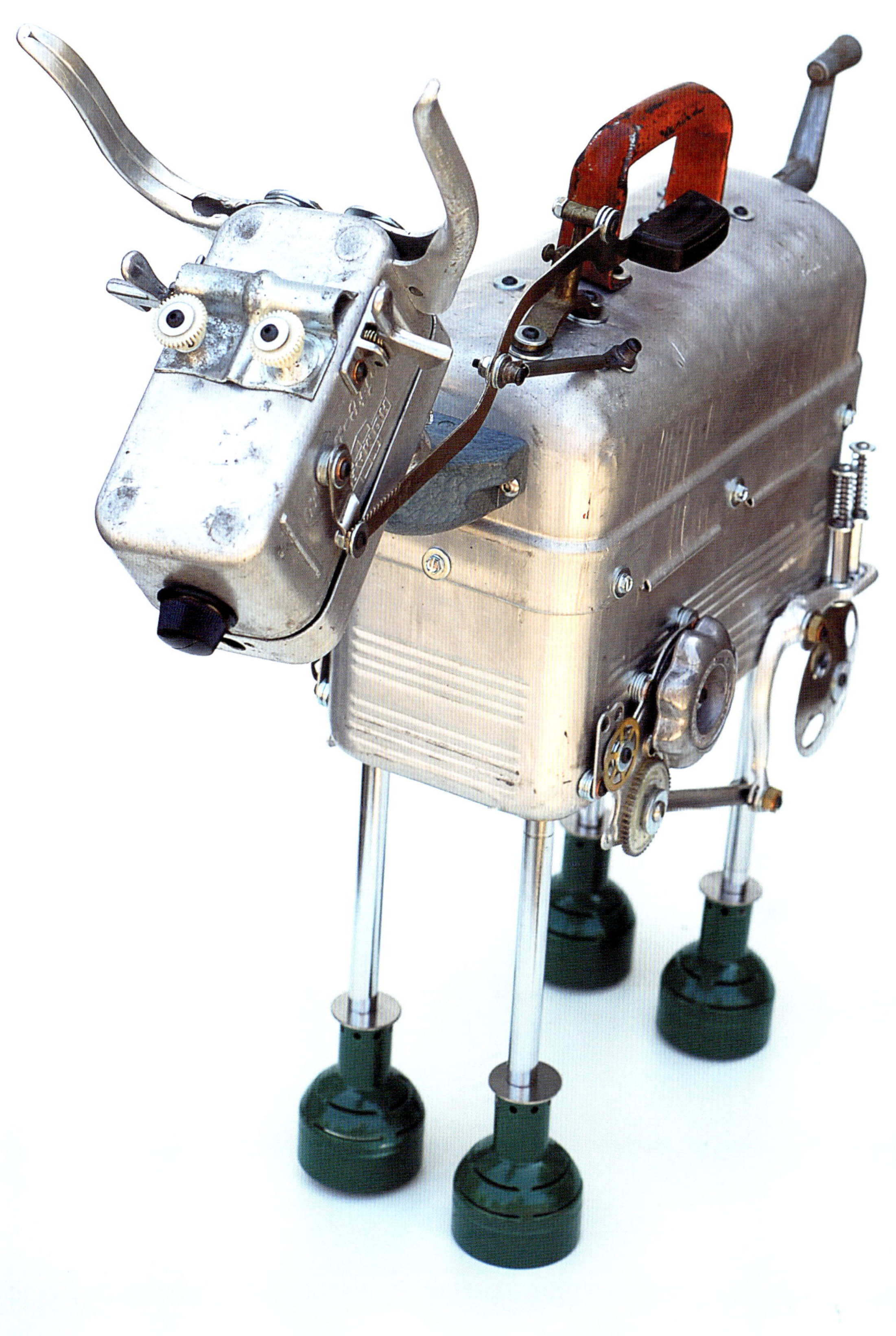

Steampunk Steer – 22" x 22" A vintage aluminum lunchbox, camp flashlight, a pair of bicycle hand brakes, and an old vacuum cleaner flange. (2008)

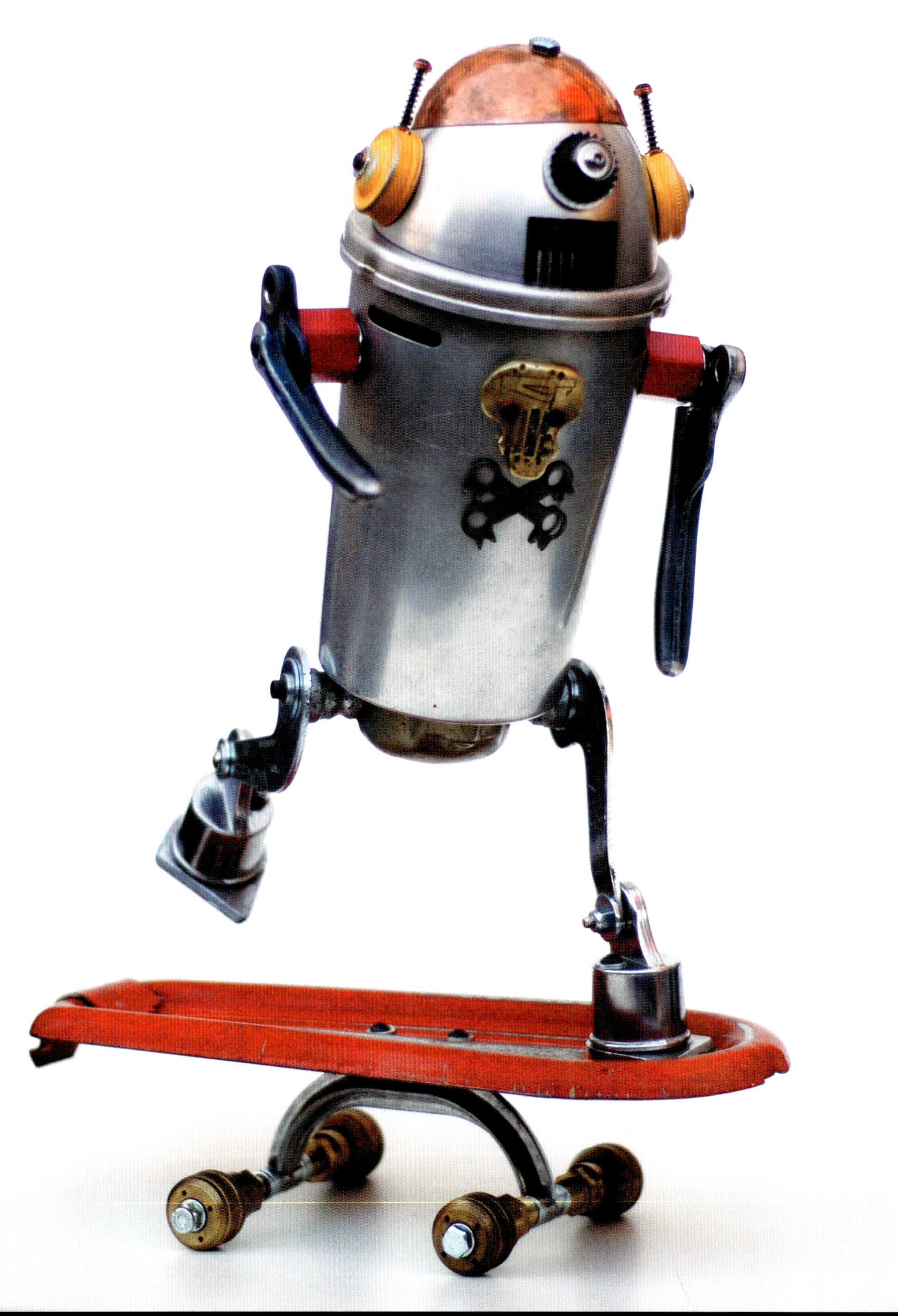

RoboSkater – 19" x 14" copper measuring cup, aluminum track light shade, a pair of old Kodak film container lids, part of an old typewriter, aluminum kitchen steamer, ceramic insulators, welding clamp arms, 4-wood brass face plate, electric drill body part, coaster brake arms, cyclone fence caps, vintage bicycle rear rack, golf pull-cart parts, and four brass air hose female couplers... gnarly dude! (2008)

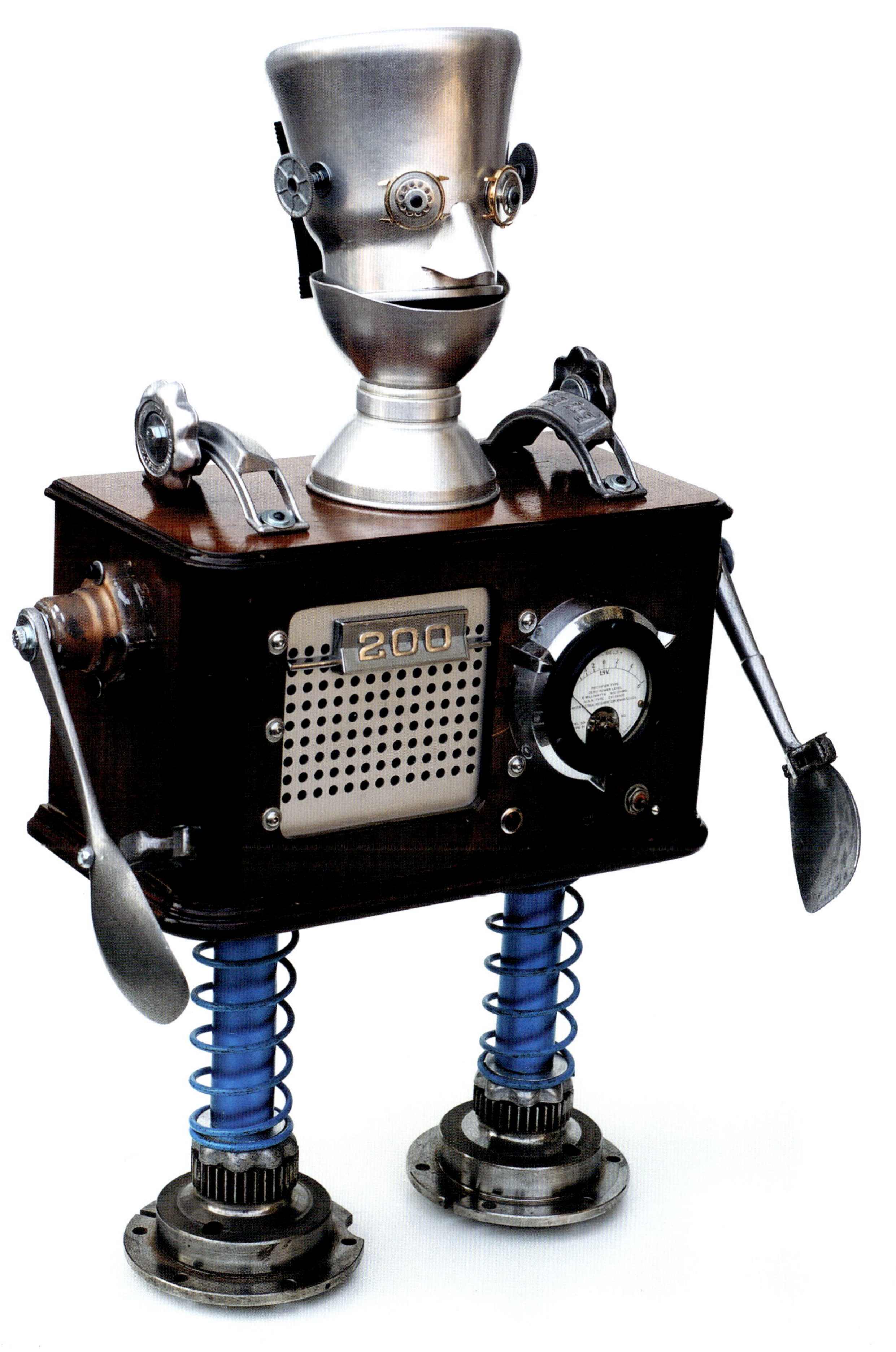

Silvertone Radio Robot – 28" x 20" coffee pot, sewing bobbins, wrist watch lens, golf pull-cart parts, propane tank valves, Silvertone wooden radio cabinet, ice cream scoops, amp gauge, alligator clips, relay baton, auto differential, and old pogo stick springs (2008)

MICHIHIRO**MATSUOKA**

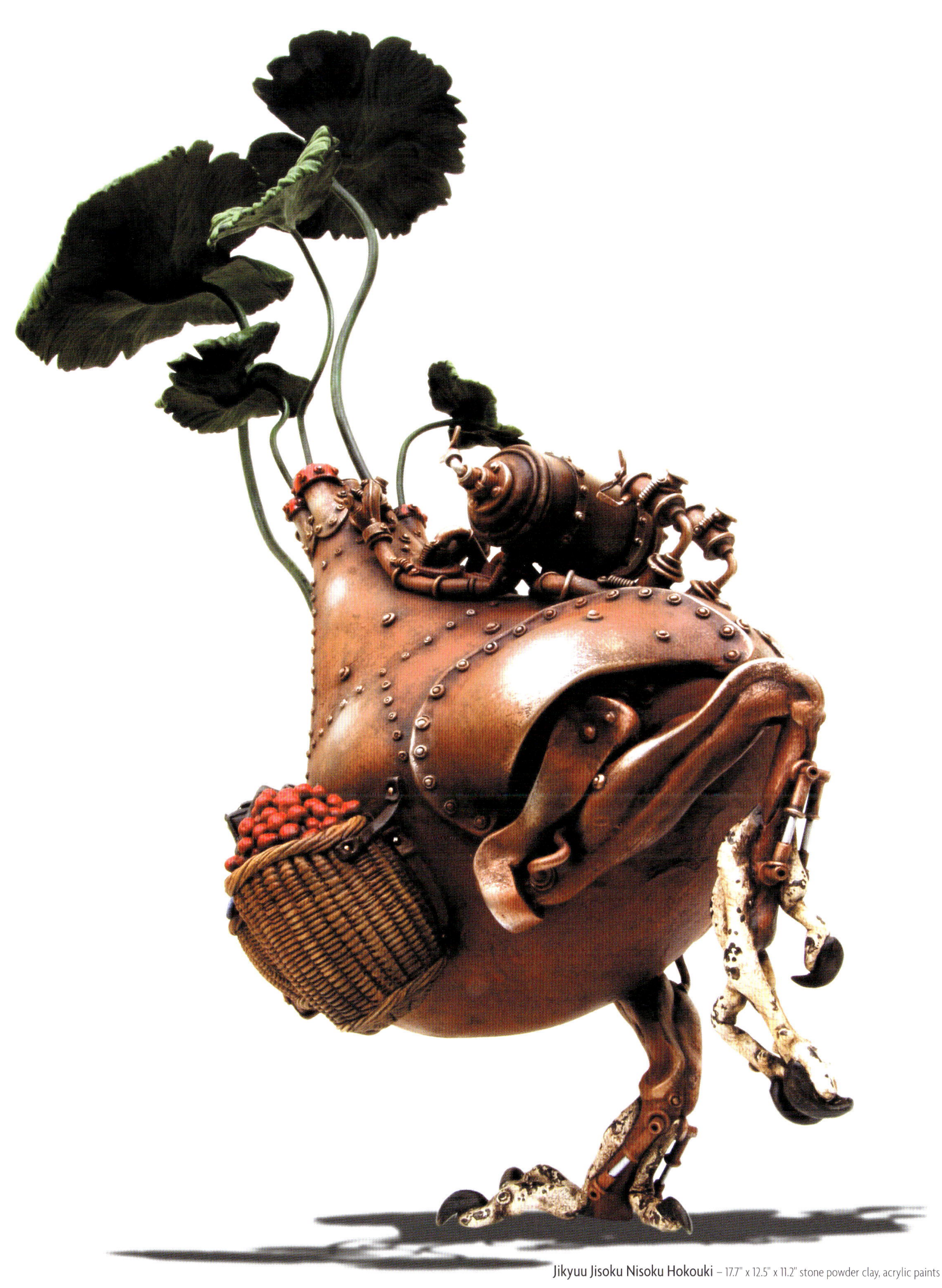

Jikyuu Jisoku Nisoku Hokouki – 17.7" x 12.5" x 11.2" stone powder clay, acrylic paints

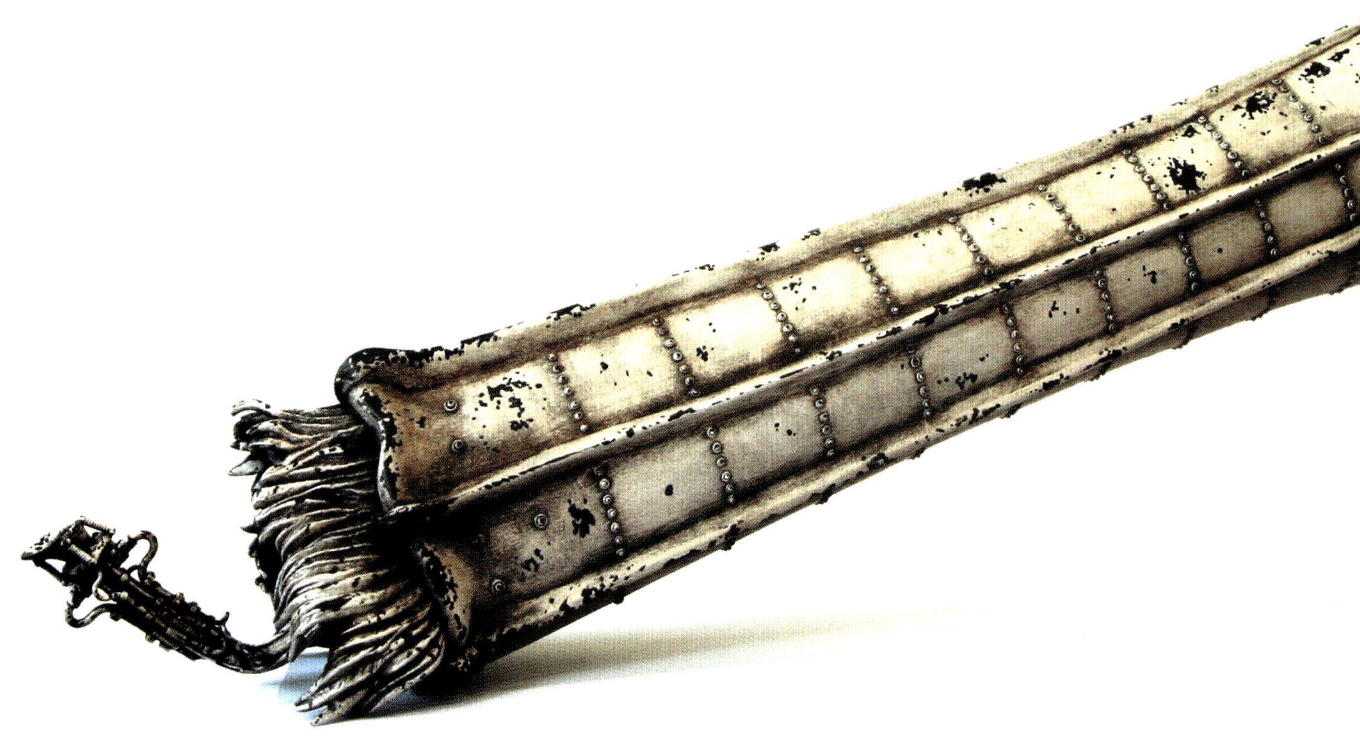

Michihiro **Matsuoka**

Born in 1969 in Japan, Matsouka finds inspiration from his childhood memories and deteriorated devices. Creating worn out devices that fuse animals and fish with machinery, Matsouka primarily uses stone clay for his work, but will incorporate other materials that seem to be suitable. The sculptures are meticulously finished with acrylic paint, which aids his desire to express the progress of time.

Matsouka's work has been featured in twenty-five exhibitions throughout Japan.

A Resonant Tower – 38.5" x 25.5" x 17.7" stone powder clay, acrylic paints

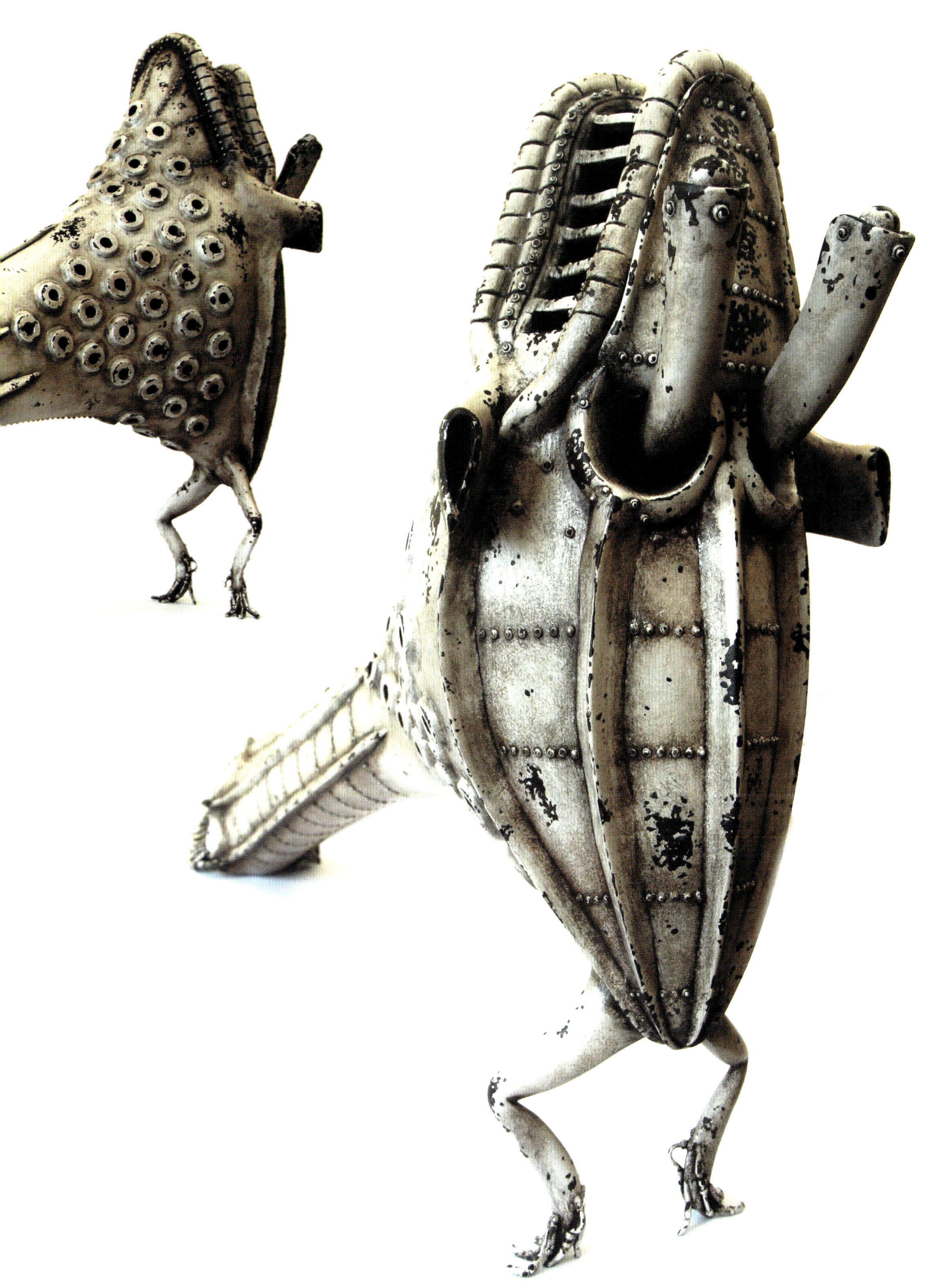

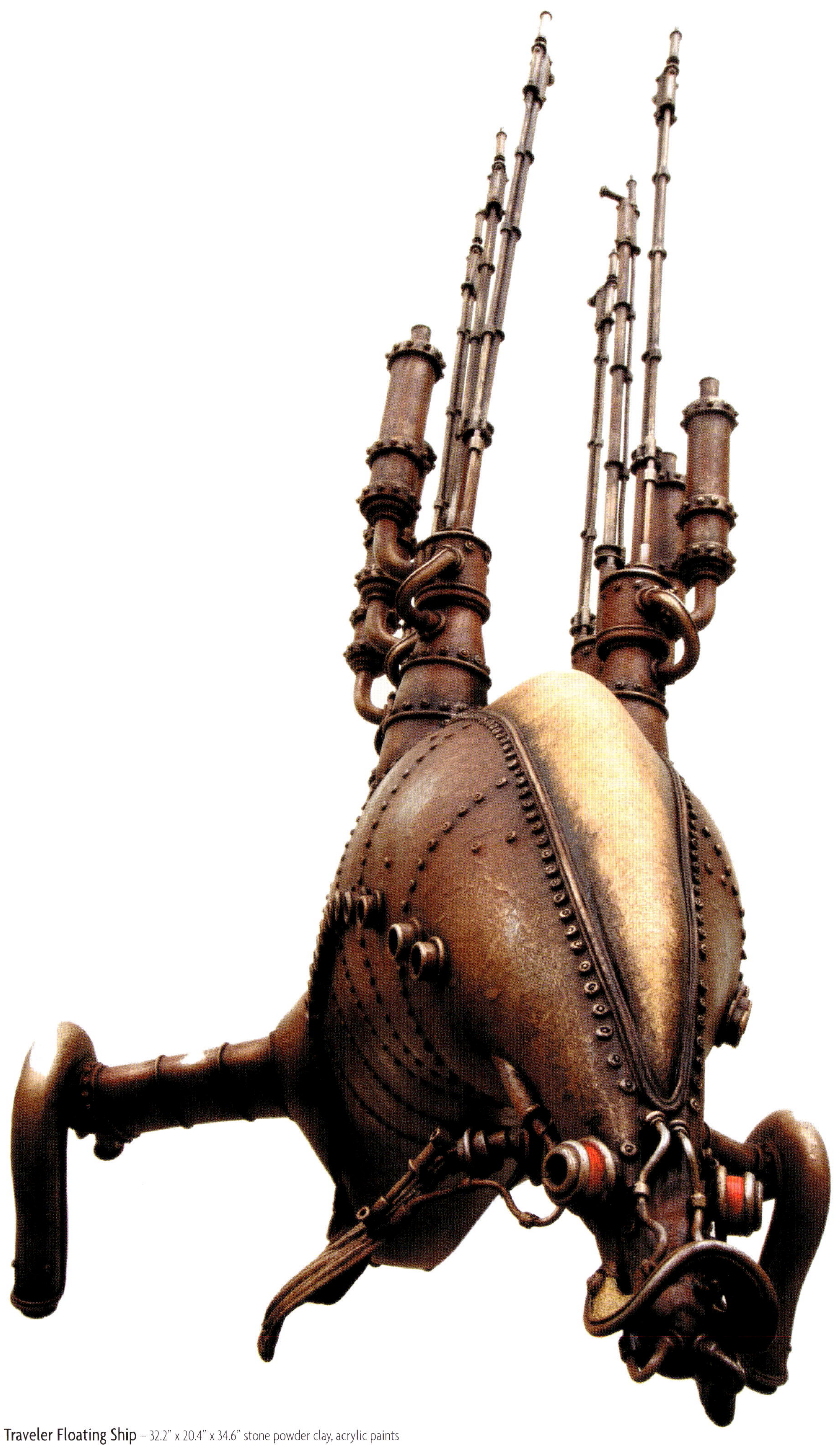

Large-Scale Traveler Floating Ship – 32.2" x 20.4" x 34.6" stone powder clay, acrylic paints

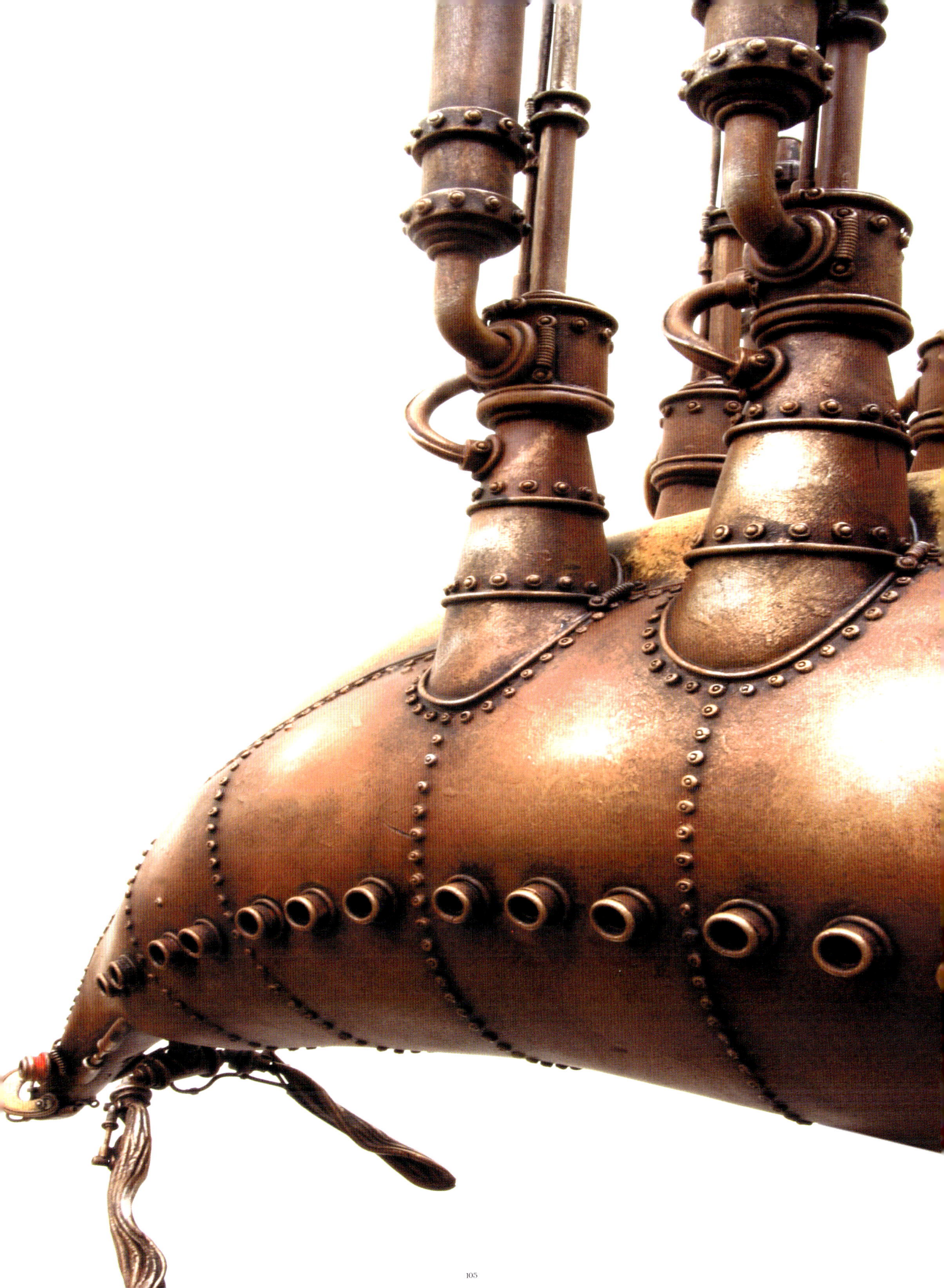

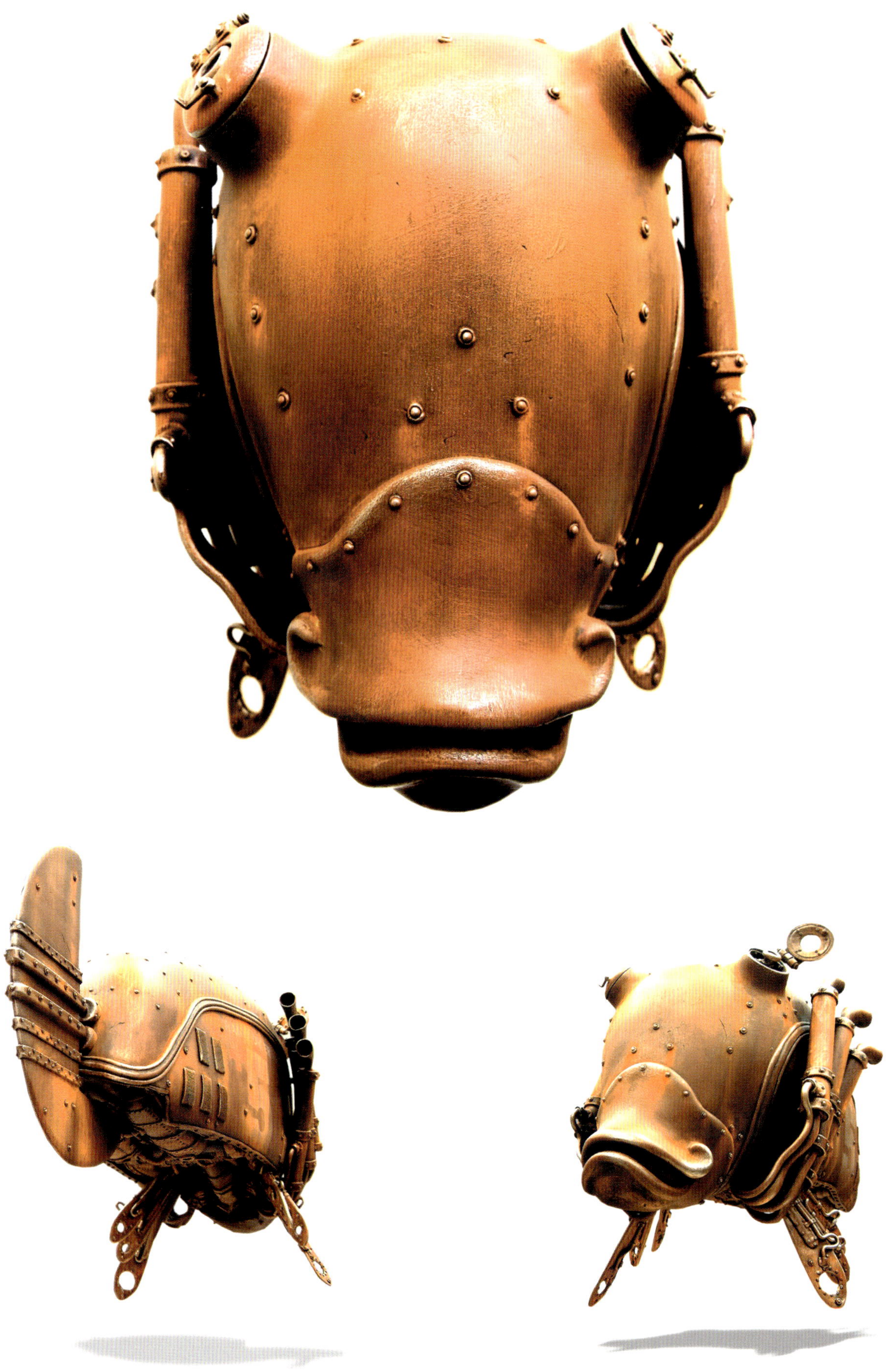

Dugong – 21.2" x 12.5" x 12.9" stone powder clay, acrylic paints

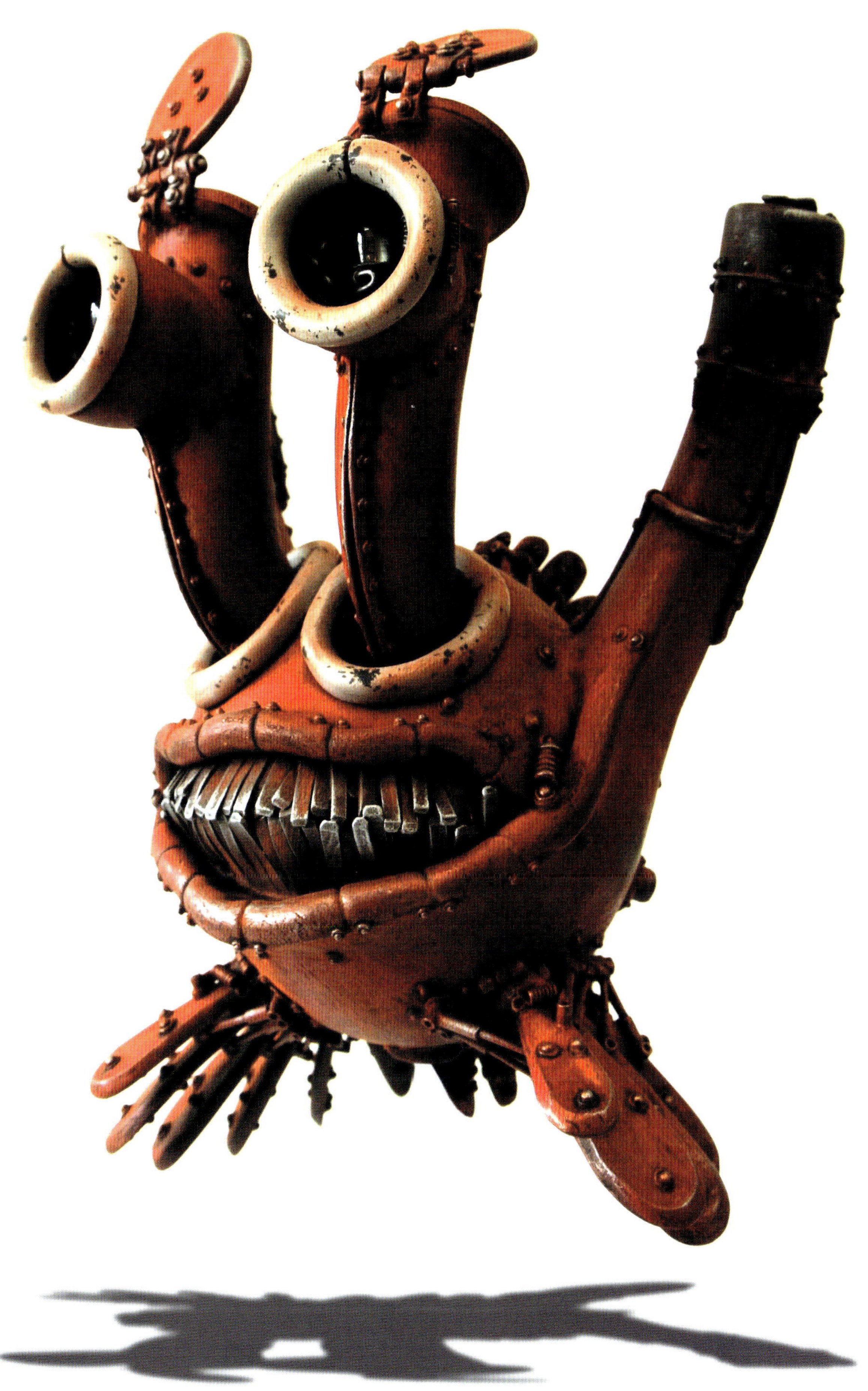

Mantis Shrimp – 17.7" x 17.7" x 15.7" stone powder clay, acrylic paints

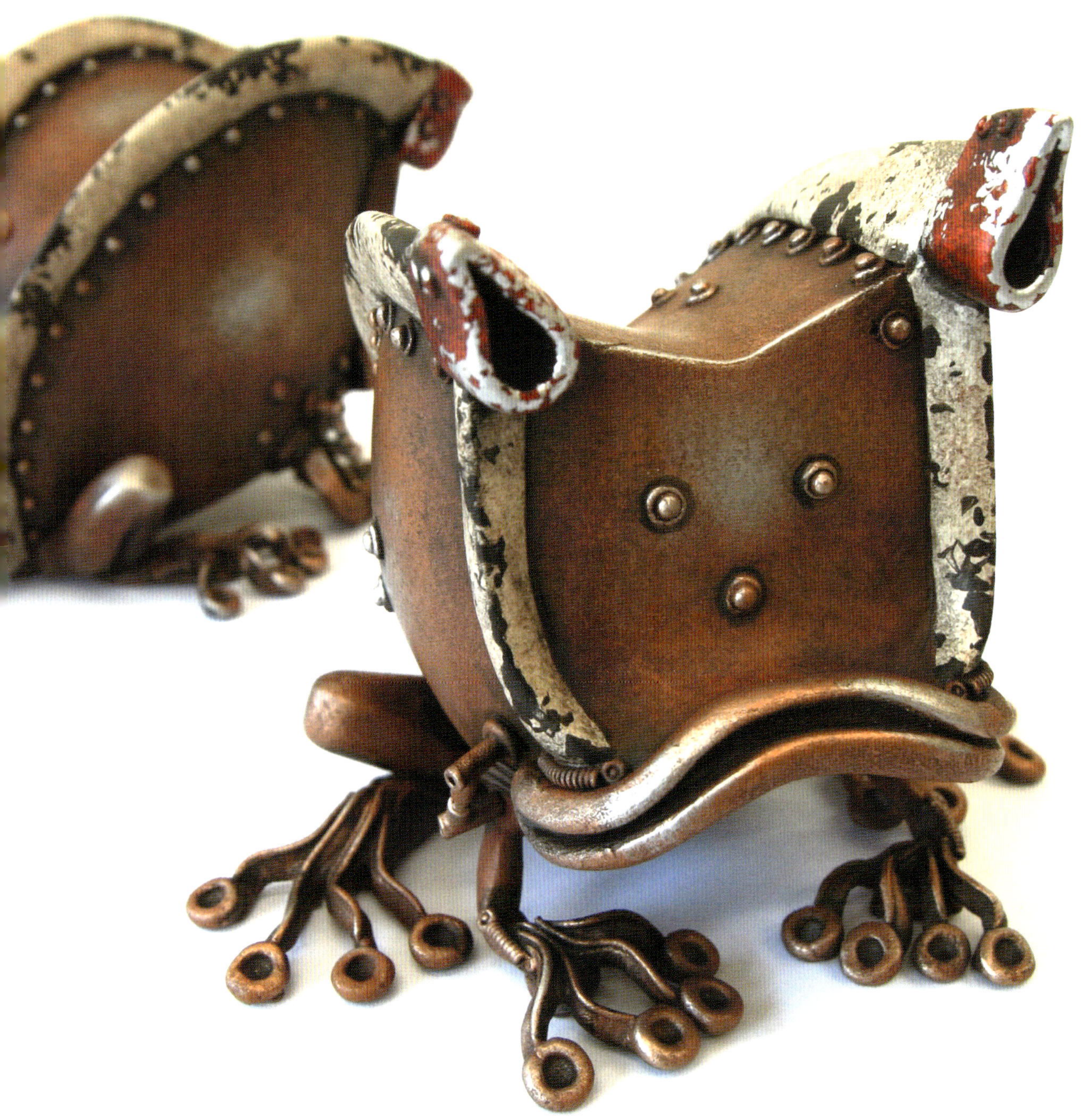

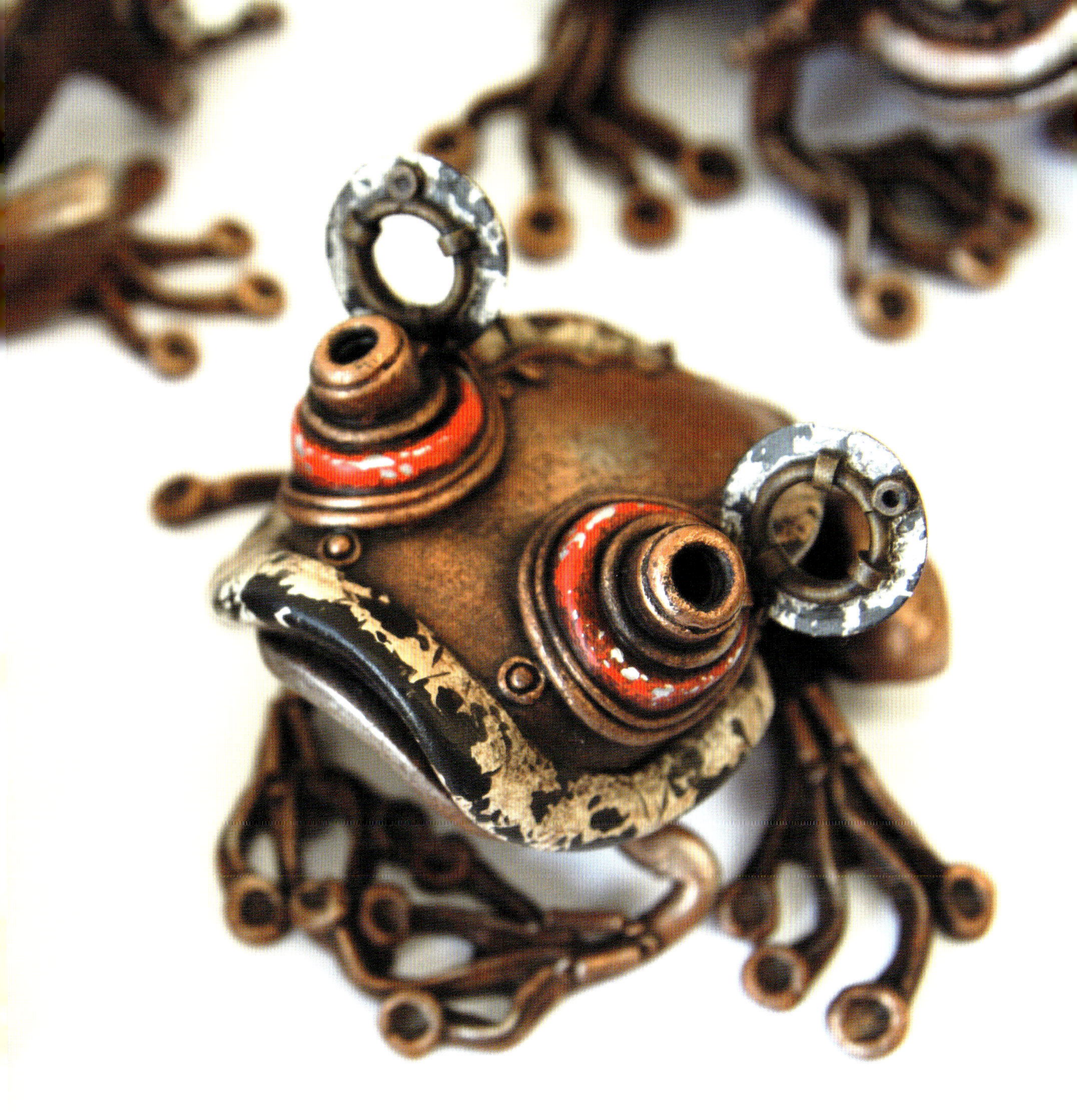

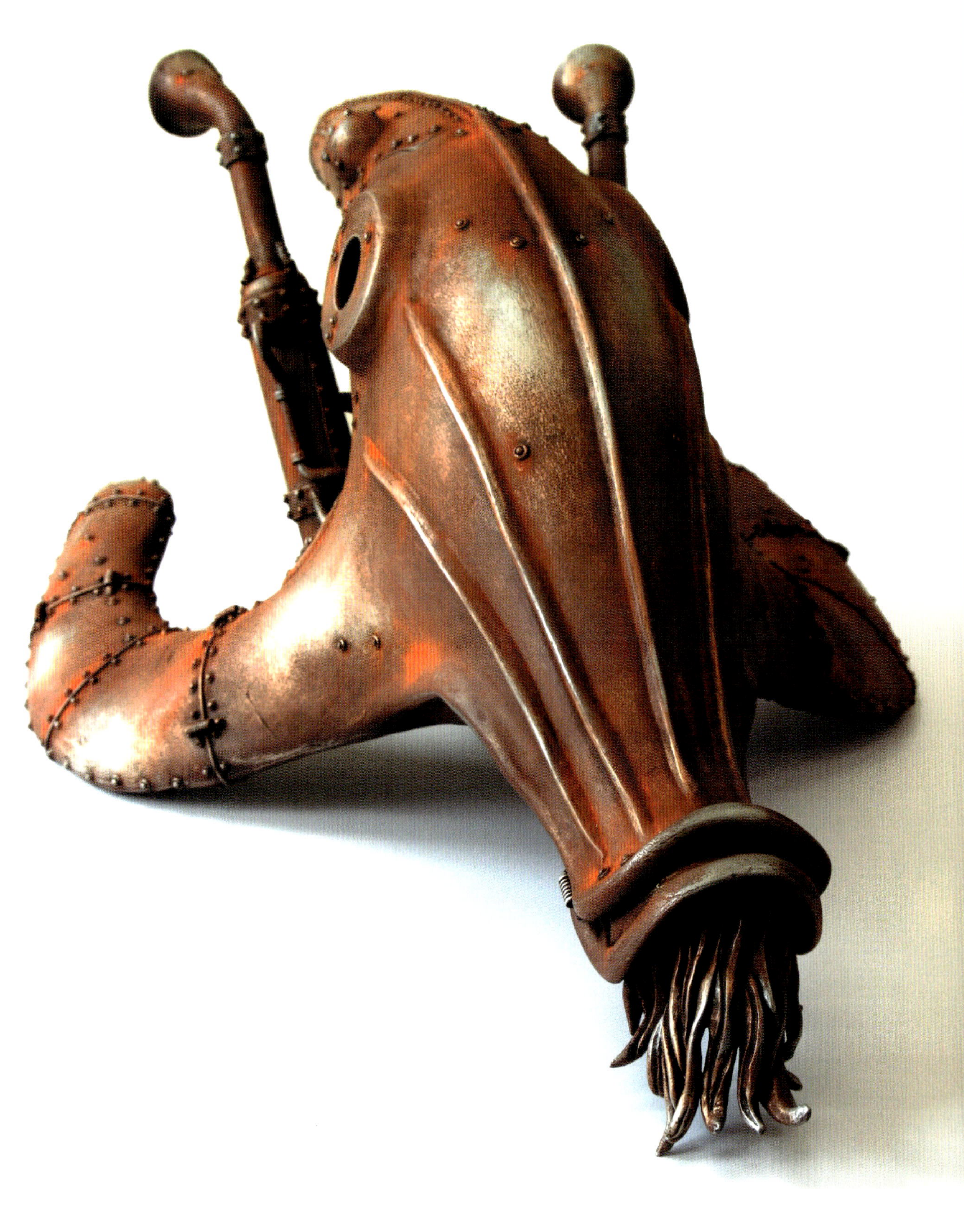

Clipper – 31.4" x 19.6" x 15.7" stone powder clay, acrylic paints

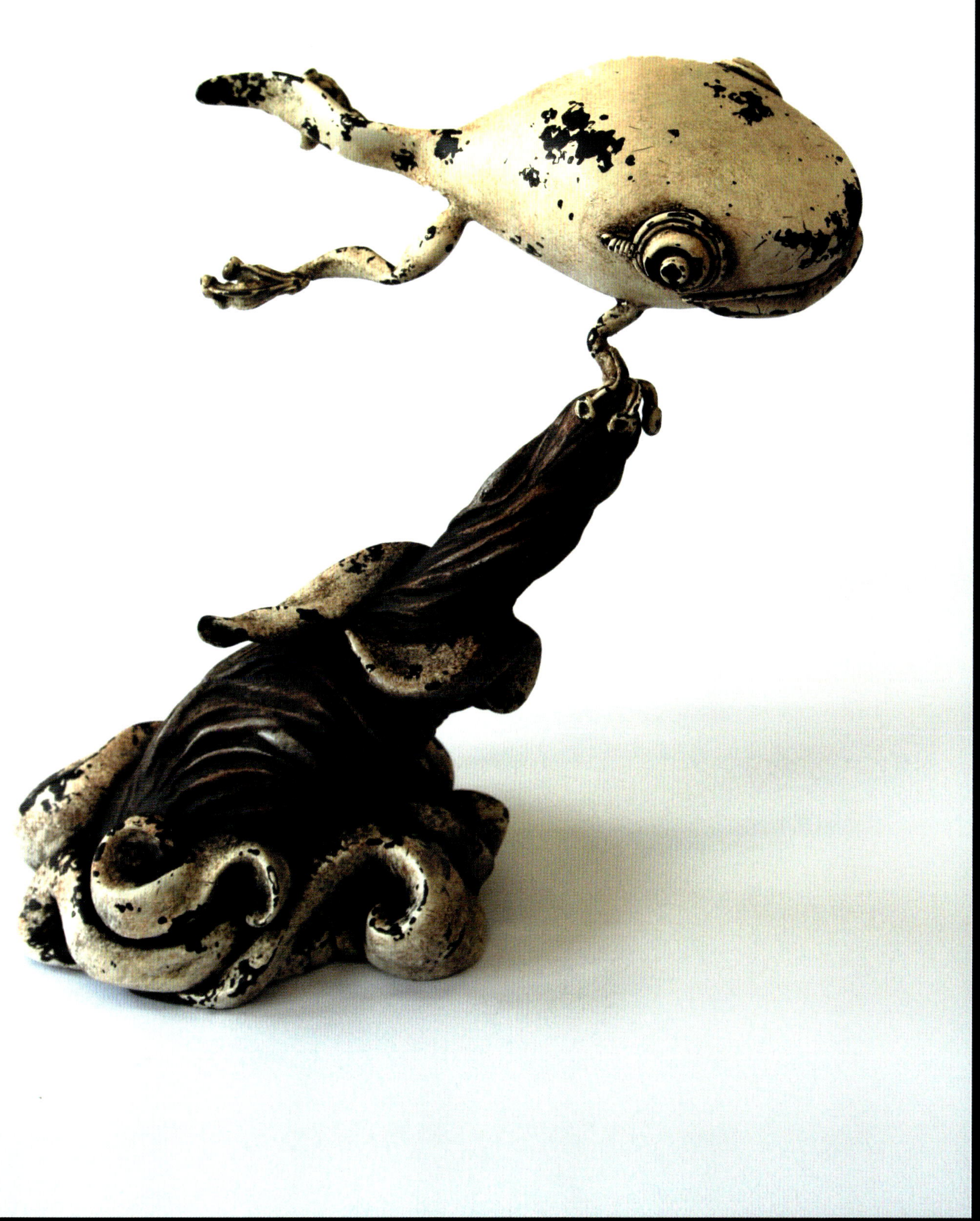

A Ladle – 10.2" x 437" x 5.7" stone powder clay, acrylic paints

JEREMY**MAYER**

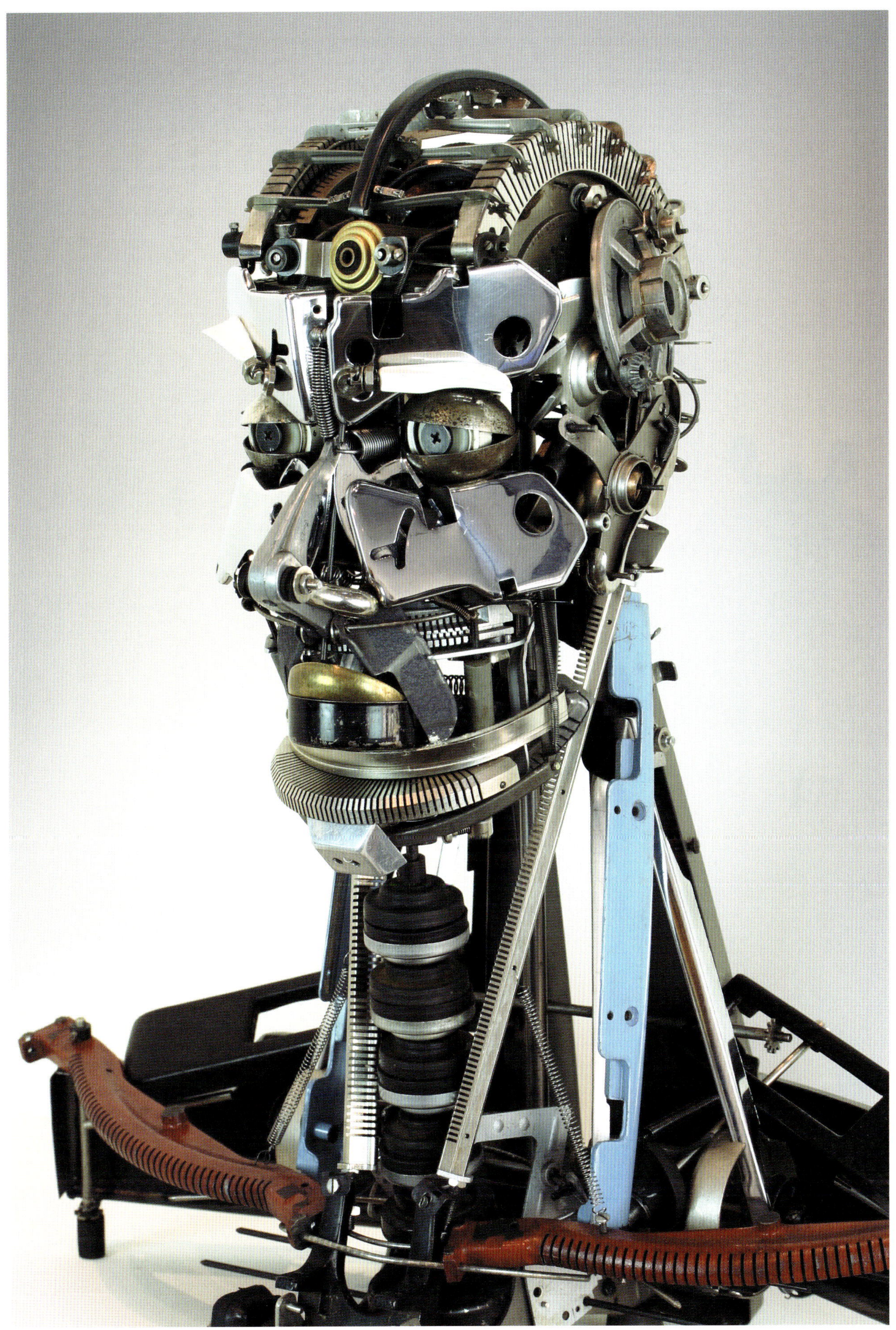

Bust III – typewriter parts (2008)

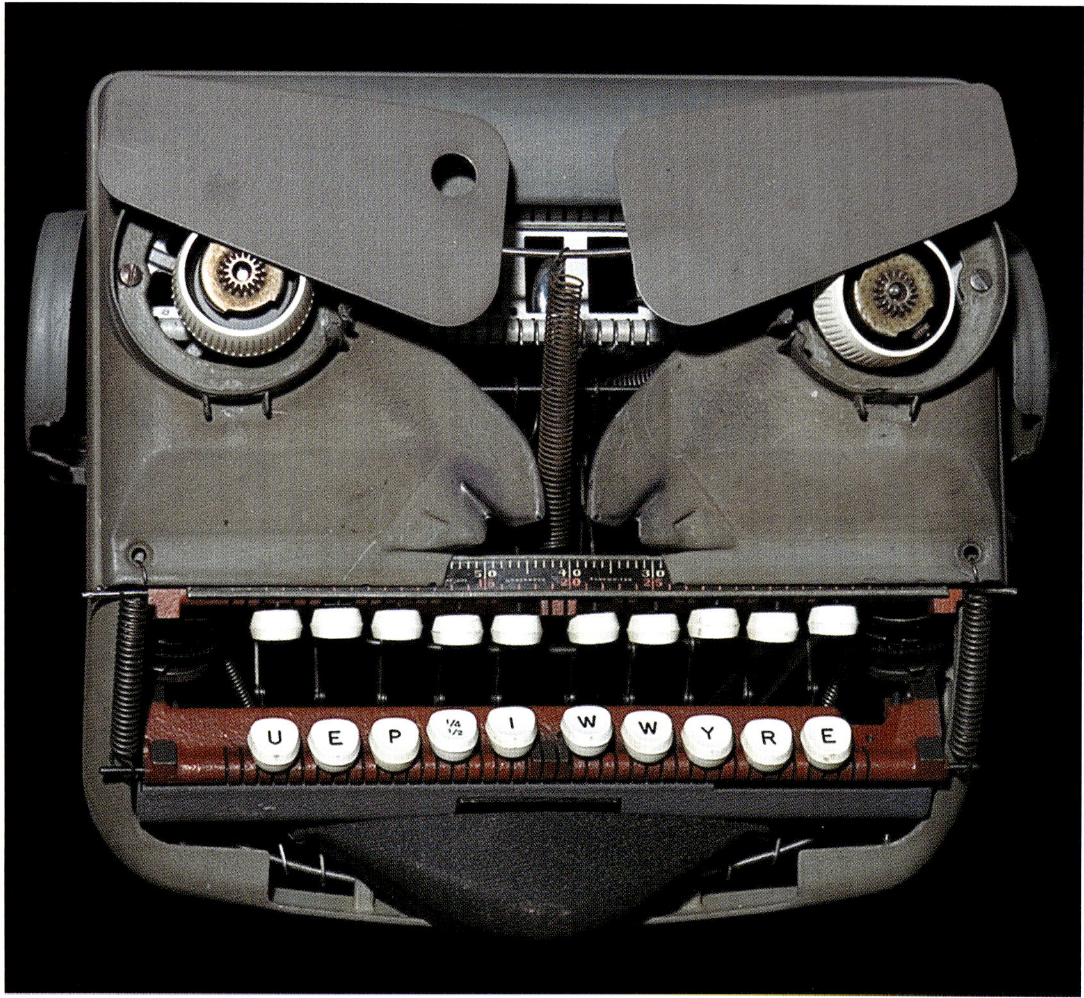

Jeremy **Mayer**

Jeremy Mayer disassembles typewriters and then reassembles them into full-scale, anatomically correct human figures. He does not solder, weld, or glue these assemblages together. The process is known as cold assembly.

Interested in assembly, particularly in nature, Mayer pays very close attention to the strong current in science and technology flowing inexorably toward an emulation of natural systems. Over the years, he has watched the advances in molecular engineering and biotechnology with giddy anticipation and also with a faint ping of trepidation. Mayer loves the sciences and science fiction, both disciplines which often stress the importance of considering the ramifications of implementing new technologies. These interests figure greatly into his sculpture and drawings.

Mayer began working with typewriters in 1996 while living in a small town in Iowa. However, his intense interest in the devices dates back to when he was ten years old and wanted to take apart his mother's 1920's Underwood. Mayer sees the typewriter as a product of nature even though it's made of cold metal and human hands. He uses the typewriter in his work as a natural material such as stone or wood. Mayer's work reflects his fascination with the raw material and interest in science and science fiction together with the subtleties of the human form.

He currently lives and works in Palo Alto, California.

Mask III – typewriter parts (2005)

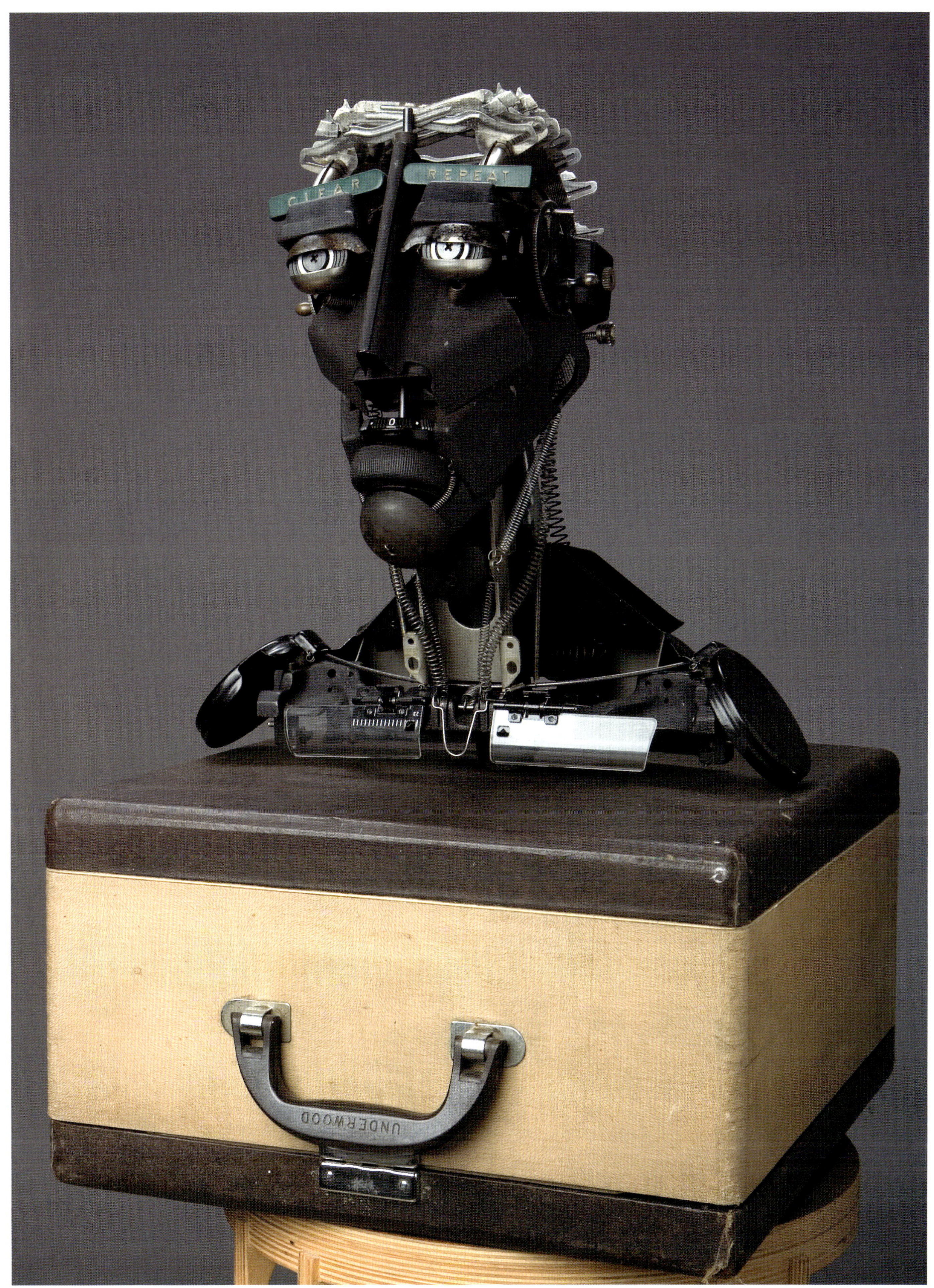

Bust II – 16" x 18" x 24" typewriter parts

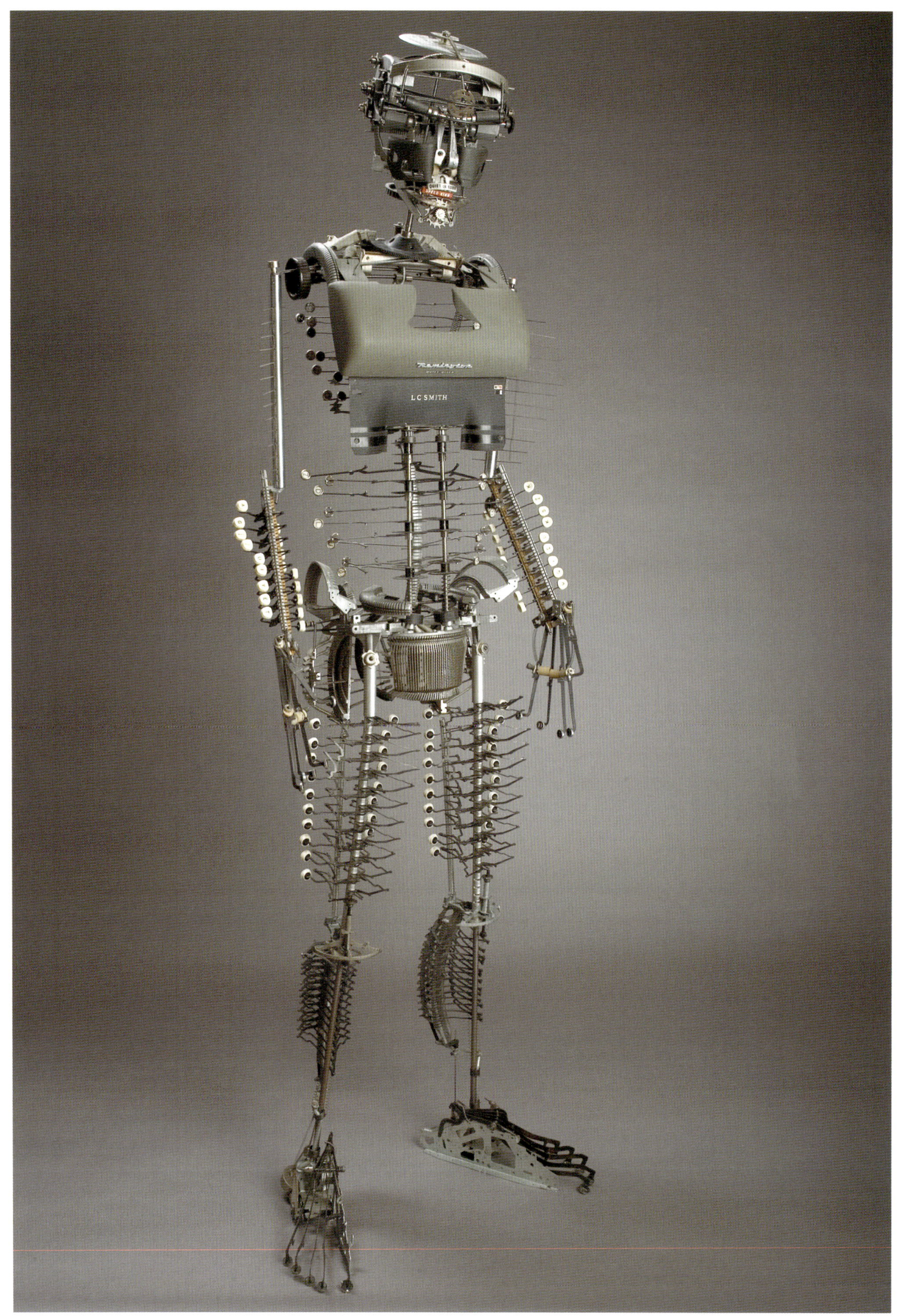

Nude – 27.6" x 23.6" x 59.1" typewriter parts (1995)

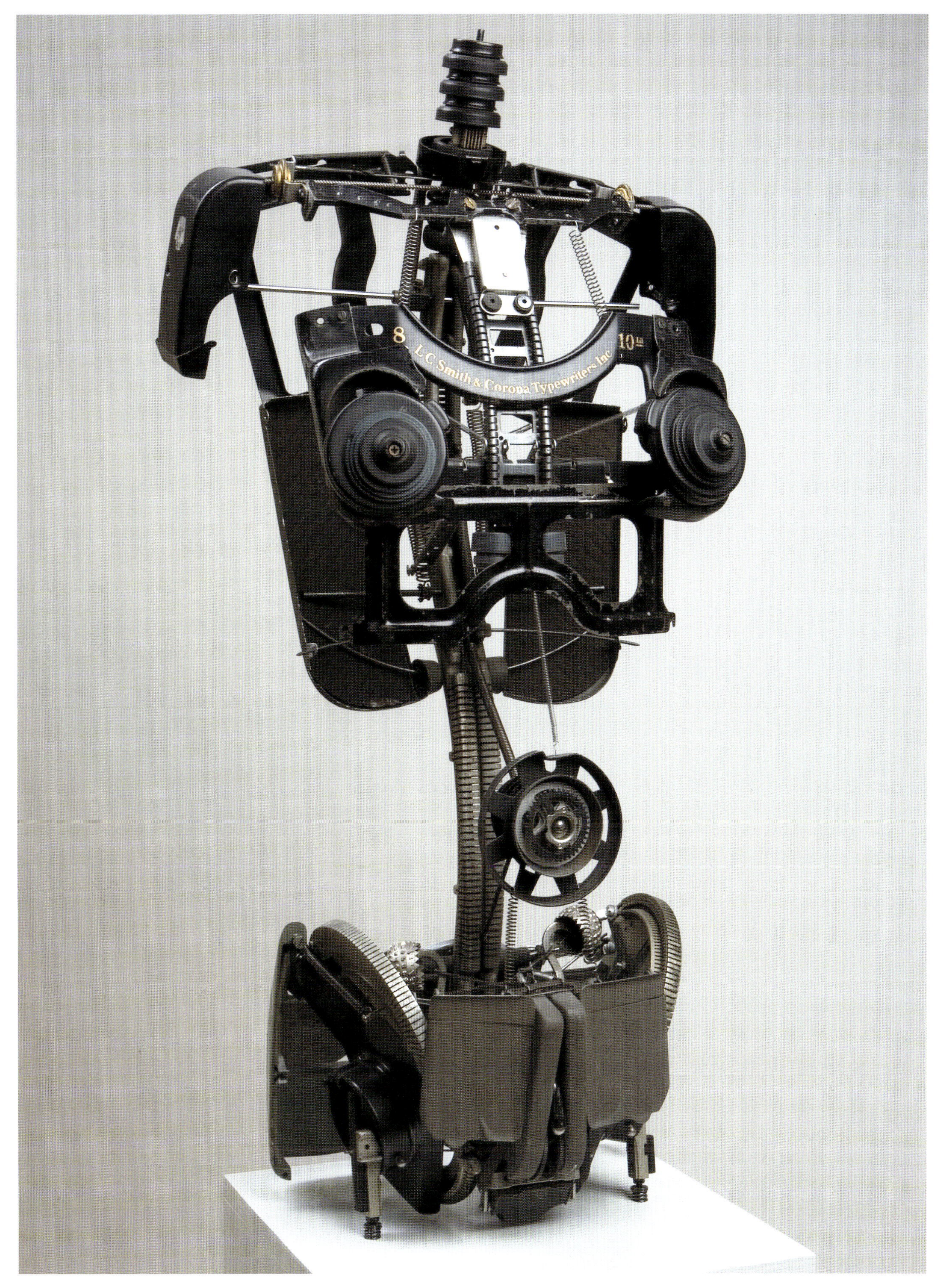

Torso I – 17.7" x 11.8" x 35.4" typewriter parts (2003)

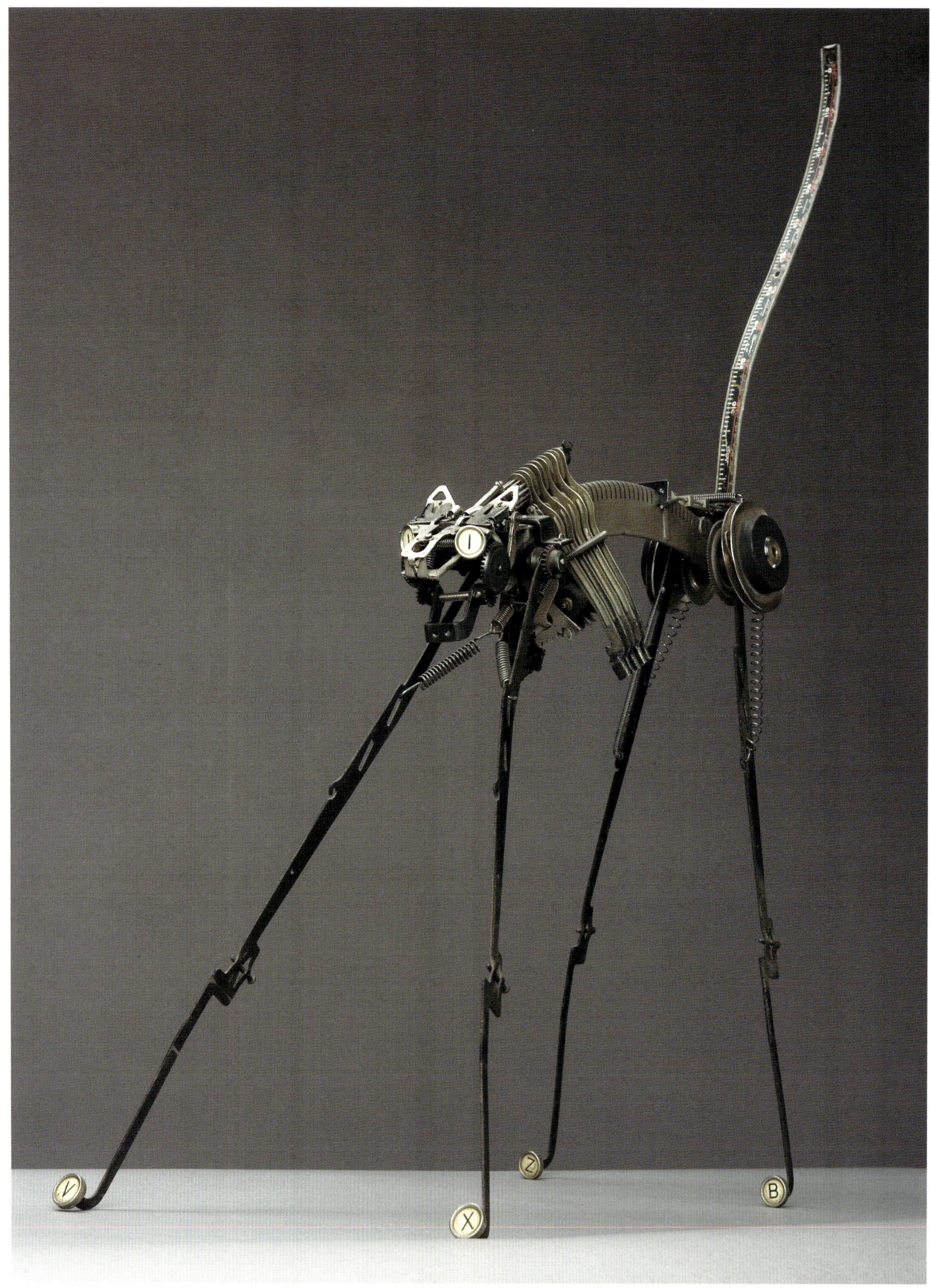

Cat X – 18" x 11" x 22" typewriter parts (2000)

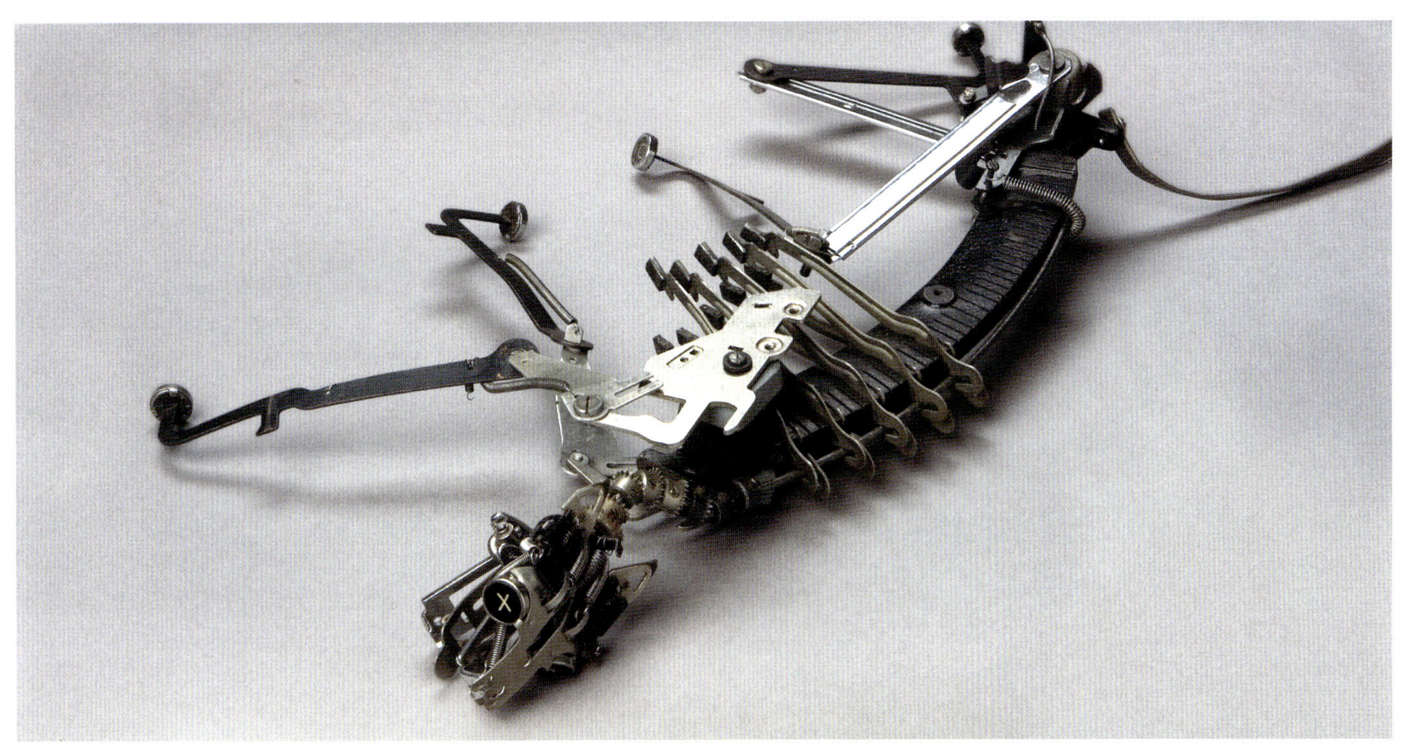

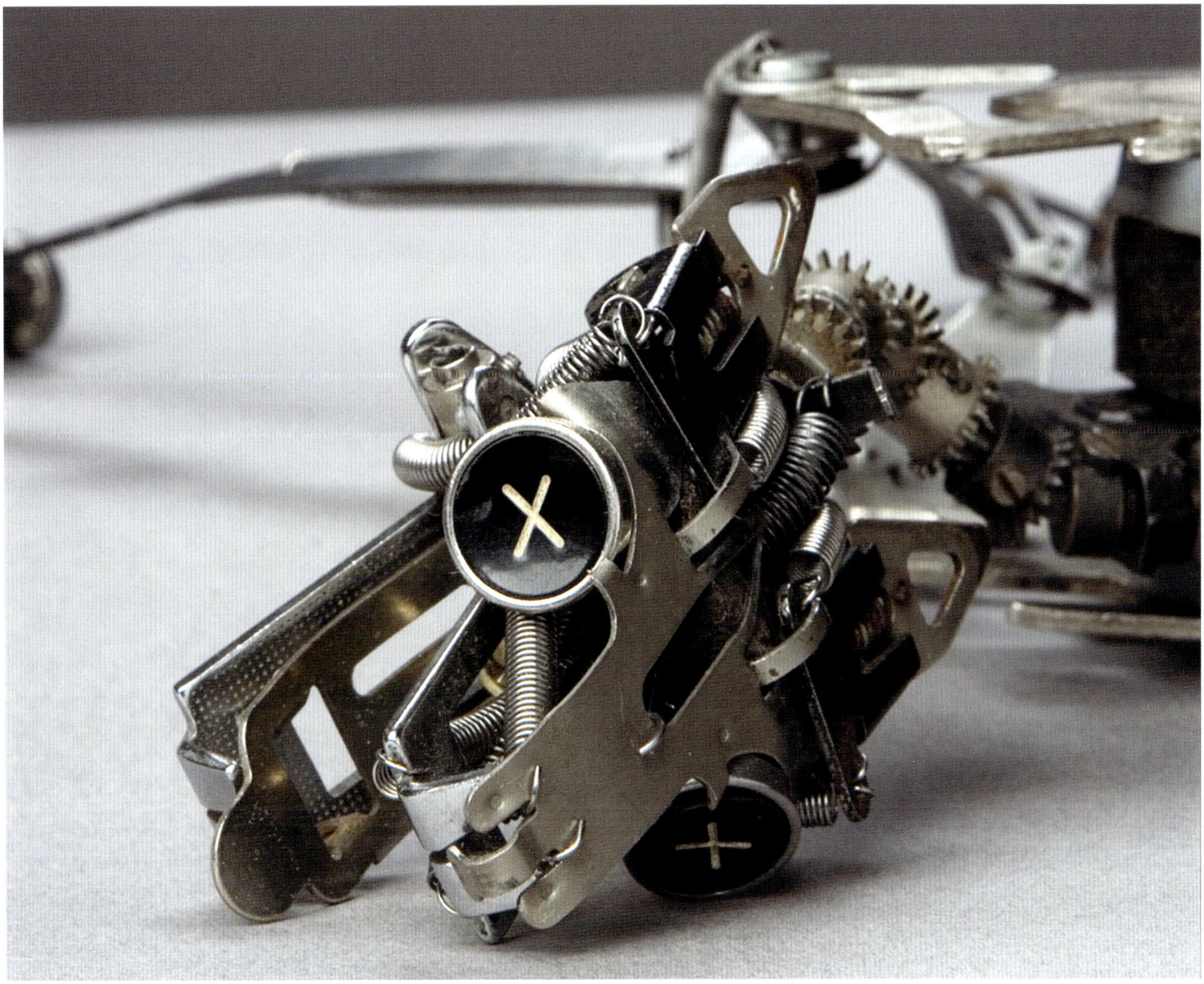

Dead Cat I – 16" x 12" x 3" typewriter parts (2004)

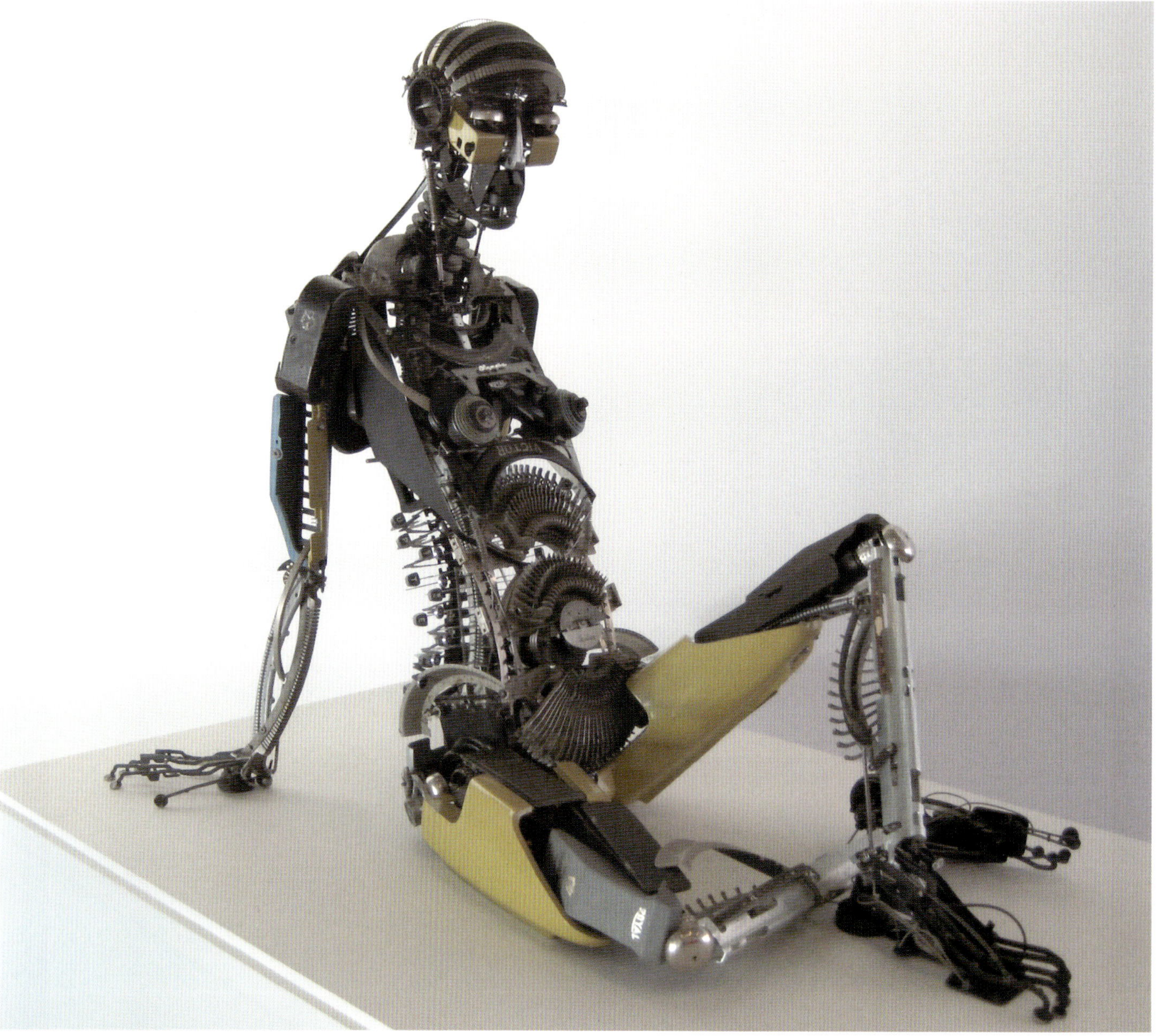

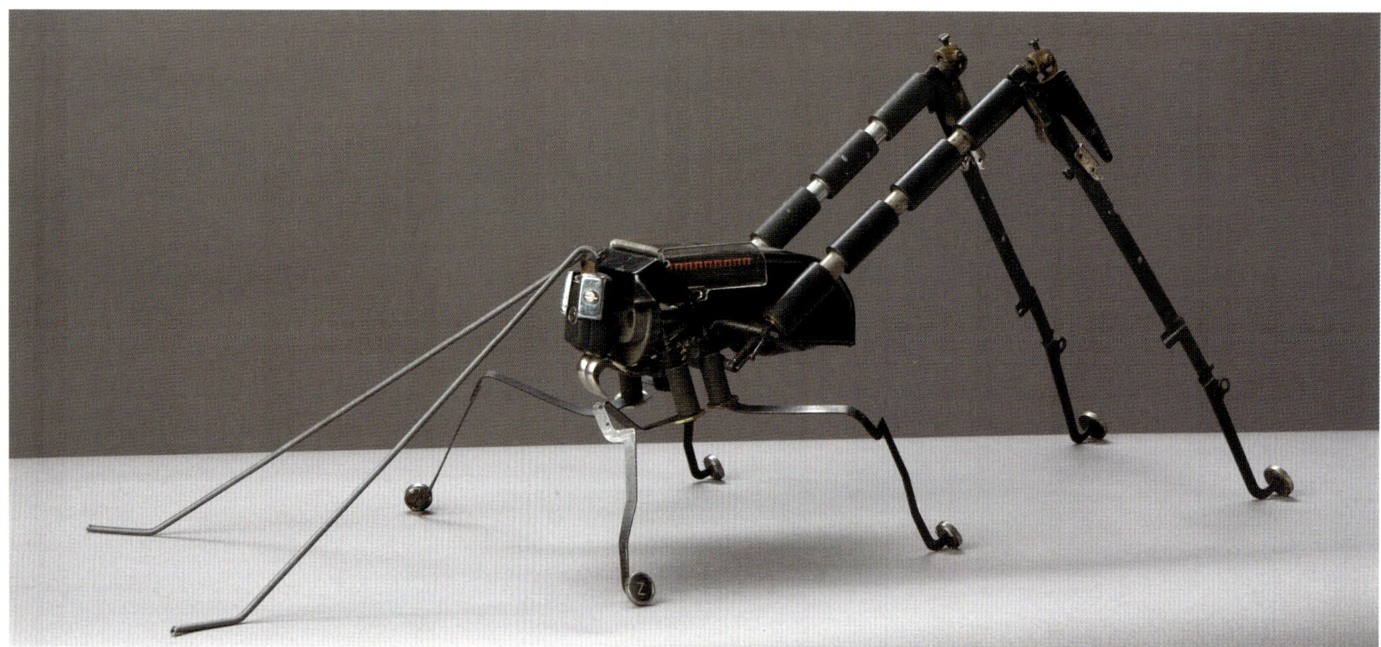

Nude III – typewriter parts (2007) (top)
Cricket III – 23.6" x 11" x 9.8" typewriter parts (2008) (bottom)

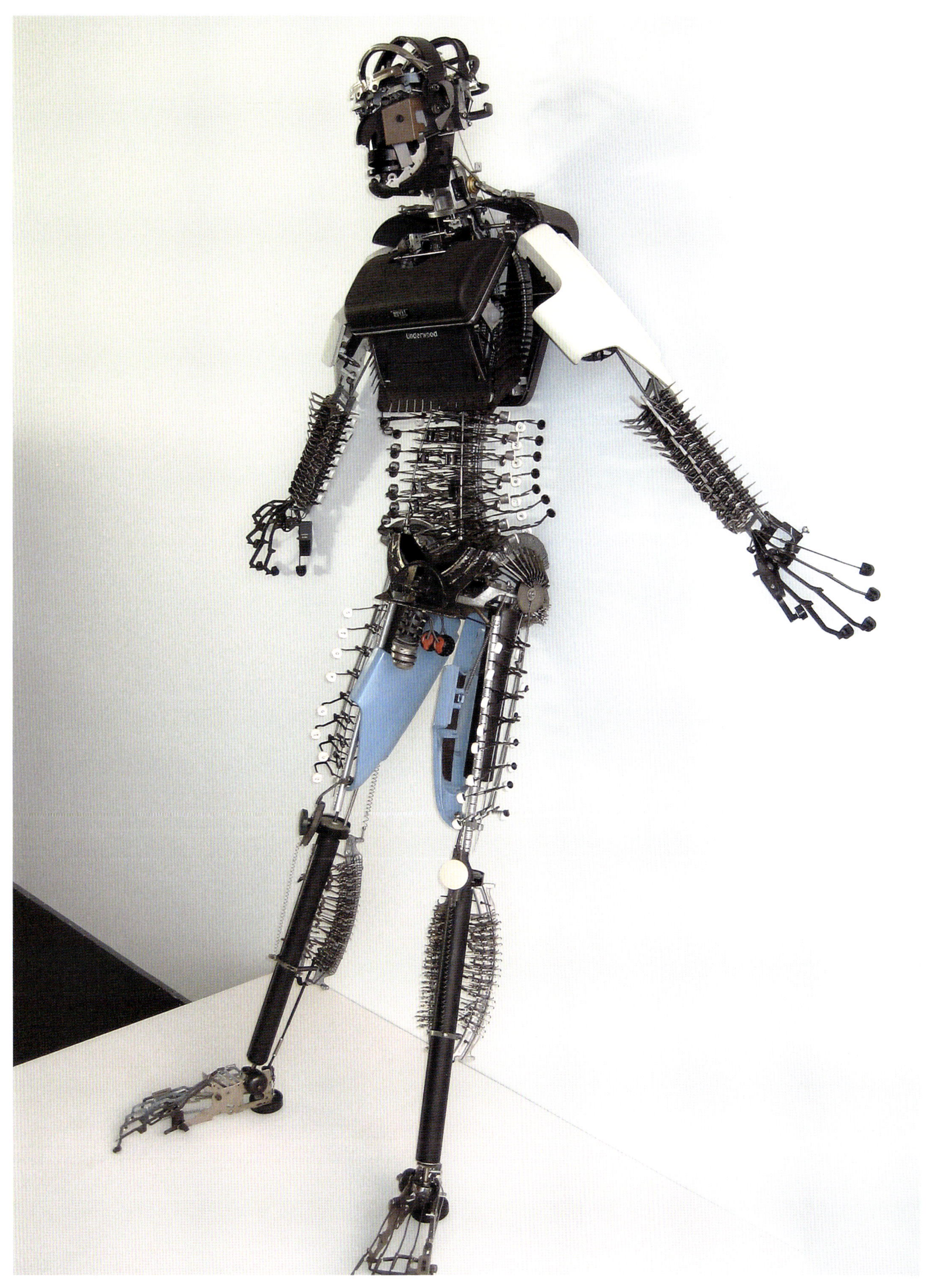

Nude II – 55.1" x 15.7" x 55.1" typewriter parts (2000—2001)

RICH**MULLER**

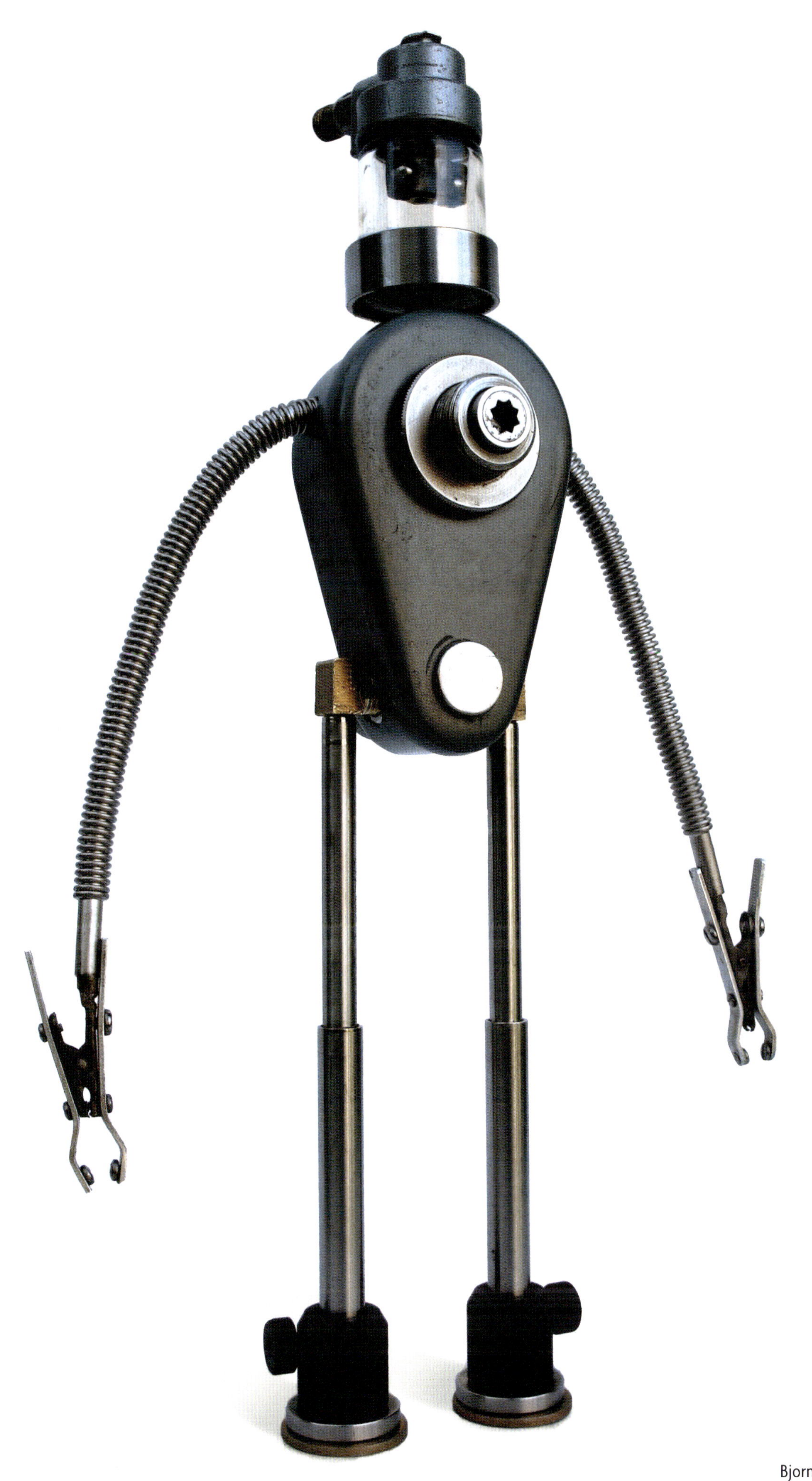

Bjorn – 15" x 6" x 3" (2009)

Rich **Muller**

My grandfather, a first generation American, lived with my family when I was a kid and he loved nothing more than to tinker in the workshop, fixing things and repeating his favorite jokes and bits of advice. He would scan the vast stores of itemized 'junk' that he had accumulated in his shop, and then hold up some oddity he had been searching for and utter one of his primal mantras. "You see that," he would say to me while sagely waggling the item "it was junk when I found it—but it is gold when you need it!" So it was from my grandfather that I learned the enjoyment of workshop repairing, and I still hesitate before throwing something away, knowing that whatever it is, it might someday be just what I need ("Gold when you need it").

Los Angeles—where I live and work in the aerospace industry and make my robots—is my artistic collaborator and provides an extremely fertile terrain from which to mine raw robot materials. Flea markets, swap meets, and garage sales abound; semiconductor, telecom, and biotech laboratories regularly get set up and later torn down; and we have a subculture of Hollywood set-decorators and artists who rapidly outfit—and then generously dispose of—the latest Buck Rogers landscapes. These sources complement nicely the local avionics and electronics surplus outlets that peddle all manner of retro equipment. On a good day I can find anything from bakelite knobs to rocket nose-cones.

It has been great fun to put together and present my family of little guys. People typically see each robot first as the character it is meant to be. As they look closer, they can also enjoy the history and variety of the constituent elements that take new shape together.

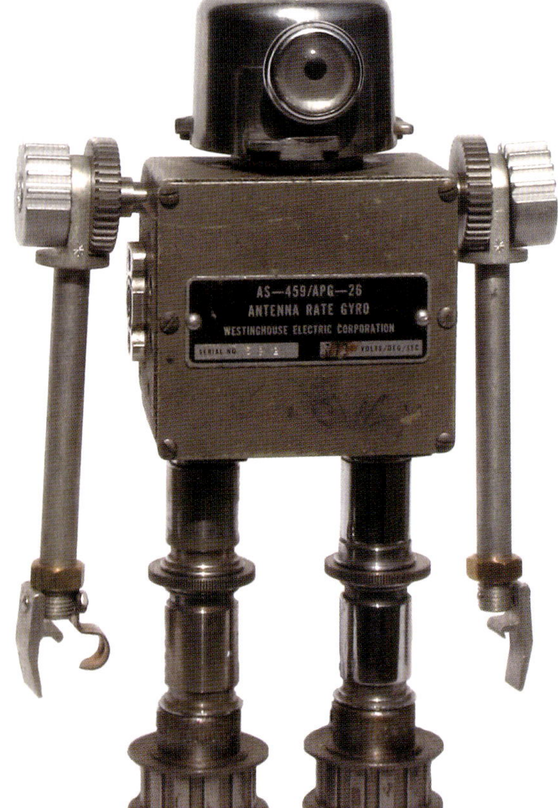

Gyro – 19" x 6" x 4" (2007)

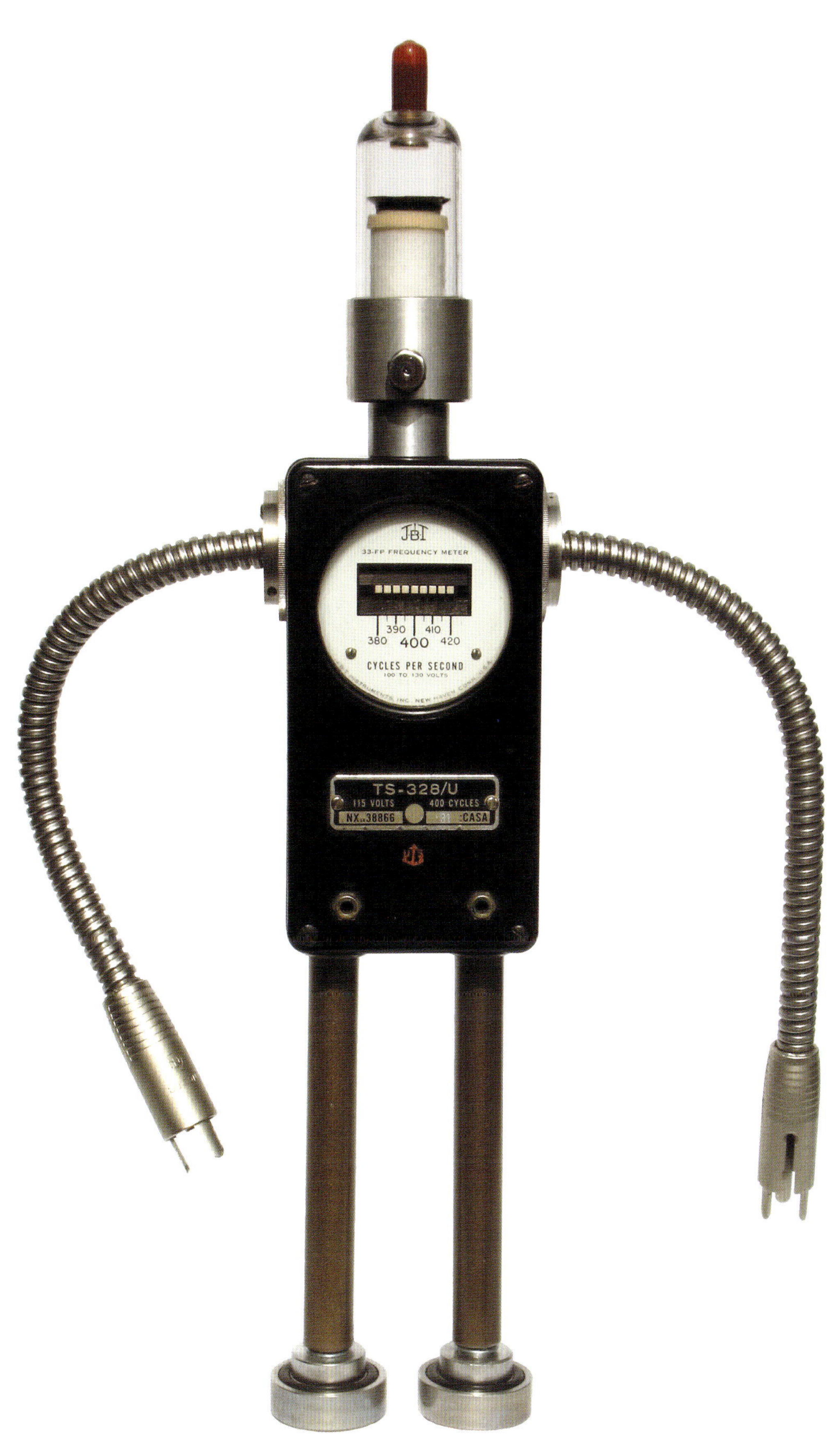

J.B. – 17" x 9" x 3" (2007)

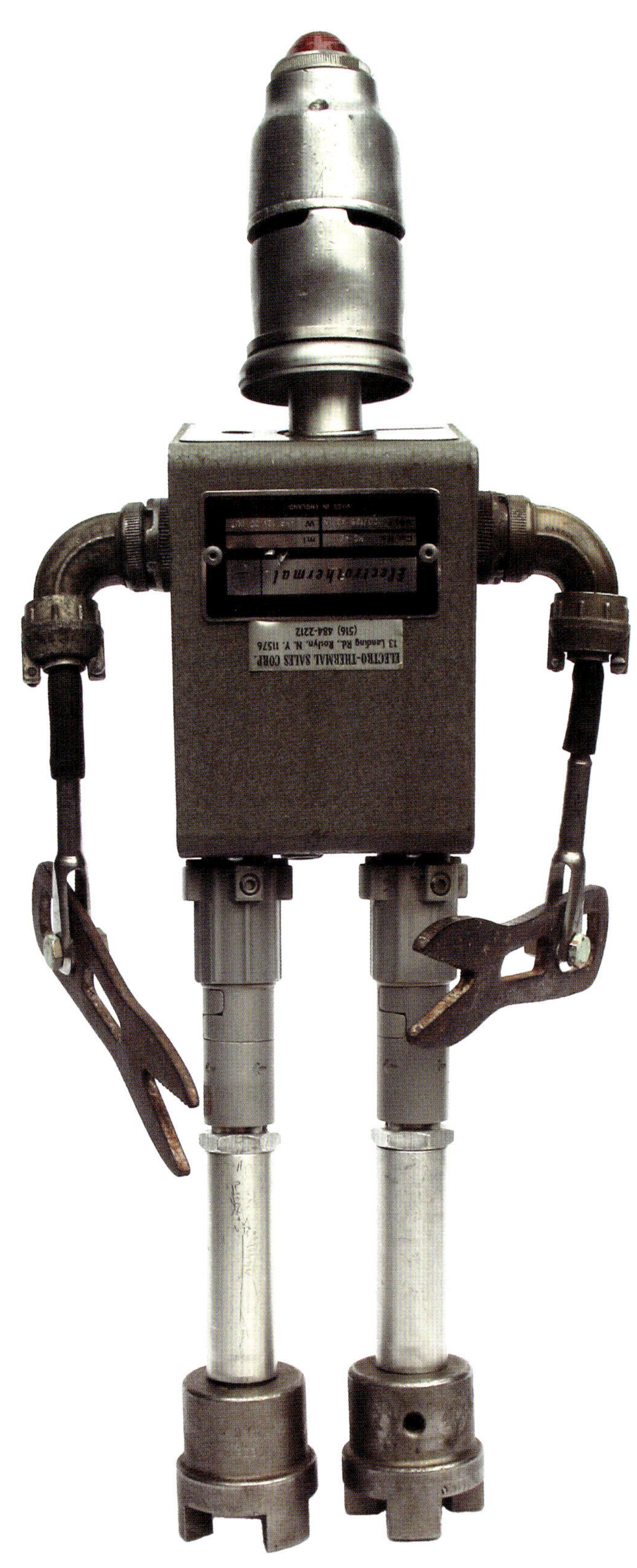

Electro – 20" x 8" x 4" (2007)

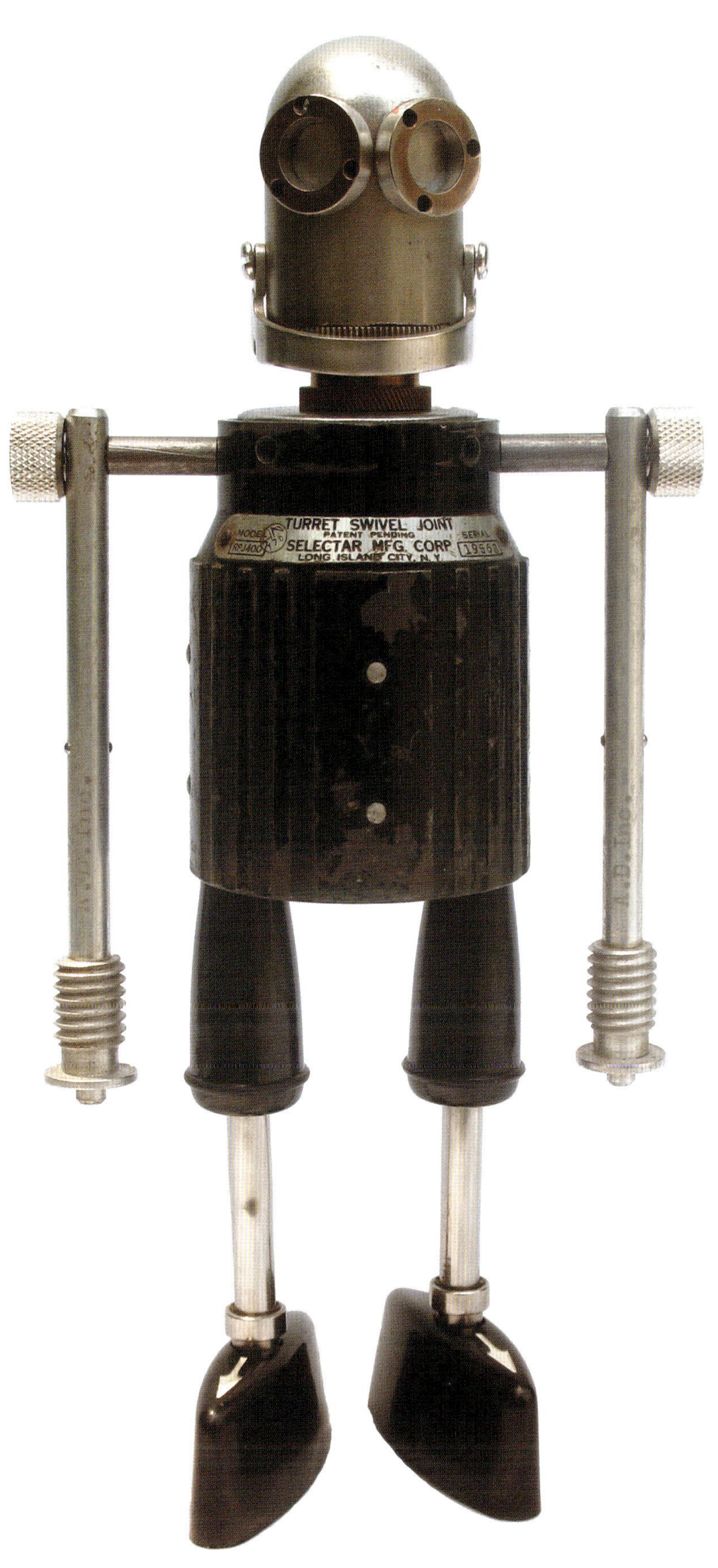

Cosmo – 8" x 4" x 2" (2008)

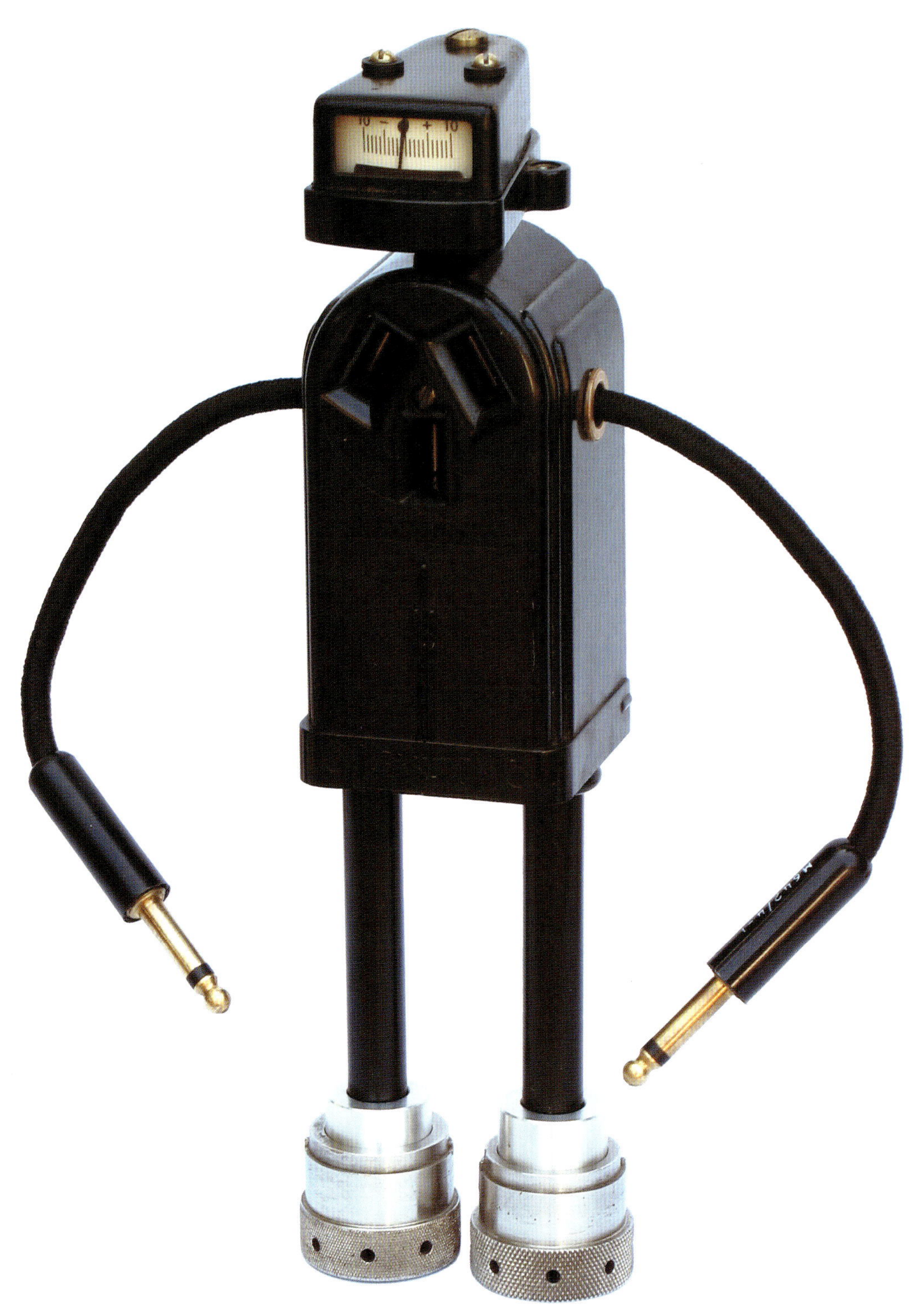

Levit – 11" x 6" x 3" (2007)

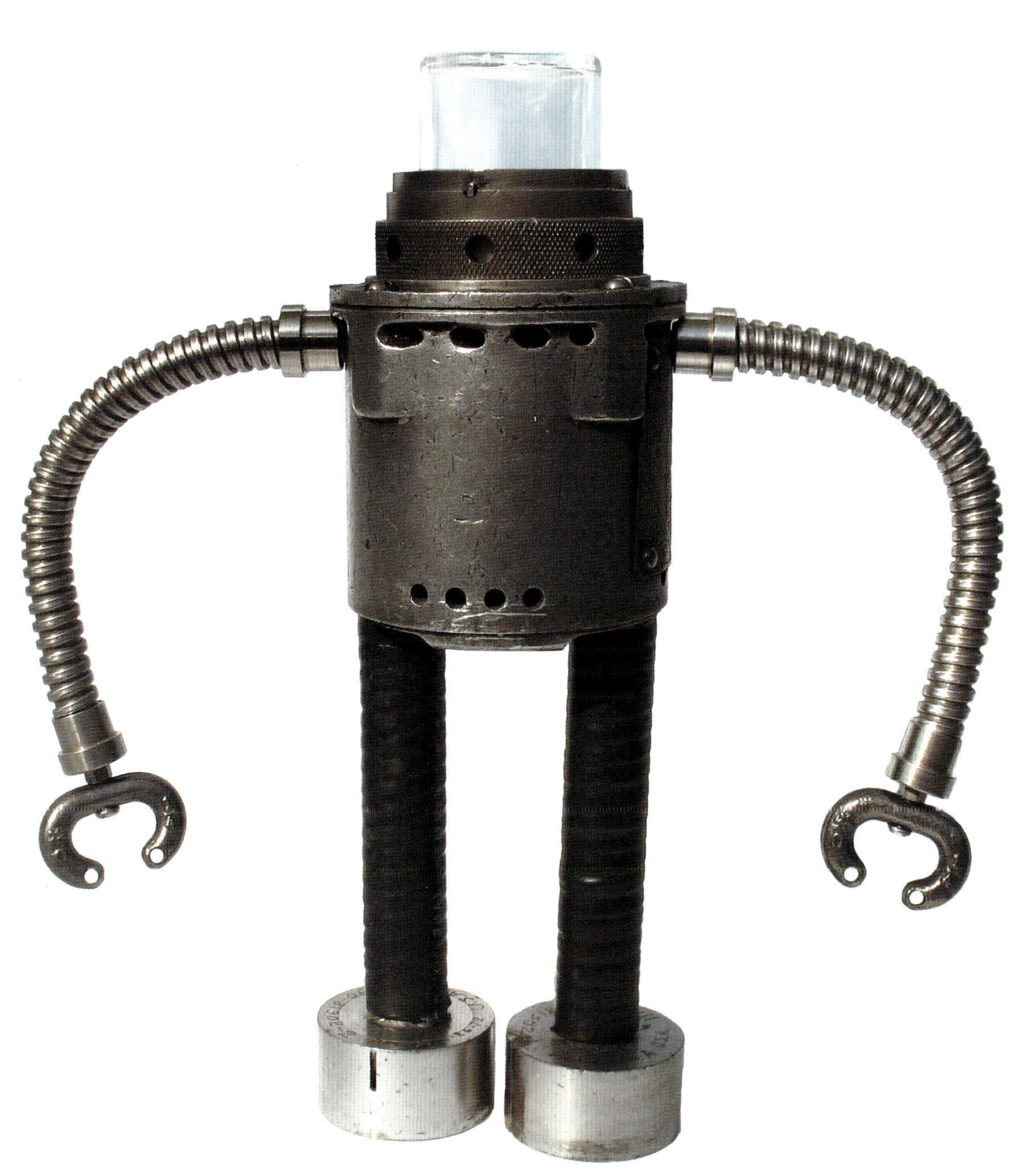

Thor – 10" x 10" x 4" (2008)

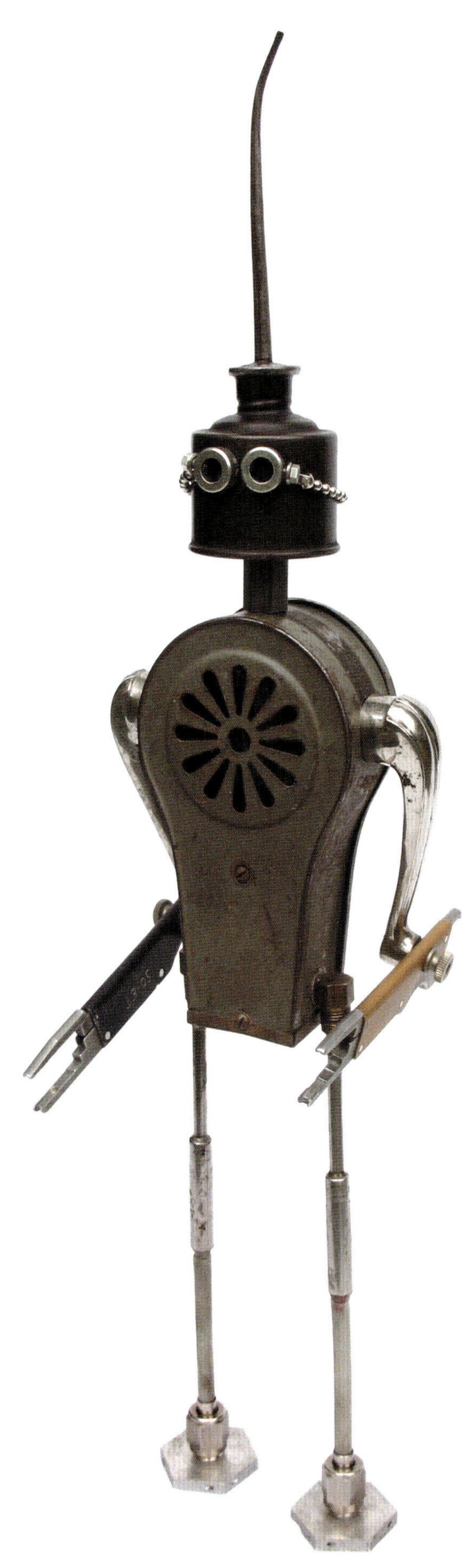

Slim – 19" x 5" x 4" (2007)

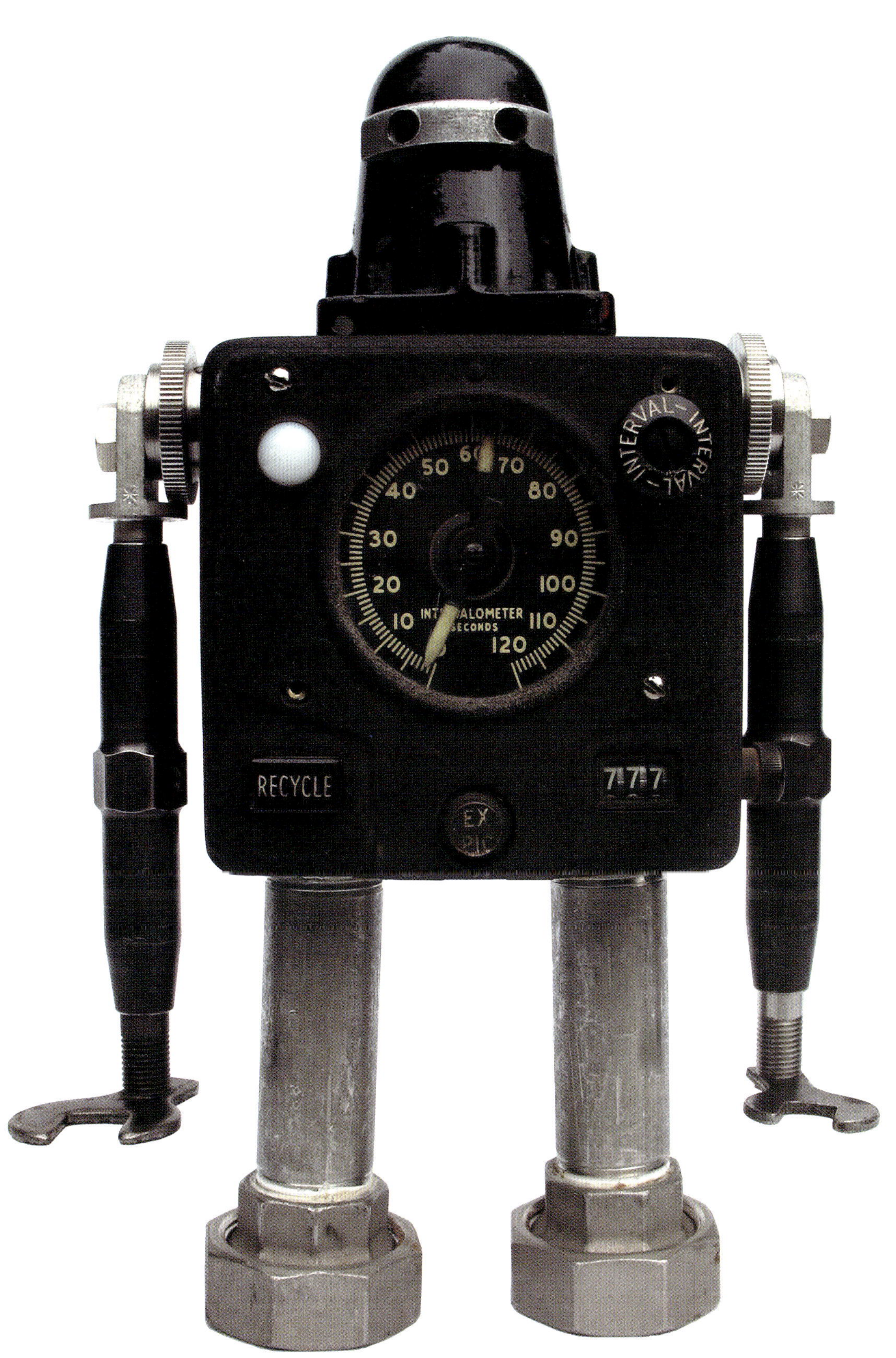

Ollie – 11" x 7" x 5" (2007)

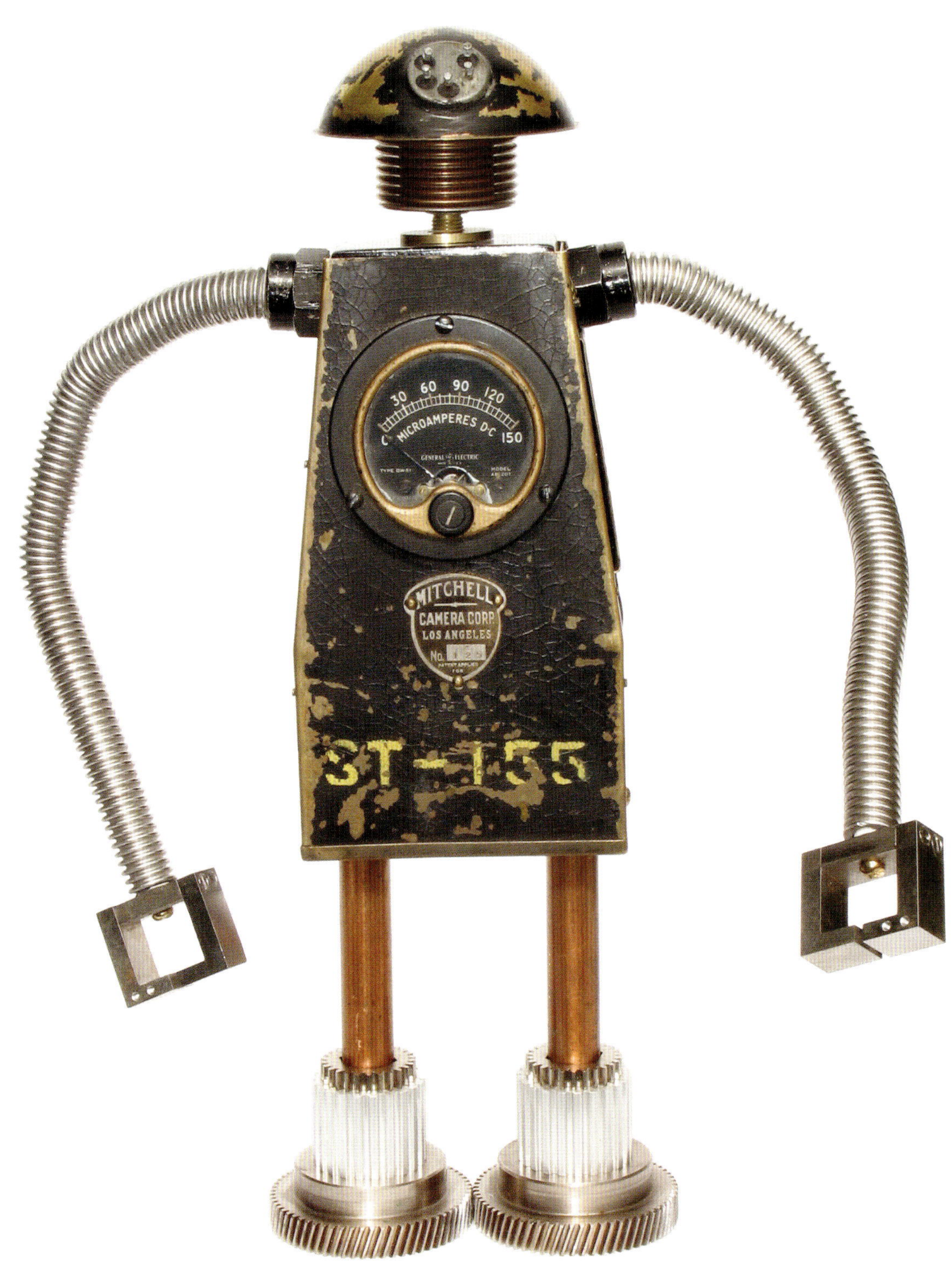

Mitch – 14" x 11" x 3" (2007)

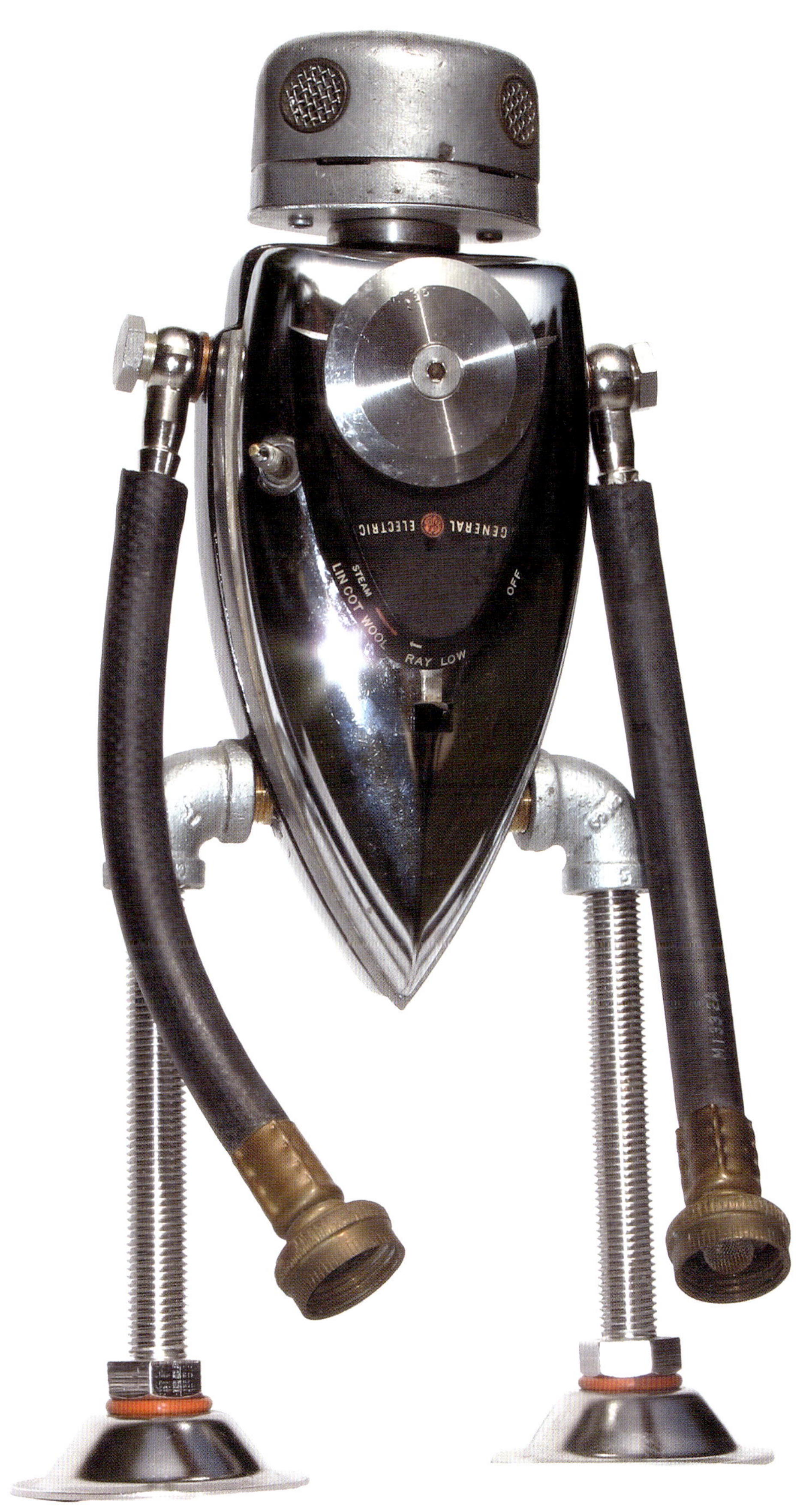

Iron Man – 14" x 6" x 3" (2007)

OLIVIER**PAUWELS**

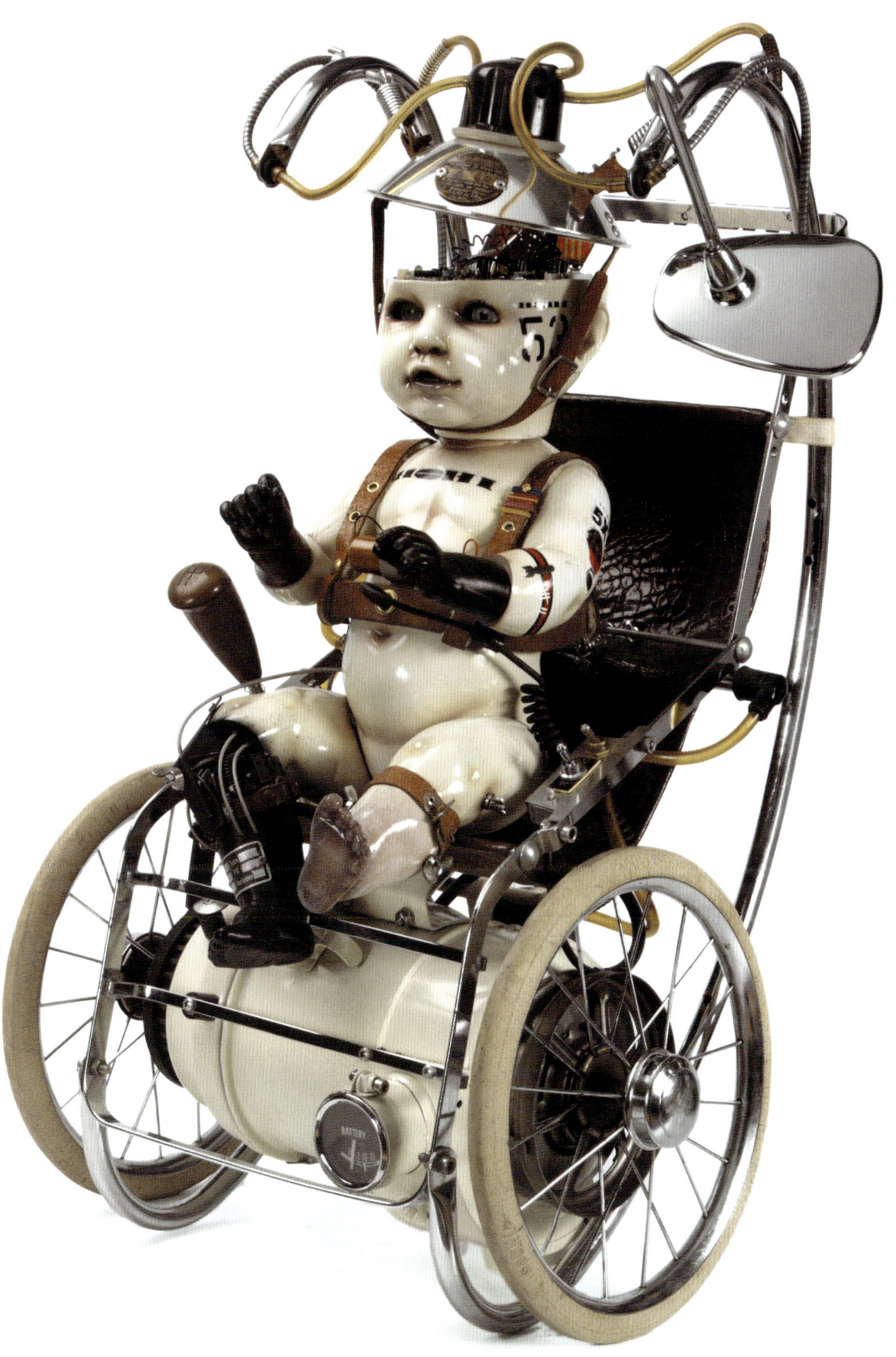

The Veteran Cyberbaby – 35.4" tall

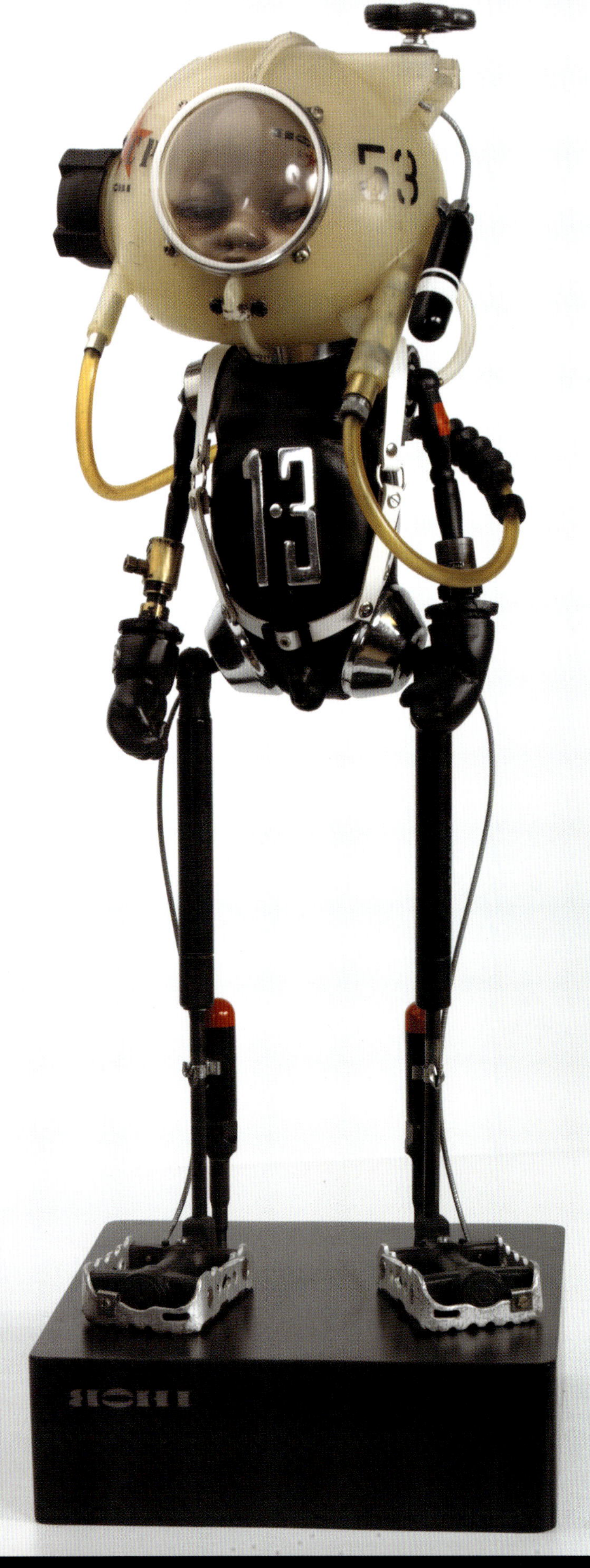

The Mars Diver – 27.6" tall

Olivier **Pauwels**

Olivier Pauwels aka BOHI (°Oostende 1974)

During his childhood his grandfather told him stories about World War II and Nazism. These stories had a tremendous effect on Olivier Pauwels. They would also influence his oeuvre. He has been painting and making sculptures for about 15 years now. A vital moment in this artistic career was when the young artist came in contact with puppets because of a school assignment. While browsing the attic he became fascinated by puppets and the bizarre world that he created around them. But he didn't only come across puppets. He also found instruments and numerous apparatuses, an old radio for example. He dismantled those instruments, linked their components, and created a being without realizing his first cyberpuppet was born.

His skilful hands gave shape to his creatures and at times it has made him shiver. His grandfather's stories concerning war and brainwashing kept haunting him. His creatures were a protest against cloning. Changing life and nature irritates him immensely.

A classical doll serves as the base figure for his creations. Every creation is cast in polyester and painted. Next, recuperated materials and objects are attached to or implanted on their bodies. Some of the attributes on his creations move so that one day the army of puppets might jump into action. Since they were all made from recuperated material, they are already considerably battered and therefore show no fear. They would carry out orders seamlessly when their creator commands them. One day, somewhere, perhaps.

Olivier Pauwels creates fascinating cyberpuppets that carry the cruelties of former days, today, and tomorrow inside them. His creations have to make spectators think. And yet Olivier Pauwels is not a doomsayer. He is trying to warn us of what might happen one day but still cherishes what is beautiful, inside and outside.

He is creating a particularly dualistic artistic world because next to the strong message, and sometimes cruel nature, the puppets are and still remain dolls. Moreover, there is always that pinch of humor, their attitude, their thin legs, and so on.

Olivier Pauwels continues to surprise.

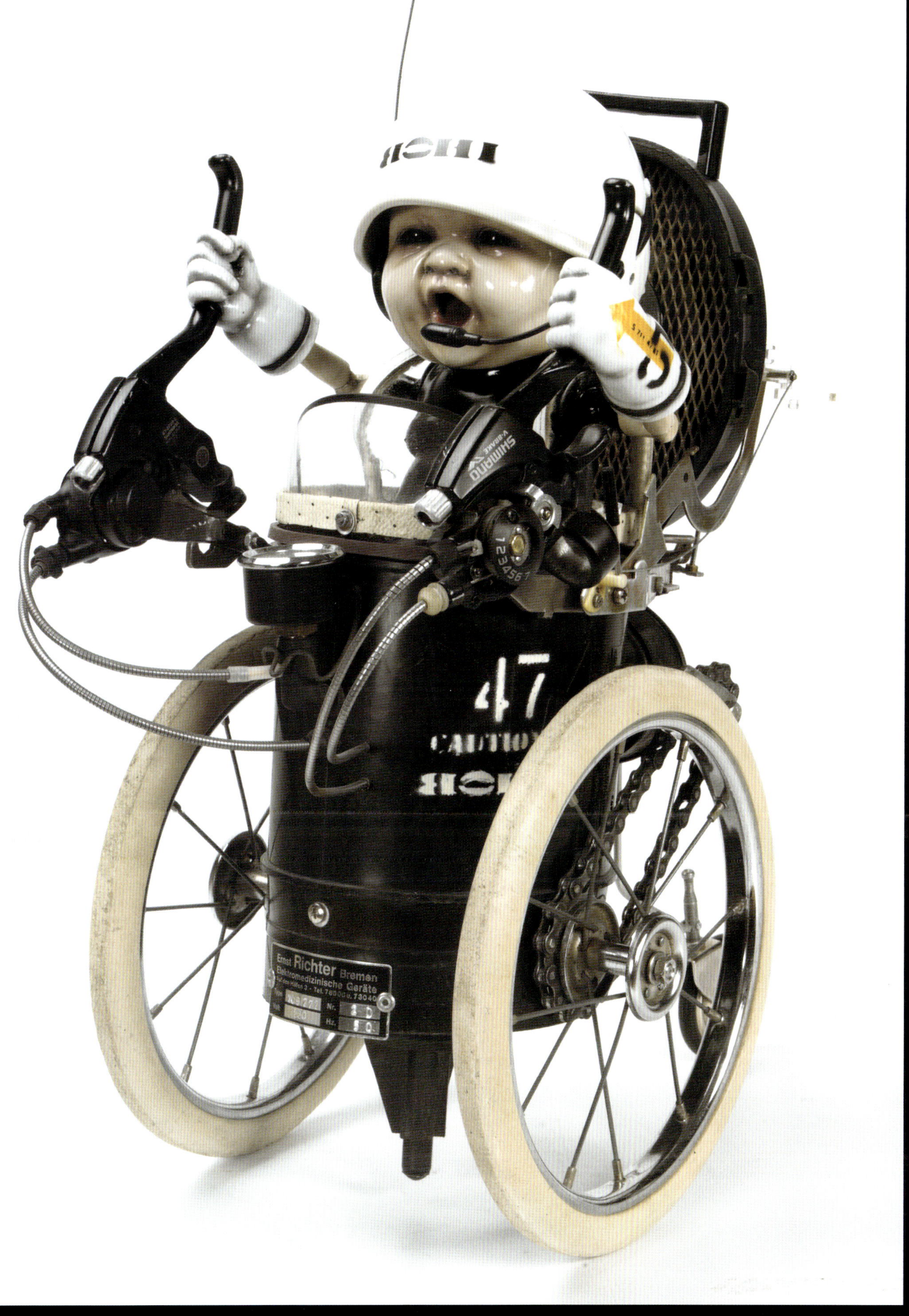

THOR
SHIMANO V-BRAKE
47
CAUTION
THOR
Ernst Richter Bremen
Elektromedizinische Geräte

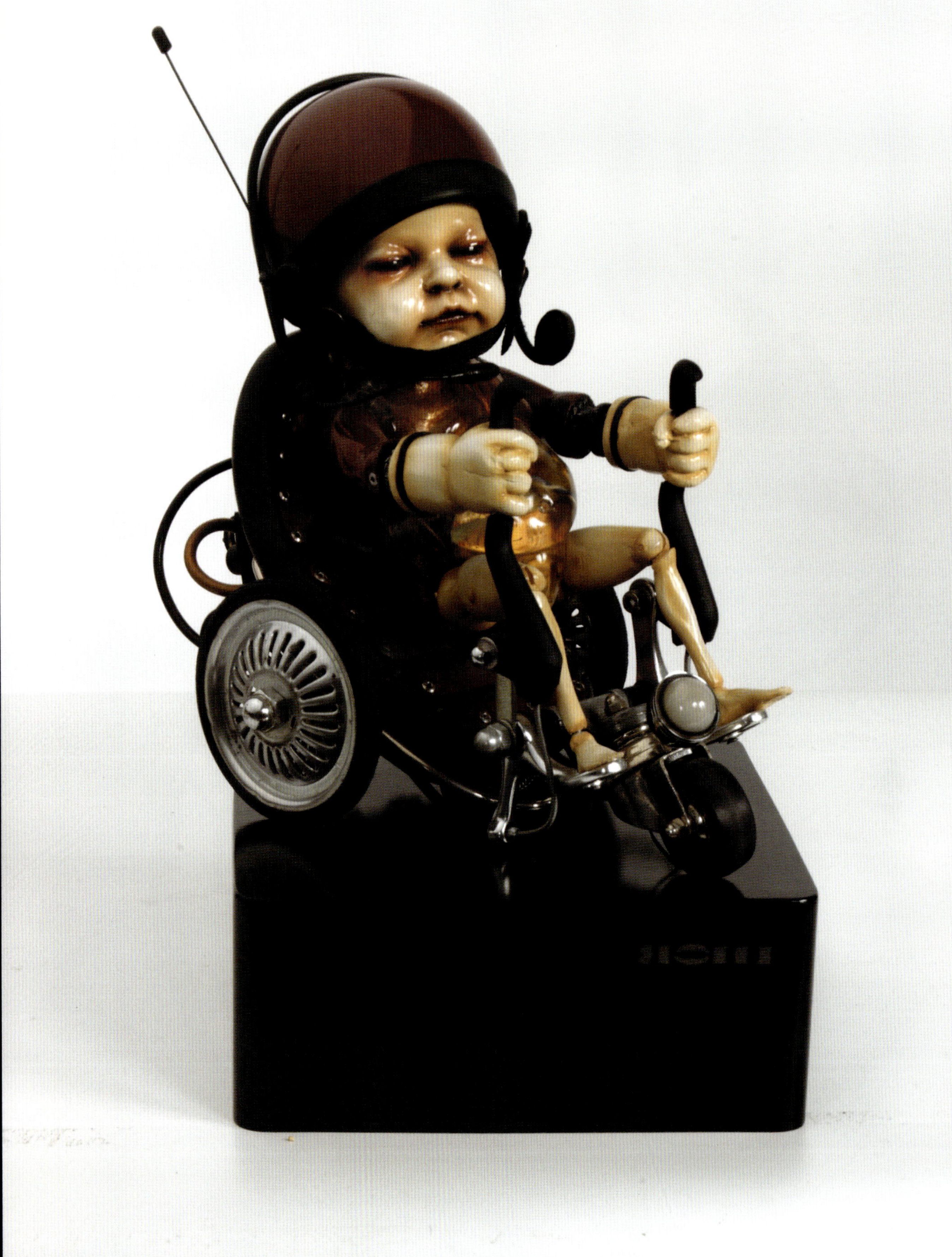

The Patrol – 16.5" tall

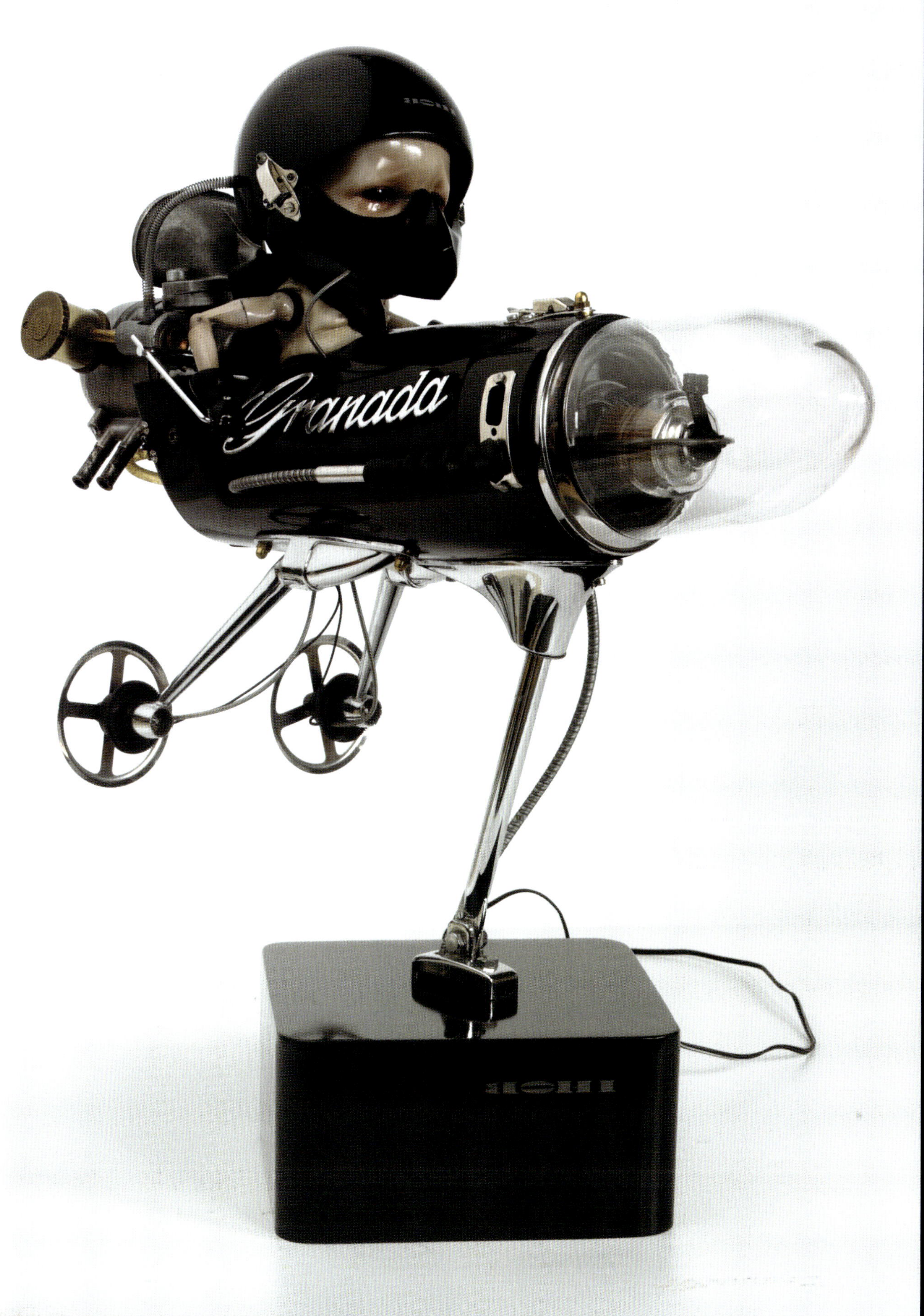

The Granada Rocket – 23.6" tall

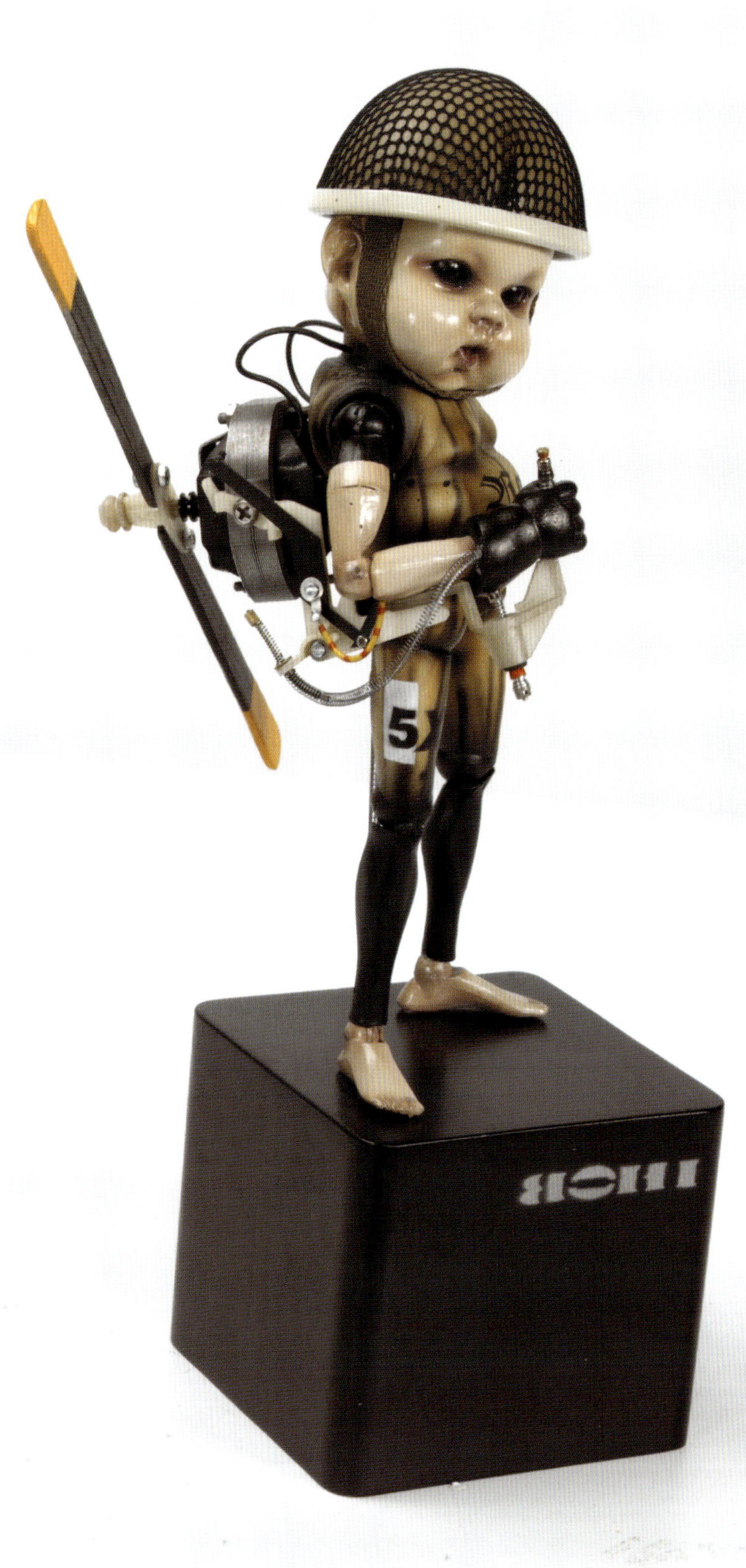

The Flight Lieutenant

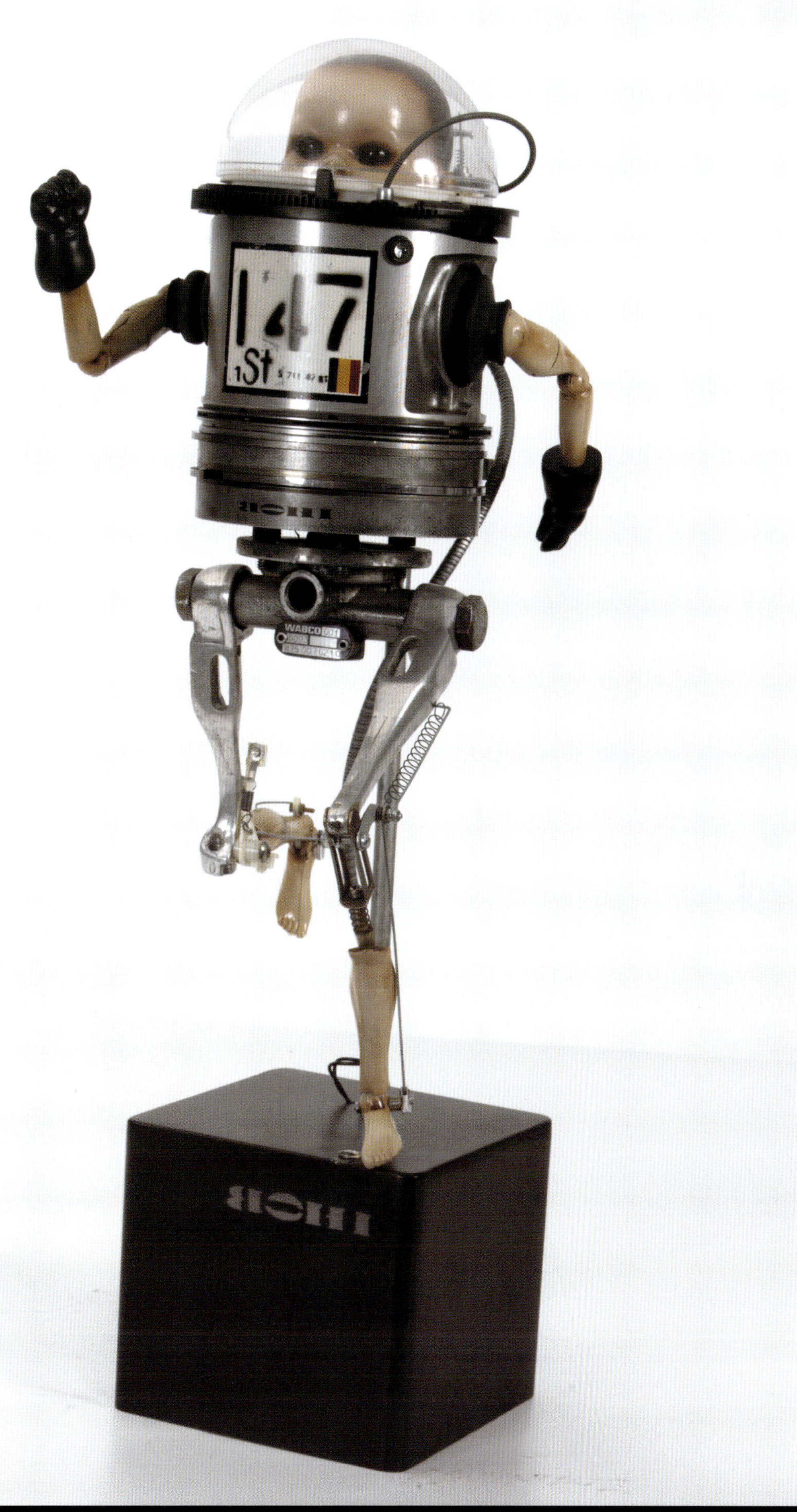

The Epo Runner – 15" tall

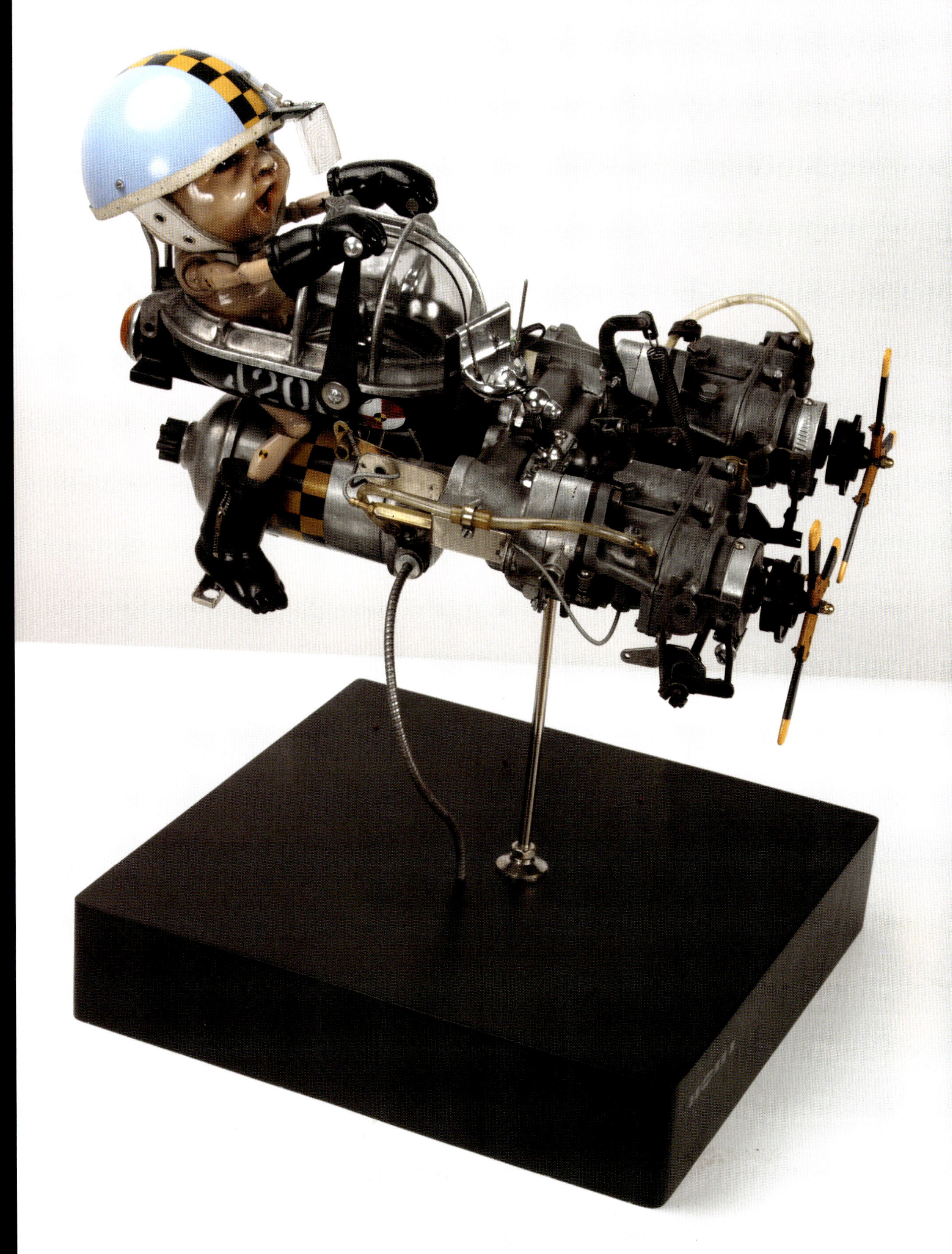

Kamikaze Dummy – 25.6" tall

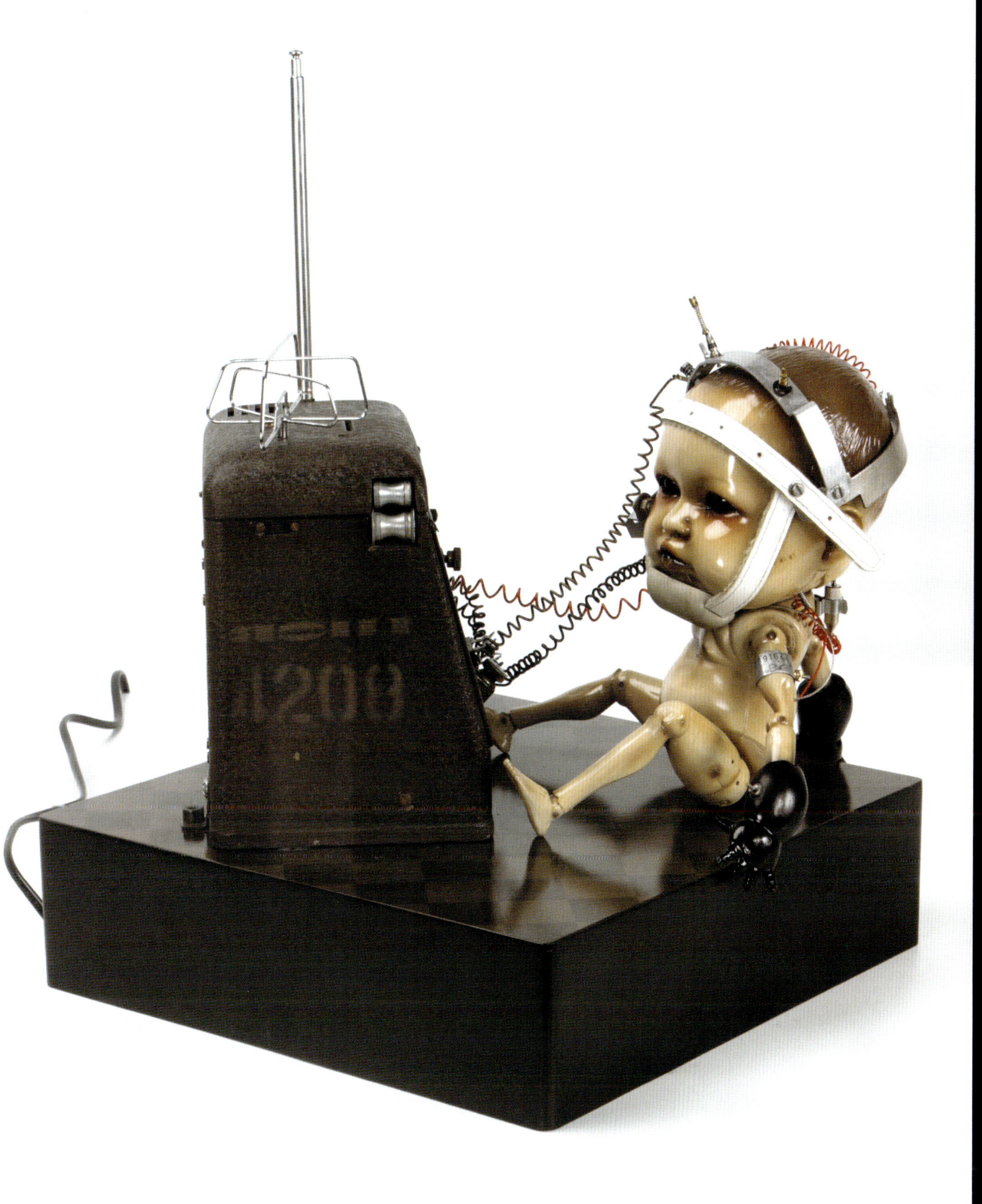

Propaganda Box – 11.8" tall

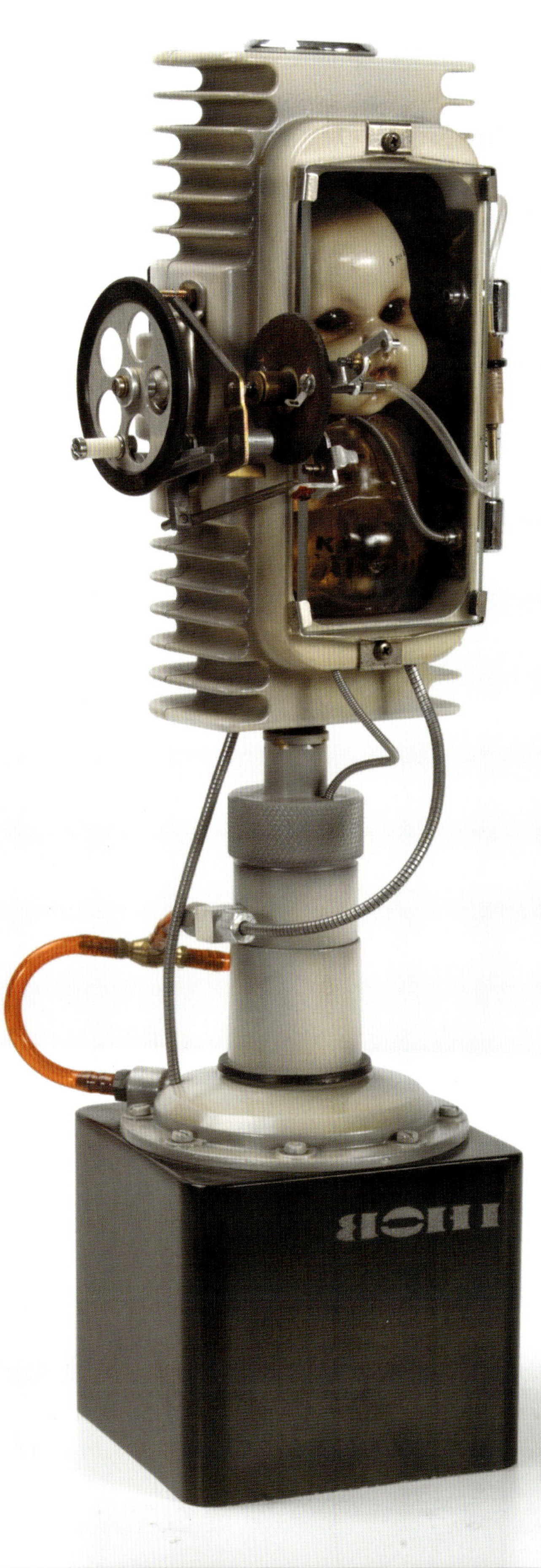

Holding Chamber – 17.7" tall

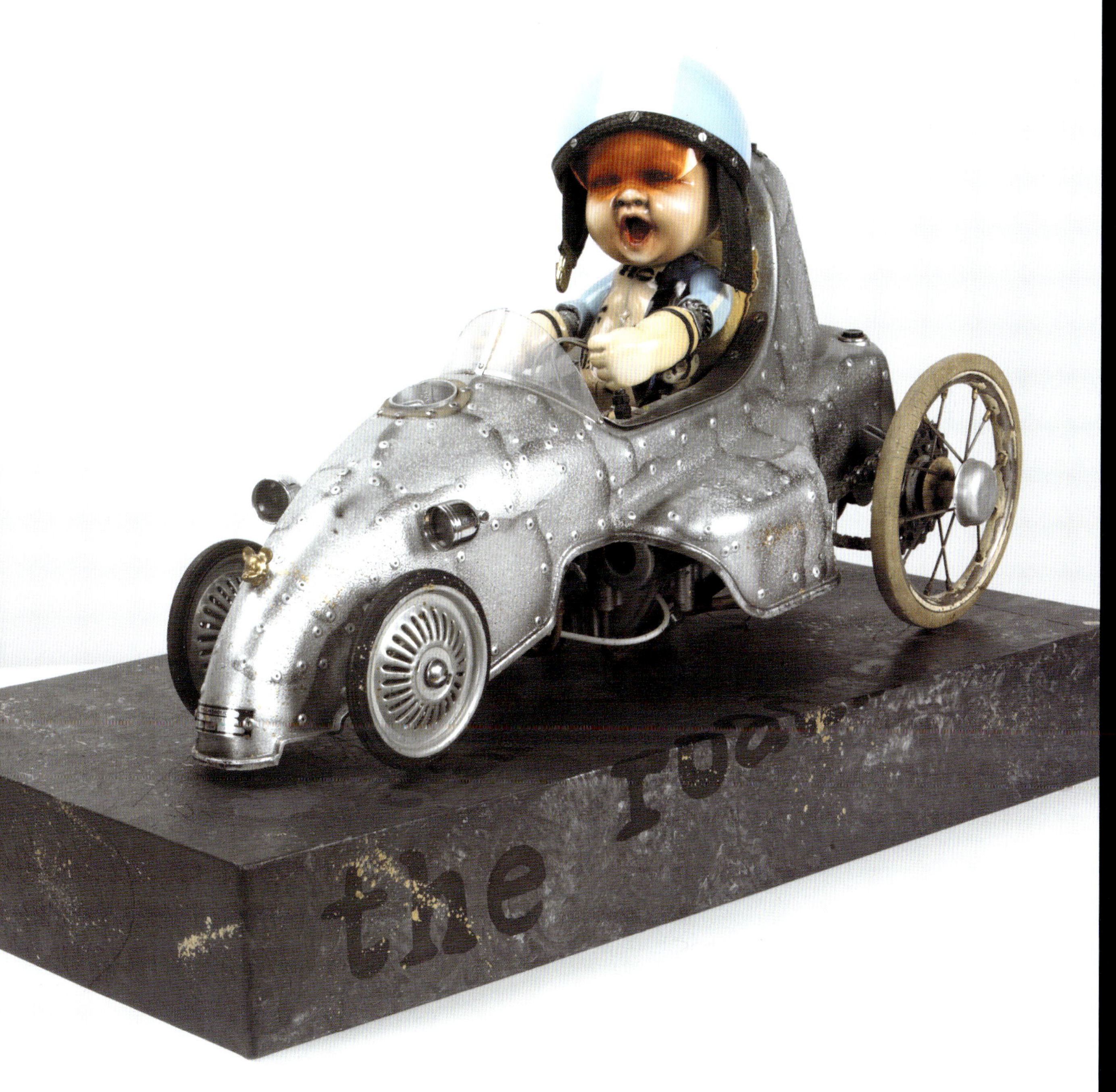

the road

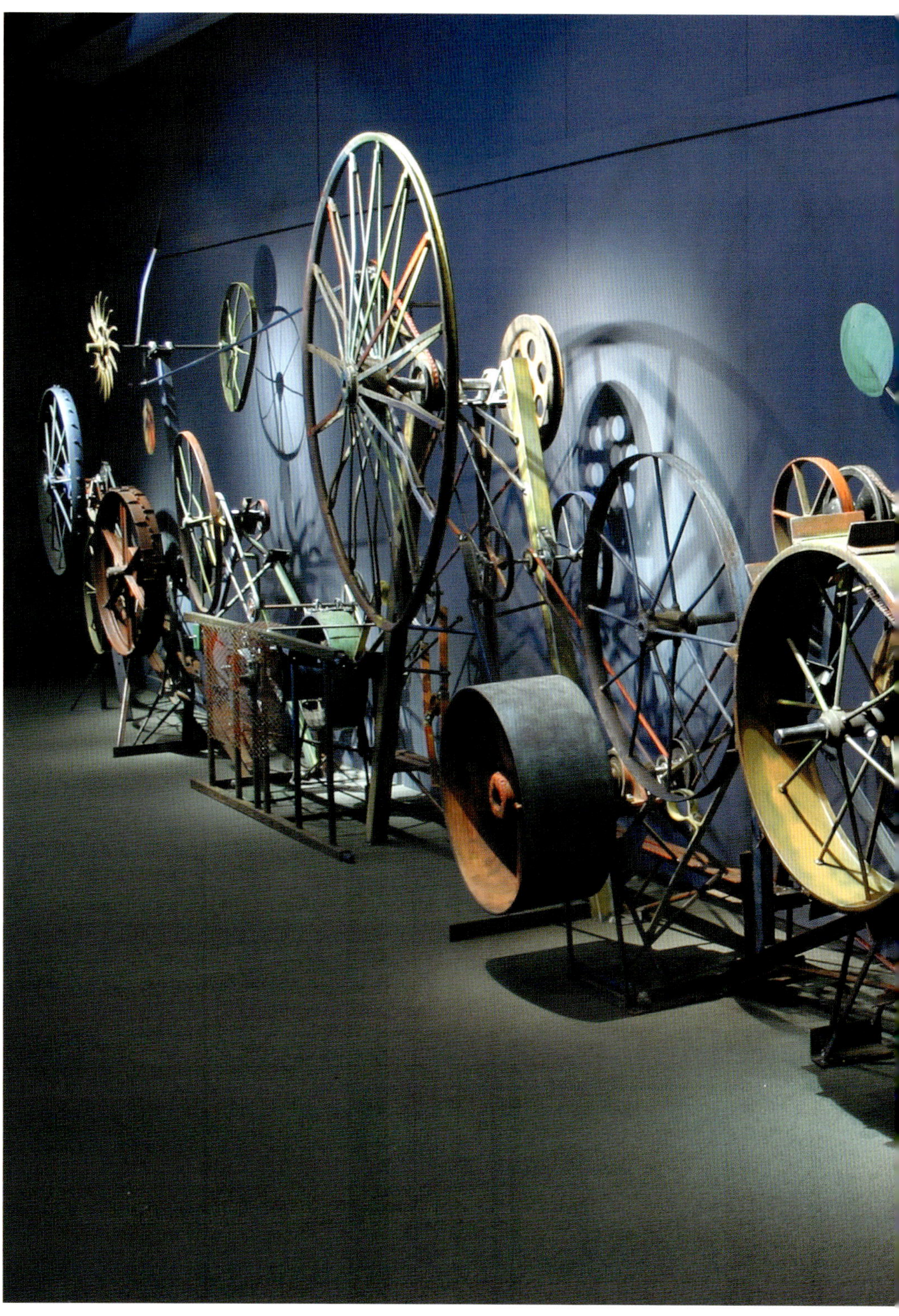

Driving Force – 40'8" x 3' x 1' (2006)

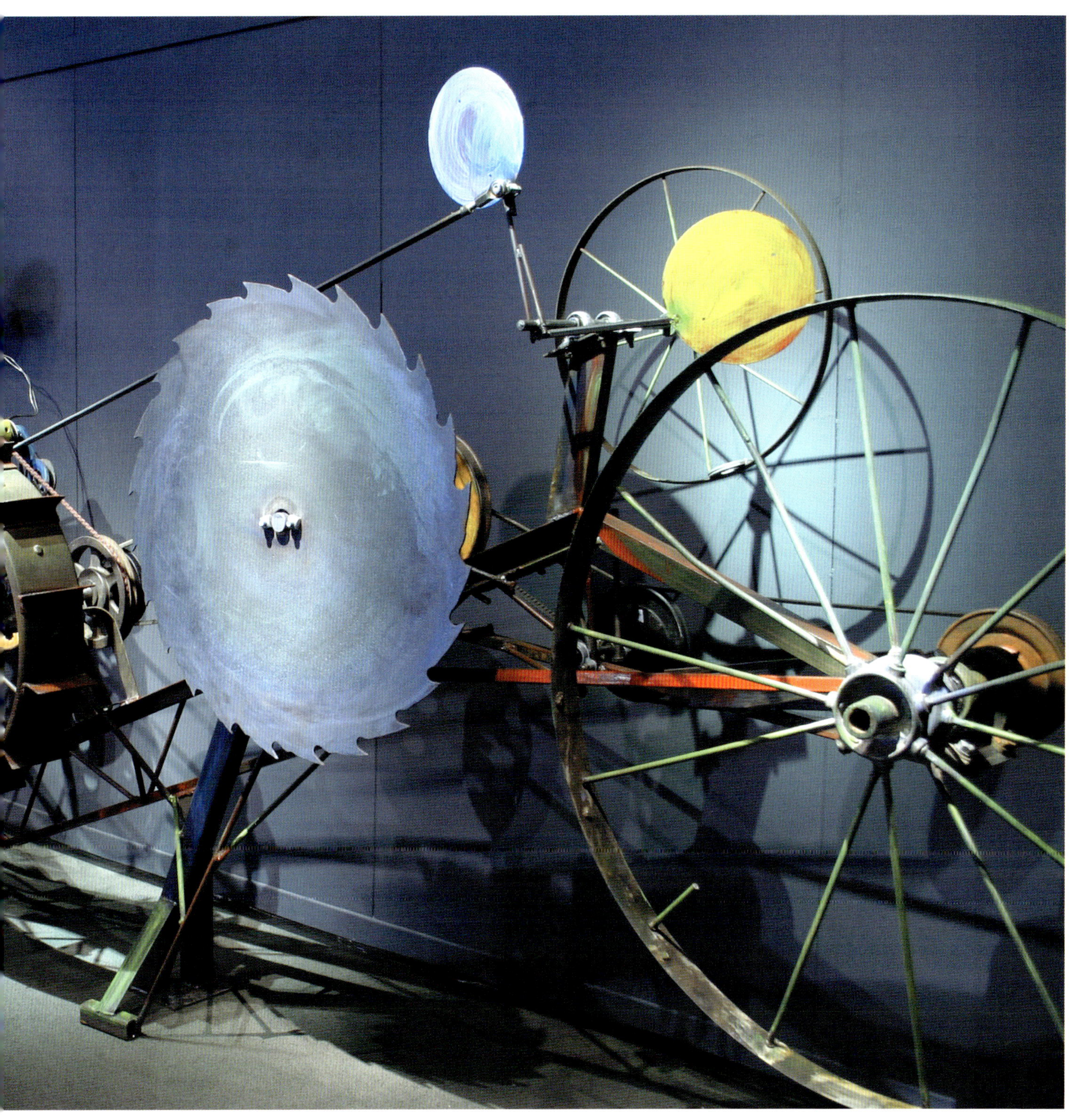

ANDREW**SMITH**

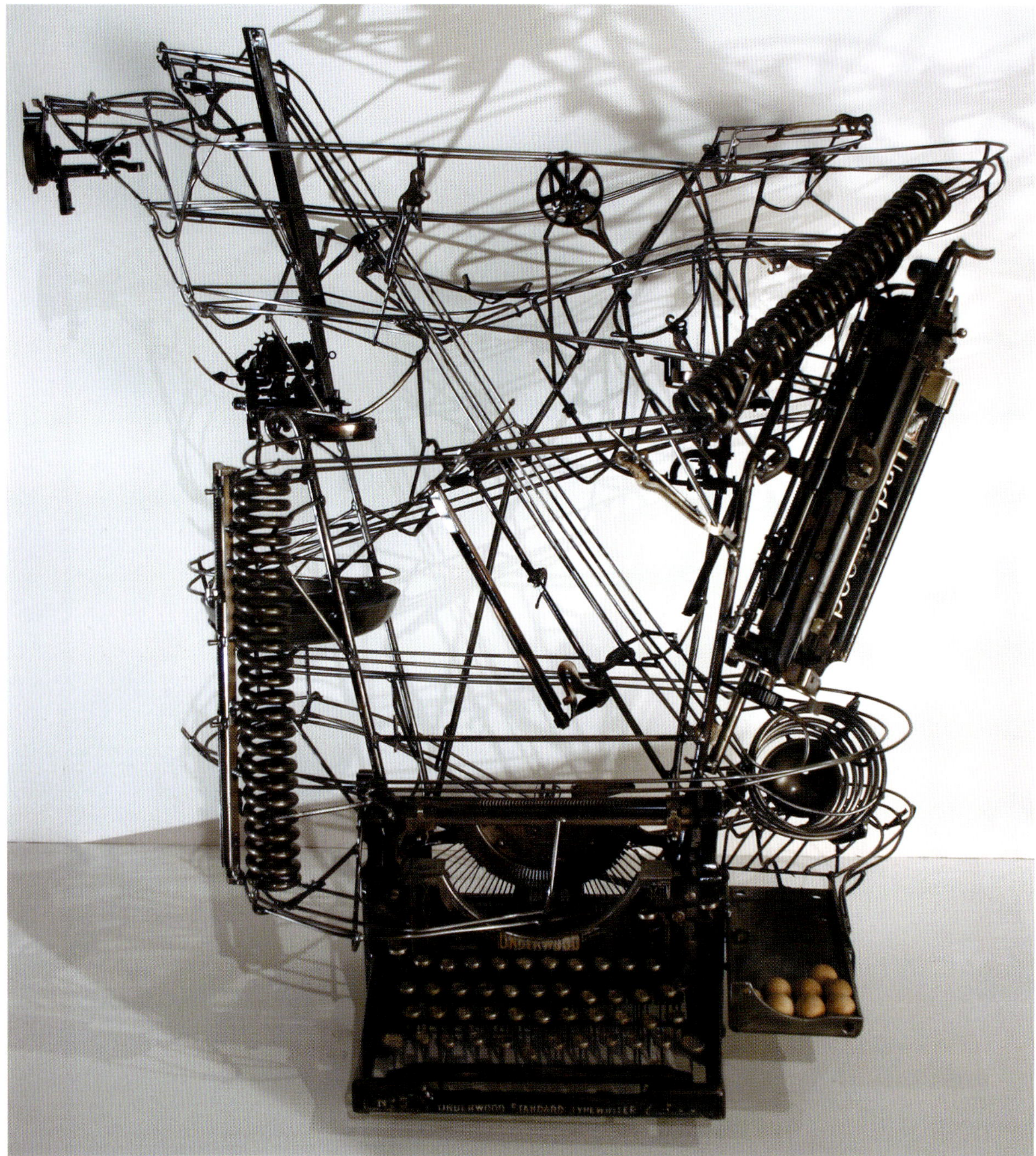

Andrew **Smith**

Andrew Smith's intricate sculptures meld industrial motifs with organic elements to present works of fascination and fancy. His art seems to be a rediscovery of life's simplicities. Smith's sculpture has quickly gained national attention through various exhibits and commissioned works. In 2007, he was approached by the National Inventors Hall of Fame to exhibit his work in the show "Art of Invention, Invention of Art," located at the US Patent and Trademark Office Museum in Alexandria, Virginia. The largest work in the show is titled *Driving Force* and is a forty-foot-long kinetic sculpture that incorporates a series of large, brightly colored wheels and shapes, all powered by a single motor.

Smith has built a reputation on creating objects of curiosity. Yet, he retains the ability to create sculptures on a small scale. It is this wide range that has exposed Andrew to so many different types of projects and experiences in his career. His works include elements such as a water cylinder with a pod-like shape rising and falling as it fills with air, or sculptures that launch smoke rings across the room, or even a "tornado in a can." His works seem to grow as they are being built, in a "form follows function" sort of way. Young and old alike are continually drawn to his work.

Smith was born in 1978 and raised in Highland, Utah, the son of a well-known and highly respected sculptor and painter. Growing up in this environment gave him a wide exposure to the world of art. At age 21, Andrew began to seriously pursue his interest in sculpture. It has been described as a "celebration of curiosity." As Andrew explains, "I like to incorporate moving elements into my sculptures, something that draws people in and makes them wonder how it works. I want to encourage people to step into a new frame of mind where they can see forms and shapes in places they normally wouldn't."

Typewroller v 1.5 – *24" x 36" x 20" (2008)*

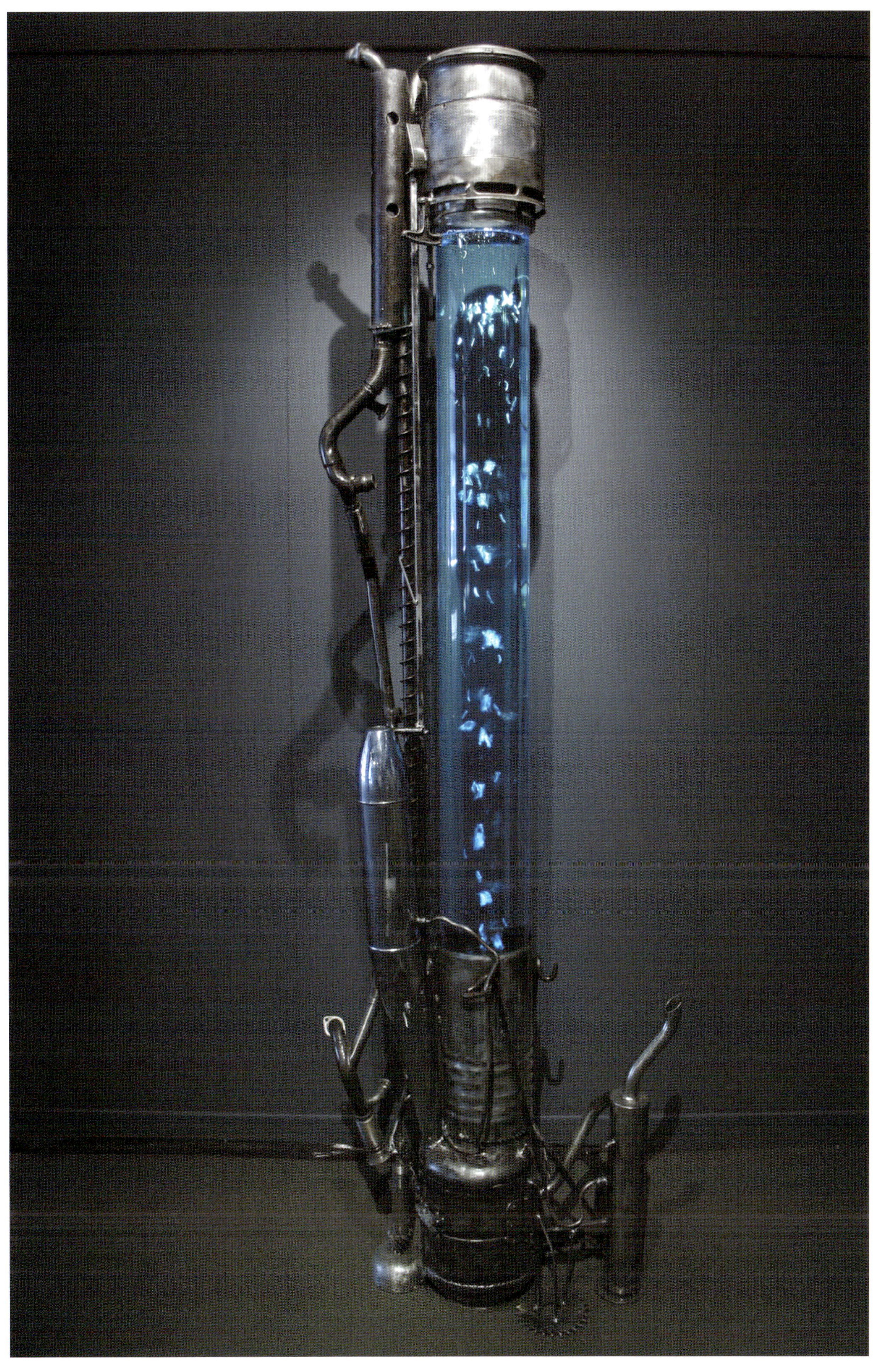

Bubbler #1 – 1'8" x 7' x 2' (2006)

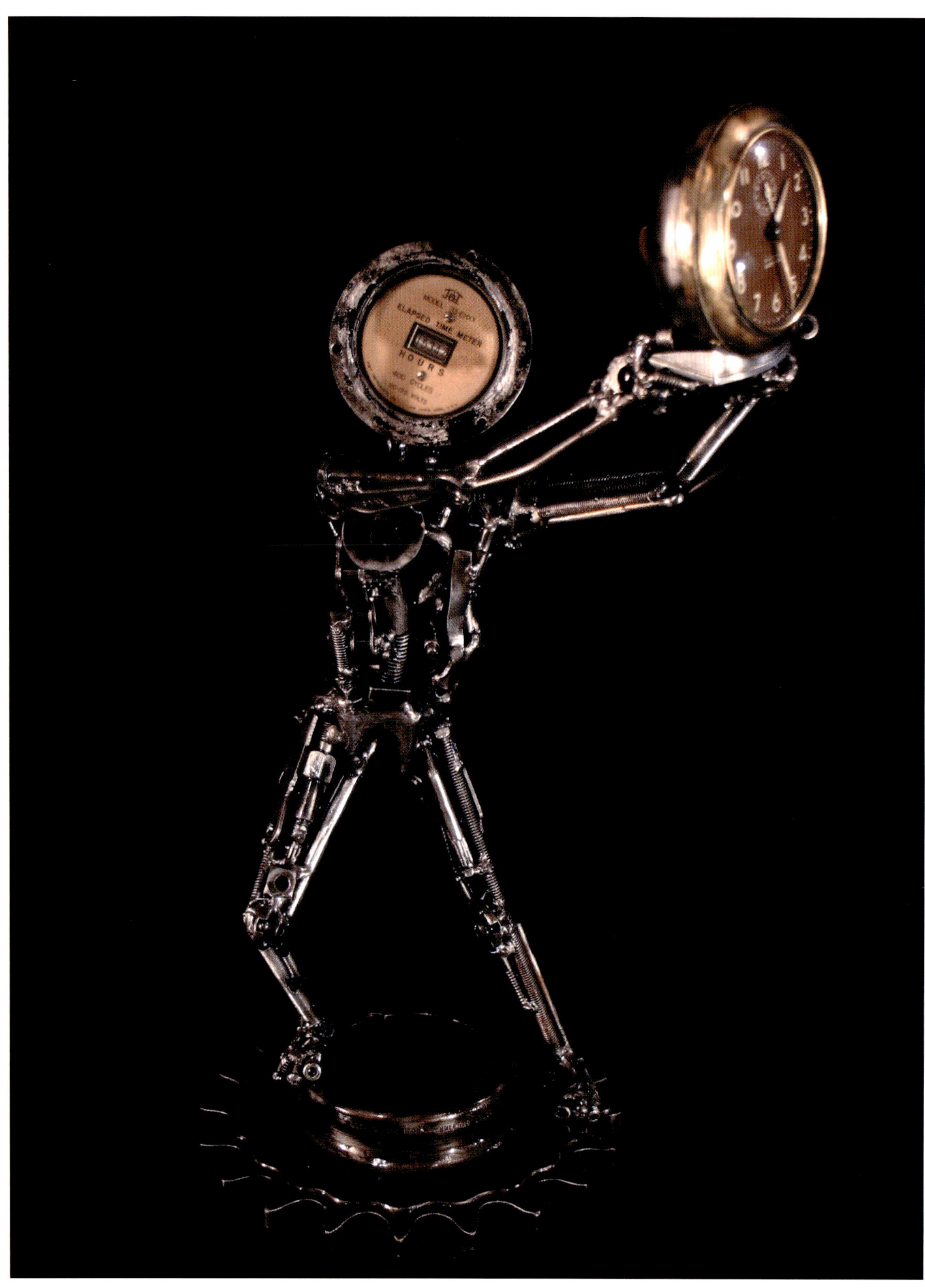

Elapsed Time – 9" x 19" x 12" (2008)

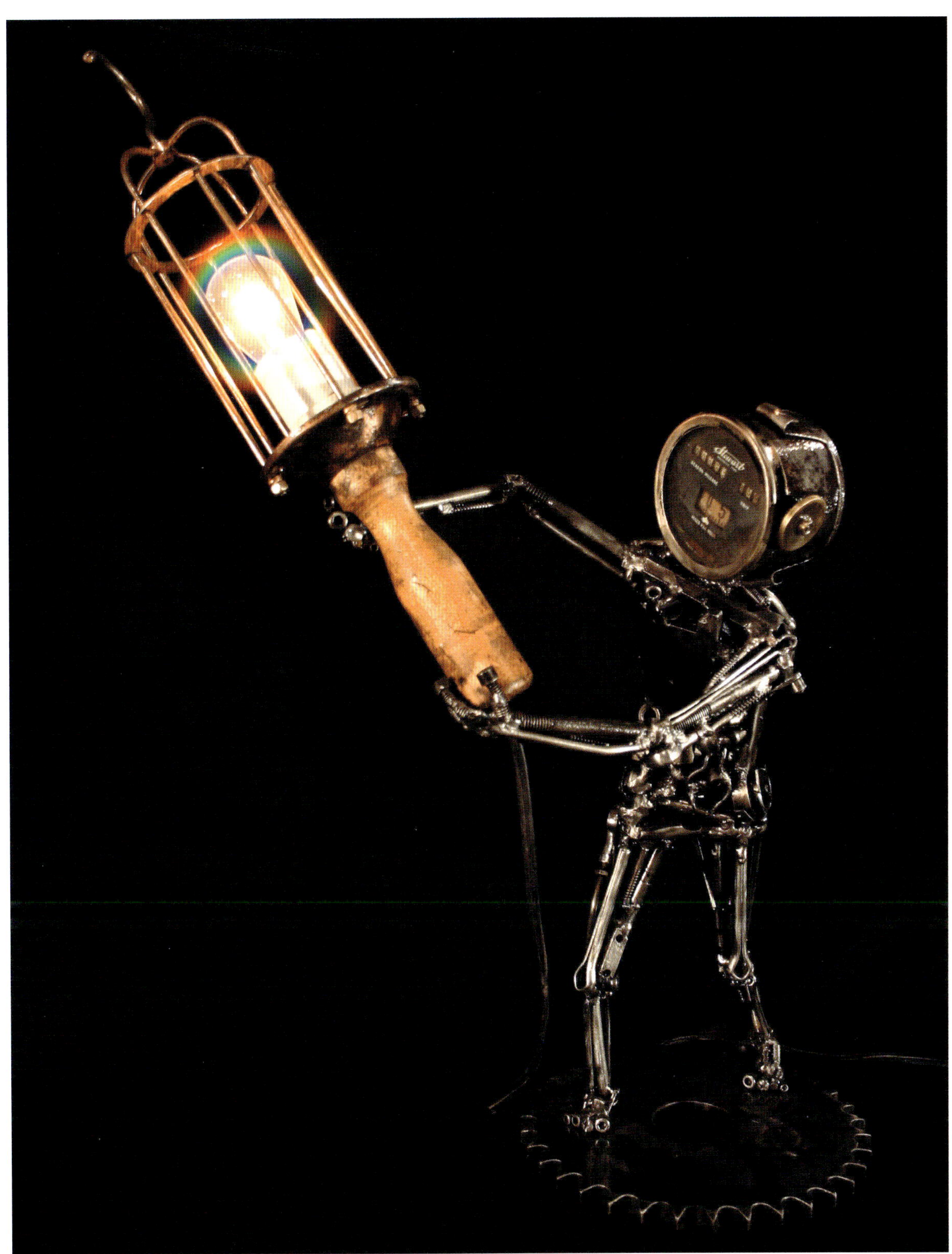

Left in the Dark – 18" x 24" x 16" (2008)

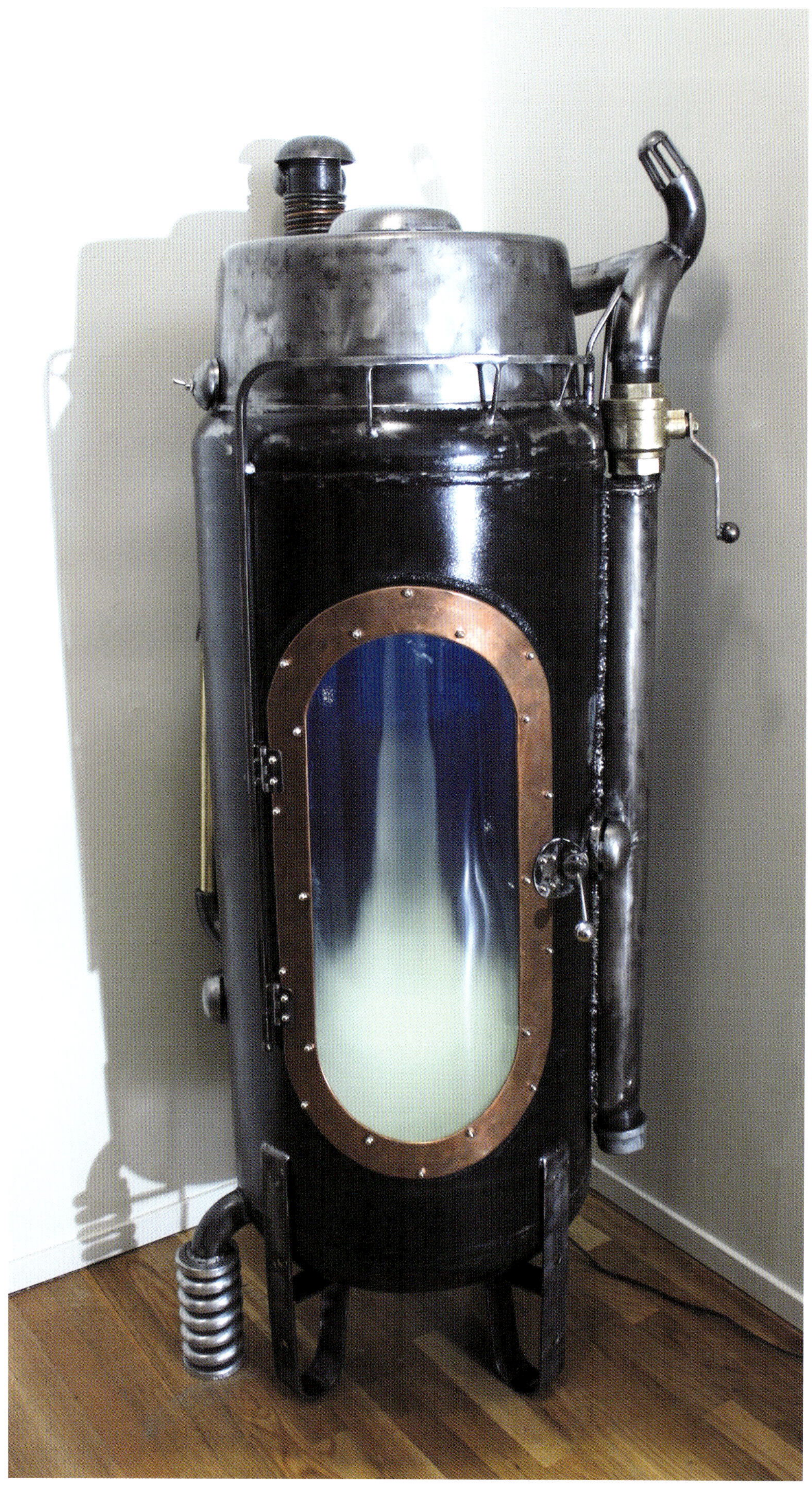

Tornado II – 2' x 5'6" x 2'

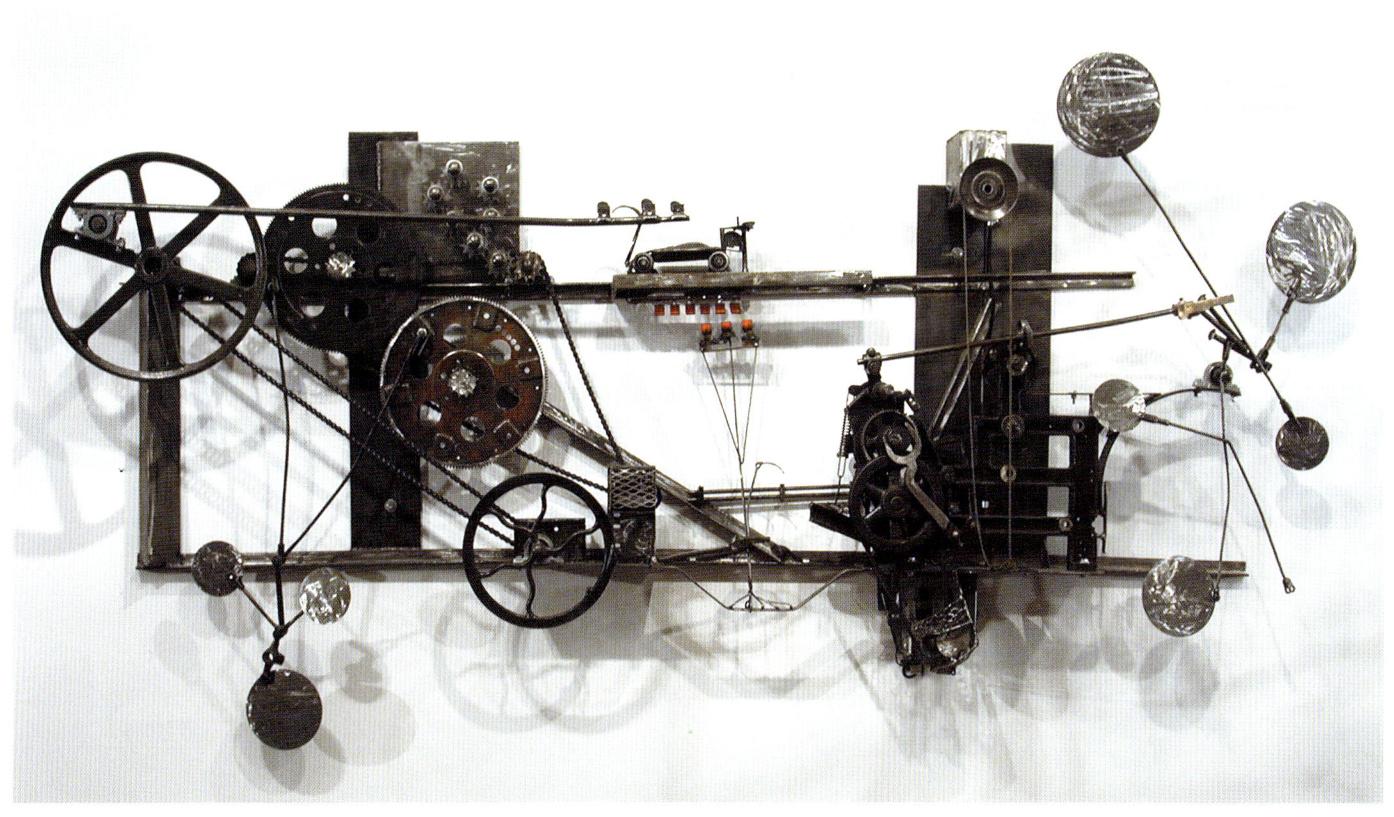

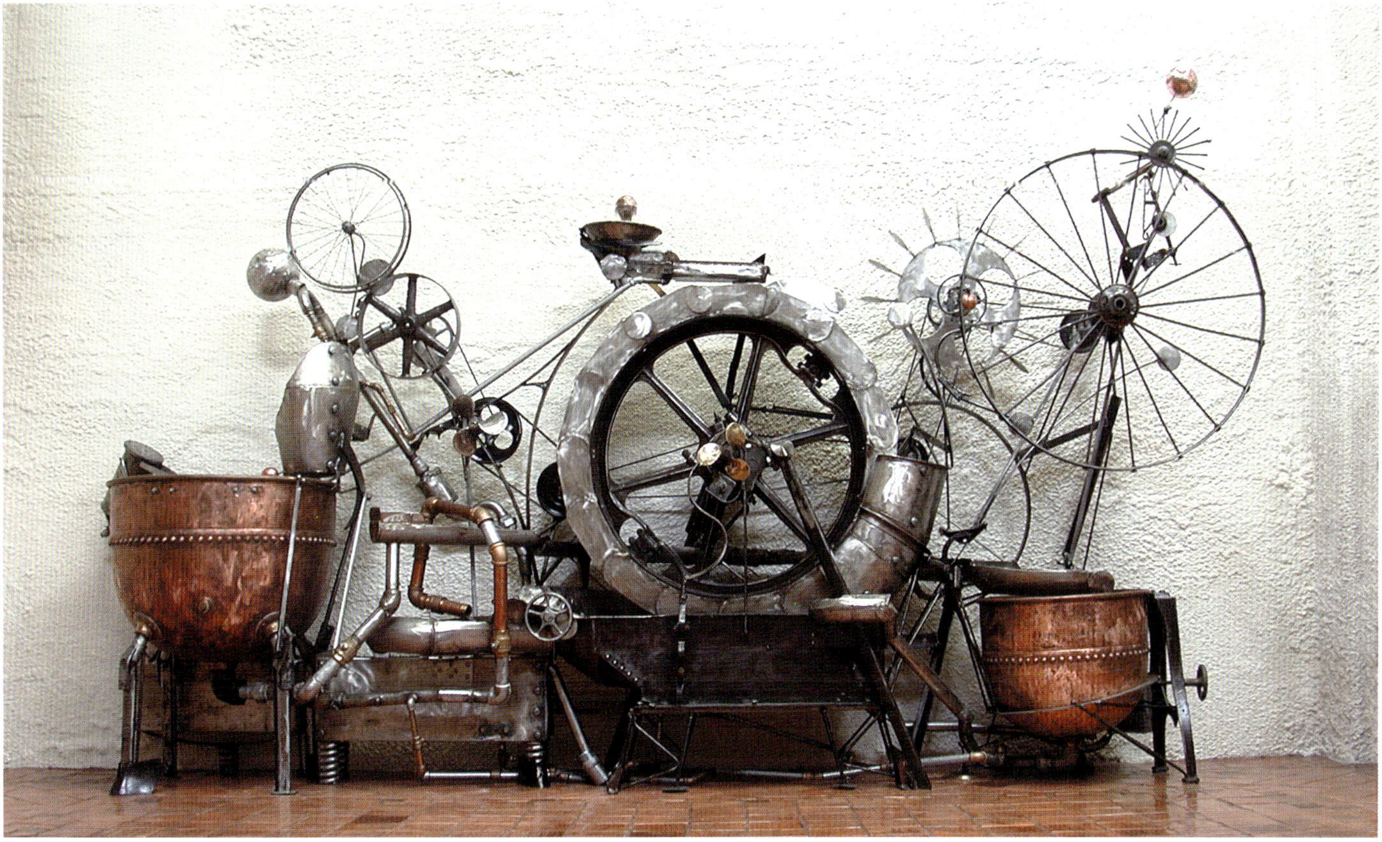

Geared Up – 9'4" x 5'4" x 1' (2001) (top)
Moon Pool – 14' x 8' x 4' (2004) (bottom)

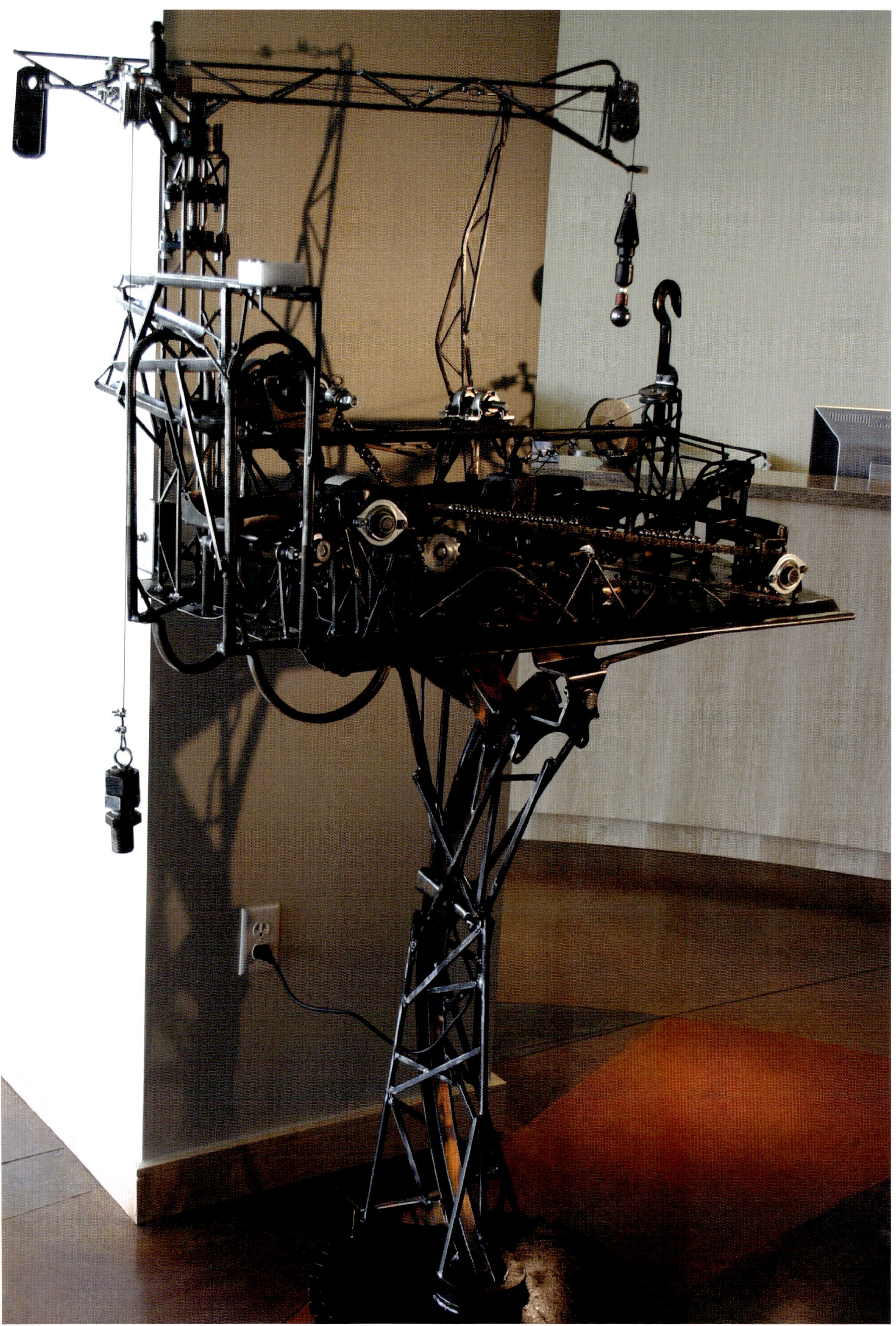

Nine to Five – 42” x 72” x 32” (2007)

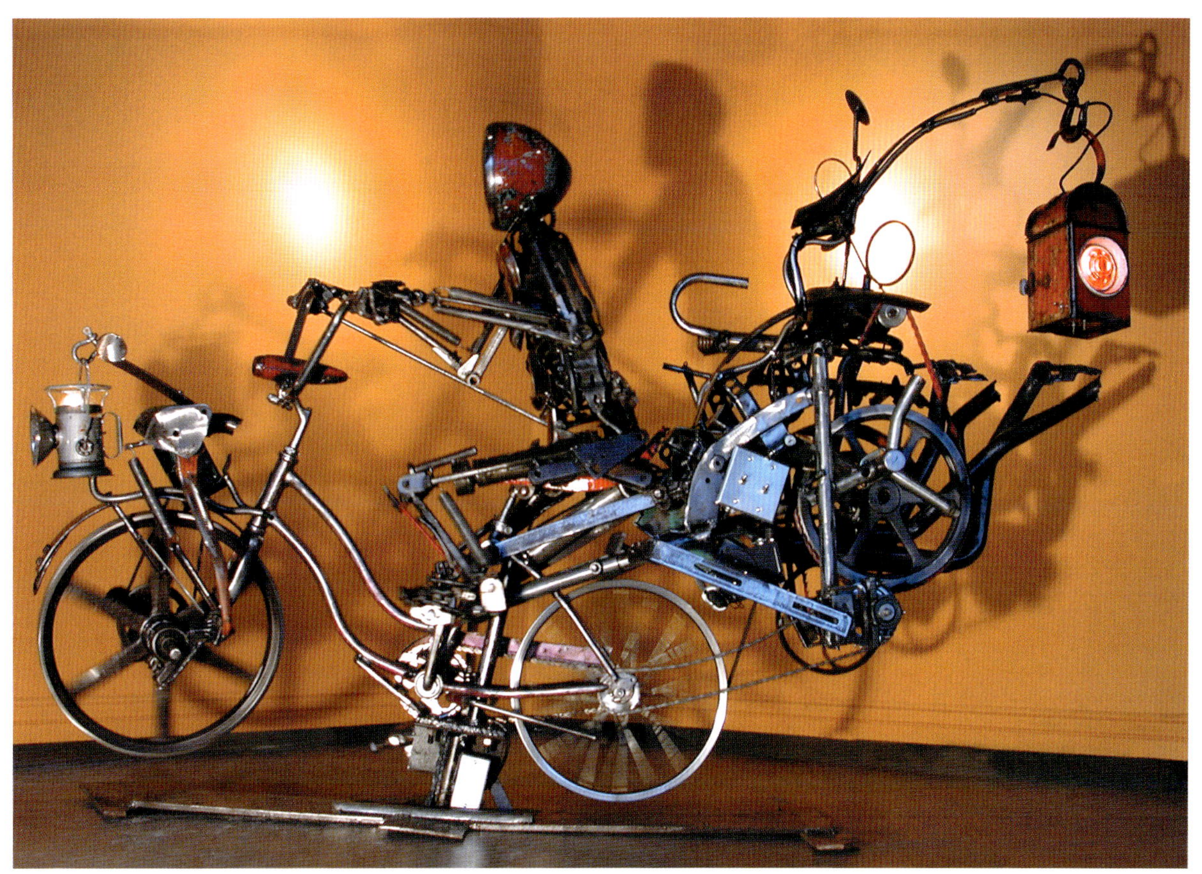

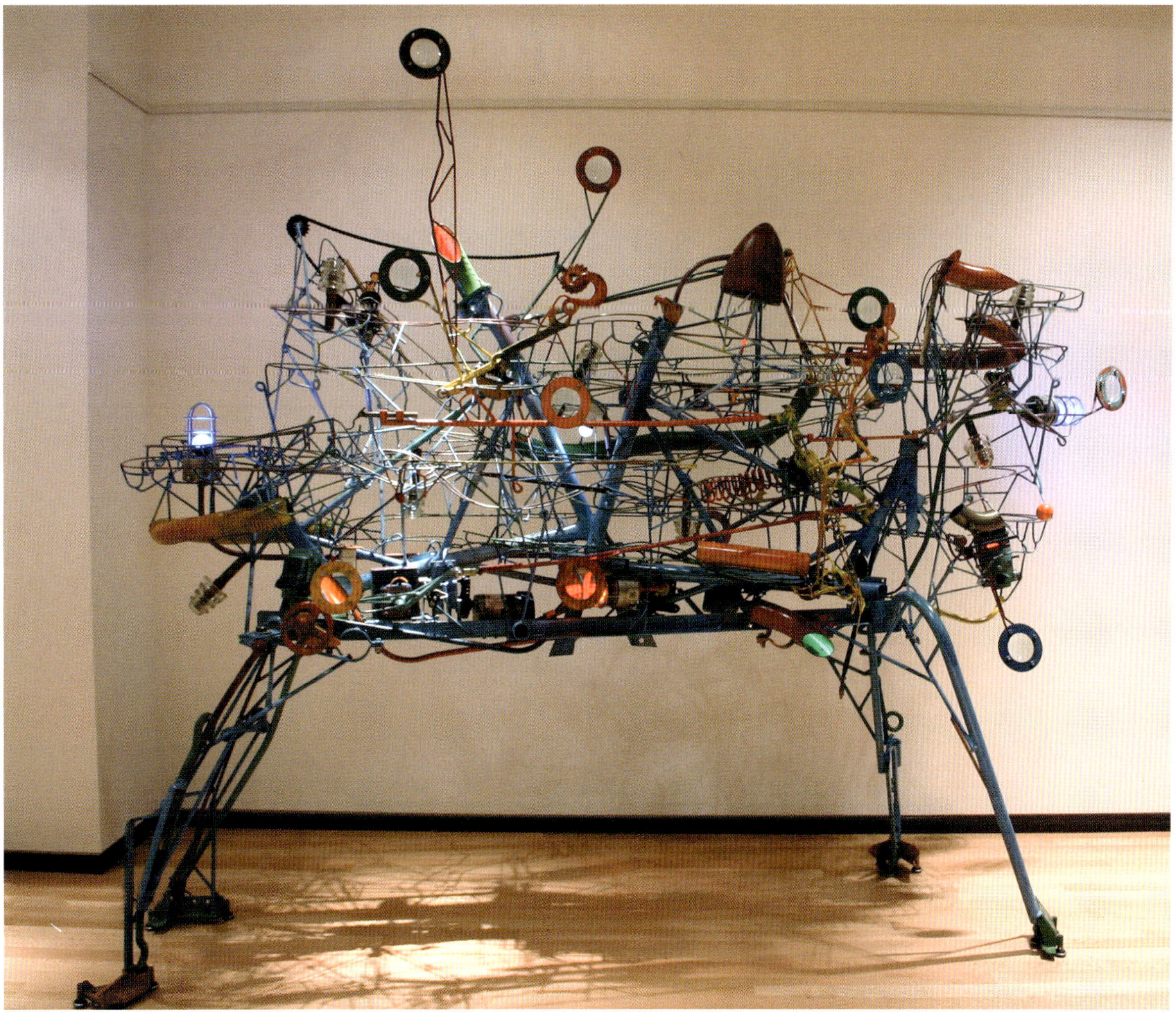

Long Road Ahead – 8' x 5'6" x 2' (2002) (top)
High Rise Billiards – 9' x 8' x 4' (2007) (bottom)

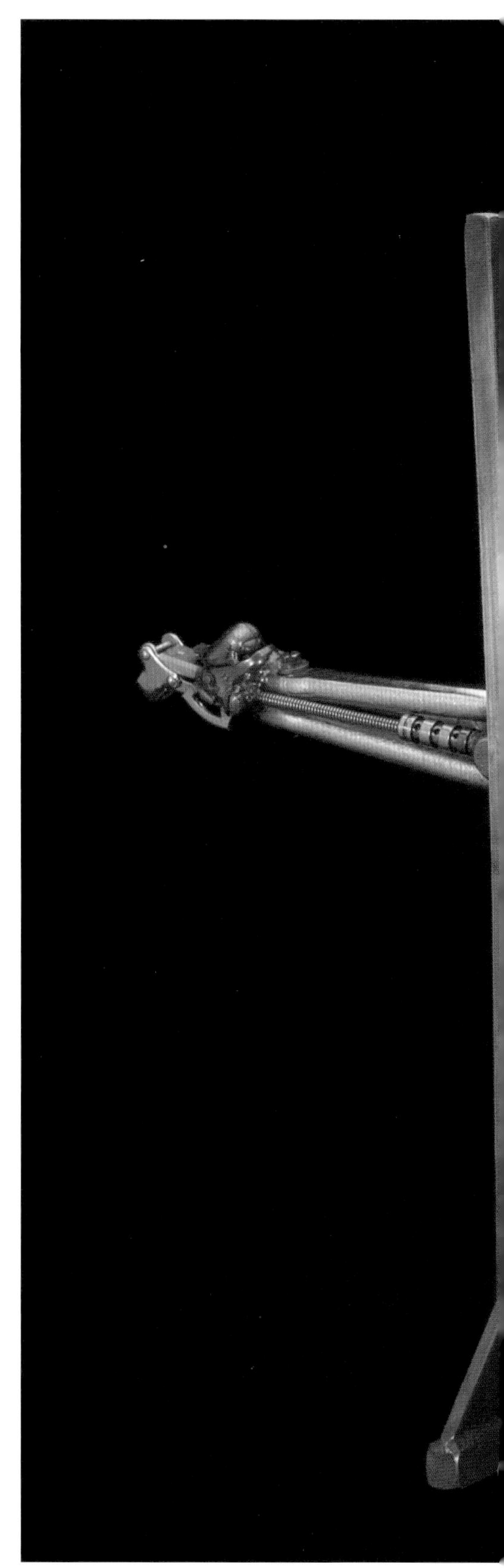

LEWIS**TARDY**

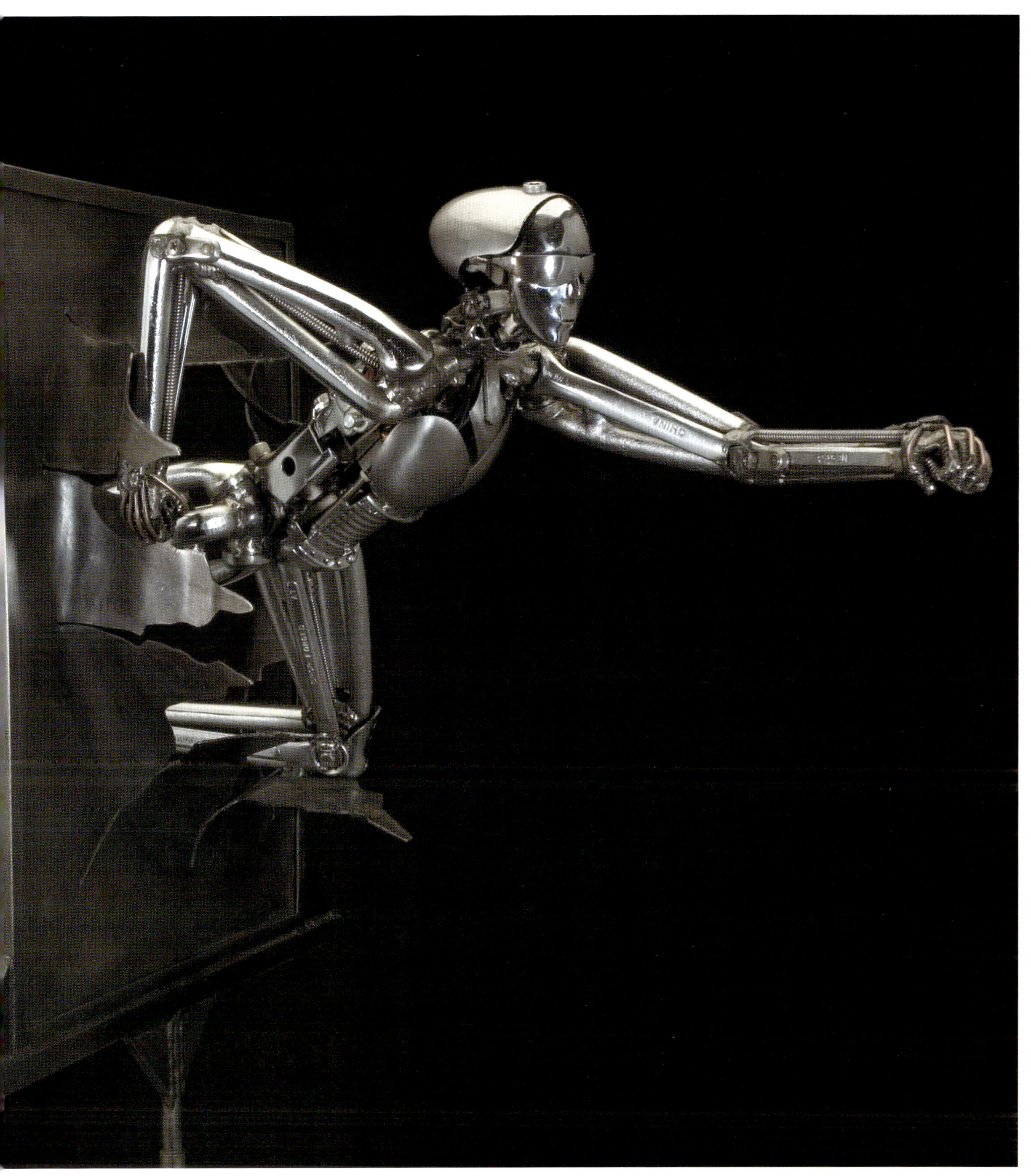

Breaking Through – 15" x 20" x 10" bicycle parts, wrenches, and surgical tools (2007)

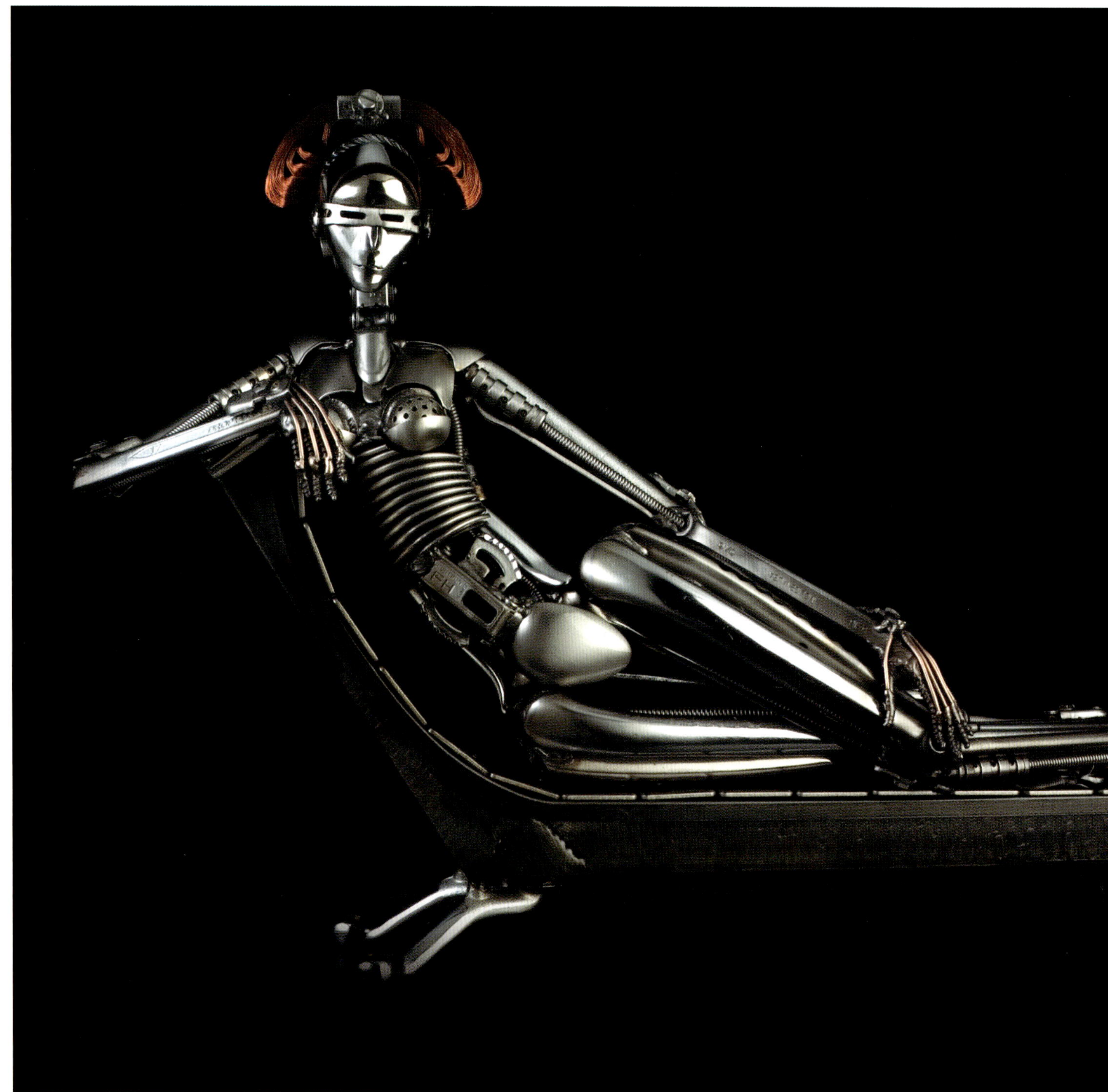

Lewis **Tardy**

The biomechanical styles of Lewis Tardy's sculptures have evolved throughout a lifetime of experiences, creating life and motion out of static scrap metals.

"Growing up, art wasn't necessarily emphasized in my family, but somehow it took root. Most of my eight siblings had a considerable amount of talent. We all spent quite a bit of time sketching and drawing to entertain ourselves, as well as being a bit competitive about it too. As a kid, I liked drawing cartoons, planes, and cars. Later, I began to focus on the human form. Along with that, I had an early introduction to things mechanical. My father was a Mr. Fixit guy and a service repair manager for a company manufacturing the 'old style' adding machines. As a young kid, he used to keep my brothers and me busy disassembling the un-repairable examples of these contraptions. I was fascinated by the complex engineering, the gears and linkages that made these things work. Later in my teen years I moved into working on cars and playing with the internal combustion engine. I believe my interest in things mechanical, combined with the love of illustrating the human form are most significant to the evolution of my art today."

Reclining Woman – 10" x 20" x 6" bicycle parts, wrenches, stainless steel, and copper wire (2008)

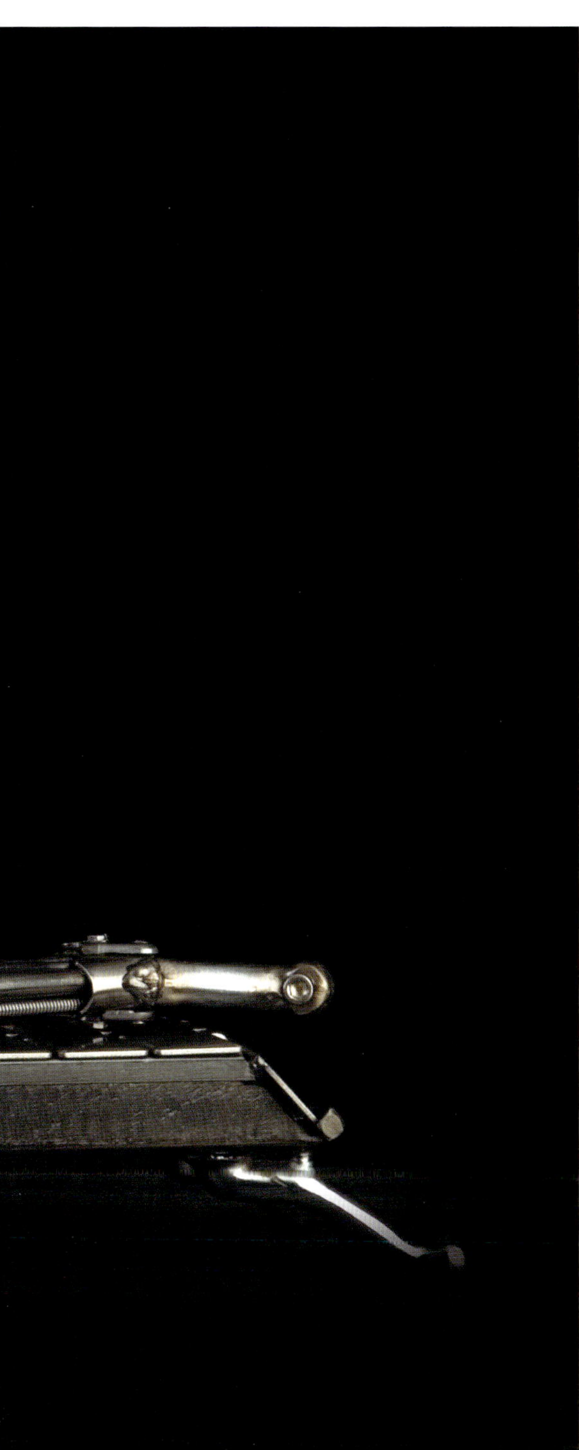

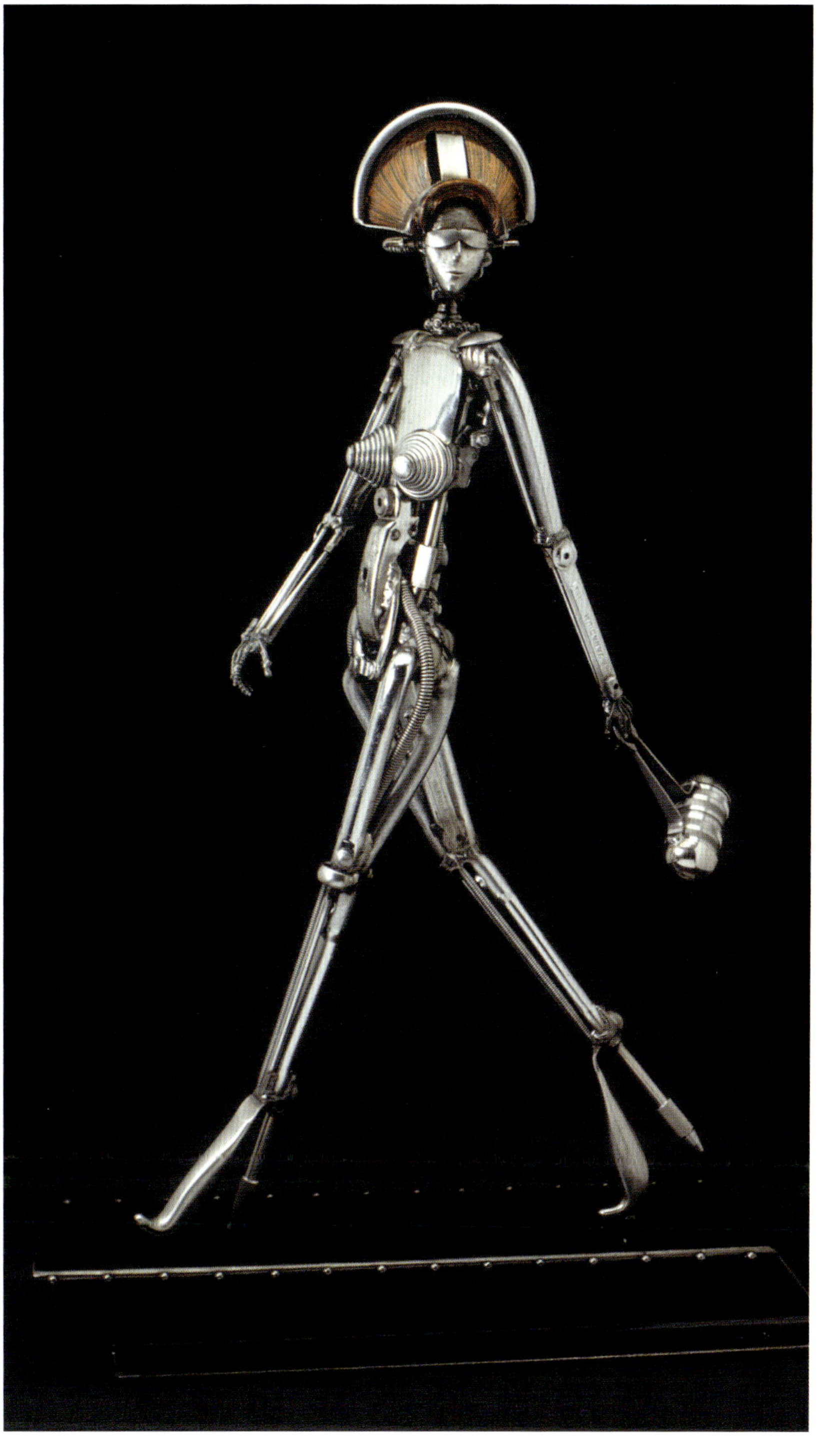

Kalamazoo, Michigan, has been home since 1965. Shortly after graduating high school, Tardy began studying graphic arts and photography. He has always been drawn to the visual arts, but with a technical element. While looking for his calling, Tardy stumbled upon it in 1985, and began working as an assistant in a sculpture studio. Creating fantastic visions with the tools and processes he was already comfortable with helped Tardy to answer the call. He spent several years there, learning technique and developing his own vision before striking out on his own.

The combination of found-steel materials coupled with a mixture of commentaries including sexuality, levity, motion, strength, and attitude result in this unique expression of Tardy's vision. Significant inspiration comes from shapes and designs discovered within the found parts and materials, which take shape in human and animal subjects alike. On many occasions, a single shape or part will inspire and become the building block of a whole Idea.

Cyber Strut – 30" x 24" x 7" bicycle parts, wrenches, stainless steel, and copper wire (2001)

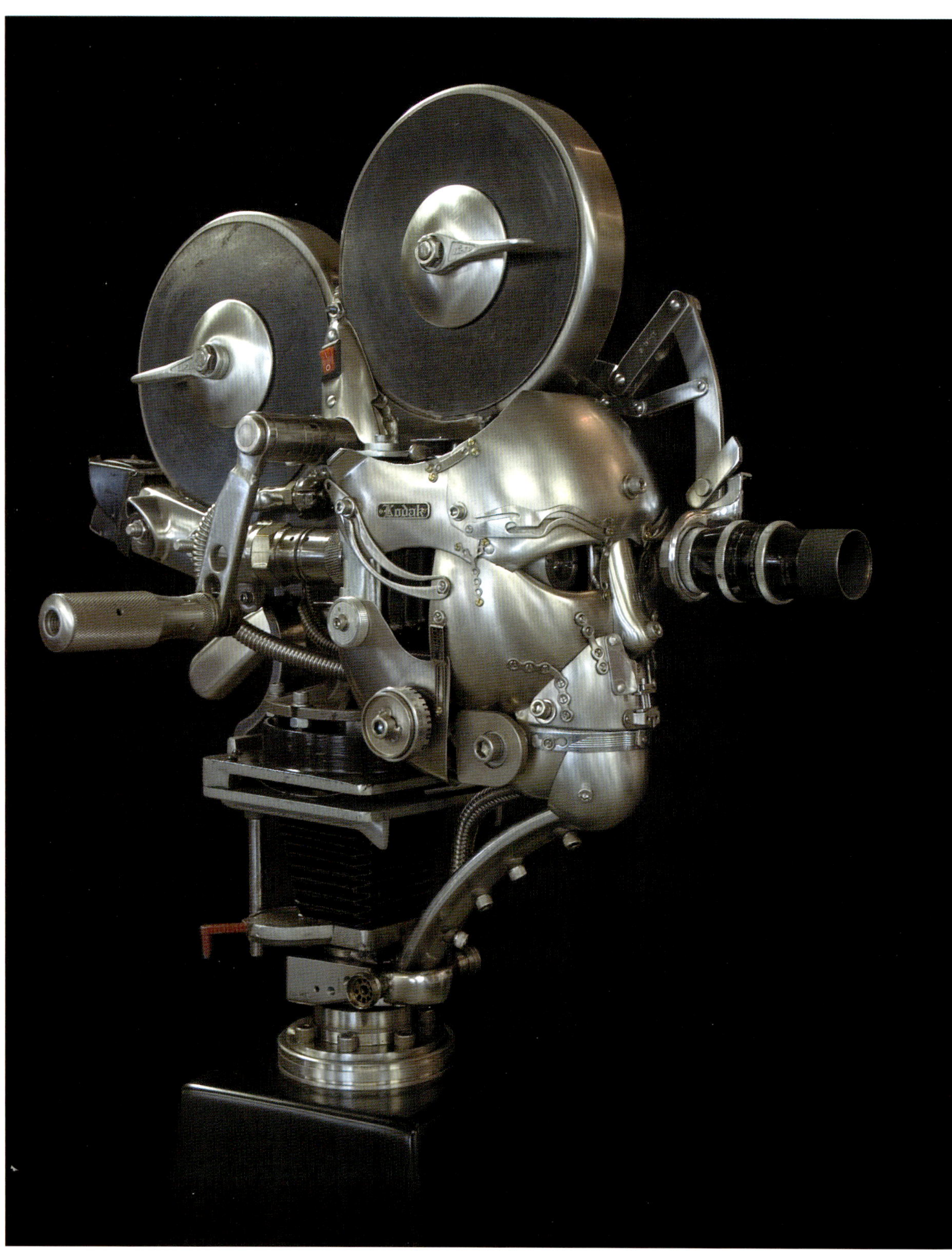

Celluloid Consciousness – 23" x 21" x 13" camera parts, titanium implants, and stainless steel (2008)

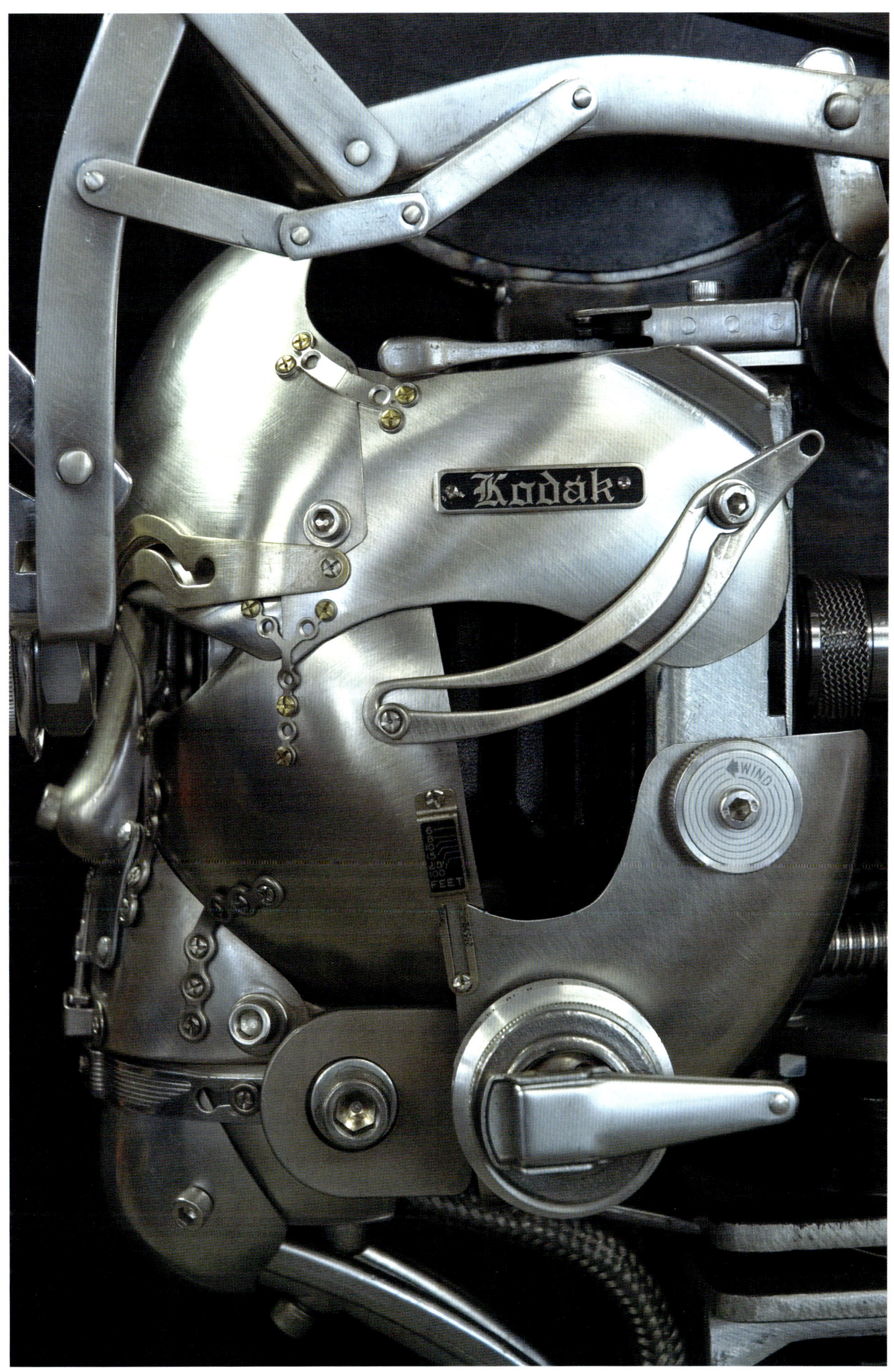

Celluloid Consciousness – detail

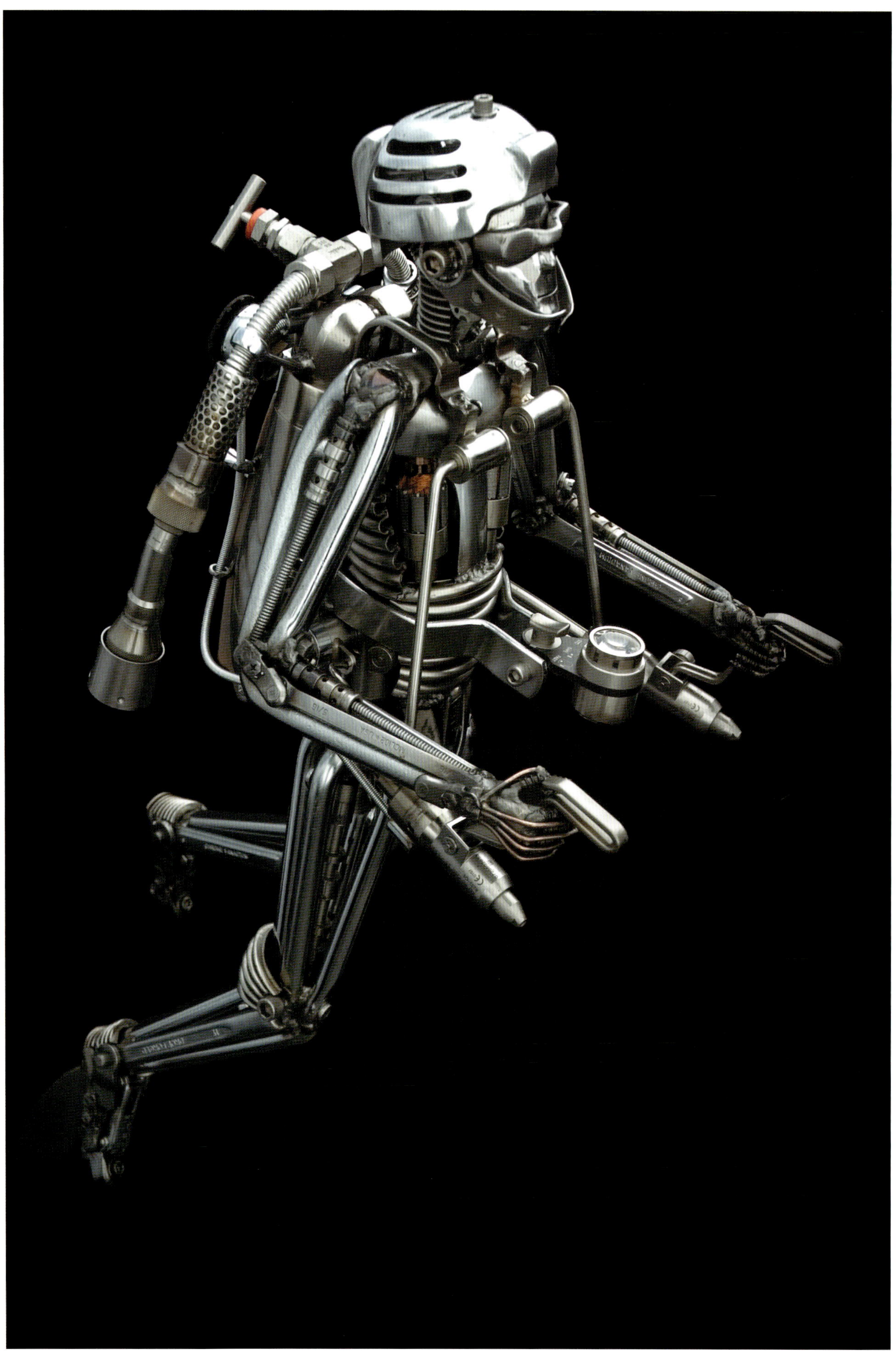

Globe Trekker – 36" x 25" x 12" bicycle parts, wrenches, surgical tools, and electric drill housing (2008)

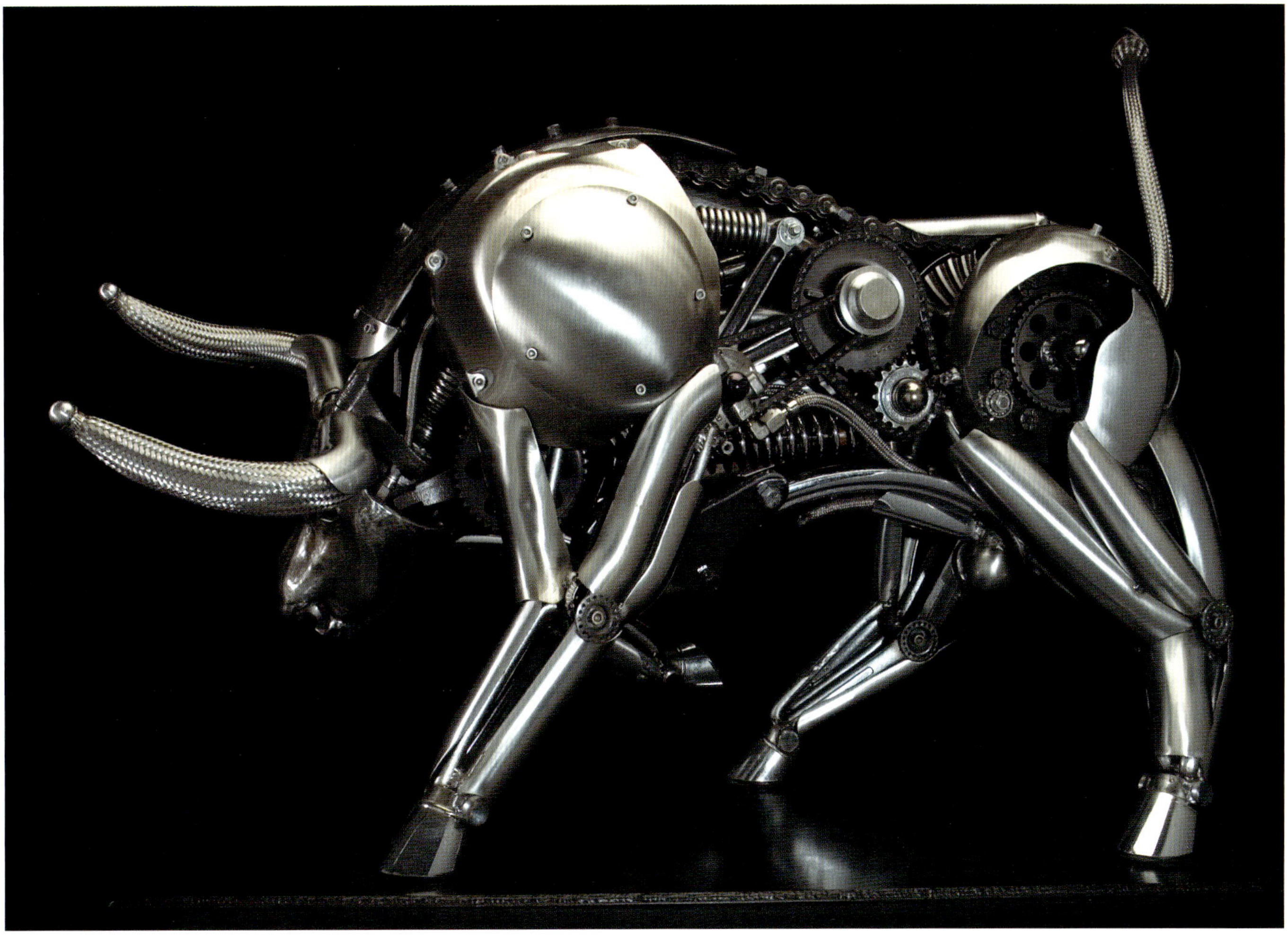

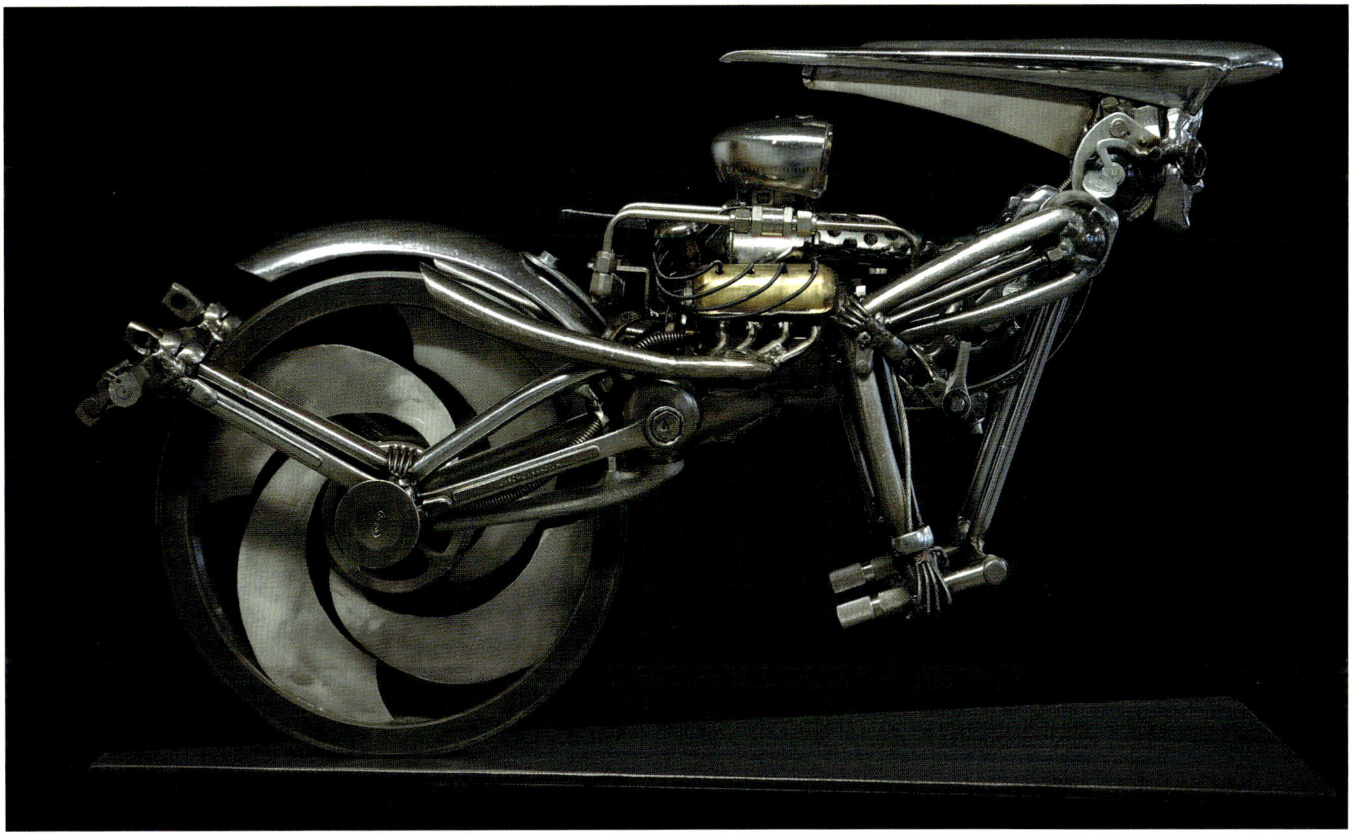

Raging Bull – 30" x 40" x 20" bicycle, motorcycle and auto parts, wrenches, and springs (2007) (top)
Otto – 25" x 32" x 12" bicycle, motorcycle and auto parts, wrenches, and surgical tools (2005) (bottom)

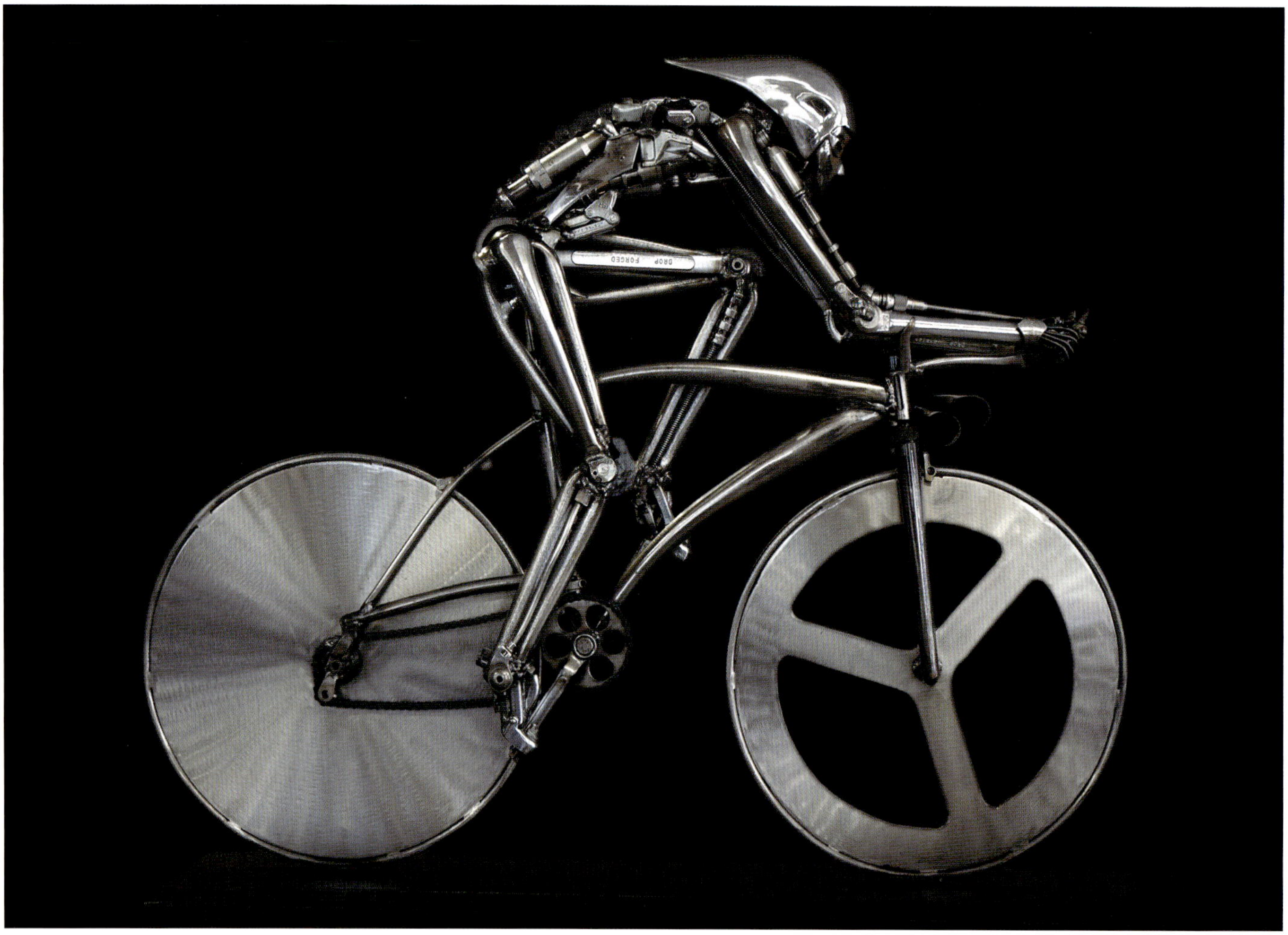

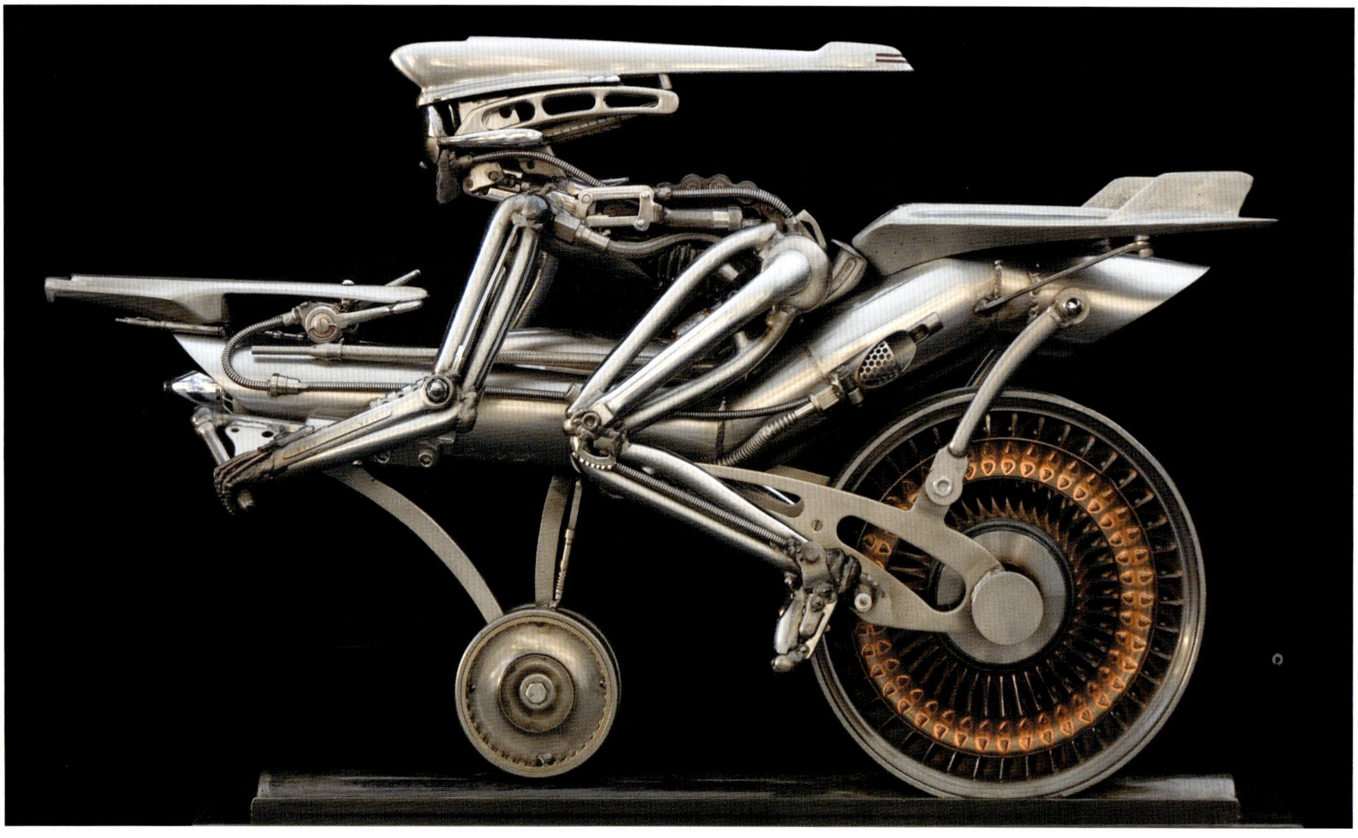

Velodrome Sprint – 22" x 30" x 10" bicycle parts, wrenches, and surgical tools (2007) (top)

Turbo – 25" x 32" x 12" bicycle, motorcycle and auto parts, wrenches, and surgical tools (2007) (bottom)

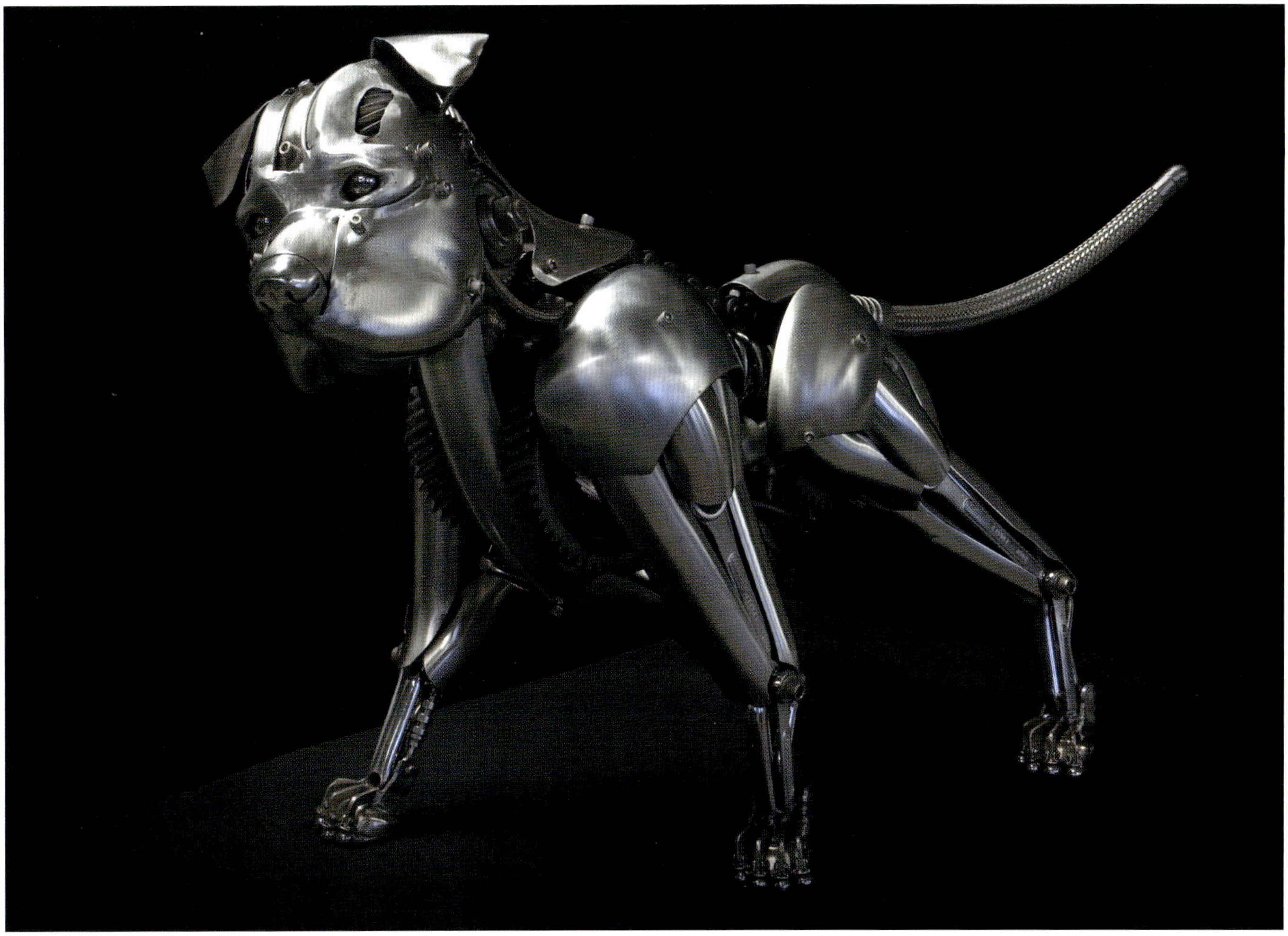

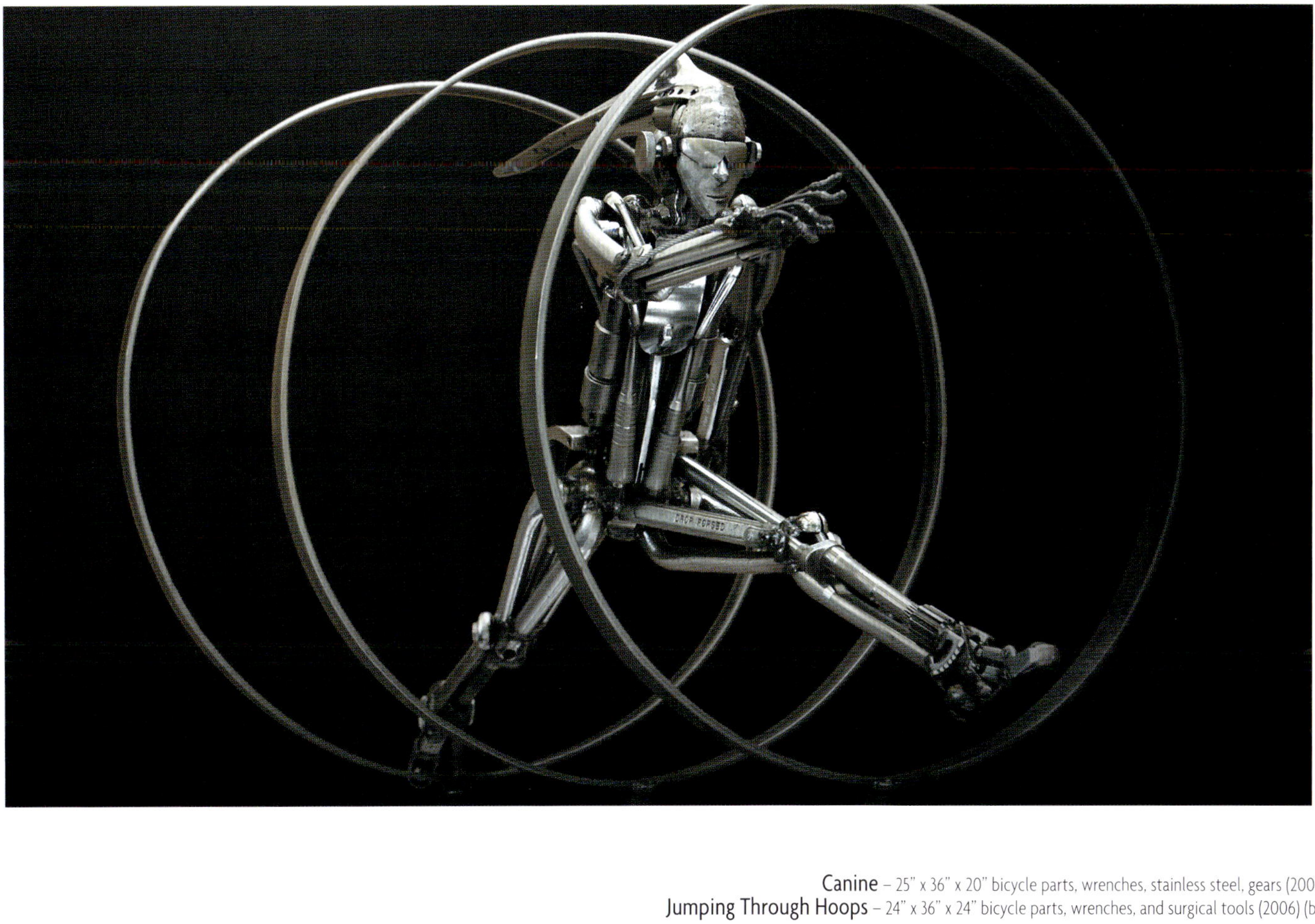

Canine – 25" x 36" x 20" bicycle parts, wrenches, stainless steel, gears (2008) (top)
Jumping Through Hoops – 24" x 36" x 24" bicycle parts, wrenches, and surgical tools (2006) (bottom)

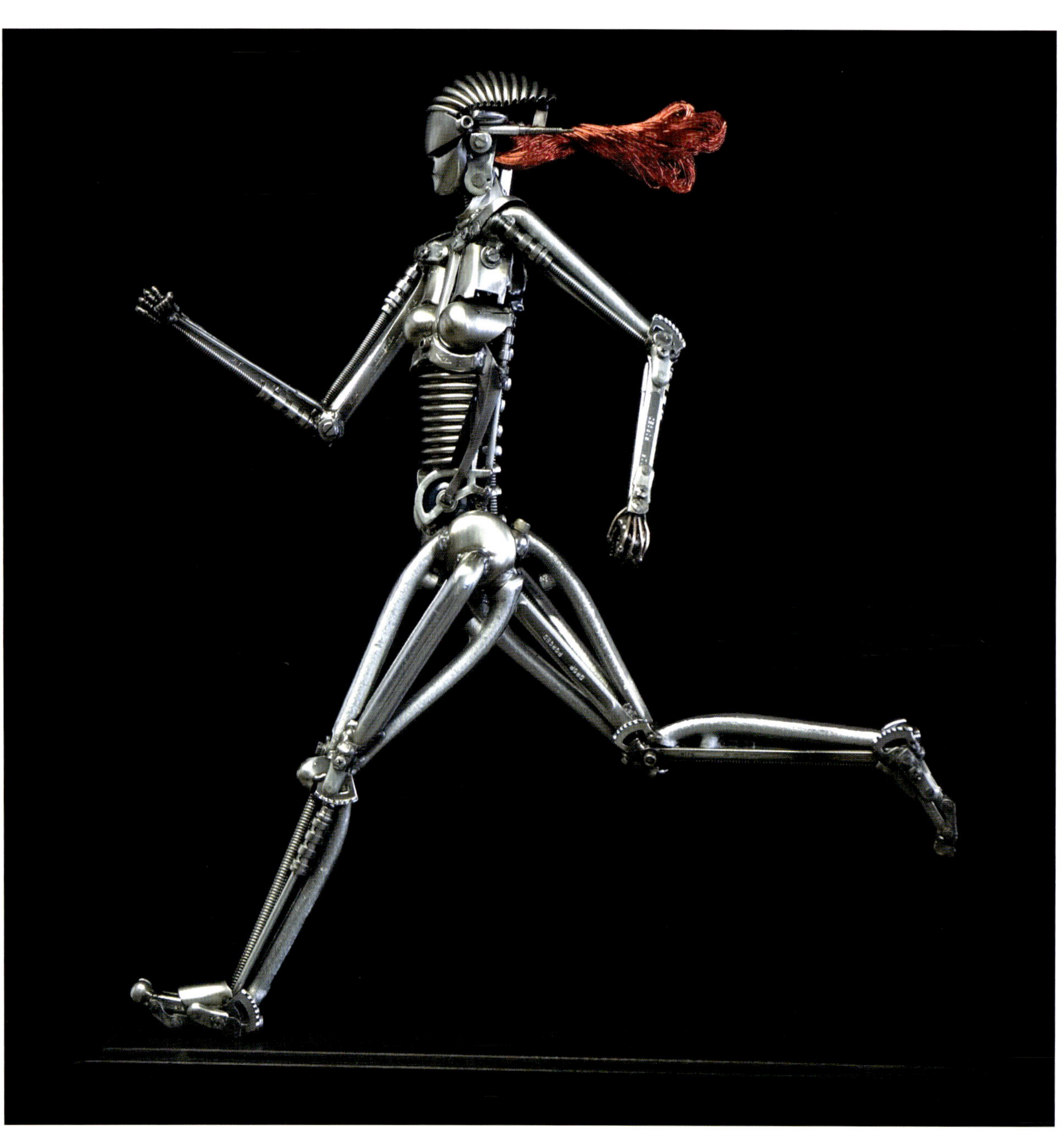

Marathon Woman – 28" x 24" x 7" bicycle parts, wrenches, surgical tools, and copper wire (2009)

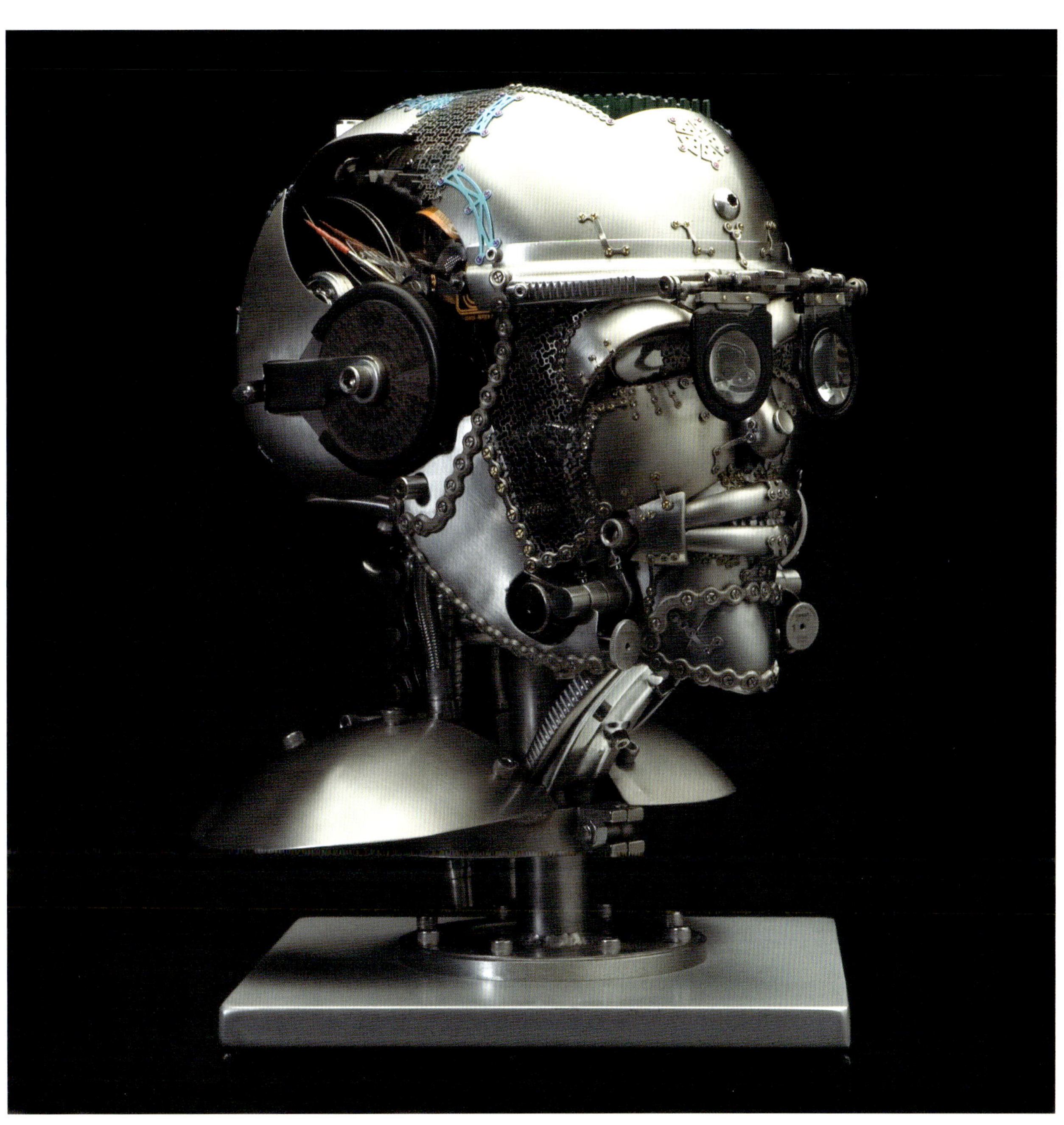

Reconstruction – 20" x 15" x 15" titanium craniomaxillofacial reconstruction plates, surgical tools, and stainless steel (2006)

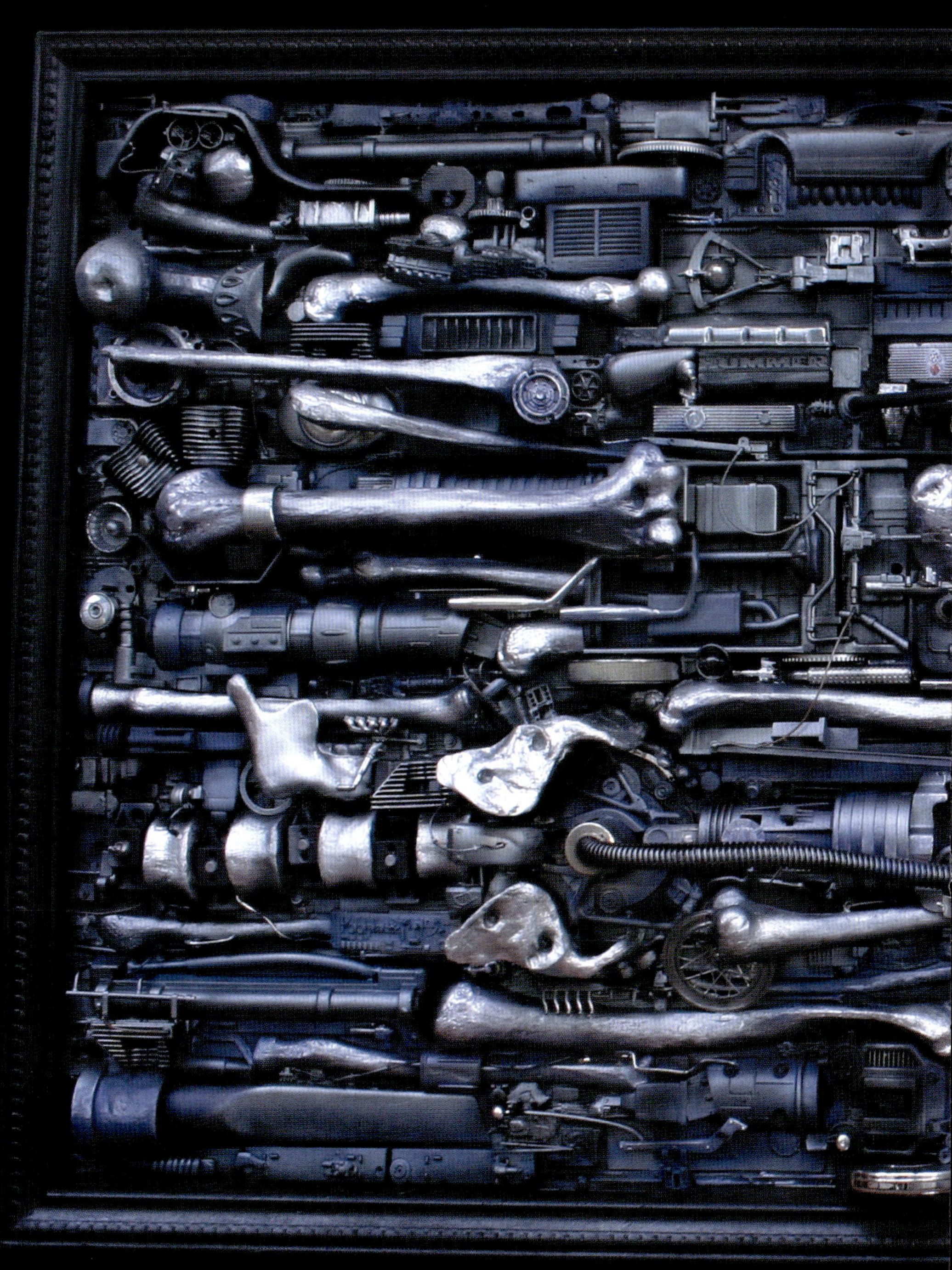

JUD**TURNER**

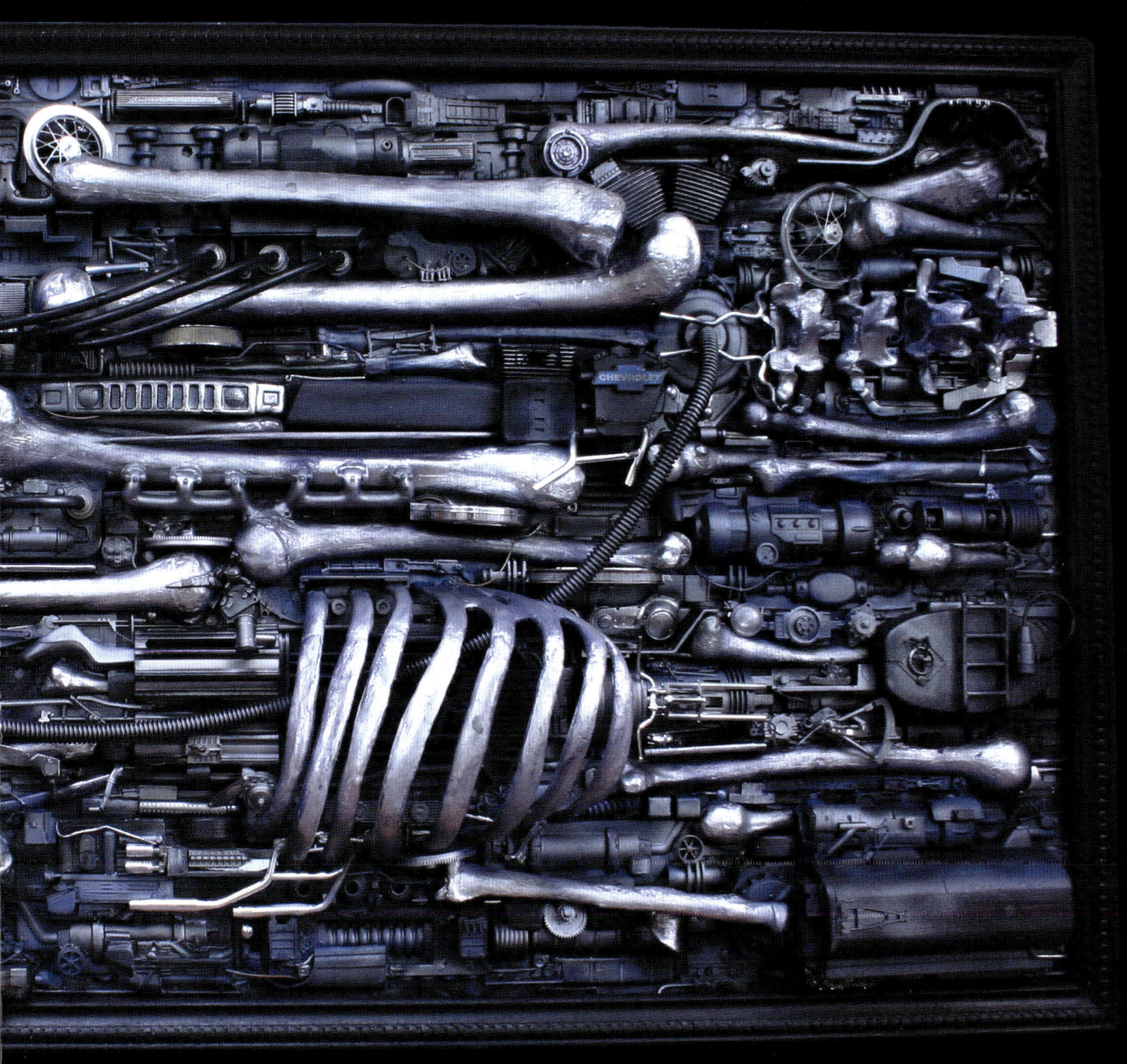

Internal Combustion – 34" x 38" x 8" mixed media assemblage (2008)

Jud Turner

Quantum physics tells us that apparently solid objects compose vast empty spaces, populated by tiny particles whose individual relationships create the whole. And that a single particle can exist in two separate places during one moment in time.

Jud Turner explores such dichotomies in his sculpture. Using welded steel and found objects, he creates artwork which embraces opposites—the tension between humans and nature, the perils of balancing biology and technology, or the combination of ancient fossils with modern machinery. He also engages contradictions by the materials he chooses—human forms that appear solid and realistic, but which were made with a delicate surface of thin wire, allowing the viewer to see through the figure, or by mixing the sense of scale in a piece using large items alongside tiny pieces.

Turner places a high value on craftsmanship and surface appearances. He tries to balance realism with a stylization that allows him the freedom to push concepts into the deepest levels of the viewer's perception. While his vision can tend towards the darker side of human nature, Turner's work is infused with a sense of humor which can make difficult subjects easier to approach.

Born in Eugene, Oregon, on November 17, 1969, a high premium was placed on education and creativity when Turner was growing up. He has always drawn, painted, and sculpted—trying to make some sort of tangible record of his experiences and impressions of the world. He received training in drawing and painting at the University of Oregon under Professor Ron Graff and the late Professor Frank Okada, both renowned artists and educators. In the early 1990s, he transitioned to sculptural works as his main artistic output, focusing on direct welded steel work and found-object assemblages.

Currently, Jud Turner lives and works in Eugene, Oregon, with his wife, Melissa, and their two cats.

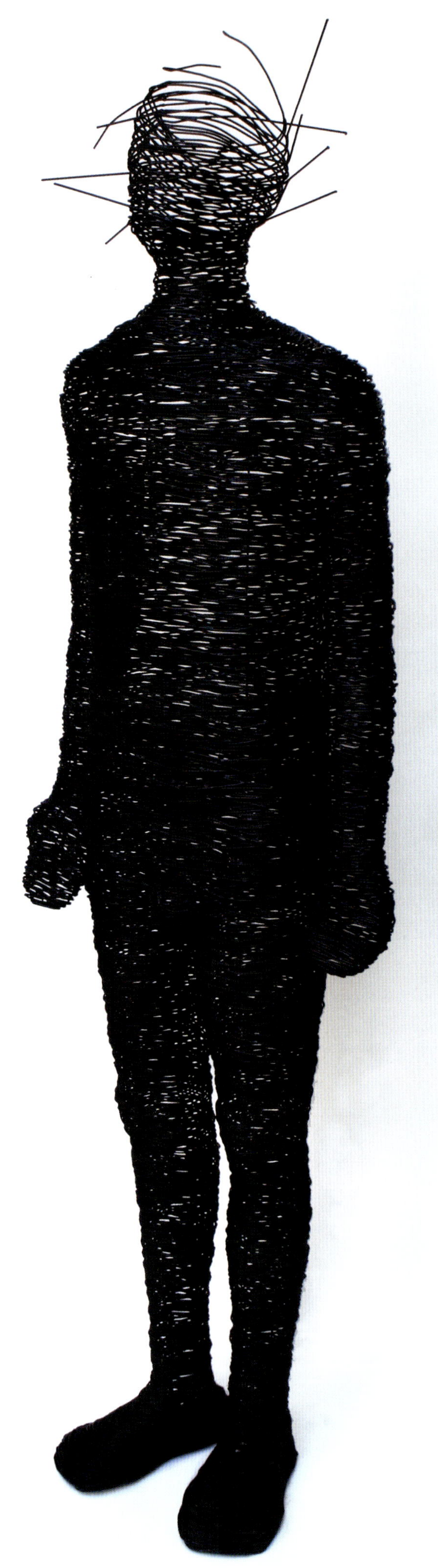

I Am – 5'10" x 2.5' x 2" welded steel 3/32 rod (2008)

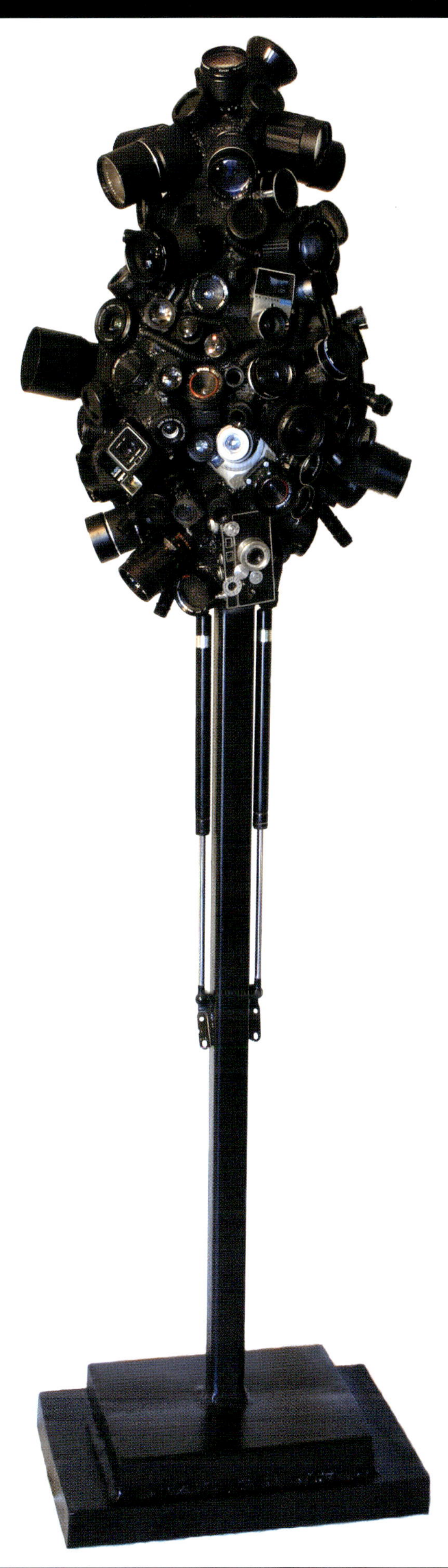

The Panopticon (War is Peace Freedom is Slavery Ignorance is Strength) – 6.5' x 2' x 1.5' found objects, welded steel, silicone, camera lenses (2006)

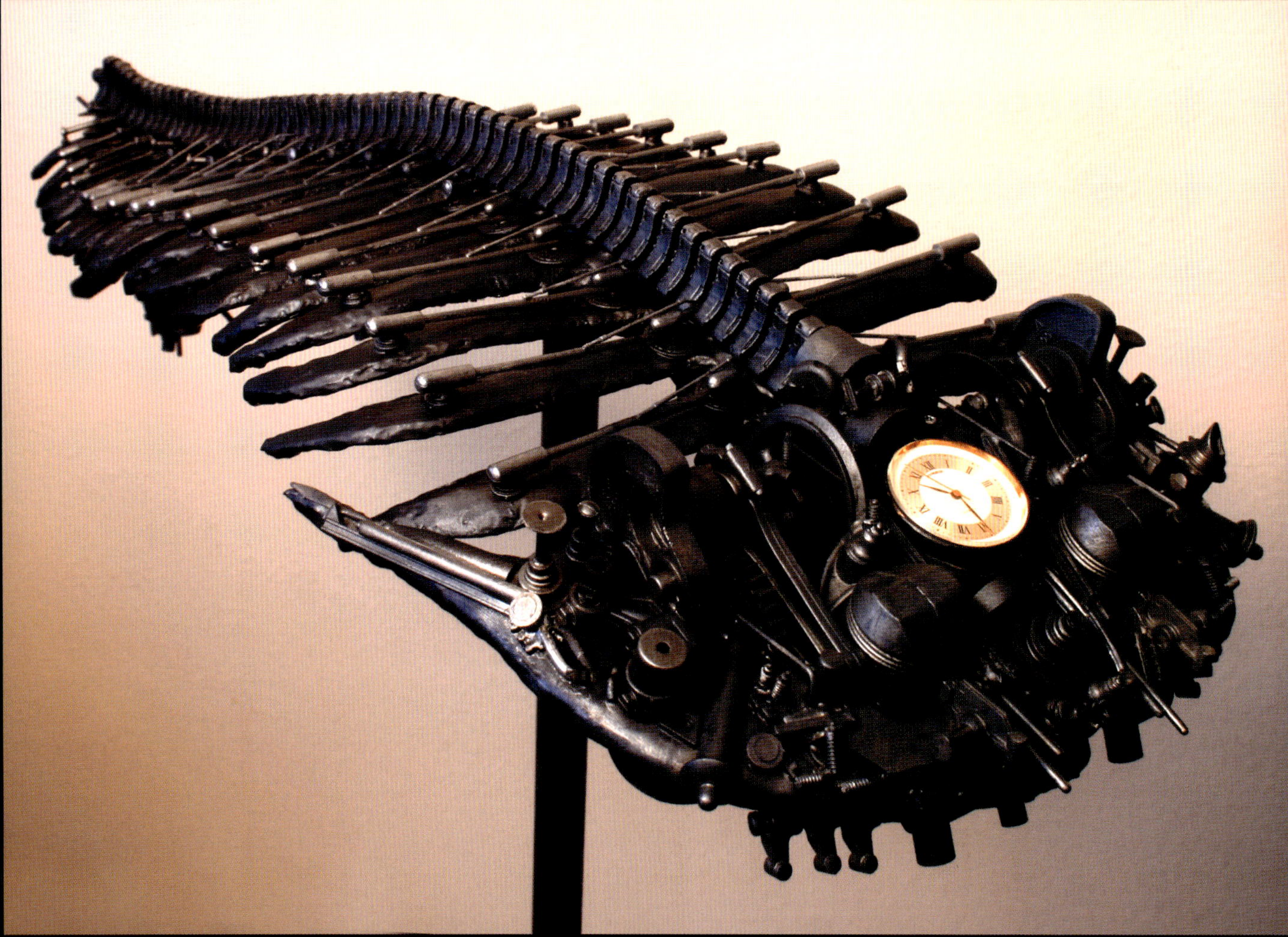

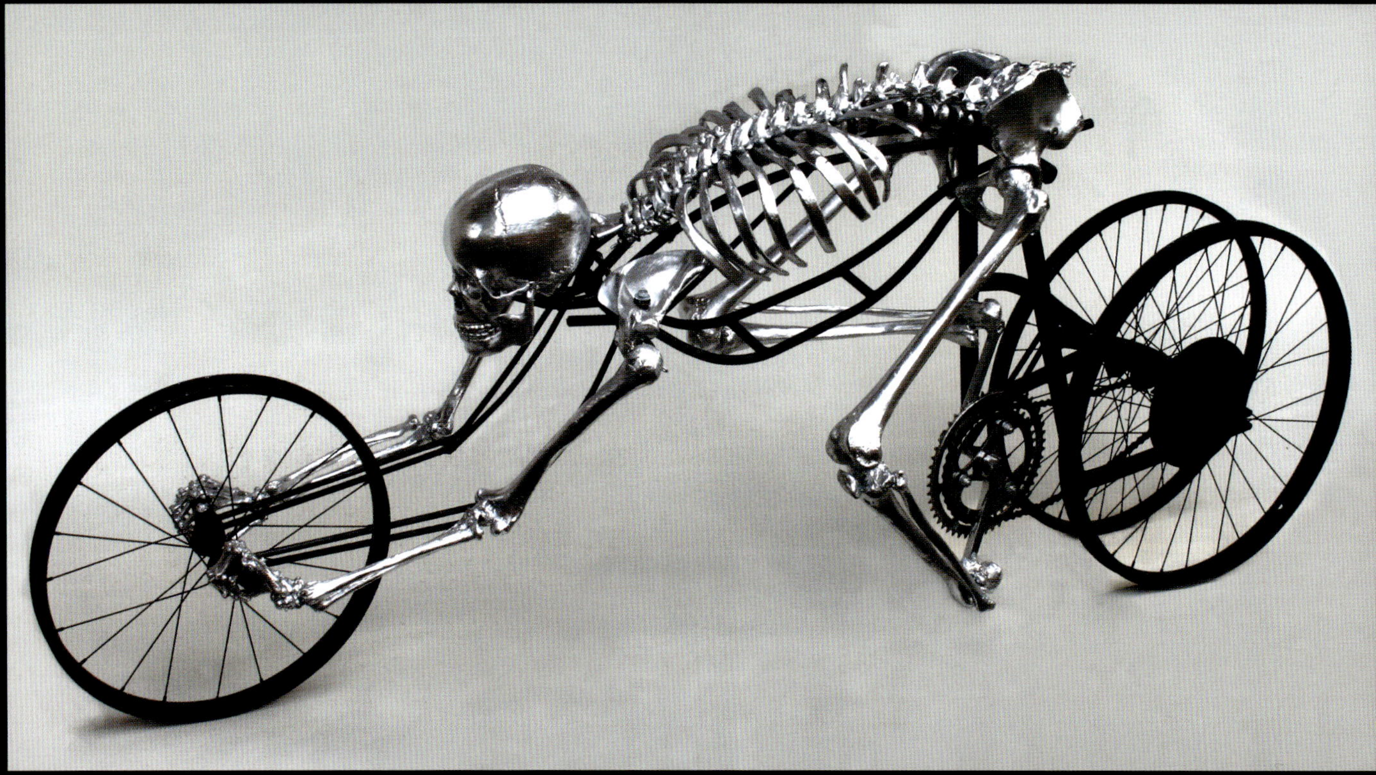

Trilo Temporalis – 24" x 10" x 7" welded steel, found object (2009) (top)

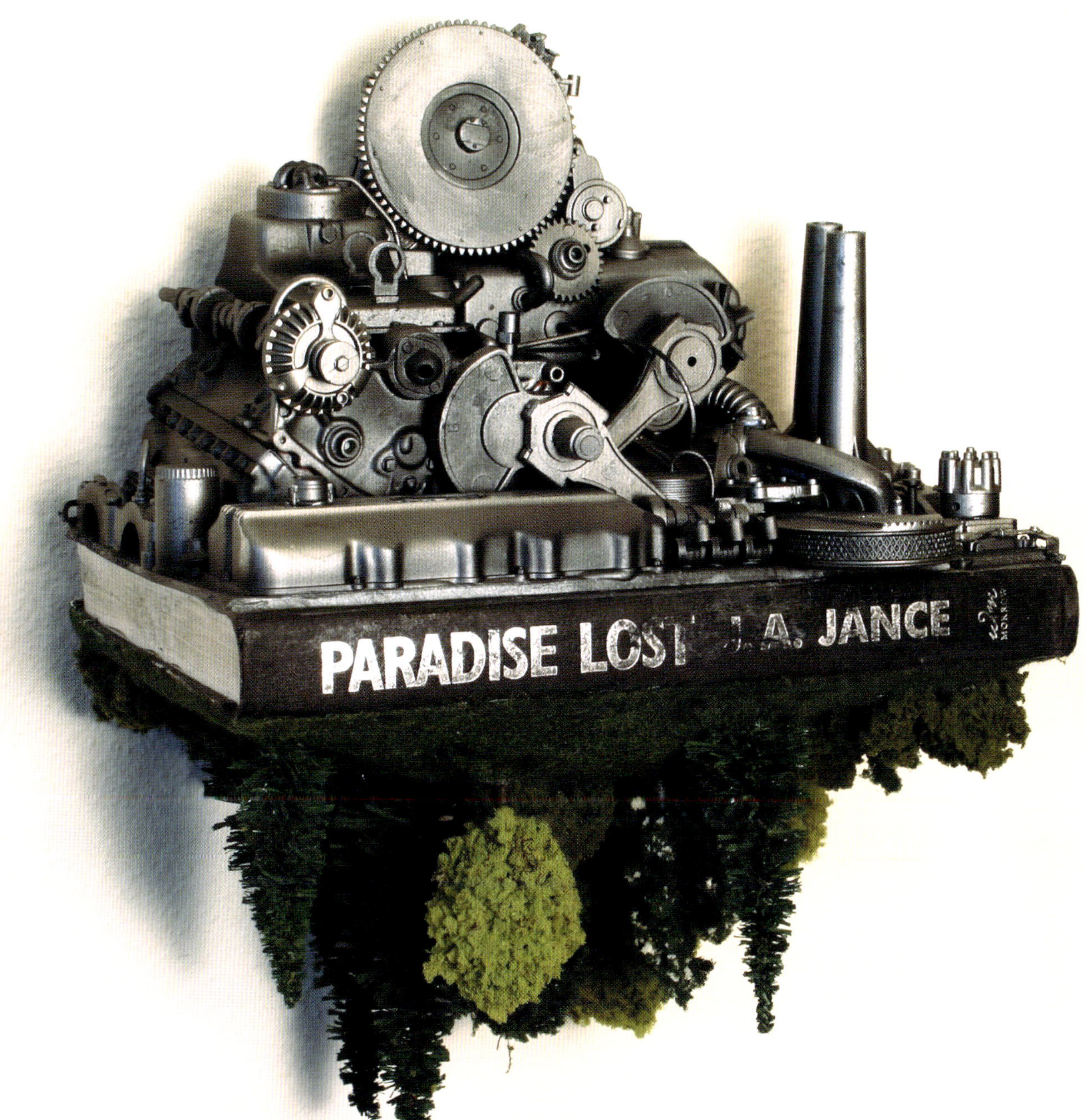
PARADISE LOST J.A. JANCE

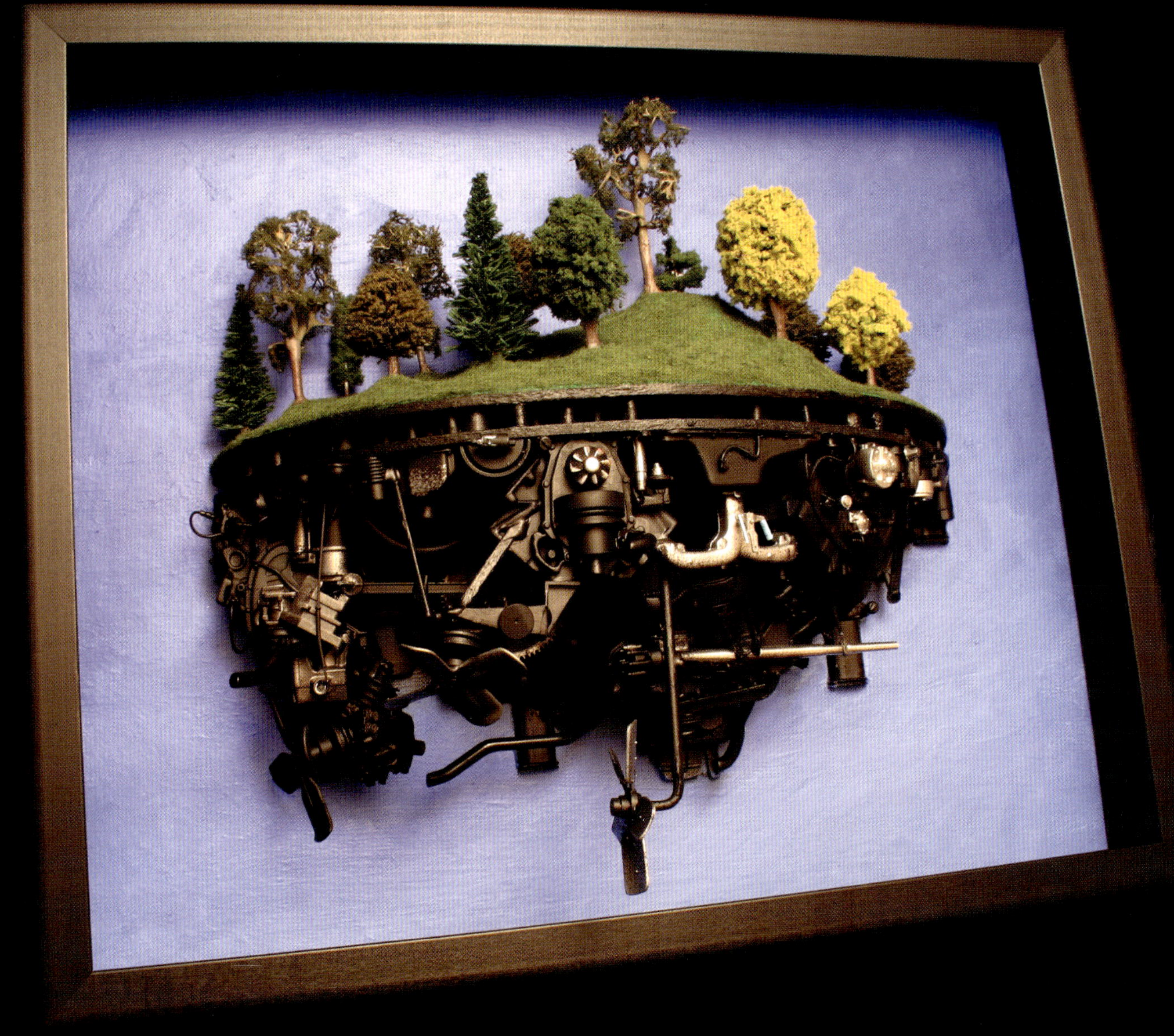

Round Up – 16" x 20" x 8" found object (2008)

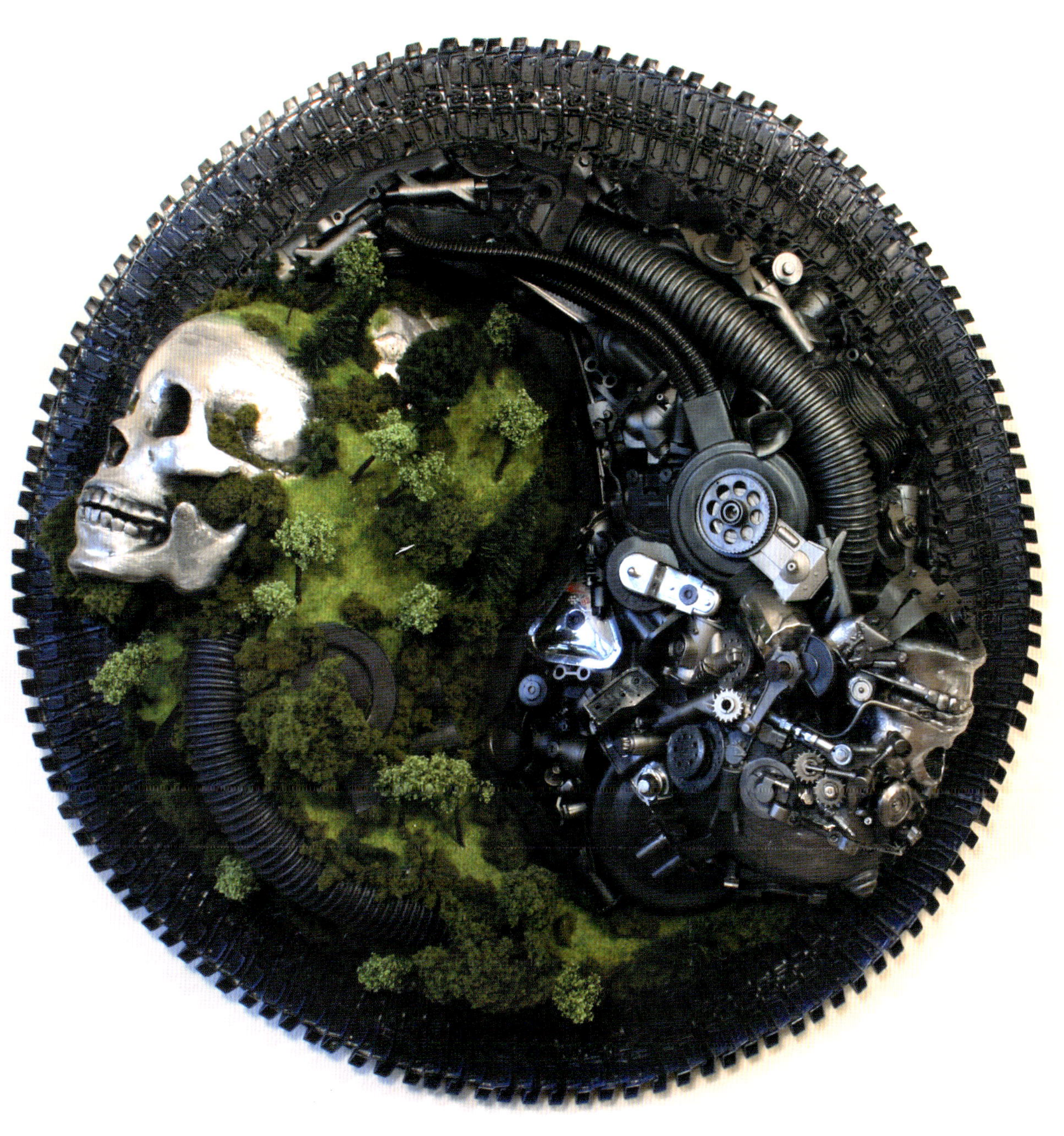

Spring Sprang – 30" x 10" found object (2009)

Photo Credits:

Page 29—Photo by Robert Hakaski, Visual Machinery

Pages 30, 31, 33-35—Photos by Amanda Dutton, Synesthesia Photo

Pages 39, 41,45—Photos by Sibila Savage

Pages 37,40, 42, 44, 46 & 47—Photos by Cameron Platt

Page 49—Photo by Larry Strong

Pages 58-69—Photos by Muriel Thies

Acknowledgments:

Cover and Book Design by Gregory Brotherton

Co-Edited by Amy Brotherton and Justin Eisinger

Book Production by Robbie Robbins